THE
PHILADELPHIA
GARDEN BOOK

THE
PHILADELPHIA
GARDEN BOOK

A Gardener's Guide
for the
Delaware Valley

Liz Ball

COOL
SPRINGS
PRESS

Ball, Liz
    The Philadelphia garden book : a gardeners guide for the Delaware Valley / Liz Ball.
        p.   cm.
    Includes bibliographical references (p.   ) and index.
    ISBN 1-888608-46-3
      1. Landscape plants--Pennsylvania--Philadelphia Region.
    2. Landscape gardening--Pennsylvania--Philadelphia Region.
    I. Title.
    SB407.B3   1999
    635.9 ' 09748 ' 1--dc21   99-18614
                                     CIP

Cool Springs Press, Inc.
2020 Fieldstone Parkway
Suite 900210
Franklin, Tennessee 37069

First printing 1999
Printed in the United States of America
10 9 8 7 6 5 4 3 2 1

Horticultural Nomenclature Editor: Gary Keim

Cover design by Christa Schoenbrodt

Visit the Cool Springs Press website at: www.coolspringspress.com

DEDICATION

To Charles O. Cresson, dear friend and patient gardening mentor,
who has generously shared with me his extensive horticultural knowledge,
his abiding enthusiasm for gardening, and many special plants.

ACKNOWLEDGMENTS

ONE OF THE GREAT GOOD FORTUNES of my life is to have discovered gardening in a place that abounds with friendly, enthusiastic gardeners and horticulturists. I am indebted to these wonderful people for the uncounted hours I have enjoyed in their company and in their gardens learning through their informal sharing of their wisdom and expertise. I am also grateful for the many stimulating formal conferences and lectures offered to me and other Philadelphia-area gardeners by institutions such as the Morris and Scott Arboretums, Longwood Gardens, and the Pennsylvania Horticultural Society (PHS).

Special thanks to Judy McKeon at the Morris for her insights on growing roses in this region and to Barbara Klaczynska of Gardens Collaborative, who has generously shared its resources. Thanks to Lisa Stephano, Joe Soprani, and Erin Fournier at PHS for their help in assembling resource lists. Thanks to Carole Ottesen for her expertise on ornamental grasses and always to Jeff Ball for his understanding and moral support.

Another great good fortune that I have enjoyed is writing this book for Cool Springs Press. Thanks to Roger Waynick and Hank McBride for their belief in the importance of regional gardening information and their confidence in me. Thanks especially to managing editor Jan Keeling for counseling me along the way with unfailing optimism and cheerful encouragement. Thanks also to Gary Keim for his valuable input and horticultural edits.

Finally, I also have the great good fortune to have in my life Rick Ray, to whom I am deeply indebted for his unfailing support and patience as well as his generosity in sharing his enormous knowledge of woody and herbaceous plants.

THE
Philadelphia
GARDEN BOOK

CONTENTS

FOREWORD

MORE THAN ONCE OVER THE YEARS I have reflected on the paradox that sometimes the more familiar something is, the less you really understand about it. In these instances it is often a matter of perspective; the subjectivity of dailiness crowds out the objectivity of distance.

So it was that growing up in this horticultural heaven called variously the Delaware Valley, Southeastern Pennsylvania, or the Greater Philadelphia area, I was not aware of how special it was. I assumed everyone played in the woods as a kid, walked to school in the shade of huge trees, and lived in a neighborhood where most people had colorful, abundant gardens. I assumed everyone had a mother or aunt who belonged to the garden club and referred to the shrub out front as the *Ligustrum* or some such word. Didn't everyone live within a few miles of a garden center, go to a world-class flower show every year, and routinely visit a place such as Longwood Gardens?

Living in other regions of the country as a young adult helped me realize that the incredibly rich horticultural world that I had taken for granted was virtually unique to our area. Gardening friends, among them many talented professional horticulturists who live and work in this area and guard its green heritage, have furthered my understanding, generously helping me learn more about plants and gardening here. And writing this book has helped me achieve the broader perspective and truly appreciate the geographical and historical foundation of this horticultural heaven.

This book incorporates several themes. It is first a practical guide to growing 175 specific plants of various kinds that grow well and appropriately in this region. Also, it suggests the diverse uses of plants, not just as ornamental features in a designed residential land-scape, but as essential elements of a balanced, natural ecological system that is predicated on plant and animal diversity and sensitivity to the soil environment. Finally, it pays tribute to the role that

Foreword

passionate plantsmen and gardeners from this area, historical and contemporary, have played in developing and maintaining our rich horticultural tradition.

This book is intended for both newcomers to the area and long-time residents. It is for both novice gardeners and experienced gardeners who want more geographically focused horticultural information. It is also for home owners who simply want to know how to take better care of their yards. It is not intended to replace more technical books on specific plants such as roses and specific techniques such as pruning, which go into more depth. It does not cover ancillary topics such as landscape design or seed starting and other forms of propagation. Only a few of the hundreds of plants that do well in this region could be included, and these were chosen because they are attractive, relatively low maintenance, and have successful track records here. They are garden-worthy plants that are representative of the wide range of those commonly used and available in Philadelphia, Bucks, Delaware, Chester, and Montgomery Counties.

INTRODUCTION

*D*ESCRIBING THE PHILADELPHIA AREA as the "Cradle of Liberty" has become something of a cliché. The idea that it is also the "Cradle of American Horticulture" is not so widely appreciated and accepted. Yet anyone who lives here long comes to gradually understand that this area is as special horticulturally as it is historically. The seeds of both traditions were sown by a community of thoughtful, passionate settlers, many of them Quakers, who shared Enlightenment values, curiosity about the natural world, and a commitment to knowledge, especially about plants of all kinds. Fundamentally the Philadelphia horticultural world was always, and continues to be, about trees. And in their shade there grew a rich and diverse gardening tradition, known and appreciated worldwide, that continues to define the Philadelphia area.

THE PLACE

The trees of the Eastern Seaboard's hardwood forest have always covered the rolling Piedmont Plateau on which much of the Philadelphia area is located. The accumulated humus from eons of fallen leaves from a rich assortment of stately deciduous and evergreen trees created fertile, well-drained, spongy loam over the region that literally and figuratively nourished the seeds of its horticultural tradition. Except for a few areas where shale is very close to the surface, or where the sandy soil of the coastal plain extends across the Delaware River from New Jersey, the soil in the Delaware Valley tends to be wonderfully rich, somewhat acidic, and fertile.

Through the ages, trees have flourished here and moderated a climate that has provided ample rainfall, hot, sunny summers, and relatively mild, but real, winters. Depending on whether the prevailing winds bring Gulf Stream or Arctic temperatures, winters may be intermittently somewhat harsh, but these vagaries (including the occasional ice storm) notwithstanding, conditions in this region have always favored the cultivation of a wide variety of plants. Situated nicely between North and South, it is cold enough to provide the necessary chill for Northern plants, yet mild enough to accommodate many Southern ones. The earliest Philadelphia-area gardeners, the Lenni Lenape community of Delaware Indians, cultivated pumpkins, corn, and many other edible native plants that flourished here.

THE PEOPLE

The towering trees that sheltered the Lenni Lenape for thousands of years greeted William Penn when he arrived to survey the 45,000 square miles of forested land granted to him by King Charles II as payment for a debt he owed Penn's father. The great forest inspired William Penn to call his colony Pennsylvania, or Penn's Woods, to honor both his father and this inspiring natural phenomenon. Under the huge oaks and maples of this woods, he negotiated treaties with the Lenni Lenape so that he could create parcels of land to grant to the Quakers whom he encouraged to emigrate from England and participate in his "Holy Experiment."

As fundamental to his vision of this colony as a place of religious freedom was Penn's desire to have it be a "greene countrie towne" where trees continued to dominate the landscape. Reflecting his devotion to trees, Penn's detailed plan for the layout of Philadelphia specified that several main streets be named for them. To this day Walnut, Chestnut, Pine, Spruce, and Cherry Streets are at the hub of life in the city. Also, according to his plan, four city squares were set aside for recreation. Today Rittenhouse, Franklin, Washington, and Logan (now a circle) Squares create green oases in the center city under the benign eye of William Penn himself, memorialized as a sculpture atop City Hall.

Although the Swedes, the Dutch, and some English had already settled and farmed parts of this area for three generations prior to Penn's grant in 1681, the later Quaker arrivals most enthusiastically responded to its natural wonders and laid the foundation for its horticultural prominence and tradition. The conviction of members of

Introduction

the Society of Friends that one way to know and understand God was to know and understand His natural creations stimulated the interest of Quakers in gardening in England. In the New World many also gardened enthusiastically. Some intensely studied and collected the fascinating flora they found here, their Enlightenment-era confidence in reason and order fueling their exploration. As they prospered in the New World, Quaker businessmen built estates, as Penn did at Pennsbury Manor, where they indulged their interest in growing plants and displaying them in gardens.

It is a tree, the Franklinia, that shall be forever associated with the Delaware County Quaker farmer John Bartram, who best typifies the confluence of Quaker and Enlightenment sensibilities that so inform the development of horticulture in the Philadelphia area. It was a daisy in the path of his plow, however, that initially awakened his interest in botany. Before long, the modestly educated farmer gave himself over to the task of systematically collecting, studying, and cultivating native plants.

So extensive were his activities and travels that King George III recognized Bartram as Royal Botanist for the mainland North American colonies. He and his son William, a trained naturalist who shared his passion, identified and introduced more than 200 of our native plants into cultivation in Europe. On his new farm fronting the Schuykill River, Bartram and his son raised as many plants as they could, including the aforementioned Franklinia tree (named for friend Benjamin Franklin). John Bartram was saluted by Linnaeus, who was busy developing a system for categorizing and naming plants, as "the greatest natural Botanist in the world."

After his father's death, William continued to travel and collect plants, and he sold plants and seeds from his garden to contemporary horticultural enthusiasts such as Thomas Jefferson. He issued the first mail-order catalog, a single sheet of paper, or "broadside," which evolved by 1807 into a small, bound booklet for the public. Among Bartram's customers were the Painter brothers, Jacob and

Minshall, Quakers who farmed 700 acres near Media in Delaware County. Before they were finished indulging their love of trees, they had planted more than 1000 of them on the property. Their property is now part of Tyler Arboretum, the oldest and largest arboretum on the East Coast.

Trees were also the great love of the Pierce brothers, Samuel and Joshua, who as early as 1798 began planting them in stately rows on their Kennett Square farm. Quakers, and avid collectors of unusual as well as familiar trees, they gradually turned their farm, originally granted to their great-grandfather by William Penn, into a fine arboretum that was prominently mentioned in horticultural publications by 1830. By the late 1800s the Pierce property had evolved into a recreational park with gardens, featuring boating, picnicking, and other Victorian pastimes.

Ultimately, a love of trees impelled Pierre Samuel duPont to purchase Pierce's Park after it had deteriorated to the point that the trees were destined for a sawmill. Having found an outlet for his love of gardening, this enormously successful businessman personally designed and supervised the gradual development of the Pierce property into the renowned Longwood Gardens.

The devotion of Quakers to trees and gardening is evident today everywhere in the Philadelphia area. It is no coincidence that the campuses of Quaker colleges in the area—Bryn Mawr, Haverford, and Swarthmore—are also the sites of arboretums. The grounds of the Friends' meeting houses that dot the environs are also shaded by great trees, and the great homes of affluent Quaker businessmen, preserved and restored, testify to the enthusiasm for gardening of these "founding fathers" of horticulture.

THE TRADITION

Trees were, and continue to be, emblematic of the rich horticultural potential of the Philadelphia area, and the Quakers were the initial spiritual and practical energizing force for the introduction of gardening, collecting, and cultivating plants here. The tradition has also been nurtured by many other forces, however. Through the 19th and 20th centuries, new arrivals to this area have embraced its rich potential for gardening.

The descendants of Eleuthère Irenée duPont, who came from France after its revolution and established a gunpowder factory along the Brandywine River, inherited his love of gardening. Like Pierre, who established Longwood Gardens, others built mansions and planted their grounds in gardens, profoundly influencing the gardening aesthetic in the Philadelphia area.

The Bartrams' idea of sending seeds through the mail was adopted by 18-year-old W. Atlee Burpee, who parlayed a $1000 loan from his mother in 1886 into a seed company. He was concerned that plant varieties that immigrants from Europe and elsewhere were accustomed to growing were not suited to the soil and climate in this country. He set about identifying and developing strains that were. He established Ford Hook Farm on a site recommended by Luther Burbank near Doylestown as a testing ground for new varieties that he found in his travels and developed through hybridization. Eventually, his Burpee Seed Company would become a household word throughout the country, greatly influencing both food and ornamental gardening.

About the same time, Rabbi Dr. Joseph Krauskopf, who shared Burpee's concern for the success of Jewish and other immigrants who would depend on farming in this country, established a special school for them in Doylestown. In 1896 he purchased a 100-acre farm there, built a building, and hired two teachers for his National Farm School. Over 100 years it has evolved into a full four-year college that features programs in food industry, biology and chemistry, and liberal arts. In its present incarnation as Delaware Valley College it continues its mission to teach gardening through its Horticulture and Ornamental Horticulture Departments.

Introduction

Formal education in the art and science of horticulture would be made available to women in the Philadelphia area at the Pennsylvania School of Horticulture for Women, established in 1891. For several decades it offered career opportunities to liberate women under the direction of women of superb capability such as Louise Bush-Brown. After World War II, its mission and role as a teaching institution and landscape were taken over by Temple University, which incorporated it into its suburban campus at Ambler as its School of Horticulture and Landscape Architecture.

THE PRESENT

The Pennsylvania Horticultural Society (PHS), founded in 1827, has been from the beginning a major force in perpetuating the gardening legacy of the Philadelphia area. Through the decades by means of exhibitions, contests, demonstrations, workshops, and lecture programs, it has disseminated information about contemporary horticulture. Further, it has honored the tradition of Penn's "greene countrie town" by pioneering programs in urban horticulture. In the 1960s, PHS started the Philadelphia Green program, which encourages community gardening projects and stimulates the interest of residents in gardening in their yards. In the 1970s, the Society added a Public Landscapes program, which works with partners to restore and maintain public green spaces such as the Azalea Garden in Fairmount Park, the grounds surrounding the Philadelphia Museum of Art, and gateways to the city of Philadelphia.

With this "green" tradition, it is not surprising that Philadelphia is the site of one of the largest urban parks in the world. The nearly 9000-acre present-day Fairmount Park had its beginning in 1854 when the Act of Consolidation extended the city limits to include stretches of the Schuykill River and several streams. In 1867 seven miles of rocky formation and hardwood forest along the Wissahickon Creek where the Lenni Lenape once fished became part of Fairmount Park. Over the years numerous other parcels of land have been incorporated into the park. Many of them protect stream corridors, provide areas for recreation and the enjoyment of nature, and preserve the disappearing natural flora that so fascinated the early Quaker settlers and others.

YOUR GARDEN

Those of us who already garden or are starting to garden here in the Philadelphia area are heirs to this rich horticultural tradition. Rather than be intimidated by it, be inspired by it. Almost nowhere else in this country are conditions so favorable and information so available. Also, perhaps not since the early Quaker days have the residents of this area been so acutely aware of how important it is to preserve the natural resources that we enjoy. While gardening here is a healthy pastime, a source of creative expression and personal pleasure, it is simultaneously a contribution you can make to the preservation of the legacy of the "greene countrie towne."

PLANT PROFILE

Every plant entry within the chapter features a "plant profile" box with information such as mature size, bloom time, light requirements, and special features. The following symbols indicate full sun, partial shade, and shade:

Full Sun   Partial Shade   Shade

SPECIAL FEATURE SYMBOLS

For quick reference, some of the plants' features are indicated by symbols on the right-hand page:

Attracts Butterflies or Moths

Attracts Hummingbirds

Edible Fruit, Flowers, or Plant Parts

Fragrant or Scented

Seeds or Fruit for Birds and Other Wildlife

Good for Cut Flowers

Multi-Season

Water Plants

Supports Beneficial Insects

Evening Garden

Ornamental Pods, Seedheads, or Fruit

Old-Fashioned

 Did You Know?

Many plant entries end with a "Did You Know?" information box that offers information about the plant's uses, nomenclature, history, or other information that is little known or just plain interesting.

CHAPTER ONE

Annuals

A NNUALS ARE THE FLOWER MAINSTAY of most residential
landscapes. How can you not love plants that knock themselves out
to flower as furiously as they can for as long as they can? Annuals such as
spider flowers, cosmos, and nasturtiums are under a biological imperative
to produce as much seed as possible in one season to assure future generations. They literally burn the candle at both ends, giving their all to flower
and seed production at the expense of root development and energy storage. Those that do not succumb immediately to frost, expected any time
after October 15 in the Philadelphia area, soon die of exhaustion anyway.

Some annuals are called hardy—seemingly a contradiction in terms—
because they tolerate a bit of frost in the fall before dying. Cleomes and four
o'clocks, among others, leave behind tough seeds that can survive winter,
then cold and soggy thaws, to germinate in the spring in the yard. Other
annuals, such as geraniums, are really perennials by nature, structured to
invest in root systems and store energy for the future, but they are too tender to survive cold winters. They are called tender perennials. Gardeners in
places such as the Philadelphia area grow them for their wonderful flowers,
then treat them as they would regular annuals, letting them die in the cold
in the fall. In some cases, they dig them up, pot them, and grow them
indoors on a windowsill over the winter.

ANNUAL ASSETS

Annuals, whether acting as vines, ground covers, or bedding plants, deliver
just about any color. Because most deliver it nonstop all season, their
dependability is unmatched by other flowering plants. Reliable color means
the yard will have a consistent look all season. It means a steady supply of
blooms for indoor arrangements. It means regular visits from butterflies,
hummingbirds, and honeybees all summer, and seed-eating birds in the fall.

CARING FOR ANNUALS

Annuals require cultural techniques suited to their go-for-broke natures.
Steady blooming over many, many weeks requires steady nutrition to stay
healthy and stress free. Slow-acting granular fertilizer mixed into their soil
at planting time assures consistent, uniform nutrition over this long period.
It can be supplemented during periods of stress (such as when pinching

petunia stems back in midsummer to rejuvenate the plants) by a spray or watering of diluted liquid fertilizer for a quick boost.

Typically, annuals have shallow, fibrous roots that need watering more frequently than deeply rooted permanent plants. Mulching their soil to retard evaporation of its moisture extends the time between necessary waterings. If they think they have produced enough seed to assure a new generation, annuals will stop flowering. Pinching off faded flowers interrupts seed production, forcing them to bloom more.

Annual seedlings are relatively inexpensive. Because of this and their short life expectancy, pest and disease control is less of an issue than with large, permanent shrubs or perennial plants. In the face of insect attack, gardeners can cut back the entire annual plant and let it renew itself. It is easier and safer to pull up seriously ill plants and replace them with other annuals than to treat the ailment.

In the following plant entries, starting seedlings indoors is not discussed for several reasons. One is that, in most cases, commercially grown ones are readily available and of high quality. Another is that many annuals germinate so easily and quickly outdoors that there is not much time to be saved by early indoor starting. The main reason, however, is that growing sturdy, healthy seedlings requires another whole set of skills and equipment. It is a wonderful, rewarding activity that enhances, but is not essential to, outdoor gardening.

Alyssum

Lobularia maritima

Other Names: Sweet Alyssum, Snowdrift

Mature Size: 2 inches tall; 18-inch-wide
  mounds

Bloom Time: May to October

Flower Color/Type: Pink, while, lilac; floret clusters

Features: Old-fashioned; fragrance; attracts butterflies; evening garden

Light Requirements:

Color photograph on page 201.

*L*ike a sprinkling of snow or perhaps a layer of lace, alyssum covers the ground with loose mounds of tiny clusters of white florets. Their delicate presence is easy to take for granted until the subtle honey scent wafts by and announces their presence. Low-growing, dark-green, narrow leaves set off the flowers at the tips of soft, delicate stems. Though fine-textured, alyssums are sturdy, their Mediterranean heritage making them tougher than they look. Drought tolerant once established, they are excellent plants for bedding, rock gardens, edging, and containers. They may droop somewhat in the heat of Philadelphia summers, but they recover promptly and bloom until, perhaps through, the first light frost.

WHEN TO PLANT

Plant seeds directly into the garden as directed on the seed packet in early April when the soil has dried out and warmed a bit. Seeds germinate quickly; plants bloom in 7 or 8 weeks. Transplant young plants in pots from the garden center in May.

WHERE TO PLANT

Alyssum likes full sun as long as the site does not get too hot at midday in summer. Plants with lilac flowers appreciate some shade to prevent their color from fading. Although it prefers soil rich in organic matter, alyssum will settle for ordinary soil as long as it is regularly moist but well-drained. Alyssum is especially appealing in between stepping-stones, along walks and drives, or tumbling over rock walls.

HOW TO PLANT

Cultivate the soil down 8 to 10 inches, add a handful of a granular slow-acting all-purpose fertilizer, and mix in organic material if the soil is heavy. Plant seeds as directed on the packet. Do not cover them with soil. Dig planting holes for small seedlings about as deep as and slightly wider than their rootballs when they are removed from their containers. Set each plant in its hole so that it is at soil level. Fill in the hole with soil, firming it gently around plant stems, then water well. Space plants about 6 inches apart to allow for their decorous spread over the season.

CARE AND MAINTENANCE

Water alyssum when rainfall is scarce. As its stems lengthen over the season and threaten to flop, shear or clip stems back 2 inches to revitalize the plant. A watering of very diluted liquid fertilizer at this time will boost the plant's energy as it strives to resume flowering. If at the end of the season, blooms are allowed to mature to pods with seeds within, alyssum may self-sow and appear next spring as long as the soil is not disturbed.

ADDITIONAL INFORMATION

Good for containers, alyssum flops gently over edges of window-boxes and softens sides of planters. Its fine texture contrasts with larger-leafed, coarser annuals such as geraniums.

ADDITIONAL SPECIES, CULTIVARS, OR VARIETIES

There are many choices of alyssum as seeds, fewer as retail seedlings. 'Wonderland' series offers mixed colors. 'New Carpet of Snow' is dwarf and spreading in white. 'Tetra Snowdrift' is tall and makes good cut flowers. 'Oriental Night' is deeper lilac; 'Easter Bonnet' has mixed colors.

 Did You Know?

Pale or white flowers that reflect the waning light in their luminous petals assure some pleasure in the garden at the end of long workdays or during evenings of entertaining. Long-blooming annuals such as alyssum are staples of evening gardens, which also feature moonvine, lilies, nicotiana, night-blooming tropical water lilies, and silver- or gray-foliaged plants. Plants with fragrance, variegated foliage, and trees and shrubs with pale bark and/or fragrant flowers such as daphne and lilac contribute to the wonderful experience of an after-hours garden.

Begonia, Wax

Begonia semperflorens-cultorum hybrids

Other Names: Fibrous-rooted Begonia,
  Bedding Begonia

Light Requirements:

Mature Size: 6 to 15 inches tall; 8 to
  10 inches wide

Bloom Time: June to October

Flower Color/Type: Red, white, pink; single or double cups

Features: Variously colored foliage; evening garden

Color photograph on page 201.

This annual is all that it can be and then some. Neat and tidy enough to excel at formal bedding designs and edging chores, it is so versatile and adaptable that it accommodates shady nooks, all kinds of containers, and life indoors as a houseplant. Furthermore, it blooms all summer, then into fall and possibly past light frost without missing a beat. Wax begonias have dense, crisp, rounded, or tapered foliage. Waxy and glossy surfaced, their leaves may be bright green, deep bronze, maroon, or variegated. Flowers of tall begonia varieties are 1 to 2 inches wide; those of dwarf types are 1 inch wide. They bloom in clusters at joints in the fleshy stems where leaf stems branch off, and they have 4 rounded petals and 2 narrower ones that resemble wings.

WHEN TO PLANT

Plant homegrown or commercial seedlings in May when danger of frost is past and the soil has warmed and dried out.

WHERE TO PLANT

Wax begonias, especially the bronze- or maroon-foliaged ones, can handle full sun. It helps if the temperature is below 90 degrees Fahrenheit and they are well watered. Otherwise, they do best in some shade. Too much shade causes leggy stems because they have to stretch for light. Begonias accept almost any type of soil that is rich in organic matter that will help it hold moisture, yet drain well.

HOW TO PLANT

Loosen the soil down 8 to 10 inches, digging in organic matter and a handful of granular slow-acting all-purpose fertilizer to provide consistent and uniform nutrition all season. Dig a planting hole about as deep as and slightly wider than the rootball removed from its container. Set the plant in the hole so that it is level with the surrounding ground. Fill in the hole with soil, firming it gently around plant stems, and water well. Space plants about 6 to 10 inches apart in groups of 3 in beds; pack them in closely in containers. Use soilless potting medium laced with granular slow-acting fertilizer in containers that have drainage holes in the bottom.

CARE AND MAINTENANCE

Water begonias during dry periods to maintain steady bloom. Those in pots or under trees competing with their roots for soil moisture will need more frequent watering and feeding. Begonias are self-cleaning, dropping their blossoms when they fade, so they do not need deadheading. Pinch back their brittle stems midseason, if necessary, to make plants more compact. In October either dig up begonias and pot them for life indoors as houseplants, or wait until after frost kills them and clean them up for the compost pile.

ADDITIONAL INFORMATION

Begonias in moist, woodland settings may suffer slug damage on their leaves. To make plants for next year, pinch off young stems, and root them in a glass of water. Pot them, and put them on a bright windowsill or light table until planting time outdoors.

ADDITIONAL SPECIES, CULTIVARS, OR VARIETIES

There are many choices of wax begonias. Study mail-order catalogs and seedlings on display at the garden center in the spring to make selections. Tuberous begonias (*Begonia* × *tuberhybrida* hybrids) are described in the bulb section.

Did You Know?

Hardening off plants that have spent time indoors is critical to their successful transition to outdoor living. Begonias, coleus, geraniums, and other annuals wintered over as houseplants or raised indoors from rooted cuttings need gradual acclimatizing to sun and air temperatures. Put flats or pots outdoors in a sheltered area for a few hours daily, then bring them inside. Increase the time outside each day over a week or two, eventually leaving them out overnight. Then plant them in the garden or in outdoor containers.

Coleus

Coleus × hybridus; Solenostemon scutellarioides

Other Name: Flame Nettle
Mature Size: 6 to 30 inches tall; 12 to
   18 inches wide
Bloom Time: Midsummer to autumn
Flower Color/Type: Blue, lilac, white; insignificant floret spikes
Features: Multicolored, variable foliage

Light Requirements:

Color photograph on page 201.

The color from their nonstop flowering is the greatest asset of most annuals. Coleus contributes riotous color, but it is its foliage that is the standout. Commonly used in England in elaborate Victorian-style bedding designs, coleus has come into its own in this country as a versatile, dependable garden plant. Initially a bit flashy and coarse, sort of like a gaudy Hawaiian shirt at a formal party, coleus was relegated to shady corners. Now, newer coleus blend better with other plants and can take some sun. These bushy, upright plants feature foliage in an astounding variety of shapes and colors. Heart-shaped, oval, or filigreed, some leaves are edged with teeth or fringe. They may be white, cream, yellow, chartreuse, green, bronze, purple, red, or rose, often combined or edged with contrasting colors. Many coleus are dwarf, eminently suitable for lush, tropical container plantings similar to those on display at Scott Arboretum, Chanticleer, and Longwood Gardens.

WHEN TO PLANT

Plant seeds, seedlings, commercially rooted cuttings, or plants wintered over indoors as houseplants in May when all danger of frost is past and the soil has warmed a bit. Plant stems rooted in water or plants in pots from the garden center anytime in summer.

WHERE TO PLANT

Give dark-colored coleus some light shade; newer, brighter types do best with considerable sun. They all like average soil of any type that is well-drained. Over-rich soil causes floppy stems and may affect foliage color.

HOW TO PLANT

Dig the soil down 8 to 10 inches to loosen and aerate it. Mix in granular slow-acting all-purpose fertilizer to provide uniform and consistent nutrition for the season. Add organic material such as peat moss or compost to improve soil drainage if necessary. Dig a planting hole about as deep as and slightly wider than the coleus seedling's rootball, and set it in the hole so that its top is level with the surrounding soil. Fill in the hole with soil, firm it gently, and water well. Space plants 1 to 2 feet apart to allow for their mature width.

CARE AND MAINTENANCE

Using 2 or 3 inches of organic mulch will keep their surrounding soil moist and discourage weeds. Water coleus during periods of drought, especially plants located in sun and/or in containers. Pinch off flowers to encourage more foliage. Pinch back stems that are long and leggy to a pair of leaves to encourage compactness. Limit fertilizer to the initial planting dose to avoid excess tender foliage, which attracts aphids. Coleus are extremely vulnerable to cold, so take stem cuttings or pot plants to bring indoors for houseplants by early October when frost threatens.

ADDITIONAL INFORMATION

In the fall root pieces of stems from plants with desirable foliage in a glass of water on a windowsill. Plant them in a pot of soil promptly once substantial roots appear. Since coleus is actually a tender perennial, it can survive as a houseplant indoors and go back into the yard in May.

ADDITIONAL SPECIES, CULTIVARS, OR VARIETIES

Coleus are available in seemingly infinite foliage variety. Choose appealing colors from among prostrate and semiprostrate forms as well as full-sized upright plants at the local garden center.

 Did You Know?

Scientists define a plant both botanically and horticul-turally. Its botanical definition is based on how a plant's reproduction system is structured. Thus, coleus is a tender perennial because it lives for more than 1 year where winters are warm. Its horticultural definition is based on how a plant functions in the garden. In our climate coleus dies when frost arrives, so it is effectively an annual. For gardeners, the horticultural definition is the one that counts.

Corn Poppy

Papaver rhoeas

Other Names: Field Poppy, Flanders
  Poppy, Shirley Poppy
Mature Size: 2 feet tall; 1 foot wide
Bloom Time: Late May into June
Flower Color/Type: Pink, red, salmon, and white; cup
Features: Evening garden; old-fashioned; attracts bees

Light Requirements:

Color photograph on page 201.

Corn poppies are the slim, colorful poppies in the delightful wildflower mixes that cheer drivers near turnpike interchanges, highway cloverleafs, and median strips. Their airy, fragile beauty often stops traffic wherever they grow. Domesticated for the garden, they are called Shirley poppies after the English town where they were painstakingly bred in the 1880s. Shirley flowers are up to 3 inches wide, featuring water-colored, tissue-paper petals. Some have distinctive black blotches in their centers; some are double petaled; others are streaked or edged in white. They float at the tips of pliable, leafless, hairy stems above their dark-green, finely divided papery leaves. They produce prodigious amounts of pollen, which their brightly colored petals boldly advertise to insects galore. They bloom for only a few weeks, during which they are perfect accompaniments to bulbs such as Asiatic lilies, or naturalized in fields and in informal beds for a cottage garden look.

WHEN TO PLANT

Technically, corn poppies are hardy annuals, which means their seeds can stand cold. They sow themselves after they bloom, and their seeds survive all winter. Gardeners can sow seeds in late March or early April, even before the soil warms. Since they bloom in 60 days, expect traditional red poppies for Memorial Day. Sow more seeds at 2- or 3-week intervals for the all-season flower color most annuals deliver.

WHERE TO PLANT

Plant corn poppies in full sun. They take any well-drained soil, even somewhat alkaline. Plant seeds or seedlings directly into the designated area in the garden. Because of their taproots, they are tricky to move later.

HOW TO PLANT

Because the early-spring soil in the garden is too wet to dig without harming it, scratch its surface to create a shallow seedbed. Sprinkle poppy seeds, perhaps mixed with sand to make them more manageable, on the disturbed soil. Then barely cover them with a ⅛-inch layer of very fine soil or compost, and moisten the seedbed. To naturalize poppies in meadows, sow seed randomly over mown or bare-soil areas either after Thanksgiving or in early March.

CARE AND MAINTENANCE

Thin emerging poppy seedlings so that plants are 6 inches apart. Spread a thin layer of organic mulch on the soil between them to discourage weeds and retain moisture. There is no need to fertilize them. After flowers fade, remove the greenish seedpods to encourage more flowering. Leave pods from the last flush of bloom to encourage self-seeding.

ADDITIONAL INFORMATION

Corn poppies do not have any significant pest or disease problems. Picked when their buds are just barely open, flowers have a short, but wonderful vase life. Dried seedpods are useful for floral crafts.

ADDITIONAL SPECIES, CULTIVARS, OR VARIETIES

Although there are many kinds and colors of Shirley poppies—a result of natural hybridizing in the field—there are few named ones: 'Mother of Pearl' ('Fairy Wings') is shorter, more compact at 10 to 14 inches tall; it and double-flowered 'Angel's Choir' do not have black centers.

Did You Know?

When John McCrae wrote, "In Flanders fields the poppies blow between the crosses, row on row . . . ," he was referring to a stunning sea of red corn poppies that sprang from soil trampled by embattled soldiers in World War I. Later in the area consecrated as a cemetery for those who fell on the western front, the deep-red poppies eerily symbolized the blood that had flowed there. Today, the artificial "Buddy" poppies that veterans sell around Memorial Day commemorate the tragedy, the place, and the Flanders poppies.

Cosmos

Cosmos bipinnatus

Other Name: Mexican Aster

Mature Size: 4 to 6 feet tall; 2 to
  3 feet wide

Bloom Time: June through September

Flower Color/Type: Red, pink, rose, magenta, white, or bicolor; daisylike

Features: Old-fashioned; evening garden; attracts butterflies and
  beneficial insects

Light Requirements:

Color photograph on page 201.

This old-fashioned flower is enjoying something of a comeback these days. For many gardeners it has never gone away, although it may have been taken for granted. Like many annuals, it is tough and agreeable as well as beautiful and is easy to grow. An open, branching, sturdy plant, it features pastel-colored, daisy-type flowers with yellow centers. Up to 3 to 4 inches across, the flowers bloom above airy, finely divided, ferny foliage. Fully mature plants have a blowzy, informal look that suits their role as fencerow, open field, and median strip plants. They are also delightful at the back of a flower border, where their lack of good posture is not too noticeable, or in a cutting garden.

WHEN TO PLANT

Plant seedlings or directly sow seeds into a prepared bed in the spring when all threat of frost is past, usually mid-May. Transplant potted plants from the garden center anytime during the growing season, but the sooner the better.

WHERE TO PLANT

Cosmos love full sun. Any average soil that drains well and is slightly on the acid side is fine. They do fine in sandy soil at the Shore. Standard-sized ones look best behind other plants; dwarfs in the foreground are see-through.

HOW TO PLANT

Loosen the soil down 8 to 10 inches, digging in organic matter or coarse sand to improve drainage if necessary. Skip fertilizer if the soil is decent because too much nitrogen makes cosmos rangy. Sow seeds as directed on the seed packet, or dig planting holes large enough to accommodate the root systems of cosmos seedlings. Tip them out of their containers, and set them in their holes so that the tops of their soilballs are level with the surrounding ground. Fill in the hole with soil, firm it gently, and water well. Space plants about 1 foot apart to allow for their branching.

CARE AND MAINTENANCE

A thin layer of organic material spread as a mulch over the bare soil around cosmos seedlings keeps it moist and discourages weeds. Eventually, taller cosmos will need staking, unless their young stems are pinched back early on to encourage compactness. Cut flowers frequently or pinch back center stems periodically to maintain compactness. Deadheading spent blooms will stimulate new flowering all season.

ADDITIONAL INFORMATION

Cosmos make great cut flowers for indoor arrangements. To encourage reseeding, leave some flowers at season's end, and do not disturb the soil over the winter.

ADDITIONAL SPECIES, CULTIVARS, OR VARIETIES

Sonata series cosmos are dwarf at 2 feet tall and mixed pink and white. Versailles series cosmos are large at 3 feet tall with larger flowers, ideal for cutting. Bicolor 'Candy Stripe' is white with red edges on petals. Seashell series flowers have petals that curve in to form tubes, in a variety of colors. Psyche series cosmos have a double row of petals. Yellow cosmos (*Cosmos sulphureus*) is shorter, has yellow or orangish, single or double flowers, and has slightly wider leaves. Bright Lights Mixed has double flowers. 'Sunny Red', dwarf at 2 feet tall, is an All-America Selection winner with bright-scarlet, single flowers that fade to orange.

 Did You Know?

Both Painted Lady (Cosmopolitan) and Monarch butterflies visit cosmos. Painted ladies migrate from northern Mexico in the spring, sometimes flying in groups of thousands low to the ground. Capable of flying more than 600 miles, they are sometimes seen out over the Atlantic Ocean. Many settle in our area in the spring and breed and die here. They are mostly black-patterned orange with white wing tips and black dots on the edges of their back wings.

Four O'Clock

Mirabilis jalapa

Other Names: Beauty-of-the-Night, Marvel of Peru

Mature Size: 2 to 3 feet tall; 2 feet wide

Bloom Time: July until October

Flower Color/Type: Yellow, rose, white, red; trumpets

Features: Old-fashioned; scented; evening garden; attracts hummingbirds

Light Requirements:

Color photograph on page 201.

Some people believe that a flower garden is not a true garden unless it includes four o'clocks. Certainly, once they are planted, they are there for the duration because of their reliable self-seeding. They have great appeal late in the day, their fresh, newly opened, perky 1- to 2-inch trumpet flowers brightening the waning light and providing a last stop for local hummingbirds before the sun sets. Attuned to the sun, they do not open on cloudy or rainy days. Their tough roots and sturdy stems testify to their staying power, taking pollution, dust, and a certain amount of drought in stride. By the end of summer, they are virtually bushes, so give them space.

WHEN TO PLANT

Four o'clocks will plant themselves in the garden by dropping their seeds in the fall. Grow the resulting seedlings in place next spring, or transplant them elsewhere in the yard. An alternative is to collect the hard, black seeds from faded flowers and either start them indoors or sow them directly in a bed outdoors in the spring when the soil has warmed. They are so fast growing that starting them indoors early does not provide much time advantage.

WHERE TO PLANT

Four o'clocks like full sun, but will accept some shade. They do fine in ordinary soil that is well-drained. Plant them as edging along high walls, in flower borders, or in mixed borders where they can serve as temporary shrubs by late summer.

HOW TO PLANT

Dig the soil down 8 to 10 inches to loosen it. A handful of a granular slow-acting all-purpose fertilizer mixed into the soil at this point will sustain four o'clocks all season. Dig a planting hole about as deep as and slightly wider than the seedling's rootball, and set it in the hole so that it is level with the surrounding ground. Fill in the hole with soil, firming it gently, and water well. Plant seedlings or thin existing ones to at least 1 foot apart to allow for the four o'clock's mature size.

CARE AND MAINTENANCE

Four o'clocks are truly low maintenance. They need no ongoing care except watering in a severe drought. If plants begin to flop over from the weight of their dense branching, cut them back some, or stake them. Pull up unauthorized seedlings before they become established. After frost blackens four o'clock stems, pull them up and discard them.

ADDITIONAL INFORMATION

The primary pest problem of four o'clocks is Japanese beetles in July. Brush them off foliage into a jar of soapy water. Cut back marred foliage. Because four o'clocks are actually tender perennials, their tuberous roots will survive the winter indoors, although it is not usually worth the trouble to dig them up.

ADDITIONAL SPECIES, CULTIVARS, OR VARIETIES

'Jingles' is a smaller, denser plant and has striped flowers.

 Did You Know?

Four o'clocks are the ultimate pass-along plant. Their seeds are so large and convenient for gardeners to collect and pass along to friends and neighbors that commercially grown seedlings are rarely available at local garden centers. Seeds are available, though, in retail outlets and mail-order catulogs every spring.

Geranium

Pelargonium × hortorum

Other Names: Zonal Geranium, Storksbill, Annual Geranium, Bedding Geranium

Light Requirements:

Mature Size: Up to 2 feet tall and wide

Bloom Time: June to October

Flower Color/Type: Shades of red and pink, white, salmon, and bicolor; clusters of small flowers

Features: Old-fashioned; attracts hummingbirds

Color photograph on page 201.

Common geraniums are voted by the American public into the top 10 most popular annual plants every year. They show no sign of losing favor as the backbone of millions of windowboxes, hanging baskets, planters, and light-post and mailbox beds. Their flowers attract all of the attention—small florets clustered in 5- to 7-inch balls of rich-hued color, large enough to be seen from a distance. They bloom at the tips of stiff, bare stalks, their crisp, upright habit lending an air of formality to the proceedings. Geranium leaves typically have reddish-colored rings or "zones," although some may be plain green or variegated green and cream. All this, and an easygoing nature that takes pollution, dry soil, and partial shade in stride, explains why geraniums are so loved.

WHEN TO PLANT

Plant new plants or those rooted from last year's plants in May when the air and soil are warm. Full-grown plants can be planted anytime all season.

WHERE TO PLANT

Geraniums thrive on full sun. They manage fine in average garden soil with some organic matter to help it drain well. They prefer a more neutral pH, but rarely get it in Philadelphia-area gardens where soil tends to be on the acidic side.

HOW TO PLANT

Add organic material and granular slow-acting all-purpose fertilizer to the garden soil when loosening it down about 12 inches. Dig each planting hole about as deep as and slightly wider than the rootball of the plant when it is removed from its container. Set each plant in its hole so that it is level with the surrounding ground. Firm the soil gently around plant stems, and water well. Use groups of 3 plants, spaced about 1 foot apart for best effect in a mixed flower bed. Adding granular slow-acting fertilizer to soilless potting mixes when planting in containers will provide uniform, consistent nutrition to geraniums and their companions all season.

CARE AND MAINTENANCE

Whether they are in containers or in the garden, geraniums like a wet-dry watering cycle. Allow their soil to dry out a bit before each watering. Remove spent flowers by breaking off their stiff stalks at their base near the main stem. Doing this encourages new blooms and grooms the plants. Mulch garden geraniums to discourage weeds. If slow-acting fertilizer was not provided at planting time, add water-soluble fertilizer as directed on its label to their water every few weeks to keep them blooming vigorously. As the first fall frost nears, bring plants indoors to overwinter as houseplants or to store bare root on drying lines in a cool basement for a source of plants and/or cuttings for next spring. Those that remain in the garden can handle a light frost, but will succumb to a hard one.

ADDITIONAL INFORMATION

Geranium stems will root in a glass of water or damp sand.

ADDITIONAL SPECIES, CULTIVARS, OR VARIETIES

Ivy-leaved geraniums (*Pelargonium peltatum*) have 5-lobed leaves resembling those of English ivy on trailing stems, ideal for containers. Showy geraniums (*Pelargonium × domesticum*) include those called Martha Washington, Regal, or pansy-flowered geraniums. Their upper flower petals often sport dark blotches of color that contrast with the richly hued rose, lilac, pink, or white flowers.

 Did You Know?

Scented geraniums are the lesser-known geranium cousins. Usually planted in pots, their flowers are less showy, but their foliage is remarkable. Various types have curled, frilled, or finely cut leaves that smell like lemon, pineapple, coconut, rose, nutmeg, or peppermint. They are used to flavor cakes and jellies, and they are dried for potpourris.

Impatiens

Impatiens wallerana

Other Names: Busy Lizzie, Patience Plant

Light Requirements:

Mature Size: 6 to 24 inches tall; 8 to
  12 inches wide

Bloom Time: June to October

Flower Color/Type: Shades of red, pink, salmon, orange, and white,
  bicolor; single, double

Features: Shade bloomer; attracts butterflies

Color photograph on page 201.

What did we do before there was impatiens? This one plant has changed the look of Philadelphia-area residential landscapes where large, gorgeous shade trees are common and shade is a fact of life. Impatiens, named for the tendency of its seedpod to impatiently split open at the slightest touch, offers a dazzling array of colorful flowers with 5 flat petals backed by a thin, spurred bract. Hybrid types offer more elaborate double-flowered, iridescent, white-edged, and longer blooms; more colors; uniform size; and variegated foliage. Some are low growing, whereas others grow more upright. Impatiens are perfect for containers in shady spots and for woodland settings among ferns and hostas.

WHEN TO PLANT

Directly seed impatiens into the garden in late May, or if you are impatient for impatiens, transplant seedlings or potted plants from the garden center instead.

WHERE TO PLANT

They can handle some (morning) sun if they must, but impatiens prefer bright indirect light or shade. A woodland setting with moist, well-drained soil is ideal. They like soil a bit toward neutral but seem to manage just fine with the more acid soil typical in the Philadelphia area. Their shallow roots suit them for planting under trees and shrubs.

HOW TO PLANT

Dig and loosen the soil down 10 to 12 inches, mixing in organic material and a sprinkling of granular slow-acting fertilizer at the same time. Dig the planting hole about as deep as and slightly wider than the rootball without its container. Set the plant in the hole so that it is level with the surrounding soil, then fill in the hole with soil and firm it gently around plant stems. Water well, and spread organic mulch on the bare soil near each plant to discourage weeds. Set plants about 1 foot apart in groups of 3 to heighten the impact of their color.

CARE AND MAINTENANCE

Thirsty impatiens droop alarmingly. Try to water before they are under such stress. Maintaining the mulch in the garden bed helps because it retards evaporation of moisture from the soil. Impatiens in containers with soilless medium need frequent checks for moisture, especially if they receive any sun. Pinch stems back to keep plants more compact. If there is no slow-acting granular fertilizer in their soilless planting mix, impatiens in containers will need diluted liquid fertilizer in their water every 2 weeks.

ADDITIONAL INFORMATION

Occasionally, young impatiens develop aphids on their tender growing tips. Simply pinch off the infested tips, and discard them.

ADDITIONAL SPECIES, CULTIVARS, OR VARIETIES

Dazzler series plants are 8 inches tall, with large flowers. Swirl series flowers are edged with a contrasting color. Balsam impatiens (*Impatiens balsamina*) has old-fashioned, pretty, double flowers growing on upright stems among the leaves. New Guinea hybrids have narrower, pointed, variegated foliage and tropical-colored flowers. They tolerate more sun, but still prefer shade. 'Tango' is an All-America Selection. Jewelweed or snapweed (*Impatiens capensis*), a wild cousin, is native to our woods and shady roadsides. It is shallow rooted and succulent with tiny, yellowish orange flowers that hummingbirds visit.

 Did You Know?

Catalogs sometimes use specialized terms to describe impatiens and other plants:

Picotee—*flower petals edged with a strong, contrasting color. It is from the French language, meaning "to prick or dot."*

Eye—*the center of a flower blossom that is a different color from the petals.*

Series—*a group of similar plants, usually hybrids, that are not identical.*

Larkspur

Consolida ambigua

Other Names: Annual Delphinium,
  Rocket Larkspur

Mature Size: 2 to 5 feet tall; 2 to 3 feet wide

Bloom Time: June through October

Flower Color/Type: Shades of blue, pink, white, lilac; single or double

Features: Attracts hummingbirds

Color photograph on page 201.

Light Requirements:

Larkspur is the next best thing to delphinium, which struggles in the Philadelphia area because of our warm nights. It, too, provides vertical interest with upright, floret-covered spires in wonderful shades of blue, pink, or white. Larkspur florets may be single or double, and they are about 1 inch long and spurred. They are arrayed along the upper parts of stems above feathery, soft-green, 4-inch-long leaves. Finely divided into many narrow leaflets, the foliage of massed larkspurs creates a misty effect that contrasts well with coarser-textured foliage of neighboring plants. Sometimes flowers are tightly clustered along the stems; other times they are widely spaced. Use larkspur as a filler in a flower border for a cottage garden look or in a cutting garden.

WHEN TO PLANT

Larkspur does not like transplanting, so either work with very young plants in May, or plant seeds directly into the garden. Sow them in late fall after frost or in the very early spring. They can handle cold, if the soil is workable, taking about 20 days to germinate.

WHERE TO PLANT

Plant larkspurs where they will get full sun. They do fine in decent garden soil of any type that is well-drained.

HOW TO PLANT

Prepare the planting bed by loosening the soil down 6 to 8 inches and mixing in a handful of a granular slow-acting all-purpose fertilizer to give the new plants a boost. Add organic matter to improve soil drainage and moisture-holding capacity if needed. Sow seeds as directed on the seed packet, or plant seedlings in holes about the size of their rootballs. Thin seedlings about 10 to 12 inches apart to allow for their mature width.

CARE AND MAINTENANCE

Mulch the bare soil around larkspur seedlings to discourage weeds and retard evaporation of moisture from the soil. Water them regularly until they are established and then whenever rainfall is scarce. Cut off faded flower heads to groom the plants and stimulate continued flowering. Allowed to dry and form seeds, larkspur will self-sow and come up on its own next year. The seeds of hybrids may produce plants that do resemble the original plant, however. Larkspur tends to decline and die back after flowering. Tall, blossom-heavy plants will need staking so that they do not fall over in wind and heavy rain.

ADDITIONAL INFORMATION

Larkspurs air dry easily and hold their color well. Cut stems with about half of their florets open and half buds. Strip the leaves from the stems, and hang them in bunches in a warm, dry place. **Note: All parts of larkspur are poisonous.**

ADDITIONAL SPECIES, CULTIVARS, OR VARIETIES

Dwarf Rocket series has double flowers and grows 1 to 2 feet tall. Plants of the Giant Imperial series branch readily low on 2- to 3-feet-tall main stems; they have double flowers that are ideal for cutting.

Did You Know?

Wherever they grow, larkspurs attract the local humming-birds. Ruby-throated hummingbirds are the only species east of the Mississippi River, so they are the ones that visit Philadelphia gardens. Migrating to and from their homes in Central America, they regularly fly across the Gulf of Mexico. They arrive here in May and leave anytime after July. Both males and females are iridescent green on top, white below. The male has the trademark ruby bib as well as olive-tinted sides. Ruby-throats nest in open woodlands, parks, and gardens near their favorite flowers. The size of demitasse cups, their nests are made of downy plant material, lichen-covered leaves, and such, anchored with spider webbing. They nest in hickory, hornbeam, oak, pine, and tulip trees, raising 1 or 2 broods of 2 eggs each season.

Marigold

Tagetes species and hybrids

Other Names: African/American Marigold, French Marigold, Signet Marigold

Light Requirements:

Mature Size: 8 to 36 inches tall; 10 to 20 inches wide

Bloom Time: June to October

Flower Color/Type: Shades of yellow, orange, mahogany, white, bicolor; single, double

Features: Attracts butterflies; edible; evening garden

Color photograph on page 201.

Their various common names notwithstanding, marigolds are from Mexico. They have a long history in gardens in the United States, though. Their intense color, many forms, and reliability qualify them as dependable summer standbys, lasting well into fall when their colors coordinate beautifully with autumn hues. Marigold foliage is composed of finely cut, green leaflets and is notorious for its distinctive musky smell. The flowers are from ½ to 4 or 5 inches wide, a size for every landscape and garden use. The American, formerly African, marigolds are the tallest and are good for small hedges to divide the garden area, edging for walks, backdrops for shorter flowers, and cutting. Their hybrids, triploid types, have 4- to 5-inch-wide double blossoms and withstand heat very well. Smaller French and signet marigolds are great for edging, containers, and interplanting with vegetables.

WHEN TO PLANT

Plant homegrown or garden center plants outdoors in mid May when the weather warms up. Marigold seeds are easy to handle and germinate in no time. They bloom in 8 weeks. Plant garden center plants for the larger American types.

WHERE TO PLANT

Marigolds thrive in sun and love hot, southern exposures. They will take any soil of poor to average fertility that is well-drained. With ample moisture they can handle the reflected light and heat of paved surfaces.

HOW TO PLANT

Dig the soil down 8 to 10 inches, and add organic matter to improve its drainage if necessary. Add a handful of a granular slow-acting all-purpose fertilizer. Sow seeds as directed on the seed packet, or dig planting holes about the size of transplant rootballs. Set each plant in its hole so that it is level with the surrounding ground. Fill in with soil, firm it gently, and water well. Space tall types about 15 inches apart, the smaller ones 8 to 10 inches apart.

CARE AND MAINTENANCE

Water marigolds when rainfall is sparse. Avoid overhead watering of American marigolds, which causes their flowers to deteriorate rapidly. A 2- or 3-inch layer of mulch on the soil discourages weeds and retains soil moisture. Stake tall American types to protect them from wind and rain storms. Clip off faded marigold flowers to groom the plants and prevent reseeding.

ADDITIONAL INFORMATION

Watch for caterpillars and Japanese beetles on American marigolds. Control aphids by pinching off the infested plant part or by spraying insecticidal soap according to label instructions. Marigold foliage may have a gray mildew coating, more unsightly than dangerous. If foliage and flowers turn yellow and are stunted, however, pull up plants immediately, and put them in a plastic bag in the trash. Disinfect any tools in a solution of hot water and household bleach.

ADDITIONAL SPECIES, CULTIVARS, OR VARIETIES

American/African marigold (*Tagetes erecta*), the Lady Hybrid series, is an All-Time Gold Medal All-America Selection winner. 'French Vanilla' is the first hybrid white marigold 24 inches tall, and has flowers 3 inches wide. Afro-French or triploid hybrid 'Nugget Supreme Yellow' is long flowering. French marigold (*Tagetes patula*) 'Golden Gate' and 'Queen Sophia' are All-America Selections. Grand Prix Mix flowers are double, 3 inches wide. Signet marigolds (*Tagetes tenuifolia*) are more open with lacy leaves and single ½-inch flowers. 'Lemon Gem' has lemon-scented foliage.

 Did You Know?

Marigolds are almost synonymous with the W. Atlee Burpee Seed Company in Warminster, Pennsylvania. Since 1915 the company has been at the forefront of marigold breeding. It awarded a $10,000 prize to an Iowa gardener who helped develop a white one. For all its efforts, the company did not succeed in getting the marigold chosen as the national flower (that honor belongs to the rose).

Nasturtium

Tropaeolum majus

Other Name: Indian Cress
Mature Size: 8 to 12 inches tall; 2 feet wide
Bloom Time: June to October
Flower Color/Type: Mahogany, red, orange,
yellow, white; single, double-spurred cups
Features: Old-fashioned; evening garden; attracts hummingbirds; edible

Light Requirements:

Color photograph on page 201.

Gardeners cannot resist planting nasturtiums somewhere in their yards. They were routinely included in Thomas Jefferson's garden plan at Monticello. Part of their appeal is their versatility because the dwarf-mounded, semitrailing, and trailing forms of nasturtium literally cover just about any landscape situation. Also, they are low maintenance. Their bright, zesty flowers and interesting foliage account for most of their appeal, however. Nasturtium flowers have 5 creased petals with slightly frilled tips and spurred bases in exuberant jewel colors. They bloom at the tips of slim, flexible, pale-green or bluish green stems that nestle among similarly stemmed lily pad–type leaves. Newer forms of nasturtium feature pastel-colored flowers that rise above the foliage and have no spurs. Use nasturtiums for edging, hanging baskets, and screens for eyesore utilities and drain pipes. As ground covers, trailing types insinuate themselves through and among other plants to weave them together or fill bare spots in vegetable beds where plants have been harvested. Their colors are just right for fall.

WHEN TO PLANT

Nasturtiums are not available as garden center seedlings because they resent transplanting. They are easy to grow from seeds. Plant seeds directly in the garden or in containers after the last expected frost in mid-May.

WHERE TO PLANT

Nasturtiums do best in full sun, but tolerate some shade well. They like decent soil, not overly rich in nutrients, but well-drained. Shore conditions are ideal. Nasturtiums will grow indoors over the winter in a cool, sunny room or greenhouse, too. Start seeds in pots of soilless mix outdoors, and then bring them inside in October before frost hits.

HOW TO PLANT

Soak seeds overnight in lukewarm water to soften their hard coatings a bit. Then plant them as directed on the seed packet in garden soil that has been loosened down 4 to 6 inches. Cover seeds with soil to provide the darkness they need to germinate. Expect leaves in 10 days or so, then flowers in 5 to 6 weeks. The size of garden peas, seeds are easily handled by kids and produce results fast enough to suit their attention spans.

CARE AND MAINTENANCE

Nasturtiums are great for weekend gardeners because they need so little attention. Water them as they get established and thereafter when conditions are droughtlike. Do not fertilize them if their soil is decent. If flowering is sparse after several weeks, allow them to dry out a bit to stress them into production. Clean them up promptly after the first dusting of frost reduces them to black mush.

ADDITIONAL INFORMATION

Watch for aphids underneath nasturtium leaves, a chronic problem. Pinch out the infested leaves and flowers, wash them with a forceful water spray, or spray them with insecticidal soap. Nasturtiums make great cut flowers for small indoor arrangements.

ADDITIONAL SPECIES, CULTIVARS, OR VARIETIES

'Alaska' has variegated leaves, green marbled with cream, and mixed flower color. Plants of the Double Dwarf Jewel series have bushy small habits, large, double flowers. Semi-tall Double Gleam Mix is an All-America Selection with double and semidouble flowers on 3-foot-tall plants. 'Empress of India' cascades with large blue-green leaves and single, brilliant-red flowers. 'Fordhook Favorite' is a trailer, with single flowers. 'Moonlight' has pale-yellow flowers. 'Whirlybird' has spurless, upturned flowers.

 Did You Know?

People have been eating nasturtiums for ages. The first truly American book on gardening, The American Gardener's Calendar, *mentions their excellence in garnishing dishes and how their pickled unripe seeds resemble capers. Spicy with a bit of bite, nasturtium leaves and petals brighten salads. Mince flower petals in cheese spreads or butter. Stuff whole flowers with tuna salad or something similar. Use only those never treated with insecticides. Pick them early in the morning.*

Nicotiana

Nicotiana species and hybrids

Other Names: Ornamental Tobacco, Flowering Tobacco

Mature Size: 1 to 2 feet tall; 1 foot wide

Bloom Time: June through October

Flower Color/Type: Red, rose, pink, white, green; trumpets

Features: Old-fashioned; fragrance; evening garden; attracts moths, butterflies, and hummingbirds

Light Requirements:

Color photograph on page 201.

Nicotianas are instantly recognizable by their narrow, tubular flowers with star-shaped flaring petals at their tips. The original lanky night bloomer, whose flowers drooped during the day, then perked up at night to release a wonderful fragrance to lure moths, is still available as jasmine tobacco. It has been joined in the garden center by newer, more compact versions of nicotiana that, though less fragrant, bear more flowers and are open in the daytime. There are also hybrids in wonderful colors that are semidwarf and bloom all season. Nicotiana flowers grow in sprays at the ends of branching stems emerging from rosettes of green leaves near the soil. They bloom all season, often tolerating the first frost to continue into early November. Some plants may even survive under mulch during a mild winter. Allowed to set seeds when flowers fade, they self-sow generously for next year. Use nicotianas as their heights suggest—middle of borders, edging, containers, along fences, or in a cutting garden.

WHEN TO PLANT

Nicotiana plants in the garden center are not likely to have buds or bloom yet. If they do, do not purchase them. Plant in May as soon as the soil is workable. Plants that have been hardened off can handle an errant light frost.

WHERE TO PLANT

Site nicotianas where they can receive full sun at least in the mornings. Some afternoon shade is fine and even enhances their colors. They like good garden soil that drains well.

HOW TO PLANT

Cultivate the soil down 8 to 10 inches, digging in granular slow-acting all-purpose fertilizer to provide uniform, season-long nutrition. Dig a planting hole about as deep as and slightly wider than each rootball tipped out of its container. Set each plant in its hole so that it is level with the surrounding soil. Fill in the hole with soil, firm it gently around plant stems, and water well. Space smaller hybrid plants about 10 to 12 inches apart, taller ones up to 2 feet apart.

CARE AND MAINTENANCE

Nicotianas are content with routine, minimal care. Water them until they are established and if rainfall is sparse. A 2- to 3-inch layer of organic mulch over their soil will discourage weeds and conserve soil moisture. Cutting their flowers stimulates more flowering and provides blossoms for indoor display. Protect favorite plants outdoors with a mulch of chopped leaves to try to overwinter them.

ADDITIONAL INFORMATION

Nicotianas are vulnerable to diseases that affect their tobacco cousins, such as mosaic virus or Colorado potato beetles, but these are not common problems in most garden settings.

ADDITIONAL SPECIES, CULTIVARS, OR VARIETIES

Jasmine tobacco (*Nicotiana × sanderae*) hybrids include the following: 'Nikki Red' (an All-America Selection); 'Domino' hybrids (pink with white eyes, lime, or assorted colors); and 'Heaven Scent Mix' (fragrance). *Nicotiana sylvestris* has narrow, white, drooping tubular flowers, 2-foot-long leaves, and 5- to 6-foot-long stalks.

 Did You Know?

True tobacco (Nicotiana tabacum) *is also ornamental. It reaches 7 feet and has pinkish blossoms. In 1560, 70 years after Columbus encountered natives of the West Indies smoking dried leaves of a certain plant called "Tobago," Jean Nicot, a French ambassador to Portugal, planted it in his Lisbon garden and harvested the leaves for snuff. He eventually introduced it into France. Thus, it began its commercial and ornamental life with the man memorialized in its botanical name,* Nicotiana. *It is also reflected in the name of the compound in its foliage that is so poisonous that it was eventually banned from use as a botanical insecticide.*

Pansy

Viola × wittrockiana

Other Names: Heartsease, Ladies-Delight

Mature Size: 6 to 10 inches tall; to
   12 inches wide

Bloom Time: March through June;
   September through December

Flower Color/Type: All colors except green, blotched, bicolor, tricolor;
   flat "faces"

Features: Old-fashioned; scented; edible

Light Requirements:

Color photograph on page 202.

There are many cool-weather flowering annuals, but pansies save the day. Their jaunty, colorful blooms ease difficult seasonal transitions. Cousins of violets and Johnny jump-ups, they are tougher than they look. Fall-planted ones can survive Philadelphia winters with no fuss. Over the years breeders have developed ever larger, more colorful flowers that face upward rather than nod and that can handle heat, too, blooming well into the summer. Plant pansies anywhere, everywhere! The large, multicolored, clown-faced ones show best in containers or rock gardens or grouped as focal points and fillers until perennials appear. The slightly smaller, single-colored ones make great ground covers, alone or among spring bulbs such as snowdrops or tulips. They hold up better in the rain.

WHEN TO PLANT

Plant young plants, if available, in the fall. They may bloom some before serious winter weather arrives. They will be ready to go with well-developed root systems in early spring. Alternatively, buy seedlings the minute they are displayed at the garden center in late winter, and plant as soon as soil is workable.

WHERE TO PLANT

Pansies do best in full sun during the cool spring and fall when they are at their peak. To encourage continued bloom over the summer, put them in some shade. They are not picky about soil type as long as it is reasonably rich, cool, moist, and well-drained.

HOW TO PLANT

Dig the soil down 6 to 8 inches or more, and add organic matter to improve drainage. For spring planting, also mix in granular slow-acting all-purpose fertilizer. For fall planting, delay fertilizing until early spring if you wish.

Dig planting holes about as deep as and slightly wider than their rootballs removed from their containers. Set each plant in its hole at soil level. Fill in the hole with soil, firm it gently around plant stems, and water well. Place pansies about 6 to 8 inches apart. Plant seedlings in windowboxes and other containers in soilless potting medium to which slow-acting fertilizer has been added. Be sure they have drainage holes in the bottom.

CARE AND MAINTENANCE
Cover the soil around fall-planted pansies with chopped leaves, straw, or evergreen boughs after hard frost to insulate the soil. Mulch spring-planted seedlings to keep their soil cool and extend their bloom period. Periodically pinch off faded flower stems to groom the plants, stimulate continued flowering, and prevent reseeding. Pull up pansies when they begin to flop in the heat, and replace them with heat-loving annuals.

ADDITIONAL INFORMATION
Pansies growing in somewhat shaded, moist sites may suffer the attention of slugs, which eat holes in their leaves and flowers. Include pansies in cutflower bouquets. As they mature, their flower stems get longer.

ADDITIONAL SPECIES, CULTIVARS, OR VARIETIES
Hybridizing over 100 years has yielded many, many kinds and colors, new ones appearing every year. Choose from among grandiflora types ('Majestic Giants') with flowers up to 4 inches across or multiflora types (Universal Hybrids) with 2½-inch-wide, more numerous flowers.

 Did You Know?

Old-fashioned flowers are those with nostalgic associations. Typically, they evoke memories of grandmother's (or great-grandmother's) garden. Usually heirlooms from before the turn of the century, they suggest times when life was simpler and slower paced on the farm or in a small town. A hallmark of old-fashioned flowers is fragrance, as found in pansies, four o'clocks, and nicotiana. Often sacrificed by modern hybrid-izers in favor of other traits such as size, color, habit, and disease resistance, fragrance turns back the clock.

Petunia

Petunia × *hybrida*

Other Name: Garden Petunia

Mature Size: 6 to 18 inches tall; 12 to 18 inches wide

Bloom Time: June through October

Flower Color/Type: Shades of pink, red, white, purple, lilac, yellow, and bicolor; single or double funnels

Features: Old-fashioned; fragrance (some); attracts butterflies, moths, and hummingbirds; evening garden

Color photograph on page 202.

Light Requirements:

If there were no petunias, they would have to be invented. In fact, botanically speaking, they were. Descendants of two South American species, they are the result of generations of crossbreeding. The most recent hybrids are wildly colorful and elaborate, featuring ruffled or fringed petals, edged and streaked petals, dark eyes in their centers, and very large or very small blossoms. Petunia flowers bloom at the tips of lax stems among simple, oval leaves covered with sticky fuzz. Many, especially purple ones, have a wonderful cinnamon fragrance early in the morning and late in the day. Petunias continue to top the list of most popular annuals year after year.

WHEN TO PLANT

Plant young plants from the garden center in May when the soil has warmed and dried out. Choose plants with healthy green foliage and swelling buds. Plant on an overcast day or in the evening so seedlings are not stressed by the sun while coping with transplant shock.

WHERE TO PLANT

Plant petunias in full sun for most abundant bloom. They accept almost any kind of soil that drains well. They prefer, but do not insist, that it be light and toward neutral. Plant ground cover types on sunny slopes, cascading ones in hanging baskets and other containers. The smaller the flower size, the smaller the overall plant.

HOW TO PLANT

Acclimate seedlings raised indoors to the outdoors by setting them out during the day for a few hours for a week or two prior to planting, increasing the time until they stay out all night. Prepare the planting area by digging the soil down 8 to 10 inches and mixing in granular slow-acting all-purpose fertilizer to provide steady nutrition all season. Add organic matter to improve the soil's water retention and drainage if necessary. Dig the planting hole about as deep as and slightly wider than the petunia seedling's rootball with its container removed. Set each plant in its hole level with the surrounding ground. Fill in the hole with soil, firm it gently around plant stems, and water well. Group upright plants about 12 inches apart in flower borders.

CARE AND MAINTENANCE

Petunias are shallow rooted, so they need regular moisture from rain or the hose to do their best. Without slow-release fertilizer in the soil, they will need a snack of diluted liquid fertilizer every month or so while they are in high gear. They bloom at the tips of stems, which become progressively longer with each successive flower. Pinch leggy stems back by half to stimulate more bloom.

ADDITIONAL INFORMATION

Do not grow petunias near their vegetable cousins, such as tomatoes, potatoes, or eggplant, because their pests, whiteflies and flea beetles, like petunias, too. Petunias in containers may need daily watering in summer. Double-flowered types are very susceptible to flower damage from overhead watering or rain.

ADDITIONAL SPECIES, CULTIVARS, OR VARIETIES

Gardeners may choose from hundreds of petunia varieties. Decide on the type, then the color to narrow the choice. Many have been All-America Selections over the years. Milliflora types have small, 1-inch flowers and are ideal for containers. Multifloras are 2 to 3 inches (improved ones are called floribundas). Grandifloras have huge, 5-inch blooms, and double grandifloras are even larger. 'Purple Wave', a 1995 All-America Selection, and others in the Wave series carpet the ground with blooms.

 Did You Know?

Hybrid plants are more expensive than open-pollinated ones because they are painstakingly hand-pollinated to assure that the correct parents are paired. This must be done each year with the same parents under scientifically controlled conditions to assure uniformity. Hybrids typically offer more unusual plants, more colors, fancier shapes, and enhanced disease and weather resistance.

Portulaca

Portulaca grandiflora

Other Names: Moss Rose, Sun Rose

Mature Size: 6 to 10 inches tall; 6 to
  12 inches wide

Bloom Time: June through October

Flower Color/Type: Shades of pink and red, orange, yellow, white;
  single or double cups

Features: Low water demand

Light Requirements:

Color photograph on page 202.

Portulaca is the agreeable, easy-care plant that is perfectly happy decorating the hottest, most inhospitable site on the property. Its desert heritage enables it to survive with aplomb, producing waves of brightly colored flowers at the tips of its trailing stems all summer. Up to 2 inches wide, the flowers open wide during sunny days and close at night or on cloudy days. When they fade, they drop off, leaving behind tiny seeds for a new crop of portulaca next year. New, fancier hybrids offer double flowers and more of them, but their self-sown plants may not resemble them. Portulaca foliage is succulent and narrow, like needles, and it and the stems may be green or tinged with red or bronze. Use portulaca as a filler in sunny beds where other plants go dormant by midsummer, in rock gardens, between stepping-stones, and in containers. Massed as a ground cover, it will obscure embarrassing bare spots in the yard.

WHEN TO PLANT

Portulaca needs heat to thrive. Plant young plants from the garden center in late May when the weather starts to get warm. They will bloom before seedlings self-sown by last year's plants.

WHERE TO PLANT

Site portulaca in full sun to provide the heat it needs. It actually prefers sandy, lean soil that drains well. Plant it where nothing else will grow.

HOW TO PLANT

Prepare the planting area by scratching or digging the soil down 4 to 6 inches, deeper if it needs sand or gravel mixed into it to improve its drainage. Either sow seeds as directed on the package, or dig a planting hole about as deep as and slightly wider than each portulaca seedling's rootball without its container. Set each plant in its hole so that it is level with the surrounding ground. Fill in the hole with soil, firming it gently around plant stems, and water well. Space portulaca seedlings 6 to 8 inches apart.

CARE AND MAINTENANCE

Portulaca does fine on whatever moisture comes from rain. Use no fertilizer or mulch. A bit of weeding may be necessary until plants really spread.

ADDITIONAL INFORMATION

Portulaca has no pests or diseases.

ADDITIONAL SPECIES, CULTIVARS, OR VARIETIES

Cloudbeater Hybrids flowers are double, nonclosing. 'Sundial Peppermint' flowers are bicolored pink and red. Sundial Hybrid Mix flowers come in many bright colors. Purslane (*Portulaca oleracea*) is a weed relative and often turns up where portulaca grows. It has flatter, rounded leaves and little yellow flowers that produce copious seeds if permitted. Its foliage is edible.

 Did You Know?

Plants with a desert heritage are suited to life without much moisture. Some, like portulaca, are succulent, their fleshy stems and leaves filled with moisture-retaining sap, and coated with wax to prevent drying out. They not only survive drought well, but require little water, period. Other plants have physical characteristics that identify them as low-water-demand plants in a landscape setting. The adaptations are most often in their foliage because that is where plants lose moisture most as they transpire. They may have small leaves or thorns instead, or finely divided leaves that reduce the surface area exposed to sun. Many have silver or gray foliage that reflects heat and light, hairs on their leaves that shade leaf surfaces and trap dew, and leaves with aromatic oils that are volatile in heat to envelop the plant in a protective haze. Low-water-demand plants often have fleshy, deep roots, or taproots, to store moisture and trailing habits to keep them close to whatever soil moisture is present.

Red Salvia

Salvia splendens

Other Name: Scarlet Sage

Mature Size: 1 to 3 feet tall; 1 to
1½ feet wide

Bloom Time: May through October

Flower Color/Type: Red, purple, salmon, maroon, cream; spiked clusters

Features: Attracts hummingbirds

Color photograph on page 202.

Light Requirements:

Red salvia is impossible to overlook in a residential yard or garden. Its upright posture and the richness and brightness of its red flowers make it such a standout that most neighboring plants retire into the background under its intensity. A little red salvia goes a long way unless you want to lure hummingbirds—then plant a bed of it. This plant seems made to order for hummers, its narrow, tubular flowers crowding along tall stems and facing outward for easy access. They contrast wonderfully with the heart-shaped, medium-green foliage below. The traditional salvias are tall and red flowered; newer, more garden-compatible varieties have more rounded habits, dwarf or intermediate height, and a range of softer colors. Use various size salvias to line walks and walls or in tubs and windowboxes.

WHEN TO PLANT

Transplant homegrown or garden center plants in May when all danger of frost is past and the soil is warm and drier. Choose an overcast day or late hour so that direct sun will not stress newly planted seedlings.

WHERE TO PLANT

Full sun is best for the most intense color and fullest shape of the red salvias. Those of other colors can take a bit of shade. Salvias need moist, but not soggy, soil because they withstand lots of summer heat. Choose a site that takes advantage of their heat tolerance, for instance, poolside planters or south-facing windowboxes.

HOW TO PLANT

Prepare the planting area by digging the soil down 8 to 10 inches and mixing in granular slow-acting all-purpose fertilizer to provide steady nutrition all season. Sow seeds as directed on their packet, or dig planting holes about as deep as and slightly wider than the salvia plants' rootballs with their containers removed. Set each plant in its hole so that it is at the level of the surrounding ground. Fill in the hole with soil, firm it gently, and water well. Space tall salvias about 2 feet apart; medium and dwarf types proportionally less.

CARE AND MAINTENANCE

Typical of most annuals, red salvias have shallow root systems and appreciate regular moisture from rain or sprinkler. Using 2 or 3 inches of organic mulch on their soil helps it retain moisture. Deadhead spent flowers. Pinch back stems of tall varieties to stimulate branching. Newer, more compact types branch automatically. Stake tall salvias to keep them neat and safe from winds of summer storms.

ADDITIONAL INFORMATION

Use red salvias as the centerpiece of a red, white, and blue garden. Plant them behind white petunias, then plant low-growing blue ageratum in front. Red salvias do not make good cut flowers because their color fades. Air dried, they hold some color but lose the brightness.

ADDITIONAL SPECIES, CULTIVARS, OR VARIETIES

'Firecracker' and 'Hot Stuff' are dwarf, under 1 foot tall. 'America' is mid-sized to 20 inches. 'Salsa Mix' is a color assortment. 'Splendens Tall' is later flowering and 30 inches tall. Scarlet salvia (*Salvia coccinea*), a native red sage, has a more informal habit and grows 3 to 4 feet tall. 'Lady in Red', more compact at 2 to 3 feet, was an All-America Selection in 1992.

 Did You Know?

Plants reveal many of their problems through their foliage. Is red salvia foliage:

- *Drooping or wilting?* Dryness.
- *Yellow on lower leaves, dull or grayish on upper?* Nutritional deficiency.
- *All pale?* Whiteflies.
- *Pale and/or curled?* Aphids.
- *Punctured with ragged holes?* Slugs.
- *Stippled with pale dots or discolored?* Spider mites.
- *Black and soft all over?* Frost killed.
- *Gray blotched or coated?* Mildew.

Snapdragon

Antirrhinum majus

Other Name: Garden Snapdragon

Mature Size: 6 to 30 inches tall; 8 to 18 inches wide

Bloom Time: June through October

Flower Color/Type: White, yellow, pink, orange, rose, lavender; jaw shaped

Features: Old-fashioned; scent; butterfly larval host

Light Requirements:

Color photograph on page 202.

The snapdragon is one of those plants fondly remembered from childhood, but not as frequently grown in home gardens now as in the past. That is unfortunate because these classic staples of florist bouquets are also sturdy, colorful garden plants. Their distinctive flowers are 1 to 1½ inches long, with 2 upper petals and 3 lower petals forming "dragon jaws." They are compactly clustered along narrow, tall stems above fine-textured, green foliage. Available in almost every color except blue and black, snapdragons open gradually from the lower to the upper stem, creating spires of pastel colors. Newer hybrids have fancy butterfly and double azalea-type flowers that are more open faced with fluted edges. Use dwarf-sized snaps for edging, traditional bedding, containers, or rock gardens. Intermediate-sized ones are perfect for a mixed flower border, tucked in among shrubs or along fences. Like the tall ones, they are good for larger containers and cutting. They are technically tender perennials and commonly survive mild winters in Philadelphia-area gardens.

WHEN TO PLANT

Sow seeds outdoors as soon as the soil is dry enough to cultivate. Snapdragon seeds do not mind some chill. Wait to plant young plants from the garden center with at least 4 sets of leaves until early May.

WHERE TO PLANT

Snapdragons like full sun, even though during our peak summer weeks the heat may stop their growth temporarily. They will resume when temperatures moderate. They can take some shade and virtually any type of soil that drains well here so that water does not pool and cause stem rot.

HOW TO PLANT

Whether sowing seeds directly into the garden or planting seedlings, loosen the soil by digging down 6 to 8 inches. Mix in granular slow-acting all-purpose fertilizer to supply consistent and uniform nutrition to the snapdragons over their long season of bloom. Plant seeds as directed on the packet. Plant plants by digging holes about as deep as and slightly wider than their rootballs when removed from their containers. Set each one in its hole so that it is level with the surrounding soil. Fill in the hole with soil, firm it gently, and water well. Space tall snapdragon plants about 1 foot apart, dwarf ones about 8 inches, to assure good air circulation when plants are mature.

CARE AND MAINTENANCE
Water young snapdragons until they are well established. Then water only in the absence of regular rainfall when they are so dry that their foliage starts to droop. A 2- or 3-inch layer of organic mulch on the soil between them will discourage competing weeds and retain soil moisture longer. Stake tall varieties to assure straight stems for cutting. Pinch off stems with spent flowers to promote side branching for bushier plants. For a return engagement, either allow snaps to self-sow their seeds, or mulch disease-free plants to encourage them to overwinter.

ADDITIONAL INFORMATION
Snapdragons are prone to rust, so choose resistant varieties, rotate plants around the yard, and avoid overhead watering. This fungal disease develops in cool, humid weather on leaves that are wet for more than 6 hours.

ADDITIONAL SPECIES, CULTIVARS, OR VARIETIES
'Tahiti' is low growing; its seeds are available as individual colors or a mixture. 'Little Darling' was an All-America Selection in 1971. 'Rocket' is a tall hybrid ideal for cutting. 'Princess White,' bicolor with a purple "lip," was a 1987 All-America Selection.

 Did You Know?

Colorful and long-blooming annual flowers are a good way to introduce kids to gardening. Seeds of sunflowers, nasturtiums, zinnias, and marigolds are easy to handle and germinate quickly. Unusual flowers such as snapdragons and pansies appeal to the imagination. Set aside a small garden plot for the children to plant and enjoy.

Spider Flower

Cleome hasslerana

Spider flowers are a contradiction of bold structure and delicate flowers; therefore, they are both interesting and attractive in the garden. They grow as tall, sturdy-stemmed, branching plants, decorated with light-green, palm-shaped foliage having 5 to 7 narrow lobes. The spider flowers themselves top each branch as loose, rounded 5- to 6-inch-wide clusters of inch-wide florets, each with several extended thready stamens that suggest spider legs. Over time, the main stem grows woody and develops thorns. This plant flowers nonstop. As successive flower heads form, its branches elongate and become laddered with seedpods from previous blossoms. Permitted to dry on the plant, they will release thousands of tiny seeds. These lanky, slightly cockeyed plants are best used informally at the back of a border, along fences and boundaries, and in cutting gardens.

WHEN TO PLANT

After planting spider flower the first year, just thin the resulting gazillion tiny seedlings in subsequent years in June when they are a few inches tall. Transplant homegrown seedlings or young plants from the garden, or sow seeds directly into the garden anytime after mid-May.

WHERE TO PLANT

Spider flowers prefer full sun; they accept some shade but become lankier. They are tough enough to handle reflected heat and sun from pavement and walls, poor soil, and neglect.

HOW TO PLANT

Whether sowing seeds directly into the garden or planting young plants, prepare the soil by digging down 6 to 8 inches and mixing in granular slow-acting all-purpose fertilizer that will supply consistent and uniform nutrition to the spider flowers over their long season of bloom. Plant seeds as directed on the packet. Plant young plants by digging holes about as deep as and slightly wider than their rootballs when removed from their containers. Set each one in its hole so that it is level with the surrounding soil. Fill in the hole with soil, firming it gently around plant stems, and water well. Space plants about 2 feet apart to allow for their mature size.

CARE AND MAINTENANCE

Water young plants until they are well established. A 2- or 3-inch layer of organic material spread on the soil between them as a mulch will discourage competing weeds and retain soil moisture longer. Although they can take some drought when mature, spider flowers do best with regular moisture provided by either rain or sprinkler. Stake fully grown plants in areas exposed to winds and storms. There is no need to deadhead spent flowers because they disappear into seedpods, but it is advisable to cut off aging, elongated flowering stems where rows of seedpods are maturing. This will control rampant reseeding, make the plant a bit more compact, and reinvigorate its blooming.

ADDITIONAL INFORMATION

If saving seeds from last year's crop, be sure to prechill them in the refrigerator for a few days before planting in May. Direct sowing them into their bed in the fall eliminates that step. Do not be surprised if self-sown seedlings all tend toward pink rather than the original color mix. Spider flowers make great cut flowers.

ADDITIONAL SPECIES, CULTIVARS, OR VARIETIES

'Helen Campbell' has all-white flowers. Burpee's Queen series offers mixed colors and separate white, pink, rose, and lavender colors.

 Did You Know?

Do not count on notorious self-sowers such as spider flowers to appear the next season in areas where preemergent-type herbicides have been used to deter weeds. These products are designed to prevent seeds from germinating and do not distinguish between desirable and undesirable ones. They do not harm plants and are often used on lawns to prevent weeds from infiltrating existing turf.

Sunflower

Helianthus annum

Other Name: Annual Sunflower

Mature Size: 2 to 12 feet tall; 2 to 4 feet wide

Bloom Time: July until September

Flower Color/Type: Shades of yellow, gold, mahogany, bicolor; double; daisylike

Features: Attracts bees, butterflies, beneficial insects, and squirrels

Color photograph on page 202.

Light Requirements:

It seems incredible that something so ridiculously easy to grow is also delightful and useful. There is a reason that sunflowers have infiltrated our culture as a decorative motif on everything from napkins to shower curtains. Native to North America, their tall but gentle presence and informal, cheery demeanor are distinctively American. The wild plants that thrive on prairie farms are too tall for other than novelties in contemporary residential yards, but now there are more refined, ornamental versions. They offer a wide range of colors, flower types, and sizes. Some are even pollenless, making them more welcome indoors as cut flowers. They all still have the remarkable stiff, fuzzy stems, coarse, bristly green leaves, and wide flower heads ringed with petals.

WHEN TO PLANT

Sunflower seeds sprout and grow rapidly, so sow them directly in the yard in May when the soil warms and dries out. Plant every couple of weeks into mid-July to extend the bloom period in the yard or to stagger the seed harvest.

WHERE TO PLANT

Sunflowers need full sun. They accept any well-drained soil, but the more fertile the soil, the bigger the flowers. Site tall ones so that they do not shade other plants—in a cutting garden, in a row as a screen, along a fence, or at the back of an informal border. Because their roots emit a growth inhibitor to which some vegetables are sensitive, plant sunflowers at least 3 feet away from them. Shorter, ornamental sunflowers integrate well into flower borders or container plantings.

HOW TO PLANT

Sow seeds as directed on the seed packet. Although established plants will not need any special feeding, a handful of a granular slow-acting all-purpose fertilizer mixed into the soil during preparation of the seedbed will give new seedlings a boost. Water seedlings if rainfall is scarce until plants are well established.

CARE AND MAINTENANCE

Do not fertilize more; too much nitrogen delays bloom. Thin seedlings—dwarf types to 1 to 2 feet apart, taller types 3 to 4 feet apart. Branching ones need more space unless they are intended for cutting. Then crowd them a bit to encourage long stems. Pinch the main stems of branching types to induce more branches. Staking tall ones with heavy flower heads prevents damage from summer rain and wind storms.

ADDITIONAL INFORMATION

Some gardeners regard squirrels as a major pest of mature sunflowers. When the back of each flower head pales to yellow, then brown, cover it with a paper bag, cheesecloth, or garden fleece tied tightly at the stem to protect the ripening seeds. To harvest seeds, cut the flowers off their stalks, and hang them to finish drying. Brush the swollen seeds from their centers and store them, or lay the seedheads in the sun to dry and let the squirrels and birds have at them. **Note: Pollenless sunflowers do not produce seeds.** Sunflowers make splendid fresh or dried cut flowers. Cut stems early or late in the day, and immediately put them in water to avoid temporary wilting of petals.

ADDITIONAL SPECIES, CULTIVARS, OR VARIETIES

'Paul Bunyan' and 'Russian Mammoth' are the tallest. 'Moonshadow' is pollenless; the closest to white, it is good for evening gardens. 'Teddy Bear' is only 2 feet tall and double flowered. 'Sundance Kid' is branching and does not need staking.

 Did You Know?

While humans like to eat the very large, striped sunflower seeds, birds prefer the smaller, black ones that are also commercially raised to produce oil. They are easier for birds to manage and for most feeders to dispense. Sunflower seed fans in the Philadelphia area are cardinals, various finches, juncoes, chickadees, titmice, nuthatches, bluejays, and grosbeaks.

Zinnia

Zinnia elegans

Other Name: Youth and Old Age

Mature Size: ½ to 3 feet tall; 1 to
2 feet wide

Bloom Time: June through October

Flower Color/Type: Nearly every color but blue and black; bicolor;
single or double

Features: Old-fashioned; attracts butterflies, hummingbirds, and small
songbirds

Color photograph on page 202.

Light Requirements:

The Mexican heritage of zinnias is reflected in their bright colors, prolific bloom, and ability to handle hot, dry weather without complaint. They are fast growers and steady bloomers. Their stiff, hairy stems are decorated with coarse, green leaves and topped by flower heads ranging from small buttons up to 6 inches across. Brilliantly colored, they are composed of flat rings of layered petals around yellow centers. Hybrid forms boast fancier flowers that resemble dahlias or shaggy chrysanthemums. Some are ruffled or bicolored. Grow these tough, easy-care annuals in a garden of their own for cutting or with other flowering plants at the back of the border. The dwarf versions are great for containers and edging. They seem to be deer resistant.

WHEN TO PLANT

Wait to plant young plants from the garden center until warm weather truly arrives in late May because they respond to heat. Sow seeds when night-time temperatures are reliably above 50 degrees Fahrenheit.

WHERE TO PLANT

Zinnias thrive in full sun. They accept any decent soil that drains well. It can be a bit on the alkaline side. Choose an open site where air circulation is good to minimize mildew problems.

HOW TO PLANT

Dig the soil down 8 to 10 inches, and mix in granular slow-acting all-purpose fertilizer to provide steady nutrition all season. Either sow seeds as directed on the package, or dig planting holes about as deep as and slightly wider than the rootballs with their containers removed. Set each plant in its hole so that it is level with the surrounding ground. Fill in the hole with soil, firm it gently, and water well. Space tall zinnias about 2 feet apart, medium and dwarf types proportionally less.

CARE AND MAINTENANCE

Water young zinnia plants while they get established, then they can manage with just rainfall if they must. Regular moisture promotes better flowering. A layer of organic mulch on their soil helps it retain moisture longer. Try to avoid wetting their leaves when watering. Deadhead spent flowers to keep more coming. Allowing some to develop mature seedheads at season's end will delight the birds. Stake tall-type zinnias to keep them neat and safe from winds of summer storms.

ADDITIONAL INFORMATION

Zinnias may develop unsightly, but not fatal, mildew on their foliage as summer progresses. Sometimes Japanese beetles attack in July. Knock them from foliage into a jar of soapy water. Bag-type traps only attract more beetles to the yard. Zinnias make great cut flowers and dry well in sand or silica. Choose fully opened blossoms before their centers produce pollen.

ADDITIONAL SPECIES, CULTIVARS, OR VARIETIES

Members of the hugely diverse zinnia clan are categorized by height. Consider these small members: 'Thumbelina' is only 6 inches tall; 'Dreamland' is 12 inches tall with double flowers; Peter Pan Hybrids are All-America Selection winners; and 'Pinwheel' has good mildew resistance. A medium zinnia is 'Cut and Come Again', which is 24 inches tall, available in mixed or individual colors. A tall one is Burpee's Zenith Hybrid series, which is 30 inches tall with cactus-type flowers in mixed colors. *Zinnia angustifolia* is finer textured and low growing for ground cover and container duty. It is free from mildew problems. 'Crystal White' is an All-America Selection winner.

 Did You Know?

All-America Selections (AAS) is an organization that tests new flower and vegetable plant varieties for vigor, reliability, and improved performance. Contenders coded by number are evaluated by professional horticulturists against proven plants growing next to them in field trials all over the United States and Canada. Annual winners proudly bear the AAS logo on their seed packets and labels and in catalogs. Visit display gardens at Peddler's Village in Bucks County, and at Longwood Gardens.

CHAPTER TWO

Bulbs

*F*OR NOVICE GARDENERS, bulbs are a good way to start gardening. For experienced gardeners, they are indispensable. No single group of plants offers so much for so little effort. Ranging from giant cannas to tiny crocuses, they provide color, texture, structure, and in many cases fragrance to a variety of garden situations. Some also respond well to "forcing" for indoor blooms during the winter, and many make excellent cut flowers. Use bulbs everywhere. Naturalize them in woodlands or lawns, mass them in drifts or island beds, showcase them in borders, or nestle them in rock gardens.

BULB BIOGRAPHY

Characterizing all plants that grow from bulbous structures as bulbs is most convenient. Actually, in addition to true bulbs, which are essentially fully formed plants in bud stage, there are corms, tubers, and rhizomes—all types of swollen stem structures. All have in common the capacity to store nutrients and energy underground so that they can survive drought and heat and (in the case of hardy bulbs) cold winters. Once planted, they appear without much fuss, moisture and rising temperatures coaxing them from dormancy according to their built-in timers. They multiply by creating tiny bulblets, or offsets, attached to the main bulb or stem that are easily separated from the mother bulb and planted individually to create new plants.

Flower bulb plants are herbaceous; the foliage of most typically ripens, then dries or dies back 4 to 6 weeks after they finish blooming. While many of the most common flowering ones are cold hardy in the Philadelphia area and provide our stunning spring display, some cannot handle even our relatively mild winters. Called tender bulbs, they are planted in the spring for summer bloom. Among them are caladiums, cannas, and dahlias. (Lilies, the exception that proves the rule, handle our winters, but still bloom in the summer.) Treat tender bulbs as annuals and replace them every year, or dig them up before frost and store them over the winter to replant in the spring.

The size of bulbs influences their performance. In most cases, larger is better (and a bit more expensive). Growers grade bulbs by size, which is typically measured as the circumference of the bulb at its roundest/widest point. Use the very largest for forcing; slightly smaller ones are fine for gardens. Except for tulips, bulk purchases of smaller- or uneven-sized bulbs are ideal for naturalizing (and a bargain).

GENERAL CULTURE

Most bulbs have similar cultural preferences—good drainage, rich soil, and lots of sun. Hardy bulbs are available at retail outlets or are shipped from mail-order nurseries in late summer and early fall. Summer bloomers are available in the spring. Plant your bulbs as soon as you acquire them; they keep better in the ground than in the shed or garage where they are often forgotten. Every type of bulb has a particular optimum planting depth, but the easiest way to proceed is to use the rule of thumb: plant at a depth 2½ times the bulb's height, measured from the bottom of the hole. For many plants, such as tulips, it pays to plant them deeper. Deep planting delays offshoots, keeping them stronger, and protects them from squirrels and rodents. Plant minor bulbs, such as snowdrops and crocuses, about 3 to 4 inches deep.

If your soil is less than wonderful, your bulbs will need a dose of fertilizer in the early fall. Sprinkle a slow-acting product formulated for bulbs on the soil as instructed on its label. The rain and snow will gradually soak it in where it will become available over time to promote strong root growth. If clumps get crowded, dig up bulbs when they are dormant, separate them, discard any that are damaged, and replant. Finally, it is critical to allow the bulb foliage to soak up the sun for several weeks after blooming is finished, no matter how unsightly it is.

Begonia, Tuberous

Begonia × tuberhybrida

Other Name: Tuberous-rooted Begonia
Type: Tender tuber
Size: Up to 12 inches tall and wide
Bloom Time: Continuous from June to October
Flower Color/Type: Red, pink, orange, yellow, white; picotee, double

Light Requirements:

Color photograph on page 202.

*T*uberous begonias bloom in the shade. Sometimes pendant, usually double, their flowers are always splendid and richly colored in primary or pastel colors. Resembling roses or double camellias in form, their velvety petals are luminous in filtered or indirect light. Blossoms appear where their glossy, pointed leaves join their succulent stems. Upright plants sport flowers 6 to 8 inches across; flowers of pendant types are 3 to 4 inches. Properly stored tubers will last many years, but young 1- or 2-year-old ones are the most vigorous.

WHEN TO PLANT

Plant tubers outdoors in the spring after any danger of frost is past and the soil has warmed. Begonias are also sold as mature plants in containers from early summer to fall. Transplant them in the garden when you bring them home, or keep them in pots and hanging baskets to decorate a porch or shaded patio. Keep pots off the ground to avoid invasion by slugs.

WHERE TO PLANT

Direct sun burns begonia flowers. They like partial shade, either as filtered light or as early-morning sun that gives way to shade as the day progresses. Site them where they have good air circulation. Orient them so that their leaves receive maximum light, since they all face the same direction.

HOW TO PLANT

Tuberous begonias are fairly forgiving about soil type, but they prefer it to be rich in humus. Start tubers in pots indoors as soon as they are available (about February). Set their hollow (concave) sides up, about 1 inch below the soil surface. When frost danger is past and the soil is warm outdoors, cultivate it down 8 to 10 inches, and mix in granular slow-acting fertilizer. Transplant potted young plants (yours or some from the garden center) so that the tops of their soilballs are level with the surrounding ground. Space them about 12 inches apart to assure air circulation and forestall mildew.

CARE AND MAINTENANCE

Tuberous begonias are a bit fussy about their conditions. They dislike frost, dry soil, soggy soil, wind, and too much sun. They are worth pampering nevertheless. They need moisture alternated with short dry periods to avoid crown rot. Because potted ones dry out faster than in-ground ones, water them more often in summer heat. Avoid wetting their foliage to prevent fungal disease. Pick off spent blossoms to stimulate flowering. To keep plants compact, pinch back leggy stems often. Upright types may need staking. When the first frost kills their tops, dig up the tubers, and store them in peat moss in an area where temperatures are constant around 45 degrees Fahrenheit.

ADDITIONAL INFORMATION

Divide overwintered tubers in the spring when new bud tips show. Cut them in half so that each half has a bud, then pot them or plant them outdoors in the ground when temperature permits. Watch for the occasional aphid blitz, and pinch off stem tips where they tend to gather. These plants struggle in our area a bit because of the heat and humidity, and they may languish by late August.

ADDITIONAL SPECIES, CULTIVARS, OR VARIETIES

Standard upright, multiflora types of tuberous begonias grow 8 to 10 inches tall and yield many small flowers. Flowers in the picotee lace strain have contrasting color on the edges of their petals plus scalloped edges. Fragrant, pendant types 'Nectarine Rose', 'Fragrant Lemon', and 'Fragrant Apricot' are ideal for hanging baskets.

 Did You Know?

You can enjoy tuberous begonias all year. Bring outdoor potted ones indoors, or pot some from the garden just before frost hits and bring them indoors as houseplants. Good drainage is essential for housebound tuberous begonias. They like a bright eastern or northern exposure and periodic watering with a very diluted liquid fertilizer.

Canna

Canna × generalis

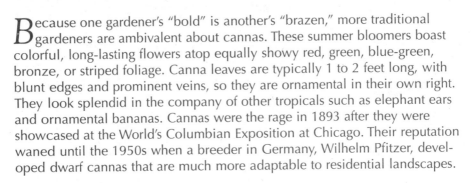

Other Name: Hybrid Canna

Type: Tender rhizome

Size: Giant over 6 feet tall; medium 3 to
6 feet; dwarf less than 3 feet tall

Bloom Time: Mid to late summer; early fall

Flower Color/Type: Pinks, salmon, red, yellow; bicolor orchid or
gladiolalike flowers

Light Requirements:

Color photograph on page 202.

Because one gardener's "bold" is another's "brazen," more traditional gardeners are ambivalent about cannas. These summer bloomers boast colorful, long-lasting flowers atop equally showy red, green, blue-green, bronze, or striped foliage. Canna leaves are typically 1 to 2 feet long, with blunt edges and prominent veins, so they are ornamental in their own right. They look splendid in the company of other tropicals such as elephant ears and ornamental bananas. Cannas were the rage in 1893 after they were showcased at the World's Columbian Exposition at Chicago. Their reputation waned until the 1950s when a breeder in Germany, Wilhelm Pfitzer, developed dwarf cannas that are much more adaptable to residential landscapes.

WHEN TO PLANT

Plant rhizomes in the spring after the soil has warmed to about 65 degrees Fahrenheit. Plant them first in pots indoors 4 weeks before the last expected spring frost (about May 15) to get a jump on the season. The sooner you plant after you purchase them, the more time the rhizomes have to grow roots.

WHERE TO PLANT

Cannas thrive on full sun and fairly rich, slightly acidic, well-drained soil of almost any type. Relegate the tall, stately ones to the back of the garden or along fences as a screen or backdrop. Smaller types mix well with annuals in a garden bed. Grow dwarf types in containers around a patio or pool.

HOW TO PLANT

Cultivate the soil down 8 to 10 inches, adding a generous dose of a granular slow-acting all-purpose fertilizer according to product label instructions. Plant the rhizomes 3 to 4 inches deep and 18 to 24 inches apart. Cover with soil, and water well.

CARE AND MAINTENANCE

To groom plants and stimulate lush flowering, pull off each faded bloom *immediately*. Cut just below its base—any farther down may cut off potential secondary flower stalks. Water cannas during drought periods; they can handle fairly damp soil. Tall types will also need staking. To store them over the winter, cut back spent stems to 3 or 4 inches, and dig up the attached rhizomes before heavy frost. Pack them, soil and all, in dry peat moss, and store in a cool, dark place that maintains 40 to 50 degrees Fahrenheit. In the spring clean off the soil and inspect them. Divide large rhizomes so that each new piece has 2 eyes or buds. Let them dry out a bit in the air overnight, then plant.

ADDITIONAL INFORMATION

Japanese beetles may be a problem after the first of July until mid-August. The best control is to pick or knock beetles off into a jar of soapy water. If the infestation is too heavy, or plants are already too tall to reach easily, spray flower and leaf surfaces with an insecticide featuring pyrethrin according to directions on its label.

ADDITIONAL SPECIES, CULTIVARS, OR VARIETIES

'Pretoria', 'Mohawk', and 'Durban' are becoming readily available. Versions of cannas that grow from seed include 'Seven Dwarf Mixed' and 'Tropical Rose' (*Canna hortensis*), which was an All-America Selection winner in 1992. *Canna glauca* is aquatic. Use it as a marginal or bog plant at the edge of a water garden or in a tub water garden on the deck or patio.

 Did You Know?

The Philadelphia Connection: A native species of canna was first spotted by Philadelphia's own William Bartram in 1777 on an exciting trip to Louisiana, which he described in his Travels *printed in London in 1792. He described the plant as "presenting a glorious show, the stem rises six, seven and nine feet tall, terminating upward with spikes of scarlet flowers." Thus began the American gardener's off-again, on-again affair with cannas.*

Crocus

Crocus vernus

Other Names: Common Crocus, Dutch Crocus

Type: Hardy corm

Size: 5 inches tall

Bloom Time: April

Flower Color/Type: White, lavender, bluish purple; goblet-shaped

Color photograph on page 202.

Light Requirements:

Most of the so-called minor bulbs such as snowdrops and squill are dainty and unassuming. Many crocuses are, too. Dutch crocuses, however, are in your face with their large-size (3 inches) and richly colored blooms with striped petals. What they lack in subtlety or humility, they more than make up for in emphatic presence. The latest of the spring-blooming crocuses to bloom, they are the least bothered by squirrels and voles, which have other plants to attend to by then. Their flowers open wide in bright sun and close tightly among their bundled, grasslike leaves at night. Count on them to multiply and spread if they like their location. A good example is the huge drifts of crocuses in February and March, just across the Delaware state line at Winterthur.

WHEN TO PLANT

Plant corms in the late summer or early fall when they become available. Prompt planting after purchase assures maximum time for root growth.

WHERE TO PLANT

Site crocuses in the sun in well-drained soil. Plant them among surface roots under the still-leafless branches of deciduous trees and shrubs. Poke them into the soil among evergreen ground covers such as sweet woodruff, ajuga, English ivy, or even lawngrass.

HOW TO PLANT

Plant crocuses 4 inches deep in ordinary soil mixed with fertilizer formulated for bulbs and cultivated down 8 to 10 inches. Plant them in individual holes, or cluster 3 or 5 corms in a single large hole. If voles are a problem, line the planting holes with wire mesh to protect the corms.

CARE AND MAINTENANCE

Crocuses seem to flourish with benign neglect. Their faded blooms sort of melt away, so they do not need deadheading. Allow the foliage to ripen and die back, even if it means delaying mowing the lawn. If flowers are targets of rodents, cover them with a low cage of hardware cloth or similar wire mesh.

ADDITIONAL INFORMATION

Plant crocuses in outdoor containers and windowboxes in the fall either alone or among dwarf evergreen shrubs. Dutch crocuses are easy to force into preseason bloom indoors. Nestle bulbs closely in a shallow, flat-bottomed bowl filled with damp gravel. Set it in a dark, cool area so that roots can develop, then bring it out into a warm room as buds show. Keep the gravel moist.

ADDITIONAL SPECIES, CULTIVARS, OR VARIETIES

'Dutch Mammoth', a hybrid, is often sold as *Crocus vernus* because it is large sized and blooms about the same time. Thomasini's crocus (*Crocus tommasinianus*), one of the earliest crocuses, is ideal for naturalizing in the lawn and will spontaneously multiply over the years. 'Whitewell Purple' is reputed to be resistant to squirrels. Greek crocus (*Crocus sieberi*) blooms during late winter, but is especially vulnerable to animal pests that pounce on the first tender new plants to appear after a bleak winter. Fall crocus (*Crocus speciosus*) blooms in mid to late October with lavender-blue to white scented flowers with yellow throats.

 Did You Know?

*Crocuses have a role in the kitchen as well as in the landscape. In some Middle Eastern cultures their starchy corms are made into flour. Saffron crocus (*Crocus sativus*) has a distinctive reddish-orange, three-branched stigma in its center. When dried, it becomes the expensive, exotic spice saffron. Although this type of crocus is not dependably hardy in our area, it is grown as a crop from southern Europe to Kashmir to provide saffron for cooks all over the world.*

Daffodil

Narcissus species and hybrids

Other Name: Narcissus
Type: Hardy bulb
Size: Dwarf 4 to 8 inches tall; standard
12 to 18 inches tall
Bloom Time: Mid-March into May
Flower Color/Type: Shades of yellow, peach, white, pink, or bicolor
cups ringed with petals

Color photograph on page 202.

Light Requirements:

The wide appeal of all kinds of daffodils is no doubt largely due to their bright, jaunty appearance at a time when everyone is sick of winter. It is also due to their interesting forms, their self-reliance, and in some cases their fragrance. For some, their ultimate virtue is that deer and rodents do not disturb them. The flowers of all types feature a central tubular "cup" protruding at right angles from a ring of 6 petals with pointed tips. They bloom at the tops of stems among long, stiff, straplike leaves. Hundreds of hybrids have been categorized by fanciers into six divisions. For most gardeners, however, the issue is simply, "How many daffodils can I fit into my yard?" The answer at Chanticleer, a public garden in Wayne, is thousands!

WHEN TO PLANT

Plant bulbs in the fall at least a month before the ground is likely to freeze hard—by early October—so they have time to grow roots. The more developed the roots, the better display next spring.

WHERE TO PLANT

Although full sun is ideal, daffodils tolerate partial sun or just bright light. Well-drained soil is a must. Create raised beds filled with soil lightened with organic material if it is clay. Daffodils bloom early enough so that they can be planted under deciduous trees and shrubs; they finish blooming before the leaves emerge and create shade.

HOW TO PLANT

Cultivate the soil at least 12 inches deep, mixing in granular fertilizer formulated for bulbs. Plant standard daffodil bulbs from 6 to 9 inches deep; plant dwarf types 4 to 6 inches deep. Plant them in clusters of 3 or more, spaced 4 or 5 inches apart, the tips of the bulbs pointed upward in the hole. In informal areas such as woodlands naturalize the planting by randomly casting handfuls of bulbs across the area and planting them where they fall.

CARE AND MAINTENANCE

Cut off spent flowers and stems when blooming is over. Allow foliage to ripen and die back naturally, even though it may look messy. Fertilize bulb beds in the fall to encourage root growth. Cover them with 2 or 3 inches of organic mulch to control weeds, conserve soil moisture, insulate soil in winter, and prevent splashing of mud onto flowers in spring.

ADDITIONAL INFORMATION

Daffodils also make excellent cut flowers. They last 4 to 6 days if stems with swelling buds are cut and immersed immediately in lukewarm water laced with a floral preservative. Many types can be forced into preseason bloom indoors, but the "paperwhites" (*Narcissus tazetta* types) are the easiest because they do not require a long cooling period.

ADDITIONAL SPECIES, CULTIVARS, OR VARIETIES

Miniatures and dwarfs such as 'Tête-a-Tête' are particularly suited to rock gardens. Dainty 'Jet Fire' and 'Peeping Tom' are popular cyclaminius types whose petals flex backward as if they are facing a strong wind. At the other extreme are the classic large trumpet daffodils, of which the enduringly popular yellow 'King Alfred' is a representative. 'Ice Follies' is a handsome white version. Although *Narcissus triandrus* hybrids are reputed not to do well in this area, 'Thalia' is a successful classic.

Did You Know?

Narcissus, the formal name for daffodil, is almost as commonly used as its informal name. It recalls the Greek myth of Narcissus, who spent his days gazing at the reflection of his handsome face in a pool of water. He was so entranced by his reflected beauty that he failed to appreciate and respond to that of the nymph Echo. She punished him by turning him into a flower destined to nod beside the pool forever.

Dahlia

Dahlia species and hybrids

Type: Tender tuber

Size: Dwarf, 1 to 2 feet tall; medium to tall, 3 to 8 feet tall

Bloom Time: Mid-June until October frost

Flower Color/Type: Yellow, orange, red, pink, purple, white, or bicolored; pompoms, cactus, double, semidouble

Light Requirements:

Color photograph on page 203.

Do not be daunted by the fact that there are more than 2,000 kinds of dahlias to choose from. Any choice will be a delight. Dahlias offer a steady riot of colorful flowers all summer, reaching their peak in September when the weather cools. Leaves may be bronze or purplish, although they are usually medium green. Their flower size varies from dwarfs typically 1 to 4 inches wide to giants as large as 18 inches. Most commonly, they are 6 to 10 inches across. After setting, buds are tantalizingly slow to open—up to 30 days—but the wait is worth it. Plant dahlias in their own bed for massed display or cutting. Or integrate them into perennial borders at the middle or back to add mass and texture, foliage contrast, and color. Use dwarfs as edgers; use tall ones in rows along fences to delineate property boundaries or to screen undesirable views.

WHEN TO PLANT

Plant bulbs outdoors in the spring after the soil has dried and warmed. The sooner you plant after you purchase them, the more time the bulb has to grow roots.

WHERE TO PLANT

Dahlias like full sun and well-drained soil. Raise the planting bed, and add organic matter to lighten clay soil if necessary.

HOW TO PLANT

Cultivate the soil down at least 12 inches, mixing in a slow-acting granular fertilizer. Dig planting holes at least 6 inches deep. Set tubers on their sides with their eyes, or buds, pointing upward. Plant them at least 1 to 3 feet apart to assure good air circulation around mature plants, which discourages powdery mildew.

CARE AND MAINTENANCE

Nondwarf types will need staking. Drive stakes into the soil at planting time to avoid harming tubers. Deadhead to promote heavy bloom. To encourage side shoots for bushier plants with more flowers, pinch out the central stem after 4 to 6 leaves form. Assure dahlias regular moisture. Because they sometimes temporarily stop blooming if the weather is too hot, mulch plants to conserve moisture, cool the soil, and prevent it from splashing on foliage during rains. Treat dahlias as annuals and allow them to die with hard frost, or dig them up and store them over the winter in moist sand, peat moss, or vermiculite in a cool place. Divide tubers in the spring when warmth causes their "eyes" to form.

ADDITIONAL INFORMATION

Jump-start dahlias indoors in pots in the early spring. Later transplant them into the garden 3 inches deeper than the pot depth. Dwarfs make good winter houseplants if they have exposure to lots of sun and/or grow lights. Dahlias make wonderful cut flowers, lasting 7 to 10 days if properly conditioned when they are picked.

ADDITIONAL SPECIES, CULTIVARS, OR VARIETIES

Some dahlias are grown from seed rather than tubers. 'Redskin', an All-America Selection winner, is a popular choice. The abundance of choices of dahlias makes it impossible to highlight any particular one.

 Did You Know?

When does a dahlia look like a mum and vice versa? Sometimes it seems as if flower breeders intend to totally confuse the poor gardener. Both dahlias and garden chrysanthemums have a variety of flower shapes—some so similar that they are often mistaken for one another. Always check the foliage to be sure.

Anemone—*pincushionlike, ray petals surround a tightly clustered center tube of petals.*

Cactus—*ray petals are curled or pointed at the tips and radiate irregularly from the center.*

Peony—*1 or 2 rows of uniform ray petals surround a central disk; some may be curled.*

Pom Pom—*petals are curved and form dense balls.*

Single—*a single row of petals surrounds a central disk in a flat plane.*

Gladiolus

Gladiolus × hortulanus

Other Names: Glad, Florists' Glad

Type: Tender corm

Size: Miniature to 3 feet; hybrid 2 to 4 feet; giant hybrid 3 to 5 feet

Bloom Time: June to October, depending on variety

Flower Color/Type: White, cream, shades of yellow, orange, salmon, red, rose, violet; bicolored/funnel shaped

Color photograph on page 203.

Light Requirements:

There is much more to gladiolus than a few spikes in a florist's arrangement. They are a real asset in the garden for color, vertical accent, and summer-long bloom if plantings are staggered. Flowers crowd the top third of the stiff stems, opening successively from bottom to tip over several days. Stiff, swordlike leaves complete the handsome display. Lacking fragrance, but little else, glads are useful where spring bulbs have died back, in a flower border or in a cutting garden. Although they are technically tender bulbs, glads often survive winters in gardens south of Philadelphia. They have returned faithfully each summer at Charles Cresson's garden, Hedgleigh Spring, for at least 20 years.

WHEN TO PLANT

Start planting in the spring when the soil is warm. Plant every 10 days to 3 weeks in succession until early July to assure flowers over the growing season. Flowers mature 8 to 10 weeks after corms are planted.

WHERE TO PLANT

Glads like full sun and well-drained soil that is rich, sandy, and slightly acidic. They will compromise on the requirements for soil as long as it is not clay, but not on the requirement for the sun. Prepare raised beds with soil lightened with organic matter if it is clay.

HOW TO PLANT

Dig the soil down 12 inches, mixing in granular slow-acting fertilizer. Planting depth varies with the size of the corm—those less than ½ inch across, go 3 inches deep; inch-wide corms, go down 4 to 5 inches; those more than 1 inch, go to 6 to 8 inches deep. For best display, plant corms in groups of 5 or more, spaced 6 to 8 inches apart. For cutting, plant individual corms 6 inches apart in rows. Aim the pointed side of the corm upward.

CARE AND MAINTENANCE

Mulch glads to discourage weeds, and keep soil evenly moist.
Water when the soil below the mulch seems dry. Tall types will
need staking. Drive a stake into the soil next to individual plants.
For those in rows, run a string the length of the row on each
side of the plants to support them. When leaves ripen and turn
yellow, dig up the corms, trim off dying stems, and allow them
to dry out a bit. Their corms multiply like rabbits, so there will
be many new ones. Gently clean off their dried husks, and store
them in bags of dry vermiculite or sand in a ventilated space
where temperatures are a steady 60 to 70 degrees Fahrenheit.

ADDITIONAL INFORMATION

Glads' nemesis is thrips, tiny insects that attack leaf sheaths
and unopened flowers. Foliage turns silvery or brown, buds
shrivel, and florets fail to open. Use a systemic insecticide product listed for thrips as directed on its label. For wonderful cut
flowers, harvest stems with the lowest flowers just opening.
Allow at least 5 leaves to remain growing on the plant.
Immediately plunge the cut stems into lukewarm water laced
with floral conditioner or citrus-based nondiet soda. Blooms
may last up to 10 days.

ADDITIONAL SPECIES, CULTIVARS, OR VARIETIES

Butterfly hybrids are only 25 inches tall and do not need staking.
Winter-hardy gladiolus (*Gladiolus byzantinus*) form more delicate
clumps and bloom in early summer. Flowers of *Gladiolus tristis*
are sweetly scented, but as winter bloomers, they are best for
greenhouses. Pixiola hybrids are specialty glads, very tiny with
2- to 3-inch florets.

 Did You Know?

*Gladiolus are named for their distinctive swordlike leaves.
The Latin word gladius means "little sword." An integral
part of Roman culture, they were reputed to be the floral
emblem of gladiators. Paintings of glads are found in the
ruins at Pompeii.*

Iris, Bearded

Iris germanica hybrids

Other Name: German Iris
Type: Hardy rhizome
Size: Dwarf 8 to 12 inches tall; tall 2 to
   3 feet tall
Bloom Time: May and June; some types are rebloomers
Flower Color/Type: Shades of lilac, purple, yellow, pink, white;
   bicolored, ruffled, speckled, splashed

Color photograph on page 203.

Light Requirements:

There is no mistaking bearded iris. With their stiff, pointed swordlike leaves and tall, rigid stems topped by elegant blooms, they are showstoppers in a spring flower border or as a specimen clump. Iris flowers, often called garden orchids, are an elaborate arrangement of 6 petals—3 erect "standards," alternately arranged with 3 drooping "falls." The fuzzy tuft of hairs on the falls are "beards." They bloom sequentially along the stalks over 2 or 3 weeks, each flower lasting only a day or two, depending on the warmth of the weather. Some are fragrant. The stiff vertical profile of clumps of irises contrasts nicely with the dainty coralbells and blowzy peonies that bloom in the garden about the same time. Grow plenty of irises so that you will have lots to cut and enjoy indoors.

WHEN TO PLANT

Plant rhizomes in August through early fall 6 to 8 weeks before the ground is likely to freeze. The sooner you plant after you purchase them, the more time the roots have to develop. Transplant potted plants anytime during the growing season.

WHERE TO PLANT

Like most bulbs, irises like well-drained soil and a very sunny location. They do fine in most soils except heavy clay. Improve clay soil by digging into it lots of organic matter such as peat moss or chopped leaves. Planting irises in raised beds facilitates soil drainage.

HOW TO PLANT

Dig and loosen the soil down 8 to 10 inches, simultaneously mixing in bulb fertilizer. Make a narrow, shallow furrow in the prepared soil, and lay each knobby rhizome horizontally so that its roots nestle into the soil indentation. Cover the rhizome with sufficient soil to bury its roots, but leave its top surface partially exposed to the sun. Water well. Space rhizomes about

12 inches apart, pointing the ends with the fan of foliage in the direction the clump of iris is to spread.

CARE AND MAINTENANCE

Fertilize irises every fall with slow-acting fertilizer or specially formulated bulb fertilizer according to package directions. Iris stems may need staking to prevent flopping if they are growing on a slope or in shade. Cut off faded iris blooms and stems, but bypass the leaves so that they can absorb sunshine all summer. If foliage flops and looks ratty, cut it back to 2- or 3-inch fans in the fall. After 3 to 5 years, bearded iris rhizomes expand into gnarled clumps and need dividing. In midsummer dig them up and separate the rhizomes, discarding any that seem soft or diseased. Replant the ones with healthy roots.

ADDITIONAL INFORMATION

Bearded irises grow well in tubs or other weather-resistant containers that are 1 to 2 feet wide and at least 1 foot deep. Borers are the most serious iris pest. They burrow into young iris leaves and excavate channels in their tissues that resemble water-soaked spots, then move into the rhizomes. An insecticide containing pyrethrum to be dusted on bulbs and soil often controls borers when used as directed. A systemic product listed for this problem will tackle borers inside plant tissues; use only as directed.

ADDITIONAL SPECIES, CULTIVARS, OR VARIETIES

Although the tall bearded iris is the most familiar and commonly used iris in residential yards and gardens around Philadelphia, there are several other bearded types. Typically available from mail-order specialty nurseries, miniature dwarfs, standard dwarfs, intermediates, miniature talls ("table irises"), and border bearded are all charming and useful in various garden situations. They rarely need staking.

Did You Know?

Because they come in a rainbow of wonderful colors, irises are aptly named from the Greek word iris, *meaning "rainbow." In Greek mythology, Iris was the goddess of the rainbow and a messenger of the gods whose path was a rainbow.*

Lily

Lilium species and hybrids

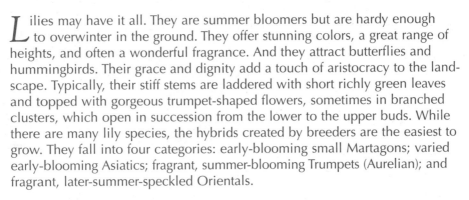

Type: Hardy bulb
Size: 2 to 8 feet tall
Bloom Time: Early summer, midseason, and
   late summer
Flower Color/Type: White, yellow, orange, pink, red; spotted, striped
   trumpets

Color photograph on page 203.

Light Requirements:

L ilies may have it all. They are summer bloomers but are hardy enough
to overwinter in the ground. They offer stunning colors, a great range of
heights, and often a wonderful fragrance. And they attract butterflies and
hummingbirds. Their grace and dignity add a touch of aristocracy to the landscape. Typically, their stiff stems are laddered with short richly green leaves
and topped with gorgeous trumpet-shaped flowers, sometimes in branched
clusters, which open in succession from the lower to the upper buds. While
there are many lily species, the hybrids created by breeders are the easiest to
grow. They fall into four categories: early-blooming small Martagons; varied
early-blooming Asiatics; fragrant, summer-blooming Trumpets (Aurelian); and
fragrant, later-summer-speckled Orientals.

WHEN TO PLANT

Plant lily bulbs in the fall or spring; transplant potted bulbs to the garden
anytime in the spring or summer. Plant bulbs kept in cold storage over the
winter immediately because, unlike most bulbs, lily bulbs are never completely dormant.

WHERE TO PLANT

Lilies like full sun, well-drained soil, and good air circulation. Take into
consideration their expected height, and plant them to best advantage. They
coordinate nicely with many perennials, but do not crowd them into an
intensively planted bed.

HOW TO PLANT

Cultivate the planting area to 12 inches deep. Add lots of organic matter to
keep soil loose and well draining. Mix in slow-acting granular fertilizer, too.
Plant bulbs at a depth three times the bulbs' diameter, measured from the
bottom of the hole (roughly 4 to 6 inches). For good mass effect, plant bulbs
6 to 8 inches apart.

CARE AND MAINTENANCE

Mulch lily beds to assure cool, moist soil and discourage weeds. To forestall the formation of seedpods, cut off faded flowers. Leave at least ⅔ of the stem so that foliage remains to ripen and die back naturally. Young lilies, those in windy sites, and those in shade that lean toward the sun may need support. Divide Asiatics that become crowded in 4 or 5 years. They transplant well with the bulb in a soilball anytime. Trumpet lilies do not truly establish until 2 or 3 years; Martagons hate to be moved at all.

ADDITIONAL INFORMATION

Try lilies with ferns, campanulas, peonies, lamb's ears, astilbes, and other garden standbys. They make good cut flowers, lasting up to 3 weeks. Cut off pollen-laden anthers to eliminate pollen stains on clothing and indoor furnishings. Pot-grown lilies rarely rebloom over a season, so plant them outdoors after blooming or discard them.

ADDITIONAL SPECIES, CULTIVARS, OR VARIETIES

The familiar Easter lily (*Lilium longiflorum*) grows well in local gardens, as does the regal lily (*Lilium regale*) with its circle of white trumpet flowers atop 6-foot stems. 'Star Gazer', a deep pink oriental lily with white-edged, speckled petals, was the top florist lily grown in Holland in 1996. Pixie Hybrid lilies are genetic dwarfs, introduced in 1985, that grow 12 to 22 inches tall with regular-sized flowers.

Did You Know?

Images of white lilies decorate frescoes and vases from Crete as early as 1500 B.C. They were a common fertility motif in ancient Greek art, incorporated into the Roman myth of Juno and Hercules. Somehow when Christians adopted the lily, it came to signify virginal purity, thus becoming the symbol of the Virgin Mary. Renaissance paintings often depict the angel Gabriel giving white lilies to Mary as he delivers his news.

Onion, Ornamental

Allium 'Purple Sensation'

Other Names: Flowering Onion, Persian Onion

Type: Hardy bulb

Size: 3 to 4 feet tall; 1 foot wide

Bloom Time: May into June

Flower Color/Type: Deep reddish-purple balls of star-shaped florets

Light Requirements:

Color photograph on page 203.

The sight of the dramatic spheres of fuzzy lavender flowers at the tips of tall, narrow stalks rising above the other plants like visitors from another planet is unforgettable. Ornamental onions are increasingly common in flower gardens—and no wonder. They sustain garden interest after the flush of spring bulbs passes and the summer show is yet to come. They continue to offer interest as their petals drop, and they dry into lovely seedheads. 'Purple Sensation' has 4-inch-wide flower heads on tall stems, at the base of which rise straplike 6- to 8-inch leaves from 1½ to 3 inches wide that age and disappear by the time the flower heads fade. Although they do not attract pests, ornamental onions do attract numerous beneficial insects, butterflies, and the occasional hummingbird, who do not seem to mind the mild scent that is reminiscent of their culinary cousins. Fortunately, deer do seem to mind it and leave these plants alone.

WHEN TO PLANT

Plant allium bulbs in the fall before the ground freezes. The sooner you plant after you purchase them, the more time the bulb has to grow roots.

WHERE TO PLANT

Ornamental onions do best in well-drained, good garden soil in full sun to partial shade. 'Purple Sensation' is the easiest to grow and most reliable of the large-headed ornamental onions. *Allium aflatunense* types have a tendency to self-sow if they are in a desirable site and their flower heads are allowed to dry on the stems. Their seedlings take many years to reach flowering size.

HOW TO PLANT

Cultivate the soil down 8 to 10 inches, and mix in bulb fertilizer. Plant individual bulbs about 6 inches deep, 12 to 18 inches apart, or closer as clusters of 3, 5, or 7. There is no need to relegate them to the back of the border, because their slim stalks make them see-through plants. Use them effectively in large borders in drifts among perennials that have silver foliage such as lamb's ears and yarrow. They will obscure their yellowing foliage.

CARE AND MAINTENANCE

If ornamental onions are shortchanged on sun, their stems may be a bit weak and will need staking. Clip off faded flower heads and stems, or leave them to dry attractively in the sun. Ornamental onions such as 'Purple Sensation' form bulblets over the years, eventually crowding the planting and reducing flower size. Divide large clumps by digging them up, gently separating the offsets from each main bulb, then replanting them more widely spaced. Offsets will bloom in 1 to 3 years, depending on their size.

ADDITIONAL INFORMATION

Ornamental onions are great long-lasting additions to bouquets, either as fresh or as dried flowers. The dried flower heads are also useful for crafts.

ADDITIONAL SPECIES, CULTIVARS, OR VARIETIES

Allium 'Globemaster' is similar but larger at 5 feet tall with 5-inch-round flower heads. Blue globe onion (*Allium caeruleum*) has much smaller flower heads at 1 to 2 inches. Star of Persia (*Allium christophii*) is more top-heavy with flower spheres 8 to 16 inches across on 12- to 20-inch stems. Smaller allium cousins such as lily leek (*Allium moly*) are ideal for rock garden situations.

 Did You Know?

Allium is Greek for "garlic." This clan includes many cousins, such as bulb onions, chives, leeks, shallots, and scallions. They share with their ornamental cousins a sturdy self-reliance, globe flowers of lilac or pinkish, twinkly florets, and a distinctive smell. Culinary use goes back to the beginning of recorded time and probably well before. Ornamental types are relative newcomers in American gardens, however. Late-summer-blooming garlic chives (Allium tuberosum) *represent a meeting of both worlds because they are ornamental and edible.*

Tulip

Tulipa gesneriana

Other Names: Garden Tulip, Darwin Tulip/hybrids

Type: Hardy bulb

Size: 18 to 24 inches tall; clumps spreading up to 10 inches

Bloom Time: Early/March; midseason/April; late/May

Flower Color/Type: All colors except black and true blue; striped, bicolor/single, double-petaled goblets

Light Requirements:

Color photograph on page 203.

The origin of cultivated or hybrid tulips is something of a mystery. They seemed to just appear in Turkey. They spread to Europe, and after centuries of growing and breeding in Holland, they evolved into modern hybrids with the familiar solitary, cup-shaped, crayon-colored blooms at the tips of tall, straight stems. Variously described as Darwin, Darwin hybrids, cottage, and hybrid tulips, these plants have not been reliably perennial. Gardeners often prefer to treat them as annuals and discard them after a single year in the garden. Newer tulips promoted as perennials are more likely to persist for several years, however.

WHEN TO PLANT

Plant tulips in the fall, anytime before the ground freezes. Do not procrastinate because bulbs planted early develop stronger roots. Store them temporarily, if necessary, in a cool place. Bulbs exposed to heat over 70 degrees Fahrenheit produce smaller flowers.

WHERE TO PLANT

Tulips like full sun and well-drained soil. Just about any soil, except clay, is fine. Add lots of organic matter such as peat moss or chopped leaves to the soil. Planting tulips in raised beds facilitates soil drainage.

HOW TO PLANT

In the fall dig the soil down at least 12 inches, and mix in bulb fertilizer. Plant tulips in groups for best effect. Dig individual holes, or dig out a bed for placing bulbs in a mass planting. Plant at least 6 to 8 inches deep. Planting as deep as 12 inches yields bigger flowers and reduces rodent damage. Aim the pointed bulb growing tips upward. Fill in the holes with soil, then water.

CARE AND MAINTENANCE

Deer love tulips, so it may be necessary to fence beds. To achieve bloom a second year, cut off stems and faded flowers, leaving all foliage to soak up sun, ripen, and collapse in a few weeks. Fertilize tulip beds with bulb fertilizer in early fall (essential) and again in early spring (desirable).

ADDITIONAL INFORMATION

Plant tulips among ground covers or low-growing spring annuals such as pansies or forget-me-nots that will mask their dying foliage later. Grow them alone or with other bulbs in containers for spring display on a porch or patio. Set bulbs with sides touching 6 inches deep in deep pots filled with soilless potting medium, and place outdoors. Keep them watered all winter. Tulips are vulnerable to "tulipfire," a bacterial blight which deforms flowers, foliage, and bulbs. It occurs in beds where tulips are planted repeatedly. It dies out if no tulips are planted in the area for at least 4 years.

ADDITIONAL SPECIES, CULTIVARS, OR VARIETIES

There are many kinds of tulips. In addition to those with classic, cup-shaped flowers, there are waterlily types called Kaufmanniana and Greigii tulips. Among the smaller, daintier species, or botanical types of tulips, are lipstick tulips (*Tulipa clusiana*) and Batalin tulips (*Tulipa batalini*). They are reliably perennial and are ideal for rock gardens. The woods tulip (*Tulipa sylvestris*) will take some shade and likes woodland situations.

 Did You Know?

When the first tulip bulbs were introduced into Europe in the late 1500s, they caused a sensation. Astute Dutch businessmen recognized the commercial potential of this tulipmania and strove to develop new and unusual types to feed the speculative market that developed among the general public. By the 1630s when the market collapsed, taking with it many fortunes, Holland remained the major producer of tulip bulbs.

CHAPTER THREE

Grasses

U NTIL FAIRLY RECENTLY, grass in residential landscapes meant turfgrass. Homes were (and are still) typically surrounded by large areas planted with turfgrass as a ground cover. A legacy from our English settlers who established grassy "commons" in the center of their villages for animals to graze on, these "lawns" became a subtle sign of status when private plots of grass were incorporated into bigger residential properties by increasingly prosperous home owners during the nineteenth century. Lawns function today as recreation areas, unifying elements to link planted areas, and as background to set off showy plants.

These days grass in the landscape is just as likely to mean ornamental grass as turfgrass. As a group, these plants offer things that turfgrasses do not—drought resistance, pest and disease resistance, seasonal color, variegated foliage, showy flowers, and minimal cutting. For some, the most important virtue of all is that they are environmentally "correct," not needing regular applications of water, pesticides, or fertilizers.

Ornamental grasses are also part of a legacy, that of early human beings who were at home on the grassy savannas of Africa, and later, that of our ancestors who settled great prairies in this country. In the frontier era Americans lived among the tall grasses and within sod houses. We continue to incorporate grasses into our culture. They are a staple of our diet and that of the grazing animals that we raise for food.

TURFGRASSES VS. ORNAMENTAL GRASSES

Turfgrasses and ornamental grasses share many characteristics. They grow in two ways. Some are runners or creepers, spreading by means of horizontal stems, or stolons, that run over or just under the soil surface, rooting as they go. Others are clumpers, spreading by means of increasingly larger clumps that sometimes give turf a tufty appearance. Both function as ground covers; both have annual or perennial varieties. Ornamental grasses, large and small, are much more versatile than turfgrasses, however. They have many landscape uses besides ground cover. They serve as vertical accents in ornamental beds and borders, substitute for shrubs, become focal points, and provide winter interest. Use them as a transition to naturalized areas and meadows, to hold stream banks, to screen views, to cover slopes that are difficult to mow, and to serve as an essential filler in meadow or wildflower mixes. To get an idea of the diversity among ornamental grasses, visit the wonderful display at Longwood Gardens.

Although both turfgrasses and ornamental grasses have warm-season and cool-season varieties, this distinction matters most with turfgrasses because lawns are expected to be green during the growing season. Warm-season turfgrasses, such as zoysia, are more at home in the South because they go dormant during cool weather and thrive during hot weather. Zoysia is truly happy (that is, green) here for only about 12 weeks out of the year. You always can tell a zoysia lawn because it is brown and dormant most of the time. In our area cool-season types are most appropriate for lawns because we water them during the relatively few weeks when it is hot and they are tempted to go dormant. They grow lushly in spring and then do very well again in fall. Sometimes a Kentucky bluegrass lawn stays green here all winter.

TURFGRASS CARE

Turfgrasses take more care than ornamental grasses. Critical to their health is decent soil. The better the soil, the better it can care for the grass, and the less you have to do. Core aerate the lawn every year or two to prevent compaction, which stifles root growth. Topdress with organic material such as compost, chopped leaves from the mulching mower, topsoil, or mushroom soil each year so that soil can hold moisture, drain well, and support microorganisms that convert nutrients to a form grass plants can use. Use a granular slow-acting fertilizer in the spring to deliver consistent, uniform nutrition to the grass over many weeks. Most important, be sure turfgrass gets regular water. If rainfall is sparse, water deeply every 10 days to 2 weeks. Frequent sprinkles only encourage shallow roots and damage grass.

Blue Fescue

Festuca glauca

Other Name: Sheep's Fescue
Type: Ornamental, cool season, clumping
Mature Size: Clumps 6 to 12 inches tall;
  12 inches wide
Foliage Color/Type: Evergreen; fine, silvery-bluish blades

Light Requirements:

Color photograph on page 203.

This most attractive colorful, low-growing grass is easy to use in the yard. Although its name suggests turfgrass—tall fescue or Kentucky bluegrass—it is definitely ornamental. Its blue color is actually a glaucous coating on its narrow foliage that is similar to that on blue spruce needles. It is great in winter when there is so little color in the yard. Its flowers are arrayed on beige spikes in late June or July and are easy to overlook completely. They are upstaged by the foliage anyway. Cut them off so they do not drain energy from the plant. Use blue fescue as ground cover, in rock gardens, or as edging. It looks good with the dwarf conifers that are becoming increasingly colorful and popular. As a cool-season grass, it may struggle a bit in full sun during our hot, humid summers, but usually does fine if it gets enough moisture.

WHEN TO PLANT

Plant divisions from a larger clump in either spring or fall. Transplant young plants in nursery pots anytime during the growing season when it is not extremely hot and humid.

WHERE TO PLANT

Full sun brings out the best color in blue fescues. They do fine in most soils as long as they drain well. They are a great rock garden plant, but they like organic matter in the typical gritty soil to help it hold moisture.

HOW TO PLANT

Dig down into the soil about 6 to 8 inches to loosen it, and mix in organic matter if needed. Dig a planting hole about as deep as and slightly wider than the rootball when the plant is removed from its container. Set the blue fescue in the hole so that the top of its rootball is at or slightly above soil level to assure good drainage. Firm loose soil gently around plant stems to remove air pockets, and water well. Space plants to allow for the eventual mature size of the particular blue fescue variety, a bit closer for instant edging.

CARE AND MAINTENANCE

Even drought-tolerant grasses need moisture while they struggle
to become established. Mulch to retard evaporation of moisture
from the soil and to discourage weeds that sometimes grow
among fescue foliage where light reaches the soil. Since foliage is
evergreen, there is no need to shear it back to the ground in the
winter or spring. Clipping unruly foliage back to about 4 inches,
though, neatens the clump. Clumps begin to look ratty in their
centers in about 3 years, signaling it is time to divide them. Dig
them up and expose their roots. Cut away chunks from the edges
with fresh foliage and good roots, and replant them. Discard the
centers where foliage has died or become sparse.

ADDITIONAL INFORMATION

Blue fescue is wonderful for planters and other containers. Its
small, neat habit and distinctive color combine well with both
vertical and trailing plants.

ADDITIONAL SPECIES, CULTIVARS, OR VARIETIES

'Elijah Blue' is the most available of the many varieties of blue
fescue. A soft, powdery blue, it grows to 8 inches tall. 'Blausilber'
has fine, bluish-silver foliage and is 6 inches tall.

 Did You Know?

*Bestowing Latin names on plants usually eliminates
confusion. While common names in the vernacular change
with the region or culture, the formal, scientific name is
universally recognized. At least that is how it is supposed
to be. In some cases the background of a plant is not well
understood, so at various times its Latin name is changed to
reflect improved understanding of its pedigree. Because a
consensus has not been reached about blue fescue, it has many
Latin names. It may also be listed in references as* Festuca
ovina, Festuca cinerea, Festuca caesia, *and several others.*

Fountaingrass, Purple

Pennisetum setaceum 'Rubrum'

Other Name: Burgundy or Red
   Fountaingrass
Type: Ornamental, clumping, annual
Mature Size: 2 to 3 feet tall; equally wide
Foliage Color/Type: Burgundy to bronze-red; fine textured, narrow

Light Requirements:

Color photograph on page 203.

*F*ountaingrass is typically grown as an annual in our region because it is not cold hardy here. Its spikes of 8- to 12-inch-long flowers nod on arching stems amid upright clumps of reddish foliage, their soft, fuzzy reddish or purplish "bottlebrushes" suggesting a spray of water from a fountain. They bloom from June to September, providing color and texture all season. Fountaingrass foliage turns rosy-gold as winter approaches and is bleached tan by December. This grass is a good size for small yards where garden space is limited. Extremely drought tolerant, it looks great with Sedum 'Autumn Joy', purple coneflower, and conifers in the background. It also makes a wonderful color accent.

WHEN TO PLANT

Plant grass overwintered indoors outside in late spring when the soil has warmed. Plant containerized nursery stock in spring when frost danger is past, or anytime during the growing season.

WHERE TO PLANT

Fountaingrass does best in full sun in well-drained soil of almost any type, including clay. It likes moist soil, so it does well near streams and pond banks. It can even take 1 or 2 inches of water over its roots.

HOW TO PLANT

Dig and loosen the soil down about 12 inches. There is no need to take special measures to improve the soil. Dig a planting hole about as deep as and about 3 times as wide as the rootball. Set the plant in the hole so that the top of the rootball is level with the surrounding ground. Fill in the hole with soil, firm it gently around plant stems to remove air pockets, then water well. Set plants 3 to 4 feet apart to allow for their gradual spread, closer to establish a mass planting.

CARE AND MAINTENANCE

Water fountaingrass well when it is first planted. Once it is established and starts to send up new shoots, it can handle typical summers. As a tender plant in our area, its roots will not survive the winter. Either pot it and bring it indoors to overwinter in a cool cellar or garage, or cut off its disintegrating flowers and leave its dried foliage in the garden for winter interest and pull it up in the spring.

ADDITIONAL INFORMATION

Purple fountaingrass does well in containers as long as it is watered regularly. Its flowers are useful fresh or dried in floral arrangements or dried for floral crafts.

ADDITIONAL SPECIES, CULTIVARS, OR VARIETIES

'Rubrum Dwarf' is more compact at 2 to 3 feet tall; it is difficult to find at nurseries. The bright green blades of annual fountaingrass (*Pennisetum alopecuroides*) are streaked yellow and brown in fall, then beige in winter. 'Moudry' has almost black flowers. Feathertop (*Pennisetum villosum*) has a shorter flowering period and habit, but smaller size.

 Did You Know?

If you like the look of red grasses, another popular warm-season grass is Japanese bloodgrass (Imperata cylindrica 'Red Baron'). A small plant featuring vertical foliage that reddens by degrees over the season, it is a stunner. Its translucent, blood-red foliage catches the autumn light as no other plant does. It does not produce flowers. Avoid tissue-culture-grown plants to assure that you do not get a greener, more aggressive version of this plant.

Hakonechloa

Hakonechloa macra 'Aureola'

Other Names: Hakone Grass, Japanese
Forest Grass

Type: Ornamental, clumping

Mature Size: 18 inches tall; about 2 feet wide

Foliage Color/Type: Deciduous; variegated gold with green streaks;
pinkish-red fall color

Light Requirements:

Color photograph on page 203.

*H*akone grass is currently enjoying considerable popularity because it is more available than ever before. It is immensely useful because, unlike most ornamental grasses, it likes shade. It creates a low clump of arching, bamboolike leaves that turn toward the light. It provides interesting textural contrast to a woodland planting of astilbes, hostas, and coleus. It makes a good edging, too. Hakone grass looks especially at home in gardens with an Oriental theme. Although it spreads by means of rhizomatous roots, it is not at all invasive.

WHEN TO PLANT

Plant divisions from large clumps in either spring or fall. Transplant containerized nursery stock anytime during the growing season.

WHERE TO PLANT

Hakone grass prefers partial shade as in a woodland setting, but it can handle some morning sun. For best results, plant it in moist, well-drained soil rich in organic matter.

HOW TO PLANT

Dig to loosen the soil down 8 to 10 inches, and mix in organic matter such as compost or peat moss and a sprinkling of granular slow-acting fertilizer. Mixed into the soil at this point, it will give new transplants a boost their first season. Dig the planting hole about as deep as and slightly wider than the plant rootball or container. Set the hakone grass in the hole so that its crown, where the roots meet the stems, is at soil level or slightly above. Fill in the hole with soil, firming it gently around plant stems to remove air pockets, and water well. Set plants about 2 feet apart to allow for their gradual spread.

CARE AND MAINTENANCE

Hakone grass does not require much care. Water new plantings well, especially during hot weather. Spread a 2- or 3-inch layer of organic mulch to discourage evaporation of moisture from the soil. It will also discourage weeds. By spring foliage is pretty scruffy, so cut it back to make way for new shoots.

ADDITIONAL INFORMATION

Hakone grass adds fine texture as a filler in containers of other shade plants. It is also effective as a living mulch under trees where turfgrass will not grow.

ADDITIONAL SPECIES, CULTIVARS, OR VARIETIES

Hakonechloa macra has plain green leaves and can handle a bit more sun.

Did You Know?

A former genus name for hakone grass is Phragmites. *It is fortunate that its name has changed because another* Phragmites *is a horrible, invasive weed and hakone grass might suffer for its reputation. Common reed (*Phragmites australis*) is choking our wetlands. A typical example is at the John Heinz National Wildlife Refuge at Tinicum and other sites along Interstate 95 near the Philadelphia International Airport. While every villain has some virtue—in this case common reed assimilates soil and water pollutants such as heavy metals—it is usually overwhelmed by its vices. Common reed drives out native plants, destroys wetlands ecosystems, and fills in streams and ponds. Do not introduce it into your landscape, lest it escape and naturalize in local drainage ditches and fields.*

Kentucky Bluegrass

Poa pratensis

Other Name: Kentucky Blue
Type: Cool-season turfgrass
Mature Size: Mow to 3 inches in summer
Foliage Color/Type: Rich blue-green;
fine textured

Light Requirements:

*T*raditionally, Kentucky bluegrass has been the gold standard for Northern lawns. It is still valued for its good color, even texture, and uniform spread. It is high maintenance, however, because it requires lots of water and fertilizer and is prone to fungal disease. Since other grass varieties improved enormously over the last decade, Kentucky blue is best used in a mixture with them, where its assets are visible and its liabilities are compensated for.

WHEN TO PLANT
Plant new lawns just after Labor Day. Kentucky bluegrass needs lots of lead time to germinate and still have a couple of months of unfrozen ground to develop deep root systems. Lay bluegrass sod or patch lawns with seed in either spring or fall. Be prepared to water at least twice a day for several weeks if it does not rain.

WHERE TO PLANT
Kentucky bluegrass does best with a minimum of 8 hours of sun daily in soil that is rich in organic matter and is neutral or just slightly acidic. Do not plant any turfgrass under trees where it has to compete with tree roots for water, light, and nutrients.

HOW TO PLANT
When establishing a new lawn or patching bare spots in an existing lawn, first improve the soil. Mix in organic matter while tilling or roughing it up. Smooth and water the area. When weeds erupt after a week, kill them with a burndown herbicide. After a week to 10 days sow seed as directed on the seed package without disturbing the soil bed, and water so that the seed stays moist at all times. Fertilizing at this time is optional. A mulch of white polyspun garden fleece maintains moisture, prevents seed from washing away in the rain, and protects the seed from birds. Continue to water grass seedlings through the fall and into winter if there is sparse rainfall.

CARE AND MAINTENANCE
Begin cutting new turfgrass when it approaches 4 inches tall. Cut it back to 3 inches until it goes dormant, then cut it at 2 inches to overwinter. Water

established Kentucky bluegrass lawns in good soil only when the grass looks limp. In poor soils or compacted soils water more often. Fertilize with a granular slow-acting product formulated for lawns in spring and/or fall. In late fall, use a product listed for "winter" to help develop strong roots. Aerate and topdress the lawn with organic material such as mushroom soil, compost, or topsoil every fall to maintain soil health. Mulch annually with leaves chopped fine by a mulching mower at the end of autumn leaf fall. Every few years mow close and overseed with premium Kentucky bluegrass or a mixture in which it is well represented to renew and thicken the turf.

ADDITIONAL INFORMATION

Because Philadelphia area soil is slightly more acid than turf-grasses prefer, spread granular lime in the fall. Do not lime at the same time as fertilizing. Kentucky bluegrass tends to get fungal diseases such as powdery mildew, fusarium, pythium, and red thread. Merion K variety is prone to rust and stripe smut. To treat chronic problems, overseed with newer seed listed as disease resistant. Use mixtures of several turfgrasses so that their specific resistances collectively assure that some grass stays green if a particular fungal disease strikes.

 Did You Know?

Regardless of the type of turfgrass in a lawn, it will develop thatch over time. This is an accumulation of tough dead grass stems and crowns that do not decompose and gradually form a mat over the soil. It blocks air and moisture penetration to the roots of the living grass plants and harbors pest larvae and pathogens. It is promoted by compacted soil and overfertilization. Rake up thatch that is thicker than ¼ inch. Core aerate and topdress the lawn regularly, and use slow-acting fertilizers to retard thatch development.

Maiden Grass

Miscanthus sinensis

Other Names: Porcupine Grass, Eulalia
  Grass, Zebra Grass
Type: Ornamental, clumping
Mature Size: 3 to 12 feet tall; as wide
  as permitted
Foliage Color/Type: Variegated silver striped, gold banded

Color photograph on page 203.

Light Requirements:

Maiden grass is the ornamental grass everyone thinks of first. It was very popular in Victorian times, so it is familiar to us from pictures. Its substantial presence as widely arching clumps of long, pointed leaf blades about ⅜ inch wide is the very archetype of an ornamental grass. Moreover, it is a grass for all seasons. It is a ghostly presence in late winter and early spring; its beige fronds near collapse as new shoots begin to form to replace them. In season the various types of maiden grass sport colorful stripes and bands of white or yellow on rich green straplike leaves, the silvery types glowing in evening gardens. It is a mainstay in late summer. When everything seems to collapse in the garden, its September flowers turn silvery and pinkish as they fluff and release their seeds. Then the foliage begins to bleach to beige again for winter. Maiden grass varieties are useful as specimens for screens, and in the middle of the border.

WHEN TO PLANT

Plant divisions cut from large clumps in the spring. Plant grass in pots from the garden center anytime during the growing season.

WHERE TO PLANT

A sunny site is best for most maiden grasses, as they tend to flop a bit in shade. They can handle almost any type of soil, even sandy. Some types will grow in shallow water as marginal plants.

HOW TO PLANT

Dig and loosen the soil down about 12 inches. There is no need to take special measures to improve it. Dig a planting hole as deep as and about 3 times as wide as the rootball. Set the plant in the hole so that the top of the rootball is level with the surrounding ground. Fill in the hole with soil, firm it gently around plant stems, then water well. Set plants 3 to 4 feet apart to allow for their gradual spread, closer to establish a hedge or screen quickly.

CARE AND MAINTENANCE

Water newly planted grass if there is no rain until it is established. Mulch it to keep soil moist. After the grass and dried flower heads provide winter interest, cut them back with hedge shears or powered hedge trimmer in the early spring to make way for new shoots. Stake floppy grass that is in overrich soil or shade. Divide clumps every 3 or 4 years. Overlarge clumps are extremely difficult to handle. Dig up the rootball, and then with an ax, saw, or sharp knife, slice through the tough matrix of roots to dislodge chunks of rooted grass from its edges. Discard the center of the rootball if it has begun to die out. Beware of sharp edges on grass blades during the season.

ADDITIONAL INFORMATION

Maiden grass flowers are good for cutting fresh for arrangements or dried for floral crafts.

ADDITIONAL SPECIES, CULTIVARS, OR VARIETIES

'Gracillimus' has narrower, finer-textured foliage with a silver midrib; 'Morning Light' has fine, silvery variegated foliage. The flower plumes of silverfeather grass (*Miscanthus sinensis* 'Silberfeder') are whiter. Porcupine grass (*Miscanthus sinensis* 'Strictus') has thick yellow horizontal bands across its blades and a stiff, upright habit. Striped eulalia grass (*Miscanthus sinensis* 'Variegatus') has vertical cream or white stripes on green blades; it flowers in late September or October and is good near water. Zebra grass (*Miscanthus sinensis* 'Zebrinus') has narrow clumps with alternating horizontal bands of yellow and white on blades, and a rusty fall color.

 Did You Know?

There is some concern in the Philadelphia area that certain forms of maiden grass are "escaping" from landscape settings and seeding into the wild. The culprit is most likely a form called banner grass or **Miscanthus sacchariflorus,** *a known runner and self-sower. At one time unscrupulous growers sold this grass, possibly under several other names, but reputable growers do not. Purchase ornamental grasses from reliable sources. Observe them to assure that they do not start seedlings around your property.*

Perennial Ryegrass

Lolium perenne

Other Name: Perennial Rye
Type: Cool-season turfgrass
Mature Size: Mow to 3 inches in summer
Foliage Color/Type: Medium green;
  medium texture

Light Requirements:

A good-looking grass, perennial ryegrass is most valued because it germinates within a week after sowing. Therefore, its roots get enough of a head start in the spring to assure that it can withstand our hot, humid summers. It is also an important component of turfgrass mixtures sown in the fall as a "nurse" grass. Its rapid germination assures us that grass will, in fact, appear. Eventually, the seed of other varieties germinates and fills in the bare seedbed. Use perennial rye to patch spots during the summer so that weeds will not move in. In the fall overseed those spots with whatever seed or mixture that constitutes the surrounding turf.

WHEN TO PLANT

Plant perennial ryegrass anytime during the growing season. Lay sod containing perennial rye combined with other turfgrasses or patch lawns with seed in either spring or fall.

WHERE TO PLANT

Perennial ryegrass does best with 8 hours of sun daily in soil that is rich in organic matter and is neutral or just slightly acidic. It is often in mixtures labeled for shade, which all require at least 6 hours of sun or bright light. Do not plant turfgrass under trees where it has to compete with tree roots for water, light, and nutrients.

HOW TO PLANT

When sowing seed mixtures in which perennial ryegrass is included, take time to improve the soil first. Till or rough it up, mixing in organic matter. Smooth and water the area to germinate the inevitable weed seeds. Kill them with a burndown-type herbicide, and then about a week to 10 days later, sow grass seed as directed on its package. Water so that the seed stays moist at all times. Fertilize with a seed-starter fertilizer, or delay fertilizing until later in the fall. Continue to water grass seedlings through the fall and into winter if there is no rain. A mulch of white polyspun garden fleece will maintain moisture, hold the seed in the seedbed in heavy rains, and prevent birds from eating it.

CARE AND MAINTENANCE

Cut new turfgrass when it approaches 4 inches tall. Cut it back to 3 inches until it goes dormant, then cut it at 2 inches to overwinter. Water perennial ryegrass lawns in good soil only when there has been little or no rainfall for more than 2 weeks and the grass looks limp. Water grass in poor soils more often. Fertilize with a granular slow-acting product formulated for lawns in spring and/or fall. Or in late fall, use a "winter" product to help develop deep roots. Aerate and topdress the lawn with organic material every other fall to maintain soil. Mulch annually with leaves chopped fine by a mulching mower at the end of autumn leaf fall.

ADDITIONAL INFORMATION

To reduce the acidity of typical Philadelphia area soil, spread granular lime on the lawn in the fall. Do not fertilize and lime at the same time. Our hot, humid summers promote fungal diseases in lawns, and perennial ryegrass is susceptible to pythium, brown patch, and red thread. While most sporadic outbreaks are usually a function of temporary weather, chronic problems indicate a need for overseeding with a newer seed variety labeled as disease resistant.

Did You Know?

Mowing tips for healthier lawns:
- *Mow with a sharp blade. Dull blades damage grass tips and promote disease.*
- *Mow tall—a minimum of 3 inches in summer—to shade the soil and conserve moisture.*
- *Mow frequently. Cut only about ⅓ of the grass height each time to avoid stressing it.*
- *Mow dry for an even cut. Wet grass clippings clump; blades bruise when stepped on.*

GRASSES

Switch Grass

Panicum virgatum

Other Name: Panic Grass

Type: Ornamental, clumping, warm season

Mature Size: Clumps to 7 feet tall;
  3 feet wide

Foliage Color/Type: Silvery-green blades; yellowish orange in fall

Light Requirements:

Color photograph on page 203.

This lovely grass is native to the tall grass prairies here in the United States. It is a classic example of how we sometimes overlook, or take for granted, a wonderful plant until it is adopted by Europeans and then reintroduced to our country. It is adaptable and easy to grow, even at the Shore. It bears airy pinkish or silvery flowers that wave in the breeze 1 foot or more above the tall, upright foliage. They appear in July, and then their seedheads last through fall into winter. The slender green to gray-green foliage of switch grass has rough edges that narrow to a fine tip. Its fall color is legendary. It is easy to imagine endless seas of it undulating across the prairie of yesteryear. In today's gardens it serves well as a specimen, background or screen, or ground cover.

WHEN TO PLANT

Plant divisions cut from overlarge clumps in either spring or fall. Transplant plants in pots from the garden center anytime during the growing season.

WHERE TO PLANT

Full sun is best for switch grass. It appreciates rich, well-drained soil, but tolerates a wide range of soil types without complaint. It can take 1 or 2 inches of water over its roots at the edge of a stream or pond.

HOW TO PLANT

Dig and loosen the soil down about 12 inches. Take the opportunity to add organic matter to the soil to enhance its ability to hold moisture and drain well. Then dig a planting hole about as deep as and slightly wider than the rootball. Set the switch grass in the hole so that the top of its soilball is level with the surrounding ground. Fill in the hole with soil, firming it gently around plant stems to remove air pockets, then water well. Set plants about 3 feet apart to allow for their gradual spread, closer to establish a hedge or screen quickly.

CARE AND MAINTENANCE

Water switch grass well while it becomes established. It can handle some drought once it has settled in the first season. Leave the grass and dried flower heads to provide winter interest in the yard, then cut them back in the early spring to make way for new shoots. In the spring, divide clumps that exceed their space or that are sagging by digging up the rootball and slicing chunks of rooted grass from its edges. Plant them in new sites.

ADDITIONAL INFORMATION

Switch grass flowers are great fresh or dried in arrangements. It has no pests or diseases.

ADDITIONAL SPECIES, CULTIVARS, OR VARIETIES

'Cloud Nine', which grows to 6 feet, has blue-gray foliage and red flowers. 'Heavy Metal' is extremely popular; it grows to 5 feet and has more columnar, bluish foliage. 'Red Rays' has red foliage. 'Squaw' is the smallest at 4 feet, with reddish color. 'Rotstrahlbusch' does not lose its upright posture with age.

 Did You Know?

Ornamental and turfgrasses, bamboos, and many other plants number among their cousins both forms that spread as enlarging clumps and those that spread by means of underground creeping roots, or horizontal rooting stems. These latter, the runners, while often very nice, useful plants, present serious problems to the gardening home owner because they need to be controlled. Rather than avoid them completely, use them judiciously in areas where there are limits to their spread, such as between a building and a paved street or walkway, in containers, or along banks enclosed by natural barriers of stone.

Tall Fescue

Festuca elatior

Other Name: Turftype Fescue
Type: Cool-season turfgrass
Mature Size: Mow at 3 inches in summer
Foliage Color/Type: Dark green; slightly coarse

Light Requirements:

*T*all turftype fescue was originally so coarse and clumpy that its use was limited to athletic fields and expanses of public turf where constant foot traffic mandated toughness over beauty. Over time breeders have developed it into a finer-textured, more uniform turfgrass. It is used alone or as a welcome addition to mixes of turfgrasses intended for residential landscapes often labeled for play areas. Its toughness and drought resistance contribute to any lawn. Always choose a premium quality seed. For areas with high use, choose a mixture of Kentucky bluegrass and perennial ryegrass with large proportions of tall fescue.

WHEN TO PLANT

Plant new lawns just after Labor Day. Tall fescue seed needs several months of cool weather to germinate and develop into seedlings with deep root systems. Lay tall fescue sod or patch lawns with tall fescue seed in either spring or fall, and be prepared to water it every few days for weeks if rain is scarce.

WHERE TO PLANT

Tall fescue needs about 8 hours of sun daily. It prefers soil that is rich in organic matter and is neutral or just slightly acidic. Do not plant it under trees. Mulch the soil under trees or plant ground covers instead.

HOW TO PLANT

When seeding or sodding a new lawn or patching bare spots in an existing one, add organic material to soil in the tilled seedbed. Smooth and water the area. When weeds erupt after a week or so, kill them with a burndown herbicide. A week or 10 days later, sow seed as directed on the seed package. Water so that the seed stays moist at all times. Fertilize now or later in the fall. A temporary mulch of white polyspun garden fleece maintains moisture, prevents seeds from washing away in the rain, protects the seeds from birds, and shelters the new seedlings. Water seedlings through the fall and into winter if rainfall is undependable.

CARE AND MAINTENANCE

Begin cutting new tall fescue when it approaches 4 inches tall. Cut it back to 3 inches until it goes dormant, then cut it at 2 inches to overwinter.

Established in good soil, tall fescue has legendary drought resistance. Water only after 2 weeks of no water or when it looks limp. In poor or compacted soils where roots cannot grow deep, water more often. Fertilize with a granular slow-acting product formulated for lawns in spring and/or fall. In late fall, use a "winter" formulation to encourage the development of deep roots while grass is dormant. Aerate and topdress the lawn with organic material every year or two to maintain good soil. Every few years mow close and overseed with premium tall fescue to renew and thicken the turf.

ADDITIONAL INFORMATION

Philadelphia area soil is slightly more acidic than turfgrasses prefer. Spread granular lime in the fall every couple of years. Do not fertilize and lime at the same time. Turfgrasses in our area suffer from fungal disease because of the hot, humid summers. Tall fescue is prone to pythium and brown patch. Use mixtures of several turfgrasses so that their specific resistances collectively assure that some grass stays green if a particular fungal disease strikes.

 Did You Know?

In the old days grass clippings created unsightly clumps on the lawn, smothering the grass beneath them unless they were raked up promptly. When they went in the trash, so did a lot of valuable nitrogen. Now, mulching mowers save us the time and effort of raking and improve the health of the lawn. Because they suspend cut blades in the air long enough to be cut several times, clippings are small enough to disappear into the turf where they fall. There they rapidly decompose and provide nitrogen—a pound over the typical season—to fertilize the lawn.

Ground Covers

ALL KINDS OF PLANTS can be ground covers because this label refers only to their function in the landscape, not any particular botanical trait. The universal stereotype of green, crawling plants hardly does justice to the world of ground covers. They may be annuals or perennials, shrubs or vines, predominantly flowering or foliage, evergreen or deciduous, sun or shade loving. Often familiar garden standbys are eminently successful and useful as ground covers. A ground cover plant is simply one that, planted en masse, effectively covers the soil, forming an attractive tapestry of color and/or texture. By means of slowly widening clumps or running roots or stems, it spreads into a protective mat. As a living mulch, it helps soil retain moisture, resist erosion, and avoid compaction.

Ground cover plants nourish and shelter the microlife that keeps soil alive and healthy. Good ground covers also suppress weeds, contribute to plant diversity in the landscape, and look attractive. Although the plants most commonly used by American home owners for ground covers are turfgrasses (see the section on grasses), they lack the versatility of ornamental plants. Many plants are more visually interesting, lower maintenance, and useful in solving problems in the yard because they can handle poorer, wetter, or shadier conditions than turfgrass can. Gardeners prefer to work with a larger palette of plants and strive to achieve decorative as well as functional goals.

What makes a good ground cover? Ground cover plants described in the following pages have many desirable traits that make them useful in our area:

- They form a thick mat over the soil fairly quickly.
- They adapt to a variety of soil types.
- They spread deliberately but not rampantly.
- They are easy to pull up to control spread.
- They have winter interest—seedheads, evergreen foliage.
- They have good foliage color, possibly variegated.
- They need little grooming or pruning.
- They hold up over many years with minimal care.
- They have a tough constitution that is often belied by a fine texture.

PLANTING
Plant individual ground cover plants as you would any plant—in decent, prepared soil that suits its preferences. (See plant entries.) Because they are

planted as mass plantings, however, spacing becomes an issue. How far apart to set them is a function of five things: the size of the transplant, the speed with which it spreads, the size of the area to be covered, the degree of your impatience in seeing the plants knit together, and the number that you can afford to buy. Nursery stock in quart containers costs more, but establishes and spreads faster. Buy fewer and plant them farther apart, and be patient. Rooted cuttings are inexpensive, but slower to spread. Buy them by the flat, plant them fairly close together, and be patient. If the area to be covered is modest and the budget is healthy, buy the larger potted plants and plant them closer together, and your patience will be rewarded sooner!

How to Use Ground Covers

Use ground covers as a low-maintenance substitute for turfgrass and as a way to protect soil. They solve all kinds of landscape problems—covering tree surface roots, controlling erosion, enduring shade, and obscuring eyesores such as old stumps and utility vents. They mask dying bulb foliage and provide variety and interest. In large areas plant lower, finer-textured plants in the foreground. Taller, coarser-textured ones are best in more distant situations. Experiment with variegated foliage to brighten deepest shade. Use those with contrasting foliage to attract attention and divert the eye from other areas. Similar colors work well to form a backdrop for specimen plants.

Flora non Grata

With ground covers there can be too much of a good thing. Some plants that have many of these assets have them in too great supply or are relentlessly overbearing. Although some may be virtual weeds that arrive in the yard unbidden, others are cultivated plants sold commercially for landscape use. Because these ground covers do not know the meaning of restraint, frustrated gardeners often refer to them as "thugs." *Unless they are grown in a container*, avoid the following:

- Barren strawberry (*Waldensteinia fragariodes*)
- Gooseneck loosestrife (*Lysimachia clethroides*)
- Mint (*Mentha* species)
- Goutweed (*Aegopodium podagraria*)
- Purple loosestrife (*Lythrum salicaria*)
- Crown vetch (*Coronilla varia* 'Penngift')
- Chameleon plant (*Houttuynia cordata*)

Ajuga

Ajuga reptans

Other Names: Bugleweed,
  Carpet Bugleweed

Light Requirements:

Type: Perennial

Height: 2 inches tall; flower spikes to 6 inches

Bloom Time: May

Flower Color/Type: Blue, white, pink florets

Foliage: Semievergreen; green, purple, bronze; silver and pinkish;
  variegated, crinkled

Color photograph on page 203.

As well known by its formal Latin name as by its common name, ajuga is a useful ground cover of the first order. It is both attractive and adaptable. It is always in danger of being taken for granted because it is so dependable. It tolerates the hot sun between stones on a patio and the shade of a woodland area. Its tightly packed whorls of colorful foliage are semievergreen during our milder winters and can withstand occasional foot traffic. Ajuga's spring spikes of tiny snapdragonlike flowers are a real bonus, and they attract eager honeybees. Best of all, it spreads with decorum and is easy to pull up when it goes out of bounds. There are many interesting versions from which to choose, and they do not seem to interest deer.

WHEN TO PLANT

Plant rooted divisions or young plants in flats from the garden center in either spring or fall. Ones that come from the garden center in pots can go in anytime during the growing season.

WHERE TO PLANT

Plant ajuga in either full sun or partial shade where the soil is very well-drained. Soggy and/or very rich soil promotes a rot in ajuga. Any ordinary garden soil is fine.

HOW TO PLANT

Dig and loosen the soil down 4 to 6 inches, and add sand or gravel, if necessary, to encourage good drainage. Dig a planting hole about the size of the ajuga roots, and set the plant into the hole so that the foliage is slightly above the level of the surrounding ground. Fill in the hole with soil, firming it gently around the crown of the plant to remove air pockets, then water well. Set plants about 6 to 8 inches apart.

CARE AND MAINTENANCE

Ajuga needs very little attention. When the tiny flowers have faded, cut off the flower spikes with hedge clippers, a string trimmer, or scissors to groom the plants and prevent their sowing seeds. As the season progresses, clip off foliage rosettes on runners that have overstepped their bounds. There is no need to mulch or fertilize, but since the roots are fairly shallow, water when rainfall is scarce. When the rosettes of leaves start to pile on each other, thin the ajuga planting.

ADDITIONAL INFORMATION

The only significant problem of ajuga is crown rot. Usually a function of excessive heat and humidity, it is most common in overcrowded patches. In a specific area the plants just suddenly melt away. Often part of a patch dies out, but not all of it. It may fill in again on its own over time.

ADDITIONAL SPECIES, CULTIVARS, OR VARIETIES

Ajuga reptans 'Burgundy Glow' has paler foliage variegated with reddish purple, green, and cream. It is the most susceptible to bitter cold. 'Catlin's Giant' has large, 6-inch-long leaves. 'Alba' has white flowers. 'Giant Bronze' has dark, burnished-bronze leaves and grows to 9 inches tall; 'Purpurea' has purplish leaves. Geneva bugleweed (*Ajuga genevensis*) does not spread, so it is good for rock gardens; upright bugleweed (*Ajuga pyramidalis* 'Metallica Crispa') is quite different with crinkly, textured leaves of lustrous reddish brown.

Did You Know?

The formal or botanical names of plants always have at least two Latin words in them. This binomial epithet, as it is called, describes the make and model of the plant. The first word is capitalized and is the name of its genus—Ajuga (or Toyota). The second word, designating the species—reptans (or Camry)—is an adjective that describes a prominent trait or commemorates the person who found or bred the plant. Be aware that reptans *or* repens *means stems that creep and root, and plant accordingly!*

Barrenwort

Epimedium species and hybrids

Other Names: Bishop's Hat, Longspur
Type: Perennial
Height: 8 to 12 inches tall
Bloom Time: Spring
Flower Color/Type: Yellow, pink, red, white, orange; spurred florets
Foliage: Heart-shaped; pale green, sometimes tinged with red

Light Requirements:

Color photograph on page 204.

Barrenworts came from Asia originally and arrived in our country by way of Japan and Europe where they have been grown since the 1600s. Their common name is derived from the resemblance of the flowers to a Roman Catholic bishop's four-cornered hat, called a beretta. Only recently have they received the appreciation they deserve as stalwarts in shady residential landscapes. Their spring daintiness belies their toughness, but the wiry stems and stiffly textured leaves that persist as winter closes in reveal it. Barrenwort foliage is not exactly evergreen, yet it adds to the winter scene if not cut back for fall cleanup. Their relatively shallow roots grip the soil tenaciously, making barrenworts useful for slopes and other areas vulnerable to erosion. They spread slowly and decorously, as permitted.

WHEN TO PLANT

Plant rooted divisions in either spring or fall. Plant potted nursery plants anytime during the growing season.

WHERE TO PLANT

Barrenwort can handle some sun, but it is most happy and useful in shade or partial shade areas. Once established, it can handle mediocre soil and some dryness, but it prefers soil that is moist and rich in organic material. It competes well with tree roots, and it is great as a living mulch around large trees with shallow or surface roots.

HOW TO PLANT

Dig the soil down 8 to 10 inches, mixing in granular slow-acting all-purpose fertilizer for a good start and organic material to improve soil drainage. Dig the planting hole large enough to comfortably accommodate the roots and shallow enough so that the plant is at the same soil depth that it was in its pot, no deeper. Fill in the hole with soil, firming it gently around plant stems to remove air pockets, and water well. Set plants about 10 to 12 inches apart to allow for their gradual spread.

CARE AND MAINTENANCE

Water during dry periods. If barrenwort is in good garden soil, there is no need to fertilize. Otherwise, a sprinkling of slow-acting granular fertilizer on the soil near the patch helps plants through the season. Cut back foliage left to provide winter interest in early spring before the tender new shoots start to unfurl from deep in the plant crowns. Divide overlarge clumps of barrenwort late in the summer when the heat subsides a bit. When patches become too large, dig up a clump to expose the roots, and cut through them with a sharp spade or knife. They are tough and wiry, so the tool must be sharp. Replant rooted chunks elsewhere.

ADDITIONAL INFORMATION

Barrenworts are virtually pest and disease free.

ADDITIONAL SPECIES, CULTIVARS, OR VARIETIES

Epimedium alpinum 'Rubrum' has red and yellow flowers. Red barrenwort (*Epimedium × rubrum*) has red flowers and heart-shaped leaves. Bicolor barrenwort (*Epimedium × versicolor*) spreads by eager runners, while Young's barrenwort (*Epimedium × youngianum* 'Niveum') is more clumping. *Epimedium grandiflorum* has heart-shaped bronzy leaves that mature to green and yellow flowers. 'Album' has white flowers; 'Rose Queen' has rosy-red flowers.

Did You Know?

Its name reminds the gardener of the conditions that barrenwort can handle if it must. It is often described as a dry shade plant. That is what the word **barren** *certainly suggests. Home owners who have lots of trees are grateful for a ground cover that can manage with the reduced water supply under them.*

Bellflower

Campanula poscharskyana

Other Name: Serbian Bellflower

Type: Perennial

Height: 4 inches tall; flower stems 6 inches

Bloom Time: Late May or early June

Flower Color/Type: Lilac-blue bells

Foliage: Semievergreen; medium green

Color photograph on page 204.

Light Requirements:

Dainty but vigorous, Serbian bellflower sprawls tidily in mounded clumps of heart-shaped, ripple-edged leaves on short stems. In late spring stems as long as 12 inches suddenly appear, and they are quickly arrayed with starry blue flowers with 5-pointed petals. At this point bellflowers' decorum slips a bit as the stems flop over with the weight of the blooms, but they are so thick that no one notices. On a stone wall or along the edge of a garden bed or walkway, these flowers steal the show from other early-summer bloomers for a week or two.

WHEN TO PLANT

Plant young plants in pots from the garden center anytime during the season when they are available. Plant rooted pieces from divided plants after they bloom in early summer. Choose an overcast day or plant in the evening so that the transplant is not stressed by the sun while it copes with transplant shock.

WHERE TO PLANT

Bellflowers can take fairly harsh conditions. They do not mind full sun, and they thrive in rock garden sites—sandy or other thin, well-drained soil. Plant along stone walls, between stepping-stones, and along paved walks.

HOW TO PLANT

Dig the soil down to 8 or 10 inches, and mix in coarse sand to promote drainage if needed. Although bellflowers do not need pampering, it is a good idea to mix in granular slow-acting all-purpose fertilizer also, so that the transplants will have a strong start. Dig planting holes roughly the size of the plants' containers. Tip them out of the containers, and set them in their holes so that they are at the same depth in the ground that they were in their pots. Fill in the holes with soil, firming it gently, and water well. Set plants about 8 to 10 inches apart. They will fill in gradually as the clumps expand and/or self-seed into nearby soil.

CARE AND MAINTENANCE

Mulch new plantings of bellflower to discourage competing weeds and maintain soil moisture while seedlings are struggling to establish. When blooming is finished, remove the stems of faded flowers by clipping them off at their base back among the foliage clump. (They will actually detach freely when grasped by hand and gently tugged.) Intermittent repeat bloom over the summer is fairly common.

ADDITIONAL INFORMATION

Use at the front of the flower bed as edging to set off minor bulbs and blend with other ground covers such as rock cress in spring. Serbian bellflower looks good under yellow daylilies.

ADDITIONAL SPECIES, CULTIVARS, OR VARIETIES

The campanula clan is large and diverse, and its many members are assets in residential landscapes. Most have the trademark bell-shaped flowers in shades of blue or white. Among the ground covers, there is also Dalmatian bellflower (*Campanula portenschlagiana*), which grows closer to the ground with similar colored flowers. It tends to bloom a bit later, in June or July. It is easily (and often) confused with Serbian bellflower.

GROUND COVERS

Did You Know?

Campanula *means "little bell." Thus it makes an appropriate family name for several related groups of plants with similar characteristics—including, but not limited to, the classic bell-shaped flowers. The family is* Campanulaceae. *Confusion may arise because of the resemblance to the genus name* Campanula. *If a Latin word has ae or eae, it is a family name. It is the job of botanists and taxonomists to determine which plants belong to which families.*

Creeping Juniper

Juniperus horizontalis

Other Names: Carpet Juniper, Rug Juniper
Type: Woody shrub
Height: 1 to 2 feet tall
Foliage: Evergreen; bluish green scales
resembling flattened needles

Color photograph on page 204.

Light Requirements:

For a heavy-duty ground cover one of the best choices is a sturdy plant such as creeping juniper. Each of these low-growing native shrubs forms a clump of dense branches that spread horizontally up to 6 feet or more into a roughly circular mound. Rather than root where they touch the soil, the stems just lie on it. Collectively, they carpet the ground with a quilt of attractive bluish-green foliage that acquires a purplish tinge in winter. It is just prickly enough to discourage shortcuts by people and pets across the area it covers. Moreover, creeping junipers tolerate all sorts of indignities such as heat, drought, seashore conditions, road salt, and mediocre soil. Female shrubs bear tiny cones, which are their flowers. They become juniper "berries" in August and last until the following spring unless the songbirds get them first. Plant minor spring flowering bulbs among junipers, which will set off their beauty, then obscure their ripening foliage after they bloom.

WHEN TO PLANT

Plant balled and burlapped plants in either spring or fall. Transplant containerized nursery stock anytime during the growing season when it is not too hot and dry. Shade new transplants their first day or two in summer.

WHERE TO PLANT

Junipers love full sun and adapt to almost any kind of soil pH and type, as long as it is not soggy. They grow on rocky escarpments and other improbable places in the wild. In home landscapes they are particularly useful on slopes to control erosion and eliminate mowing. Branches grow loose and spindly in shade. They are ideal for the house "down the Shore."

HOW TO PLANT

Choose containerized plants. Loosen the soil down at least a foot, and mix in granular slow-acting fertilizer to give transplants a boost during their first season. Take this opportunity to improve soil drainage in the entire bed by digging in organic material, too. Dig saucer-shaped planting holes exactly as deep as and slightly wider than the plants' containers. Remove each juniper from its container, and cut or loosen any circling roots. Set each plant in its hole so that its crown is at, or slightly above, soil level. Then fill in the hole with soil, firming it gently around plant stems, and water well. Set plants at least 3 feet apart, slightly closer to hurry their blending into a mat. Mulch the bare soil between shrubs to discourage the inevitable weeds during the first year. Do not pile it against juniper stems.

CARE AND MAINTENANCE
While they establish themselves, junipers need regular watering and probably some weeding. Clip off damaged or overlong branches. Never prune back as far as the bare stem because foliage will not regenerate there. After their first season they do not need fertilizing. Watch for mites, which attack when shrubs are stressed by unusually wet, dry, or hot weather. They are easily controlled by a spray of horticultural oil as directed on the product label.

ADDITIONAL INFORMATION
They are tough plants, but junipers are occasionally victimized by a tip blight known as *Phomopsis*, most commonly on plants less than 5 years old. Prune out the browned, dying twigs. Older plantings may be prone to mice damage in winter.

ADDITIONAL SPECIES, CULTIVARS, OR VARIETIES

Many low, spreading types of junipers do well in the Philadelphia area. 'Wiltoni' (blue rug) and 'Douglasii' are among them. 'Bar Harbor' is only 1 foot tall; 'Blue Mat' is prostrate at 6 inches high; 'Wisconsin', which seems to resist blight well, has 8-inch-tall purple winter foliage. A less common type, 'Mother Lode', has bright yellow foliage and grows only 2 or 3 inches tall. Local experts recommend it and Japanese garden juniper (*Juniperus procumbens* 'Nana').

 Did You Know?

An early juniper selection, 'Plumosa', is part of local horticultural history. It was introduced by Andorra Nurseries in Philadelphia in 1907 and became very popular over the years. Because it is susceptible to blight, it has been superseded in recent years by lower, more resistant, junipers such as 'Plumosa Compacta', which develops maroon foliage in winter.

Creeping Phlox

Phlox stolonifera

Other Name: Stoloniferous Phlox
Type: Perennial
Height: 2 inches; flower spikes 6 to
10 inches tall
Bloom Time: May
Flower Color/Type: Blue, white, purple, pink
Foliage: Evergreen; lustrous, dark green, oval

Color photograph on page 204.

Light Requirements:

This native woodland plant was a hit with gardeners as soon as it became available. Not only does it creep over the ground with measured speed, but the foliage mat it creates is fine textured and neat. In mid-spring it sends up perky 6-inch stems tipped with clusters of small florets that bloom for a week or more. The foliage carries on in style all summer, successfully avoiding the mildew problems that plague other phloxes. The most shade-tolerant phlox, it is ideal for edging walks and beds, and for transition areas between shade and sunny sites. It is so low growing that it does well between stepping-stones.

WHEN TO PLANT

Plant young plants in pots anytime during the growing season. Plant rooted divisions of creeping phlox in either spring or fall when an overlarge plant is divided.

WHERE TO PLANT

Plant creeping phlox in partial shade or where it gets spring sunshine under deciduous trees. It does best in woodsy soil—moist, acidic, rich in organic matter, and well-drained.

HOW TO PLANT

Aerate and loosen soil by digging down 8 to 10 inches. Add organic matter such as peat moss, compost, or chopped leaves to improve soil drainage, and mix in granular slow-acting fertilizer to give new transplants a boost during their first season. Dig planting holes about as deep as and slightly wider than the rootballs when plants are removed from containers. Set plants in their holes so that their crowns, where the roots meet the stems, are just at soil level. Fill in the hole with soil, firming it gently, and water well. Set plants 8 to 10 inches apart to allow for their gradual spread.

CARE AND MAINTENANCE

Water newly planted beds frequently until plants are established. Mulch any bare soil to discourage weeds until the plants knit together. Clip stems with faded flowers back to the foliage after bloom. Cut off unauthorized, dead, or injured runners anytime during the season to groom the patch. If the creeping phlox patch becomes too extensive or overcrowded, divide it after flowering.

ADDITIONAL INFORMATION

This phlox does not have mildew problems. If it gets too much summer sun, it may be too stressed to grow vigorously, and its leaves will become pale.

ADDITIONAL SPECIES, CULTIVARS, OR VARIETIES

There are many creeping phlox colors: 'Bruce's White' (white), 'Blue Ridge' (blue), 'Pink Ridge' (pink), 'Sherwood Purple' (purplish blue), and 'Irridescens' (lavender). Wild blue phlox (*Phlox divaricata*) is also native to our woodlands. More wispy and delicate looking, it dies back and disappears in the summer. 'Fuller's White' is a white-flowered version.

GROUND COVERS

Did You Know?

The Perennial Plant Association selected creeping phlox to be its Plant of the Year in 1990. This organization of plant growers and sellers is committed to promoting education and cooperation within the perennial plant and related industries. It sponsors research, symposia, and various publications to further these goals. Each year the association selects a perennial plant that it believes has superior qualities of appearance, vigor, and disease and pest resistance.

Deadnettle

Lamium maculatum

Other Names: Lamium, Spotted Deadnettle
Type: Perennial
Height: 8 to 12 inches tall
Bloom Time: Mid to late spring
Flower Color/Type: Pink or white
Foliage: Semievergreen; variegated green with silver/white markings

Light Requirements:

Color photograph on page 204.

One of the major assets of certain shade-loving ground covers is variegated foliage. The silvery or white streaks and blotches on the leaves of the various deadnettles brighten the ground under larger green plants such as azaleas, rhododendrons, and cherrylaurel while protecting the soil and providing foliage texture. Their stem runners grow energetically but are not invasive. The many kinds of deadnettles are quietly effective, easily controlled, attractive ground covers. As a bonus, they bear small flowers in dainty whorls at the tops of leafy spikes in late spring.

WHEN TO PLANT

Plant rooted sections from a large clump in either spring or fall. Plant deadnettle plants in pots from the garden center anytime during the growing season.

WHERE TO PLANT

Most deadnettles do best in shade, and certainly, their variegation shows to best advantage there. They can handle some sun if necessary. They prefer moist, well-drained good garden soil, but will make do with poorer, drier soil after they become established. They spread less rapidly in poorer soil.

HOW TO PLANT

Dig and loosen the soil down 8 to 10 inches, and sprinkle granular slow-acting fertilizer into it. Dig planting holes about as deep as and slightly wider than the plant rootballs, and set them in so that their crowns, where their roots and stems join, are at soil level. Fill in the holes with soil, firming it gently around plant stems, and water well. Set plants about 6 to 8 inches apart to form a mat in one season.

CARE AND MAINTENANCE

Water deadnettles well while they adjust to their site and become established. Mulch the bare soil between plants the first season to control weeds and hold moisture. After they flower, clip or shear back stem tips to forestall reseeding and to keep plants compact. The fresh new foliage growth will hold up over the rest of summer and through winter pretty well. Divide and replant in spring or fall.

ADDITIONAL SPECIES, CULTIVARS, OR VARIETIES

There are several nice versions of spotted deadnettle (*Lamium maculatum*). 'Beacon Silver' has silvery leaves edged with green, and lilac flowers. 'Shell Pink' has long-blooming pink flowers; 'White Nancy' has whitish foliage and flowers. Yellow archangel 'Hermann's Pride' (*Lamium galeobdolon* 'Hermann's Pride') has silver-tinged leaves and yellow flowers.

 Did You Know?

*When plantsmen discover a sturdy, adaptable plant that has ornamental appeal, they see a candidate for the garden. Many potentially good garden plants such as yellow archangel (*Lamium galeobdolon* 'Variegata') flunk the good citizenship test, however, because they are too rambunctious, threatening to take over the entire yard. Rather than give up on them, plantsmen look for variations of the plant that are better, in this case, more mannerly. When they find promising ones, they name them and develop them for garden use. These CULTIvated VARieties, or "cultivars," often go on to fame and fortune. 'Hermann's Pride', a clumping cultivar of yellow archangel, is a great success in the garden.*

English Ivy

Hedera helix

Other Name: Ivy
Type: Perennial
Height: 8 to 10 inches tall
Bloom Time: Fall
Flower Color/Type: Greenish white globes
Foliage: Evergreen; deep, lustrous green; variegated cream, white, yellow

Light Requirements:

Color photograph on page 204.

Just because it is the traditional basic green foliage ground cover widely used in residential landscapes, English ivy is not to be ignored. There is a reason why it is so ubiquitous—the best reason of all—it is an excellent plant. Do not let familiarity breed contempt because this ivy is not always so familiar. It goes way beyond green. There are literally hundreds of versions with foliage in every imaginable pattern of variegation, leaf shape, and leaf size. The typical ground cover is usually a juvenile form of the plant. When it is encouraged to grow and spread and climb, English ivy undergoes a transition at some point, developing a mature form. Becoming more shrubby and bearing flowers near the top of more rounded leaves, it behaves more like a bush. Its flowers bear heavy nectar and attract bees. They give way to black berries, which are poisonous.

WHEN TO PLANT

Plant potted plants anytime during the growing season, but spring and fall are best. Rooted cuttings from flats do best when planted in spring.

WHERE TO PLANT

Ivy thrives in shade or partial shade and in almost any soil type except the truly soggy. It prefers woodsy soil moist and rich in humus. Plant it under trees to protect their root zones from damage by encroaching mowers and string trimmers. Allow it to climb walls or wander between and over rocks.

HOW TO PLANT

Dig and loosen the soil down 8 or 10 inches, mixing in organic material to improve its drainage. Add granular slow-acting fertilizer to give new transplants a good start if the soil is not very good. When planting under existing shrubs and trees, dig holes carefully between roots to minimize damage. Make them as deep as and slightly wider than the plant rootballs. Set each plant in the hole so that its crown is at soil level. Fill in the hole with soil, firming it gently around plant stems, and water well. Set plants about 1 foot apart, closer if time is of the essence.

CARE AND MAINTENANCE

If rainfall is sparse, water new ground cover beds regularly until plants catch on. Mulch the bare soil between transplants to discourage weeds until the ivy knits together. Otherwise ivy needs no care except to prune runners that begin to overstep their bounds. Periodically renovate a long-established bed by mowing it with the mower set at its highest setting. Take the opportunity to improve the exposed soil by spreading organic material such as mushroom soil, compost, peat moss, or something similar. There is no need to fertilize ivy once the planting is off and running.

ADDITIONAL INFORMATION

Because we rarely have snow cover worthy of the term in our area, evergreen ivy foliage sometimes takes a beating from harsh winter sun and winds. Browned foliage will disappear when the new spring growth emerges and covers it. English ivy causes dermatitis in some people. To be on the safe side, wear gloves while handling it.

ADDITIONAL SPECIES, CULTIVARS, OR VARIETIES

A zillion kinds of English ivy are available that feature tiny or large, curly, variegated, fine, or bold leaves. 'Buttercup' won the 1988 Pennsylvania Horticultural Society's Gold Medal Award for exceptional merit and suitability for Philadelphia area gardens.

Did You Know?

Some plants are so beloved that they acquire fan clubs, called plant societies. These groups, such as the American Ivy Society, play an important part in developing and disseminating information about the care and use of the plant. Ivy society members grow and study ivy, and some also seek new varieties and propagate them. Their mission is to popularize the use of ivy, and they are a wonderful resource. For more information consult their Web site at www.ivy.org.

Flower Carpet® Pink Rose

Rosa 'Noatraum'

Other Name: Flower Carpet Rose
Type: Woody shrub
Height: 2 to 3 feet
Bloom Time: June to October
Flower Color/Type: Rose-pink; repeat bloom
Foliage: Deciduous; glossy green

Color photograph on page 205.

Light Requirements:

Unfortunately, hybrid tea roses are so high maintenance that their role in the typical residential landscape is usually limited to standoffish specimens grouped in beds of their own where they can receive intensive care. In recent years interest in roses that can be integrated into the landscape with other plants has prompted breeders to develop more useful landscape or "shrub" roses. Flower carpet pink is a standout among this group of more versatile new roses. Because it is unprecedentedly disease free and very tough, it makes a beautiful ground cover. Dense and compact, each plant spreads to about 4 feet in neat, loose mounds of stems tipped with clusters of 15 to 18 subtly scented flowers. Properly sited and appropriately watered and fertilized, a mature plant can produce 2000 flowers per season virtually nonstop.

WHEN TO PLANT

Flower carpet roses come in pots and can be planted anytime during the growing season, although springtime is best. Plant when the sun is not out to spare the transplant extra stress while it copes with transplant shock.

WHERE TO PLANT

In the Philadelphia area flower carpet rose performs best in full sun. It can take partial shade (only 4 to 5 hours of sun or all-day filtered light) and still bloom freely. It is not particular about soil as long as it is well-drained.

HOW TO PLANT

Cultivate the soil down 12 inches, and mix in a granular slow-acting fertilizer according to product label instructions. Mix in organic matter, too, to help it drain better. Dig each saucer-shaped planting hole about as deep as and somewhat wider than the rose's container. Tap each plant out of its pot, loosening any matted roots, and set its rootball in the hole so that its soil is exactly level with the surrounding ground. Fill in the hole with soil, firming it gently around plant stems, and water well. Set plants about 2 to 3 per square yard for ground cover.

CARE AND MAINTENANCE

Flower carpet roses need regular watering to develop vigorous, strong roots during the period when they are getting established. Always water during periods of drought. Mulch with a 2- or 3-inch layer of organic material to keep soil moist. In the spring prune all canes back hard to about 6 inches, fertilize, and renew the mulch. Since individual plants bloom profusely for months, they need the consistent, uniform nutrition from a granular slow-acting fertilizer every spring. It is not necessary to deadhead spent blossoms, but it is a good opportunity to cut canes back in midseason to maintain a nice shape and compactness. These plants can take hard pruning. Water and mulch roses well for the winter.

ADDITIONAL INFORMATION

Flower carpet roses are particularly useful on slopes and along walls and walkways. They are just prickly enough to discourage shortcuts by kids and mail carriers. They also do extremely well in containers and among other flowering plants in flower beds.

ADDITIONAL SPECIES, CULTIVARS, OR VARIETIES

Flower carpet white (*Rosa* 'Noaschnee') has slightly larger, camellia-like scented flowers. Flower carpet appleblossom (*Rosa* 'Noamel'), a "sport" of flower carpet pink, has deep-pink buds that develop into pastel-pink flowers. Expect yellow, red, and coral flower carpet roses in the near future.

 Did You Know?

In Germany roses are put through their paces in stringent All-Deutsche Rose (ADR) trials—one of the toughest competitions in the world. Candidates are tested six times annually for three years in nine test gardens with no chemical spraying or dusting. They are evaluated for general appearance, ease of growing, and disease resistance. Flower carpet pink won the ADR Gold Medal in 1990 with the highest rating for natural disease resistance ever given.

Foamflower

Tiarella cordifolia

Other Name: Allegheny Foamflower
Type: Perennial
Height: 6 inches tall; flower spikes to
12 inches
Bloom Time: May
Flower Color/Type: White, fuzzy "bottlebrushes"
Foliage: Semievergreen; medium green, heart shaped

Color photograph on page 204.

Light Requirements:

It is always magical when foamflower does its spring thing. The woodland floor or shade garden suddenly is carpeted in dainty, upright white flower spikes. After about two weeks they fade, and the fresh, new replacement foliage is revealed. Foamflowers carpet the area by sending out runners along the soil surface. They trail and tumble over rocks and logs and between stones with abandon, but are easy to clip off when they overstep their bounds. A spectacular show of foamflower takes place every spring at David Benner's garden in New Hope, Bucks County, where it mingles with fellow native plants—wild blue phlox and an assortment of trilliums, lily-of-the-valley, and other woodland plants.

WHEN TO PLANT

Plant rooted divisions from overlarge plants in either spring or fall when they are divided. Transplant young potted plants from the garden center anytime during the growing season.

WHERE TO PLANT

Foamflower needs shade. It does well under trees because it is shallow rooted and does not compete with them or disturb their roots. It does best in classic woodsy soil—rich in organic matter, acidic, and well-drained. Once established, it can handle mild drought and more light.

HOW TO PLANT

Dig and loosen the soil down 8 to 10 inches, mixing in granular slow-acting fertilizer and organic material to enrich it. Dig planting holes about as deep as and slightly wider than the rootballs of the transplants when they are removed from their pots. Set each plant in its hole so that its crown, where the roots meet the stems, is just at soil level. Fill in the hole with soil, firming it gently around plant stems, and water well. Space plants about 10 inches apart to allow for their gradual spread.

CARE AND MAINTENANCE

Water newly planted areas well until plants are established. In the spring deadheading spent flower spikes makes the patch look more attractive, but is not really practical for extensive areas. The flower stems are thin and relatively inconspicuous after blooms fade. There is no need to clip or deal with faded foliage; the new leaves will cover it. To acquire more plants, it is easiest to clip off rooted pieces of runners and replant anytime during the season.

ADDITIONAL INFORMATION

Typical of native plants, foamflower does not have serious pest or disease problems.

ADDITIONAL SPECIES, CULTIVARS, OR VARIETIES

'Slick Rock' has shorter, scented flowers and aggressive runners. 'Rambling Tapestry' has maroon veins in the leaves. Wherry's foamflower (*Tiarella wherryi* or *T. cordifolia* 'Collina') grows in clumps rather than sending out runners. Its flowers tend to last longer than those of regular foamflower. It has purple-tinged foliage and pink-tinged flowers. 'Oakleaf' has green leaves that resemble the leaves of an oak tree.

Did You Know?

What is better than two great plants? A plant breeder's answer to this question is: a third one that combines them! Thus × Heucherella, a hybrid of foamflower (Tiarella) and coralbells (Heuchera). Varieties of heucherella have the charming foamflower foliage and long, airy stems of tiny bell-shaped flowers which are typical of coralbells.

Ginger

Asarum europaeum

Other Name: European Wild Ginger
Type: Perennial
Height: 6 to 8 inches tall
Bloom Time: May
Flower Color/Type: Brownish, jug shaped, inconspicuous
Foliage: Evergreen; lustrous, smooth, dark green, kidney shaped

Light Requirements:

Color photograph on page 204.

The job of ground cover does not have much prestige, but some plants bring to their duty a certain polish and dignity. European ginger is such a plant. Covering the soil with a layer of its neat, glossy, kidney-shaped leaves, this plant spreads at a measured pace by means of underground rhizomes. Its flowers are all but invisible, crouching in the deep shade of its foliage, the color of the soil they nestle against. Wild ginger is both a low-profile and a low-maintenance plant that is restrained and effective.

WHEN TO PLANT

Plant divisions of rhizomes in either spring or early fall. Transplant potted plants from the garden center anytime during the growing season.

WHERE TO PLANT

European ginger needs shade. It is happiest in classic woodsy soil—rich in humus, acidic, moist, and well-drained.

HOW TO PLANT

Loosen and aerate soil 8 or 10 inches deep, mixing in granular slow-acting fertilizer and extra organic matter to improve it. Do not plant too deeply. Planting holes should be only as deep as the ginger is in its container so that its crown, where the roots meet the stems, is at exactly the same soil level in the ground as it was in the pot. Fill in the hole with soil, firming it gently around plant stems to remove air pockets, and water well. Set plants about 6 to 8 inches apart to allow for their gradual spread.

CARE AND MAINTENANCE

Water new plantings well until they are truly established. European ginger is virtually carefree. Its foliage stays nice most of the year, so there is no need to shear it for extensive renewal. Just pick off ratty leaves as needed during the season. Because it spreads so slowly, it rarely needs dividing unless it is restricted to a small space. Otherwise a patch can go up to 10 years.

ADDITIONAL INFORMATION

European ginger foliage beautifully sets off the colorful flowers of minor spring bulbs. It then obscures their dying foliage over several weeks.

ADDITIONAL SPECIES, CULTIVARS, OR VARIETIES

Canadian wild ginger (*Asarum canadense*) is our native version of this plant, growing in woodlands from New England to Alabama. Its large round leaves are deciduous and a duller green, sometimes with attractive mottling. It handles heat and more alkaline soil better than the European type, spreading about a foot a year.

Did You Know?

Here is a case where a common name is very misleading. European and native wild gingers have nothing to do with the ginger plant that produces the familiar spice. The real gingers are tropical plants (Zingiberaceae) that can be grown in our area only indoors in greenhouses or as houseplants, or outdoors as annuals. They die when frost arrives. The rhizomes and seeds of various members of the true ginger family provide cardamom, turmeric, and of course, ginger for the kitchen.

Japanese Painted Fern

Athyrium nipponicum 'Pictum'

Other Name: Painted Fern
Type: Perennial
Height: 12 to 18 inches tall
Foliage: Variably reddish, lavender,
  silvery-green fronds

Color photograph on page 204.

Light Requirements:

Perhaps because their delicate, lacy fronds give ferns a fragile look, gardeners often shy away from using them generously in the landscape. In fact, they are enormously useful as ground covers and none more so than the Japanese painted fern. It has all the virtues of other ferns, plus extraordinarily colored foliage that relieves the unremitting greenness of other plants in shady sites. It forms handsome clumps of airy fronds, with no two plants alike. The colors vary subtly from one plant to another and in varying light conditions. In optimum conditions clumps double or triple their size in one growing season, but always avoid undignified spread. Plant this fern in a woodland setting under shrubs such as rhododendron and azalea, near rocks or stone walls alone or with other ground covers such as foamflower, anemones, and sweet woodruff. It also coordinates with other ferns and spring bulbs.

WHEN TO PLANT

Plant potted nursery stock or divisions taken from overlarge clumps in late spring.

WHERE TO PLANT

Japanese painted fern can handle morning or late-day sun if it must, but prefers dappled shade. It needs soil rich in organic matter that will help it retain moisture, yet drain well.

HOW TO PLANT

Prepare soil down 10 to 12 inches by digging in organic matter and a sprinkling of granular slow-acting all-purpose fertilizer to give new transplants a good start. Dig the planting hole about as deep as the fern's container so that its crown, where its roots and stems join, is at soil level when it is set into the hole. Fill in the hole with soil, firming it gently around plant stems to remove air pockets, and water well. Set plants about 2 feet apart to allow for their gradual spread.

Care and Maintenance

Japanese painted fern is quite self-reliant once it is established. Relatively shallow rooted, it will need watering if conditions become too dry (its fronds collapse when it is thirsty). There is no need to fertilize it if it is mulched occasionally with compost or chopped leaves, which will condition the soil and provide a bit of nutrition. When the fronds die back after frost, allow them to remain on the soil as mulch until next spring. Clip them off when the new fronds unfurl in the spring. When fern clumps grow too large for their allotted space, divide them by digging up the entire plant and gently separating rooted "baby" plants at their sides to replant elsewhere. Do this in the spring.

Additional Information

Japanese painted fern is sensitive to soap-based insecticide products, so take care when spraying neighboring plants for pest insect problems.

Additional Species, Cultivars, or Varieties

Lady fern (*Athyrium filix-femina*) is easy to grow and slow spreading; it has classic green foliage. Its relative Alpine lady fern (*Athyrium distentifolium*) is ideal for rock gardens.

 Did You Know?

Along with algae and moss, ferns represent prehistoric plant life that has adapted to our modern world. They do not have typical flowers, continuing to rely instead on a primitive two-step method of reproduction. First spores, tiny dark spots, develop under the leaflets of some of their leaves. They are eventually released into the air and then settle to earth where, if conditions are right, they form a special flat structure that supports the development of male and female organs. Then fertilization takes place, and new fern plants develop.

Lamb's Ears

Stachys byzantina

Other Name: Betony
Type: Perennial
Height: 8 inches tall with flower spikes
  to 15 inches
Bloom Time: June
Flower Color/Type: Magenta florets thinly arrayed on spikes
Foliage: Silvery-white, woolly

Light Requirements:

Color photograph on page 204.

Lamb's ears generously blanket sunny sites with poor soil with wonderful, narrow, perky silver-gray foliage that so resembles a bunny's ears that it begs to be stroked. Although this plant produces striking tall flower spikes, they are more beloved by the zillions of bees that visit than by gardeners who often cut them off unceremoniously before they tilt and flop. In the end, the foliage is more ornamental than the flowers. This plant contributes a lot to a landscape, such as tenaciously gripping poor, thin soil to prevent erosion, adding texture and color to the scene, and filling hot spots where virtually nothing else will grow. A bonus is that it manages to survive the heat, the humidity, and the deer (usually, not guaranteed!) that plague the Philadelphia area.

WHEN TO PLANT

Plant divisions in the spring. Potted plants from the garden center can go into the ground anytime during the growing season.

WHERE TO PLANT

Lamb's ears prefer full sun and must be in soil that has good drainage if the plants are to avoid foliage rot. Once established, they can handle significant drought.

HOW TO PLANT

Loosen soil down 8 to 10 inches. If necessary, mix into it coarse sand, fine gravel, and/or organic material such as compost to improve drainage. Dig a planting hole about as deep as and slightly wider than the plant's rootball. Set it in the hole so that its crown, where the roots meet the stems, is at or slightly above soil level. Fill in the hole with soil, firming it gently around plant stems, and water well. Space plants about 1 foot apart to allow for their gradual spread.

CARE AND MAINTENANCE

Water new plantings until they are established. Avoid overhead sprinkling if possible. Cut off flower spikes to forestall seed production and keep foliage looking its best. If plants become overcrowded, thin them in midsummer to improve air circulation. As patches spread into unauthorized areas, clip back chunks to control them. If the center of the patch gets ratty, dig it up and cut away rotted sections, then replant healthy clumps. Plan to clean up foliage at the end of winter rather than at the end of summer because more soggy foliage will inevitably develop over the winter.

ADDITIONAL INFORMATION

Lamb's ears have a tough constitution, and their fuzzy leaves are unappetizing to most pests, crawling or four footed. Their foliage is vulnerable, however, to some rots that flourish when humidity is high. Often these problems are self-correcting, and simply cutting off affected leaves, cleaning up soggy interior foliage, and waiting for better weather do the trick.

ADDITIONAL SPECIES, CULTIVARS, OR VARIETIES

'Big Ears' has very large foliage and seems to handle heat and cold well. 'Silver Carpet' does not flower; it is strictly a foliage plant. Big betony (*Stachys grandiflora*) has pretty violet flowers on tall spikes, and it appreciates soil that is a bit richer and moister.

 Did You Know?

Lamb's ears, like so many silvery-foliaged plants, is a low-water-demand plant. When home owners in Western states began to worry about dwindling supplies of fresh water, they turned to this type of plant. Planted with others that need minimal moisture, they constitute a Xeriscape, a landscape area that needs less watering. Gardeners in the Philadelphia region are acutely aware that availability of fresh water is not just a Western issue. Designating areas for low-water-demand plants in the home landscape (especially useful where the hose does not reach) conserves water.

Lily-of-the-Valley

Convallaria majalis

Type: Perennial
Height: 6 to 8 inches tall
Bloom Time: May
Flower Color/Type: White, pink; nodding bells
Foliage: Deep green, variegated green with yellow, or white

Light Requirements:

Color photograph on page 204.

Lily-of-the-valley first seduces by its incredible fragrance, then when planted, it proves itself as a tough, attractive ground cover. Perfect for woodland and other shady sites, it carpets the area with rich, green leaves rising from tiny bulblike stems called pips. After about 3 years, the graceful, arching stems arrayed with tiny, nodding, waxy bell-shaped flowers appear each spring. Sheltered by the leaves, they infuse the area with fragrance for a week or two before fading away. Sometimes orange berries take their place, but they are not very ornamental. Later in the summer the foliage ripens, yellowing and melting back to the ground. All parts of the plant are poisonous!

WHEN TO PLANT

Plant "pips" in the spring. Transplant potted plants or divisions from an existing patch of lily-of-the-valley anytime during the growing season.

WHERE TO PLANT

Plant in a shaded area. Although lily-of-the-valley will tolerate remarkably poor soil, it prefers moist, woodsy soil that is rich in organic material, well-drained, and on the acid side. Alone or among other shade lovers such as hostas, the plants are excellent for areas under trees where grass refuses to grow and near walls, especially when they have a northern exposure. Because they tend to be invasive, it is best to give them a bed of their own rather than try to integrate them into a flower bed.

HOW TO PLANT

Cultivate the soil down 8 to 10 inches when spring soil warms and dries out a bit. Mix in granular slow-acting all-purpose fertilizer to sustain the planting over its first season. Set each pip 1 to 2 inches deep, its buds facing upward, spaced about 6 to 8 inches apart; cover with soil; and water well. Mulch the soil between plants to discourage weeds until new plants spread. They spread at a brisk pace.

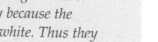
CARE AND MAINTENANCE

Lily-of-the-valley needs no care except possibly watering during a major drought. To encourage profuse flowering, fertilize with a sprinkling of slow-acting granular fertilizer each spring; otherwise do not bother. As plantings grow and spread, large clumps may need restraining. In the spring dig up crowded clumps and pull apart from them healthy-looking pips that have good roots and at least one bud. Replant them elsewhere, or give them away. After the foliage dies back, clean it up and set potted annuals in the bare spot where the lilies-of-the-valley bloomed.

ADDITIONAL INFORMATION

Lily-of-the-valley does well in containers such as patio planters and windowboxes as long as they are in the shade. Pips can also be forced indoors for the sweet smell of spring while it is still winter. Chill plants dug from the yard for forcing for 8 weeks in the refrigerator or unheated garage, then bring them into warmth that will encourage sprouting. Use flowers in bouquets with other dainty flowers that bloom about this time, such as Johnny jump-ups, creeping phlox, columbine, pansies, and sweet woodruff. Handle any mite problems with a forceful spray of water or a spray of insecticidal soap.

ADDITIONAL SPECIES, CULTIVARS, OR VARIETIES

'Fortin's Giant' has larger leaves and larger and more numerous flowers on each stem. 'Rosea' has pink flowers; 'Flora Plena' has larger, double flowers. 'Striata' has white-striped leaves; 'Aurea-variegata' has yellow-striped leaves.

Did You Know?

Lily-of-the-Valley Factoids
- *Its fragrance is the essence of the perfume Joy.*
- *It was dedicated to Ostara, the Norse goddess of springtime.*
- *Christian tradition dedicated it to Mary, and it was also known as ladder to heaven and virgin's tears.*
- *It symbolized humility and chastity because the flowers bow modestly and they are white. Thus they became a traditional part of brides' bouquets, associated with modesty and purity.*

Lilyturf

Liriope spicata

Other Name: Creeping Lilyturf
Type: Perennial
Height: 8 to 12 inches
Bloom Time: August
Flower Color/Type: Lilac to white florets on a spike; then black berries
Foliage: Semievergreen; rich green, grasslike

Light Requirements:

Color photograph on page 204.

This is one tough ground cover. It does a wonderful job covering large areas with a sea of neat, green, grassy foliage, reminiscent of overlong turfgrass. Like other plants that spread by underground roots and runners, however, it needs a controlling hand from the outset to direct and control its energy. Its uniform foliage makes a neat appearance, especially on banks where erosion control is needed or under trees where grass will not grow. Often, its late-summer flower spikes are barely visible above the arching leaves, so they cannot be counted upon for ornamental interest. The small, dark berries that appear are inconspicuous.

WHEN TO PLANT

Plant young plants in flats or rooted pieces from divisions of overlarge clumps in the spring. Plant plants in pots from the garden center anytime during the growing season.

WHERE TO PLANT

Lilyturf does best in sun, but will tolerate light shade with no problem. It likes moist soil of almost any type that is rich in organic matter, but once established, it does fine in poorer, drier soil.

HOW TO PLANT

Cultivate the soil down 8 to 10 inches, and add a handful of a granular slow-acting fertilizer to give new transplants a boost during their first season. Dig planting holes about as deep as and slightly wider than plant rootballs. Set each plant in its hole so that its crown, where the roots meet the stems, is at soil level. Fill in the hole with soil, firming it gently around plant stems, and water well. Set plants about 8 to 10 inches apart to allow for their spread.

CARE AND MAINTENANCE

Water new beds regularly until the young plants are established. There is no need to encourage lilyturf by annual fertilizing; it knows what to do. There is also no need to cut off flower spikes because they are somewhat obscured by foliage. Foliage can be left to provide cover for the winter. Then to make way for new shoots, mow it down to about 2 or 3 inches when it gets ratty near springtime. Unless it is planted between paved walks, lily-turf will inevitably spread beyond its bounds. Periodically dig up the plants that encroach on other areas.

ADDITIONAL INFORMATION

Lilyturf patches that are in particularly moist, acidic soil some-times have slug problems. A few strategically placed shallow plates of beer or baker's yeast in water will attract the slugs, and they will drown. Empty and refill traps often, especially after a rain.

ADDITIONAL SPECIES, CULTIVARS, OR VARIETIES

Blue lilyturf or monkey grass (*Liriope muscari*) forms well-behaved clumps of narrow, straplike foliage. It may be green, or green variegated with yellow, or silver variegated such as 'Silvery Sunproof'. Its flower spikes rise above the foliage and are useful as cut flowers. 'Big Blue' has lilac-blue flowers; others feature from pale to deep lilac or white.

 Did You Know?

*Mondo grass (*Ophiopogon *sp.) is often mistaken for lilyturf because its foliage is so similar. It is sometimes called lilyturf, too. Various types grow in clumps of green straplike leaves from the dwarf, 2-inch 'Compactus' to ones 18 inches tall. 'Nigrescens' ('Ebony Knight') has blackish foliage, which is striking, especially when combined with moneywort* (Lysimachia nummularia *'Aurea').*

Moneywort

Lysimachia nummularia 'Aurea'

Other Names: Creeping Jenny,
Creeping Charlie
Type: Perennial
Height: 1 to 2 inches
Bloom Time: July to August
Flower Color/Type: Yellow; cup shaped
Foliage: Evergreen; yellow-green, gold

Color photograph on page 205.

Light Requirements:

The more sun, the brighter the yellow foliage on this little creeper. Moneywort usually has green leaves, but those on 'Aurea' are much more striking in shades of chartreuse to bright gold. Perfectly wonderful for rock gardens, spaces between patio stones, edging, and containers, moneywort's flat, creeping stems root frequently at nodes where their coin-shaped leaves grow. They proceed to insinuate themselves between stems of larger plants in beds as sort of a golden living mulch. Stems encroach onto the lawn like rivulets of melted butter but are easy to lift and snip off. In the summer tiny flowers bloom on threadlike stalks at leaf nodes, visible only to the close observer. Moneywort can take some foot traffic now and then in the line of duty.

WHEN TO PLANT

Plant young plants from the garden center or pieces of rooted stems anytime during the growing season. Wait for an overcast day or until the evening to plant to minimize stress from the sun.

WHERE TO PLANT

Moneywort is truly versatile. It does equally well in full sun or partial shade. It tolerates any type of average soil. It manages in dry soil, prefers moist soil, but also adjusts to life in the water as a bog plant at pond edge without complaint.

HOW TO PLANT

Dig the soil down 4 to 6 inches, and mix in organic matter to improve its texture. If it is poor and thin, also add a handful of a granular slow-acting fertilizer to give new transplants a boost their first season. Create an indentation in the soil deep and wide enough to accommodate the moneywort plant's root system. Set the plant in the hole so that its crown is level with the soil surface, fill in the hole with soil, and water. Set plants about 8 to 10 inches apart to allow for their gradual spread.

CARE AND MAINTENANCE

Water moneywort well until it indicates that it is established by starting to send out new stems. Then water only during periods of drought. Monitor its progress overland, and clip off overambitious stems when necessary. If they have formed roots, they can be pressed into the soil elsewhere to fill in bare spots or start new ground cover patches.

ADDITIONAL INFORMATION

Moneywort was available just in time to jump on the chartreuse-and-maroon color combo bandwagon in garden design. It looks great with the purple foliage of bugleweed (*Ajuga reptans*) or black mondo grass. It echoes the yellow-green variegation in the foliage of many coleus varieties planted nearby.

ADDITIONAL SPECIES, CULTIVARS, OR VARIETIES

Moneywort, the species, has all the qualities of 'Aurea' except that its leaves are green.

 Did You Know?

Why do otherwise charming plants so often have such unlovely common names? Mugwort, barrenwort, liverwort, moneywort . . . Well, many common names were bestowed in England during medieval times when the vernacular was Middle English, Latin being the language of the educated scholars. Wort was basically an Anglo-Saxon four-letter word for "plant." Typically, plants were named for some particular physical trait or use, and then wort was attached to that word. Barrenwort was reputed to prevent pregnancy, and of course, moneywort has foliage that resembles coins. This is also reflected in its Latin name 'nummularia'. The root nomisma, meaning "coin," is discernible in the word "numismatist"—"one who collects and studies coins."

Ostrich Fern

Matteuccia struthiopteris

Other Name: Shuttlecock Fern
Type: Perennial
Height: 4 to 6 feet tall
Foliage: Deciduous; medium- to dark-green
   lacy fronds

Color photograph on page 205.

Light Requirements:

There is a good reason why ostrich fern is the most widely used fern in residential landscapes. A slow spreader by means of rhizomes, it has a unique clumping habit because the rhizome rests somewhat vertically in the soil. The stately dark-green, slightly leathery fronds grow in a vase shape from its upper tip, which constitutes a crown. They appear a bit later than those of other types of ferns and are followed by new, shorter fertile fronds. Their undersides covered with spores, they eventually dry and turn brown, persisting all winter before discharging their spores. During the growing season, subsidiary plants pop up 1 or 2 feet from the mother plant from runners that issue in all directions from each rhizome. These ferns, which are native plants, grow freely in Pennsylvania near shallow streams and boggy areas.

WHEN TO PLANT

Plant young offshoots in the spring, or transplant potted plants from the garden center anytime during the growing season as long as it is not too hot and dry. Plant when the sun is not out.

WHERE TO PLANT

Ostrich fern can tolerate some sun, but it prefers a moist, shady glen situation. It likes damp, woodsy soil; the wetter the site, the taller it grows. However, it does fine in ordinary garden soil as long as it receives reasonable moisture throughout the year.

HOW TO PLANT

Do not let fern roots dry out. Loosen the soil down 1 foot, and add organic matter such as compost, municipal sludge, mushroom soil, or peat moss to help it retain moisture. Dig planting holes about as deep as and slightly wider than fern rootballs, about 3 feet apart. Keeping as much moist soil around roots as possible, set each plant in its hole so that its rhizome is oriented properly—horizontal, but with its growth tip almost vertical. Fill in the hole with soil, firming it gently around the growing tip of the rhizome. Trim broken fronds, and mulch the soil.

CARE AND MAINTENANCE

Ostrich ferns appreciate as much water as they can get. Water during dry periods in the summer if they are not near streams or creeks. Do not worry about overdoing. Mulch them over the winter with dried fronds and/or chopped leaves. Cut off dried fertile fronds, and collect dead fronds on the ground to clean up before the new fronds (croziers) unfurl in the spring. Periodically harvest the small offshoot plants to maintain even-sized ground cover planting, to minimize crowding, and/or to control spread.

ADDITIONAL INFORMATION

Brown frond tips signal thirst. It takes two seasons of watering to get ostrich ferns truly established. They make a stunning foundation planting, replacing the traditional tiresome shrubs near doorways and along building walls. Use them to line driveways, to hold sloping creek banks, to be a woodland understory, to substitute for grass on slopes that are hard to mow, and to be a transition from a landscaped area to a wild, naturalized area.

ADDITIONAL SPECIES, CULTIVARS, OR VARIETIES

Sensitive fern (*Onoclea sensibilis*) is a close relative, so common and easy to grow that it is underappreciated as a garden plant. It can be invasive, so place it in confined areas away from delicate plants.

 Did You Know?

In the spring, the new, young fronds of ostrich ferns, called fiddleheads or crosiers, are eminently edible. Collect a few from each plant when they are only 2 or 3 inches tall and tightly furled. Store them in a plastic bag in the refrigerator until you accumulate enough, then wash off their scaly tan coating, and boil them for 3 to 4 minutes. Drain and serve them hot alone or with other buttered vegetables, cold in a salad, or with a dip.

Pachysandra

Pachysandra terminalis

Other Name: Japanese Spurge
Type: Perennial
Height: 6 to 10 inches
Bloom Time: April
Flower Color/Type: Off-white; fragrant florets on spikes
Foliage: Evergreen; lustrous medium to dark green; terminal whorls

Light Requirements:

Color photograph on page 205.

Whoever first coined the term "low-maintenance ground cover" had to be thinking of good old pachysandra. It is everywhere, and there is a reason for that. It is versatile, neat, evergreen, and easily disciplined. Furthermore, its flowers support honeybees and other beneficial insects. Pachysandra knits rapidly by underground roots into wide patches in only 1 or 2 years to create an effective year-round ground cover, even accommodating shallow tree roots. In winter its foliage tends to flop and fade to yellowish because we rarely have protective snow cover, but it recovers nicely every spring. This well-behaved ground cover is compatible with many plants. It masks the ripening foliage of bulbs planted among its foliage. Its dark leaves set off the stunning flowers of azaleas, rhododendrons, lilac, spirea, and numerous other flowering shrubs and trees.

WHEN TO PLANT

Plant pachysandra in pots or flats from the garden center in spring or during the summer if it is not too hot and dry.

WHERE TO PLANT

Pachysandra can handle a fair amount of bright light, even sun if necessary, but it prefers light to medium shade. Provide it with moist, woodsy soil that is well-drained. This plant makes an excellent living mulch under shade trees and shrubs or on a steep bank where mowing is dangerous.

HOW TO PLANT

Dig and loosen the soil down 8 to 10 inches, mixing in organic material to improve its ability to hold moisture. Add granular slow-acting fertilizer to get new transplants off to a good start. Dig planting holes about as deep as the seedling containers and anywhere from 5 to 10 inches apart. Set a plant in each hole so that its crown is at soil level. Fill in the hole with soil, firming it gently around plant stems, and water well. It is possible to transplant large, established mats of pachysandra by pulling them up gently, roots intact, and laying the entire mat in a trench made in a prepared planting bed. Press loose soil in and among rooted stems, and water well.

CARE AND MAINTENANCE

Pachysandra does fine pretty much on its own. Rejuvenate established patches by shearing it with hedge shears or by mowing it, mower blade on its highest setting, every few years in the spring. Use this opportunity to topdress the bed with organic material and/or slow-acting fertilizer, and water well. Allow leaves to fall among the plants in the autumn to enrich the soil.

ADDITIONAL INFORMATION

Yellowish foliage may mean pachysandra is getting too much light. In winter, exposure to sun may burn the foliage a bit. It is vulnerable to a fungus that causes dark blotches on leaves. Cut off the infected leaves and stems, and throw them in the trash. Thin plants to permit air circulation. Stem cuttings root easily in a glass of water or flat of damp sand.

ADDITIONAL SPECIES, CULTIVARS, OR VARIETIES

'Green Carpet' grows closer to the soil and more upright with very deep-green shiny leaves. 'Green Sheen' has truly shiny foliage. Leaves of the slightly less vigorous 'Variegata' or 'Silver Edge' are mottled with white and show to best advantage in lighter shade.

Did You Know?

Allegheny spurge (Pachysandra procumbens) *is our native version of pachysandra and is an excellent alternative. It has duller, slightly puckered gray-green foliage. Slow growing, it is semievergreen in our area, the leaves becoming tinged with red in the fall. Frost gives it a silver mottling. Flowers emerge about the same time the fresh, new leaves unfurl in spring. The whitish florets are arrayed on 4-inch stalks and are more showy than Japanese pachysandra's. It prefers shade. It has no pests or diseases.*

Sweet Woodruff

Galium odoratum

Other Names: May Flower, Bedstraw
Type: Herbaceous perennial
Height: 6 to 8 inches tall
Bloom Time: May
Flower Color/Type: White; starlike florets in flat clusters
Foliage: Deciduous; medium green

Light Requirements:

Color photograph on page 205.

The name sweet woodruff suggests all the nice things about this ground cover. It is tidy, dainty, and deer resistant. In the spring its stems are arrayed with whorls of fine-textured, deeply cut foliage and topped by delicate white, lightly scented flowers. Dried, they are variously described as vaguely vanilla or hay-scented. Throughout the first part of the summer, sweet woodruff moves quickly by means of shallow, fibrous roots to cover any and every available area of bare soil. It competes well with shallow-rooted trees because its fine roots form tough mats just below the soil surface. Its foliage provides a wonderful backdrop for spring bulbs, and it is easy to pull up as mats of roots whenever it is time to plant annuals or perennials in the space. Replant the mats elsewhere, or depend on sweet woodruff's self-seeding habit to spread it around.

WHEN TO PLANT

Plant flats of young plants in the spring; get potted plants into the ground before the summer becomes too hot and dry.

WHERE TO PLANT

Sweet woodruff does best in partial shade or areas that receive just a little sun each day. It prefers moist, but well-drained soil rich in organic matter. The better the soil, the faster sweet woodruff spreads. It gets along well with ferns and hostas, which like the same conditions.

HOW TO PLANT

Cultivate the soil down 8 to 10 inches, and mix in organic matter to improve the soil. Sprinkle granular slow-acting fertilizer over the planting bed. Dig planting holes deep and wide enough to accommodate the roots and soil of sweet woodruff transplants. Set each plant in its hole so that it is at the same depth as it was in its pot. Fill in the holes with soil, firming it gently around plant stems, and water well. Space plants 6 to 10 inches apart, depending on how many are available for the area and how fast you want them to form a mat.

CARE AND MAINTENANCE

Water newly planted patches of sweet woodruff if rainfall is scarce to help them through their first season. Keeping patches of sweet woodruff moist well into summer delays their decline each season. As the summer progresses, their foliage stems elongate and flop, appearing as if a cat has curled up among them and flattened them. Cutting or shearing green foliage back to 2 or 3 inches before this happens maintains sweet woodruff's dignity for a while longer before the inevitable dieback occurs. Rake up dead foliage in the fall, and spread 1 or 2 inches of chopped leaves over the beds as a winter mulch. If sweet woodruff spreads beyond its allotted space, simply slice down into the bed with a spade to sever the wiry roots where you want the bed to stop, and pull up the extra growth.

ADDITIONAL INFORMATION

Sweet woodruff does well in windowboxes and planters where there is not too much sun. It is a great living mulch around and under shallow-rooted shrubs such as azaleas and rhododendrons, protecting their soil and sheltering beneficial soil organisms. It is virtually pest and disease free.

ADDITIONAL SPECIES, CULTIVARS, OR VARIETIES

There are none.

 Did You Know?

A close look at sweet woodruff stems reveals that they are square. This is evidence that it a member of the huge herb clan. Its flowers play a modest role in the culinary world as a flavoring in May wine. In Germany they prepare and consume Maiwein *to observe May Day. They add flowering sprigs of* Waldmeister *(sweet woodruff) to German Rhine wine and allow it to steep awhile. Then they drink up to celebrate the arrival of May.*

Vinca

Vinca minor

Other Names: Myrtle, Periwinkle
Type: Perennial
Height: 6 to 8 inches
Bloom Time: April into May
Flower Color/Type: Lilac, purplish blue, white; 5 petals
Foliage: Evergreen; lustrous dark green

Light Requirements:

Color photograph on page 205.

Vinca is on everyone's list of reliable ground cover standbys. Dismissing it as just another plain green plant is not fair. Its small, glossy, dark-green oval leaves have a refinement lacking in some others on the list. Its measured progression across the ground by means of gracefully arching low stems that root along the way and at their tips and its lovely spring flowers set it apart, too. Energetic without being pushy, it is fairly common for a single plant to send out 100 stems in early spring. Flowers last about a month. Its roots are so shallow that it is easy to pull up when it overreaches its allotted space. In recent years wonderful variegated forms of vinca have become available, so that now it offers foliage color on its list of virtues.

WHEN TO PLANT
Plant rooted cuttings or young plants in flats from the nursery in either spring or fall. Transplant potted plants anytime.

WHERE TO PLANT
Although vinca can handle some sun, it does best in partial shade or even full shade. The less light, the darker green the foliage, and the slower its growth. It accepts soil of any type, preferring it to be woodsy and well-drained. Once established, it is amazingly drought resistant.

HOW TO PLANT
Loosen the soil down 8 to 10 inches, and mix in granular slow-acting fertilizer to give new transplants a boost their first season so that they establish quickly and start to spread. Dig planting holes about as deep as and slightly wider than their rootball, and set them so that the tops of their rootballs are at soil level. Fill in the hole with soil, firming it gently around plant stems, and water well. Space plants from pots about 1 foot apart. Space smaller ones from flats 6 to 8 inches apart to get initial coverage in one season. Mulch the bare soil between them so that weeds do not take over before the plants knit together to cover the soil.

CARE AND MAINTENANCE

Vincas do not need special care. Just water new plantings if rain is scarce during the first year when they are getting established. Snip off trailing stems that overstep their bounds. To encourage density, clip stems back to about 4 inches in early spring. Mow or shear the bed every few years to revitalize it. Spread compost or other organic material over the stubby plants and exposed soil, and water well. Sometimes vinca blooms sporadically late summer into the fall.

ADDITIONAL INFORMATION

Vinca sets off minor bulbs such as crocus, snowdrops, squill, and snowflake effectively, and then helps obscure their ripening foliage after they bloom. Then it blooms for a prolonged show. Vinca's handsome foliage and trailing stems look good in planters and hanging baskets.

ADDITIONAL SPECIES, CULTIVARS, OR VARIETIES

'Alba' has white flowers; 'Bowles Variety'/'La Grave' has large purplish blue flowers; and 'Atropururea' has deep-plum-rose flowers. 'Multiplex' is sometimes called 'Double Burgundy' because of its double deep-maroon flowers. Vincas for the more adventurous are 'Aureovariegata', with white flowers and variously patterned green and yellow leaves, and 'Argenteo-variegata', with light-blue flowers and green leaves with white edges.

Did You Know?

Q: When is a vinca not a Vinca?
A: When it is a Madagascar vinca!

Madagascar vinca/periwinkle (Catharanthus roseus) is a different plant altogether, but because its flowers and leaves resemble vinca/myrtle/periwinkle (Vinca minor), it has acquired the same common name. However, it is tropical, so it is used as an annual in our area. It is more upright and bears flowers in white, red, or shades of pink, depending on the variety, at the tops of its stems. Sometimes their centers are a contrasting pink or white. They bloom off and on over the season. The leaves have a pale vein down their centers.

Wintercreeper

Euonymus fortunei

Type: Trailing shrub
Height: 8 to 12 inches tall
Bloom Time: June/July
Flower Color/Type: Greenish white;
  inconspicuous
Foliage: Evergreen; smooth, green, or variegated with cream, yellow,
  or white

Light Requirements:

Color photograph on page 205.

Tough and versatile, this handsome shrub readily adapts to whatever situation it finds itself in. It opportunistically trails, tumbles, and climbs, depending on its site, by means of tiny rootlets that develop on its flexible stems. Over a season stems can grow 4 to 5 feet if permitted. Sometimes wintercreeper morphs into a vine and crawls up walls and tree trunks that interrupt its horizontal progress. Long-lived and very hardy, it is great for obscuring utility boxes, rocks, and stumps. Its variegated versions brighten darker areas under trees and building eaves. Like English ivy, it has both a juvenile and a mature form. The latter flowers and bears fruits and is marked by a variety of different leaf shapes. The fruits are orange-red capsules that are poisonous.

WHEN TO PLANT

Plant young plants or rooted cuttings in the spring to allow maximum time for root development before winter. Transplant larger balled-and-burlapped or containerized nursery stock anytime during the growing season when it is not too hot.

WHERE TO PLANT

Wintercreeper prefers partial shade but can handle shade. It makes do in almost any soil as long as it is not soggy. A hot, dry western exposure will stress it badly.

HOW TO PLANT

Dig into the soil 1 foot or more. Loosen it, and add granular slow-acting all-purpose fertilizer and organic material if the soil lacks humus. Dig the planting hole exactly as deep as and slightly wider than the uncovered rootball. Tip the plant out of the container or untie burlap wrappings, and set the plant in the hole so that its crown is at or slightly above soil level. (Cut away all the burlap you can reach around wrapped rootballs.) Then fill in the hole with soil, firm it gently, and water well. Set plants about 2 feet apart to allow for their gradual spread.

CARE AND MAINTENANCE

Wintercreeper shares with its euonymus cousins a vulnerability to scale, but if it is happy in its situation, it is likely to escape serious problems. If the soil is decent, there is no need to fertilize once wintercreeper is established; this avoids excessive stem and leaf growth, which attracts aphids. As it grows vigorously, especially in a confined space, wintercreeper often mounds up, its stems arching over themselves. Prune back unruly stems to keep the plant neat and in bounds. Every few years plants benefit from a major spring shearing by hand or lawn mower set at its highest setting.

ADDITIONAL INFORMATION

Severe wind chill may damage foliage in winter, even causing variegated types to turn green. A low screen of burlap or garden fleece will shelter it from winds and prevent problems. If scale appears on the leaves and stems, spray them with light (superior) horticultural oil as directed on the product label.

ADDITIONAL SPECIES, CULTIVARS, OR VARIETIES

Wintercreepers labeled *Euonymus fortunei* 'Coloratus' are especially well adapted to ground-cover duty. Their deep-green foliage turns purple in the winter, and they are vigorous growers. 'Longwood' is a good selection. Forms of wintercreeper with white, pinkish, or yellow foliage coloration are grouped as 'Gracilis'. Among the daintier, lower-growing types are 'Ivory Jade' at 2 inches tall, 'Kewensis', which has tiny leaves, and 'Minimus'; 'Sheridan Gold' has bright yellow variegation in mounds 20 inches tall. 'Radicans' is a slower grower, with more delicate leaves.

 Did You Know?

Most of our wonderful introduced (nonnative) garden plants were discovered in Europe and Asia by intrepid botanists of the nineteenth century who trekked the wilderness in search of potentially desirable specimens. The efforts of these plant hunters are often memorialized in the names of the plants. Euonymus fortunei was brought back from China by Robert Fortune, as its name so plainly indicates.

CHAPTER FIVE

Perennials

PERENNIALS ARE PLANTS THAT BLOOM season after season. Technically, woody-stemmed trees and shrubs, or hardy bulbs, fit this definition, but "perennial" usually refers to herbaceous flowering plants. Their soft stems wither or die back with frost, but their roots are cold hardy and send up new stems the next spring when weather warms.

Unlike annuals, which are programmed to produce copious flowers to make seed for next year in anticipation of sudden death at the end of the season, perennials pace their blooming and seed setting. They allow plenty of time over the summer for their foliage to collect energy and build roots to support life the following season. Therein lies the big difference for gardeners. Perennial plants do not bloom very long. Working them into a garden means accepting that all they contribute to the scheme of things for much of the season is foliage.

For this reason gardening with perennial flowering plants is regarded as more sophisticated than gardening with annuals. The interplay of foliage color and texture becomes almost as important as that of flower color, size, and height. Plants with variegated or unusually colored foliage are highly valued. Unusual plants become collectibles in an effort to enliven a perennial border that may be largely foliage a good bit of the time.

More or Less Work?

At the same time, gardening with perennials is sometimes regarded as easy when one thinks about the labor involved in digging and planting flowering annual plants every year. The perception is that perennials just pop up year after year, growing gratifyingly larger clumps to fill in the bed until, at some point, there is an automatic garden. The truth is that perennials require quite a bit of maintenance to look their best. Keeping them happy, therefore stress free, is the best way to keep them healthy and productive.

The Soil

To a great degree, soil is the key to perennial happiness. It is difficult to maintain good drainage, organic content, and nutrients in gardens where the plants are always in the way. Some perennials such as peonies, hostas, and hellebores resent being moved and are resident for decades. That is why site selection and preparation prior to planting are so critical.

Chapter Five

Mulching year-round with organic matter such as chopped leaves is the best way to improve and protect the soil over time. Mulch protects its surface from compaction from hard rains and harsh sun. It retards evaporation of its moisture, too. As it continually decomposes, mulch introduces chunky, spongy organic particles into the upper levels of the soil, which maintain its texture by creating air spaces and storing moisture. The microbial organisms that accompany the organic matter into the soil convert its nutrients into a form that plant roots can absorb.

Keeping perennials happy takes time and skill. The following plant entries address mulching, fertilizing, and watering as well as pruning tailored to a plant's particular nature, staking for support, and dividing when they become too big. Each plant responds to slightly different approaches to these tasks, so experience plays a part in getting it right in each case. Fortunately, plants are forgiving, learning is fun, and next year provides another chance for the gardener.

Artemisia

Artemisia species and hybrids

Other Name: Wormwood

Mature Size: 12 inches to 3 feet tall

Bloom Time: August to October

Flower Color/Type: Yellow; inconspicuous

Features: Aromatic foliage; evening garden; low water demand; deer resistant

Light Requirements:

Color photograph on page 205.

*E*very yard needs silver foliage to punctuate the green and set off individual plants and their colorful flowers. For this reason, members of the large clan of artemisias are important assets to a garden. Although they bear deep-yellow, buttonlike flowers, it is their foliage that is ornamental. Artemisias feature fine-textured, silvery or gray-green leaves, which are sometimes slightly woolly. Some plants are a bit shrubby, the base of their stems becoming woody over the season. Their foliage and stems typically have a distinctive resinous or medicinal smell, likely the reason why they have virtually no pests—not even deer. Drought tolerant, artemisias start the season by obscuring ripening bulb foliage and are still present to set off chrysanthemums in the fall.

WHEN TO PLANT

Plant sections of divided artemisias in either spring or fall. Transplant those in pots from the garden center anytime during the season.

WHERE TO PLANT

Artemisias require sunny sites with average, well-drained soil. Soils that are sandy or gravelly, as in a rock garden, are ideal. Soil that is a bit on the alkaline side is okay for most artemisias.

HOW TO PLANT

Dig the soil down 10 to 12 inches, and mix in coarse sand and/or organic matter to improve its drainage. Make the planting hole about as deep as and slightly wider than the artemisia's rootball, and set the rootball in the hole so that its top is level with or a bit higher than the surrounding ground. Fill in the hole with soil, firming it gently, and water well. Leave at least 18 inches between plants for good air circulation and room to spread.

CARE AND MAINTENANCE

If rain is scarce, water newly planted artemisias until they put out new growth. Then they will be quite drought tolerant. Frequent watering and heavy mulch promote rot. Fertilizing or rich soil makes artemisia stems floppy. Pinching stem tips will encourage denser growth as transplants grow. Most artemisias respond enthusiastically to a more severe cutback to about half their height in June to assure compactness. Do not cut back to where stems are woody and have no leaf buds. Unless the flowers are useful, cut them off to keep foliage looking its best. The tall artemisias may need staking. Divide overlarge clumps in the fall by digging up the rootball and cutting rooted chunks from it to replant elsewhere. Reportedly, 'Lambrook Silver' and 'Powis Castle' do not tolerate dividing and transplanting well. Wait until early spring to cut them back.

ADDITIONAL INFORMATION

Use artemisia flowers and foliage in fresh or dried flower arrangements or floral crafts. Dried wormwood stems and foliage are sometimes used as moth repellents in drawers and closets. Artemisias do well in containers with good drainage; containers are perfect for rampant spreader 'Silver King'.

ADDITIONAL SPECIES, CULTIVARS, OR VARIETIES

Silver mound wormwood (*Artemisia schmidtiana* 'Silver Mound') is fine textured and only 12 inches tall. Cut back almost to the ground by midsummer to prevent floppy stems and bare centers. White sage (*Artemisia ludoviciana*) 'Silver King' and 'Silver Queen' grow 2 to 3 feet tall, handle poor, thin soil, need staking, and are somewhat invasive. Powis Castle artemisia (*Artemisia* × 'Powis Castle') makes mounds 2 or 3 feet high and withstands humidity well. Beach wormwood (*Artemisia stelleriana*) 'Silver Brocade' has excellent round-lobed, deeply divided foliage for a spreading ground cover. Wormwood (*Artemisia absinthium*) 'Lambrook Silver' is 2 feet tall, semievergreen, and not invasive.

 Did You Know?

*French tarragon (*Artemisia dracunculus* 'Sativa') is an edible artemisia cousin. Its narrow foliage has a slight anise flavor with a touch of sweetness and is useful in vinegars, soups, marinades, and sauces (it is the star of béarnaise sauce). Crumbled fresh or dried, its leaves enhance roasted chicken, fish, and salads. A little goes a long way.*

Aster, Native

Aster novi-belgii; Aster novae-angliae

Other Names: New York Aster/Michaelmas
Daisy, New England Aster
Mature Size: 2 to 6 feet tall
Bloom Time: August through October
Flower Color/Type: White, shades of pink and purple; daisies
Features: Attracts butterflies; hosts their larvae

Light Requirements:

Color photograph on page 205.

*F*or the best fall garden, look to nature. Out in the fields and along the roadsides are billows of tall wild asters and their goldenrod companions smothered in butterflies. Long-blooming and self-reliant native asters such as the New England and New York ones offer small, colorful daisy flowers that come on strong just when summer annuals are giving up. They hold the fort until frost. Selected versions of these natives have been developed into undemanding, heavily flowered, excellent garden plants with all the virtues of their less-domesticated cousins. Use them in borders or as as edging, or naturalize them in fields.

WHEN TO PLANT
Plant young plants or divisions from overlarge plants in the spring when the soil has warmed. Transplant potted nursery stock anytime during the growing season. Choose an overcast day or plant in the evening to protect transplants from the sun while they cope with transplant shock.

WHERE TO PLANT
Asters prefer full sun. They accept almost any type of soil of average fertility as long as it is moist and well-drained.

HOW TO PLANT
Cultivate the soil down 12 inches. Although established plants do not need special feeding, a handful of a granular slow-acting all-purpose fertilizer mixed into the soil at this point will give new transplants a boost their first season. Dig the planting hole about as deep as and slightly wider than the aster's rootball. Set the rootball in the hole so that it is level with the surrounding ground. Fill in the hole with soil, firming it gently around plant stems to remove air pockets, and water well. Set plants about 2 feet apart to allow for their gradual spread. Spread a 2- or 3-inch layer of organic mulch on the soil over the root zone to discourage weeds and maintain soil moisture.

Care and Maintenance

Pinch tall New England asters starting in June up to late July to make them denser and to stimulate more flowers. A more radical cutting back of stems by half in June and again in late July delays bloom for 2 weeks, but reduces legginess. There is no need to routinely fertilize asters in decent soil that is mulched year-round. Too much nitrogen promotes excessive foliage growth and floppy stems. Unpinched tall New England types will definitely need staking. Cut asters to the ground after they finish blooming to prevent their seeding in. Spreading clumps need dividing after a couple of years. Dig them up in the spring when young shoots appear, cut through the mass of roots with a sharp spade or knife to make chunks of rooted plant with at least 3 to 5 shoots per chunk, then replant them elsewhere.

Additional Information

Aster foliage may develop mildew or rust in really humid weather. Although it mars their appearance, mildew does no real harm to established plants. Thin out crowded stems and divide overlarge clumps for next year to promote good air circulation. Asters have no significant insect pests.

Additional Species, Cultivars, or Varieties

New England aster (*Aster novae-angliae*) 'Purple Dome' makes a 2-foot mound of semidouble, purple flowers, and 'Alma Potschke' is hot pink at 3 to 4 feet tall. New York aster (*Aster novi-belgii*) dwarfs are 'Jenny' (red) and 'Professor Kippenburg' (lilac-blue).

Did You Know?

In the Victorian language of flowers, asters, or Michaelmas daisies, represented "afterthought" because they bloom so late. They are named for St. Michael's Day, which falls on September 29, relatively late in the season for flowering plants. A pleasant surprise at that time of year, the Michaelmas daisy has charmingly come to symbolize "Cheerfulness in Old Age."

Astilbe

Astilbe × arendsii

Other Names: Hybrid Astilbe, False Spirea
Mature Size: 1 to 4 feet tall
Bloom Time: Late June to early July
Flower Color/Type: White, pink, lavender,
  peach, red; floret spikes
Features: Shade blooming; ferny foliage

Light Requirements:

Color photograph on page 205.

Astilbes are particularly appreciated because they are summer bloomers, providing color in the garden long after the riotous spring flowering season that we enjoy in the Philadelphia area has passed. Among astilbe virtues are their finely cut, green or somewhat bronze leaves whose ferny texture creates a slightly blowzy, informal effect. Astilbes' main appeal, however, is their flexible, dense plumes of small florets at the tips of their stems. As woodland plants, they brighten shady areas. They are dependable, attractive background and filler plants for a border, too. In their many colors and sizes, astilbes are available for almost every home landscape situation.

WHEN TO PLANT

Plant divisions from existing plants in either spring or fall. Transplant potted astilbes from the garden center anytime during the season.

WHERE TO PLANT

Astilbes prefer the light or dappled shade typically at the edge of the woods. If they must, they can take full sun, but only if their soil is constantly moist. They do best if it is rich in organic matter, moist, and slightly acid. Shallow-rooted, they like constantly moist soil or pondside sites.

HOW TO PLANT

Loosen the soil down 12 inches, and dig in organic matter to improve its ability to hold moisture, then add a handful of a granular slow-acting all-purpose fertilizer. Dig a hole about as deep as and slightly wider than the astilbe's rootball when gently tapped out of its container. Loosen any matted roots. Set the rootball in the hole so that its surface is exactly level with the surrounding ground. Fill in the hole with soil, firming it gently around plant stems, and water well. Set plants about 2 feet apart to allow for their gradual spread.

CARE AND MAINTENANCE

Spread a 2- or 3-inch layer of organic material to keep the soil over the astilbe roots moist and rich. Astilbes need moisture, especially in summer, so water regularly whenever rainfall is scarce. Fertilize every spring with a slow-acting lawn fertilizer that is rich in the nitrogen required by astilbes. Allowing dried flower heads to remain for winter interest is optional. Leaving the dead foliage will offer some winter protection and can be cut back in spring. Astilbes need dividing every 3 or 4 years to renew their vigor. Do this after flowering during the season or in the spring when shoots first emerge.

ADDITIONAL INFORMATION

If their soil dries out, astilbes shrivel and quit for the season. Cutting off the browned foliage may generate a flush of green when moisture returns later. Astilbes make good cut flowers for fresh or dried arrangements. Cut stems when the flowers are about half open. Use silica gel or borax drying procedures to minimize shrinkage.

ADDITIONAL SPECIES, CULTIVARS, OR VARIETIES

Several types of astilbe have been hybridized to produce dozens of excellent garden plants: 'Deutschland' (white), 'Fanal' (red), 'Peach Blossom' (pale pink), and 'Rheinland' (pink). Other great astilbes include fall astilbe (*Astilbe chinensis* var. *taquetii* 'Superba'), which grows to 4 or more feet and has purplish blooms later in the summer; sprite astilbe (*Astilbe simplicifolia* 'Sprite'), which is 1 foot tall, blooms in midsummer, and was the Perennial Plant Association Plant of the Year in 1994; and dwarf Chinese astilbe (*Astilbe chinensis* 'Pumila'), which blooms in mid-summer, the lavender-pink flower spikes looming over low-growing, ferny foliage for a great ground cover.

 Did You Know?

Goat's beard (Aruncus dioicus) resembles a giant astilbe and likes the same growing conditions that astilbes do. A shrub-like 4 to 6 feet tall, it bears plumes of tiny, creamy-white florets earlier in the summer. It has a more commanding presence than an astilbe and is useful as a specimen in a partially shady site.

Baby's Breath

Gypsophila paniculata

Other Names: Chalk Plant, Perennial
  Baby's Breath
Mature Size: 2 to 3 feet tall; 3 or 4 feet wide
Bloom Time: June to August
Flower Color/Type: White, pink; single florets
Features: See-through plant; low water demand

Light Requirements:

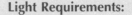

Color photograph on page 205.

*B*aby's breath is full of contradictions. Its dainty appearance belies a hardy, versatile character. It is airy and insubstantial, yet it achieves the size of a small shrub. Its flowers are tiny, yet they bloom for several weeks and make a distinct impact on the landscape. Baby's breath foliage is inconspicuous, its leaves resembling tiny carnation leaves—linear and gray-green. They are easily overlooked on the wiry, branching stems because of the galaxy of tiny, round, white florets that cover their tips. Use baby's breath as a filler where bulbs or bleeding hearts melt away or as a foil to coarser, green-foliaged plants in a border. It does well in rock gardens, too. Pink-flowered types go well with silver- or gray-leafed plants such as lamb's ears and artemisias. Try it at the front of a border as a see-through plant.

WHEN TO PLANT

Choose baby's breath plants that are in pots. Transplant them in the garden anytime during the growing season.

WHERE TO PLANT

Site baby's breath in full sun. It likes average garden soil that is not too rich in organic matter and is on the alkaline side. It must drain well. Sandy soil is fine. Choose the site well because baby's breath roots resent being moved once they are established.

HOW TO PLANT

Prepare the planting area for baby's breath by loosening the soil down 8 to 10 inches. Add coarse sand to improve drainage if necessary. Dig a planting hole about as deep as and slightly wider than the rootball out of its pot. Set the plant in the hole so that the top of its rootball is exactly at soil level. Fill in the hole with soil, firming it gently around plant stems, and water well. Set baby's breath plants about 2 to 3 feet apart to allow for their gradual spread. A thin mulch will control weeds and keep dirt from splashing onto the flowers. Do not pile it against the crown and stems of the plants.

CARE AND MAINTENANCE

In the Philadelphia area where soil tends to be on the acid side, baby's breath beds need a sprinkling of lime in the fall or wood ashes in the spring. Cut off branches when their flowers brown to stimulate renewed flowering. Baby's breath that has not been cut back at all will eventually need staking with inconspicuous sticks and string or pea stakes. In late summer, harvest the baby's breath stems and flowers, cutting them back to soil level, so other fall bloomers can fill the spot. Since baby's breath does not divide well, an attempt to propagate it this way may endanger the plant.

ADDITIONAL INFORMATION

Baby's breath is ridiculously easy to air dry for use as fillers in fresh and dried bouquets and floral crafts.

ADDITIONAL SPECIES, CULTIVARS, OR VARIETIES

Other examples of baby's breath are 'Bristol Fairy' (white), 'Pink Fairy' (pink), 'Flamingo' (mauve), and 'Perfecta' (white), which has double flowers. Creeping baby's breath (*Gypsophila repens*) is dwarf, at 6 inches tall. 'Alba' (white) or 'Rosea' (pink) makes a good ground cover. Annual baby's breath (*Gypsophila elegans*) looks similar but is short-lived, blooming for only 6 weeks.

 Did You Know?

To air dry baby's breath, pick stems when their flowers have just reached their peak. Strip off the leaves. Fasten several together with a rubber band, tape, or wire, and hang the bunches upside down in a warm, dry, ventilated room such as an attic. To dry a few stems, place them upright in a vase with no water, and let them dry out over time in a room where humidity is low. When stems become brittle and break easily, they are dry. Spritz them with hairspray to keep them from shattering.

Bee Balm

Monarda didyma

Other Names: Monarda, Oswego Tea, Bergamot

Mature Size: 2 to 4 feet tall; spreading

Bloom Time: Late June through July

Flower Color/Type: Pink, shades of red, lavender, or white; clustered tubular florets

Features: Aromatic foliage; attracts hummingbirds, butterflies, and honeybees

Light Requirements:

Color photograph on page 205.

An Eastern native, bee balm is at home in both Philadelphia-area herb gardens and perennial borders. Wherever it is, butterflies and hummingbirds have no trouble finding its brightly colored mophead flowers, which are actually rounded whorls of droopy tubular florets gracing the tops of square stems. Bee balm's leaves are on the coarse side, with fuzzy undersides, and they smell like mint when crushed. Bee balm is not as invasive as mint, but it is a bit pushy, especially in optimum conditions. Plant it in natural settings in large drifts or groupings of several plants to make it more attractive to the honeybees that make delicious honey from it.

WHEN TO PLANT

Plant rooted divisions from large clumps in the spring. Plant potted plants from the garden center anytime during the growing season. Seed-grown plants tend not to flower true to type and do not bloom until their second season because they need a chill from winter.

WHERE TO PLANT

Lavender- and white-flowered bee balms do best in full sun, but red-flowered varieties like some shade. They are not fussy about soil type as long as it is moist and well-drained. Truly damp sites make their stems taller and floppier. Their weedy, coarse texture also suits informal settings such as fence rows and wildflower plots.

HOW TO PLANT

Dig soil down 12 inches, and mix in organic matter to promote drainage and a bit of granular slow-acting fertilizer to give bee balm transplants a good start. Dig the hole as deep as and a bit wider than the plant's rootball removed from the pot. Loosen any tangled roots, and set the rootball in the hole so that its top is level with the surrounding soil. Fill in the hole with soil, firming it gently, and water well. Set plants about 2 or 3 feet apart to allow for their inevitable spread.

CARE AND MAINTENANCE

Bee balm needs minimal care. Its creeping roots are shallow, so water when rain is scarce, and maintain a layer of organic mulch over the soil to keep it moist. Taller plants will need staking. Pinch young stems to encourage branching and more compact plants, but expect somewhat delayed flowering. Deadhead spent blossoms to create a neater look and to encourage sporadic rebloom in young plants. If mildew is terrible by midsummer, cut back all the stems to the ground. In mulched, decent soil bee balm will not need routine fertilizing. After 3 or 4 years dig up large clumps of bee balm, and cut off chunks of healthy-rooted plants from their edges to replant. Discard the older center portions.

ADDITIONAL INFORMATION

Mildew, bee balm's biggest problem, coats its foliage with ugly, but not life-threatening gray in late summer. Plants stressed by drier soil seem to have worse mildew problems. Try varieties developed for resistance. Bee balm makes good cut flowers.

ADDITIONAL SPECIES, CULTIVARS, OR VARIETIES

Examples include 'Cambridge Scarlet' (red), 'Croftway Pink' and 'Marshall's Delight' (pink), 'Snow Queen' (white), and 'Mahogany' (deep red). 'Marshall's Delight' shows some mildew resistance. 'Jacob Kline' has received good reviews for mildew resistance in our area. Wild bergamot (*Monarda fistulosa*) is a cousin and native to Pennsylvania; it can handle drier, poorer soil. Spotted horsemint (*Monarda punctata*) has tiny-tiered yellow-green flowers clustered among pinkish bracts.

 Did You Know?

Native Americans taught settlers how to make a tea from bee balm leaves to treat colds, flu, and heart problems. Subsequently a staple of colonial kitchen gardens, bee balm provided a tea substitute for Earl Grey during the colonial boycott of English tea. Today bee balm's flowers and foliage are recognized as a source of antioxidants. To make tea, crush ½ cup fresh or ¼ cup dried leaves and add them to regular tea in a bag or teaball, and steep in boiling water up to 5 minutes.

Black-Eyed Susan

Rudbeckia fulgida var. *sullivantii* 'Goldsturm'

Other Name: Orange Coneflower
Mature Size: 2 to 3 feet tall; 2 feet wide
Bloom Time: July through September
Flower Color/Type: Golden-yellow; daisies
Features: Evening garden; attracts butterflies and goldfinches; deer resistant

Light Requirements:

Color photograph on page 206.

This 'Goldsturm' black-eyed Susan, the glory of late-summer Philadelphia-area gardens, is a cousin of the native annual ones of the fields and farms of the Eastern United States. It blooms beautifully over a long period with virtually no maintenance. Who could not love the classic daisy flowers with ray petals of rich yellow that ring its dark "eye"? They literally glow at the tips of heavily branching stiff stems above mounds of coarse leaves, blooming dependably, regardless of what kind of summer weather has transpired. Allowed to mature, their petals fade and their centers swell as seeds develop within and become a magnet for goldfinches. Black-eyed Susans' informal look combines well with other meadow plants such as ornamental grasses, goldenrod, purple coneflower, and wild asters. They brighten semishady areas, and it is well-mannered enough for the flower border.

WHEN TO PLANT

Plant rooted divisions from overlarge clumps in either spring or fall. Transplant containerized nursery stock anytime during the growing season.

WHERE TO PLANT

Black-eyed Susans prefer full sun, but can handle some shade. They accept average soil of any type as long as it is well-drained. Once established, they are fairly drought tolerant, especially if their soil is rich in organic matter that holds moisture.

HOW TO PLANT

Prepare the soil by digging it down 12 inches. Mix in organic material to improve its drainage, especially if it is clay. Add granular slow-acting all-purpose fertilizer to boost new transplants in their first season. Dig the planting hole about as deep as and slightly wider than the black-eyed Susan's rootball without the pot. Loosen any matted roots, and then set the rootball in the hole so that its surface is level with the surrounding ground. Fill in the hole with soil, firm it gently, and water well. Mulch newly planted black-eyed Susans to discourage weeds and help the soil retain moisture while plants get established. Plant them in groups of 3, about 2 feet apart, for a splendid show.

CARE AND MAINTENANCE

Mulched plants do not need routine fertilizing. They can handle some drought when grown to mature size by midsummer. 'Goldsturm' has no pests or diseases. Large clumps on slopes may need staking after heavy rainstorms. Deadhead spent flowers to prevent seeding in, or leave them for visiting birds. Cut back dead stems after frost, and spread a winter mulch over the area. Some green basal foliage may overwinter. Divide slowly spreading clumps every 3 or 4 years in either spring or fall. Dig up a clump, and cut off several smaller-rooted chunks to replant or give away. Discard the old, woody, or damaged portions of roots.

ADDITIONAL INFORMATION

'Goldsturm' has been chosen to be the Plant of the Year in 1999 by the Perennial Plant Association. Although black-eyed Susans spread underground by creeping roots, they also seed themselves and are likely to turn up anywhere around the yard. Unwanted seedlings are easy to pull up.

ADDITIONAL SPECIES, CULTIVARS, OR VARIETIES

'Goldquelle' has double, paler-yellow flowers. Ragged coneflower (*Rudbeckia laciniata*) is 6 feet tall; its droopy petaled, yellow flowers have green center cones. Shining coneflower (*Rudbeckia nitida*) has drooping yellow petals. 'Herbsonne' grows to 8 feet.

 Did You Know?

Gaudy gloriosa daisies (Rudbeckia hirta) *are also called black-eyed Susans. Noted for their huge 5- to 9-inch-wide yellow daisy flowers splashed with red, they bloom all summer as typical annuals. 'Indian Summer', an All-America Selection, has semidouble flowers. 'Sonora' has a wide band of mahogany across its gold petals. 'Green Eyes' has green centers. 'Toto' is a compact dwarf for containers and edging.*

Blazing Star

Liatris spicata

Other Names: Spike Gayfeather, Liatris
Mature Size: 2 to 3 feet tall; 2 feet wide
Bloom Time: July and August
Flower Color/Type: Mauve, purple, or white;
  fuzzy spikes
Features: Attracts butterflies, birds, and honeybees

Light Requirements: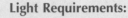

Color photograph on page 206.

Native blazing star is becoming increasingly popular in local Philadelphia gardens for many reasons, not the least of which is the colorful vertical accent it provides in the flower border. Beginning as tufts of emerging narrow, grassy leaves, this plant responds to hot July temperatures by producing a flower spike from each tuft. The 50 or so little fuzzy florets arrayed along the spike open gradually from the top of the spike downward, creating a bottle-brush that is likely to be covered with butterflies on sunny days. The seedheads that remain when the florets dry up provide winter interest and attract birds. Blazing star's rose colors are most compatible with blue-based, lilac, or magenta flowers, or flowers that are pale yellow, cream, or gold, such as its meadow neighbors in the wild—black-eyed Susans, goldenrod, coneflowers, bee balms, and shasta daisies. Ornamental grasses make good neighbors as well.

WHEN TO PLANT

Plant young blazing star plants in containers from the garden center any-time during the growing season. Plant packaged corms (roots) or divisions from larger plants in the spring. Expect plants grown from seed to vary from type and to take 2 years before producing flowers.

WHERE TO PLANT

Blazing stars prefer full sun. Ordinary soil is fine as long as it is moist and well-drained. They hate soggy winter soil. Because their tuberous roots store moisture, they can handle heat and a degree of drought.

HOW TO PLANT

Loosen the soil down about 12 inches, digging in organic material to improve drainage if soil is clay. Plant packaged corms about 2 inches deep and 1 to 2 feet apart. Dig planting holes for potted nursery stock about as deep as and slightly wider than their containers. Tip each plant out of its pot, and set it in the hole so that its crown, where the roots meet the stems, is at soil level. Fill in the hole with soil, firming it gently to remove air pockets, then water well. Set plants about 2 feet apart to allow for their gradual spread.

CARE AND MAINTENANCE

Blazing stars are pretty self-reliant. In good soil they do not need routine fertilizing. In fact, a rich diet makes the flower stems floppy, and they will need staking. Water them during prolonged dry periods. Cutting back the flower spike to the basal foliage when about ¾ of the florets have died may promote some rebloom in September. Do not cut back the foliage until it is brown and dead. To thin clumps and get more plants, divide overlarge clumps, or dig up corms and cut them into budded pieces every 4 years or so.

ADDITIONAL INFORMATION

Blazing stars have no pests or significant diseases. Foliage may show powdery mildew late in the summer. Thin plants to improve air circulation around them to reduce the problem. Cut flower stalks are great for fresh flower arrangements. They are easily air dried for floral crafts.

ADDITIONAL SPECIES, CULTIVARS, OR VARIETIES

'Kobold' has deep-rosy-purple flowers and is a bit more compact at up to 2½ feet tall. Suited to flower beds and borders, it is generally recognized as the most satisfactory blazing star of all for the garden. 'Floristan White' has cream-colored flowers and grows to 3 feet.

Did You Know?

Blazing star is a good example of how our native plants are often overlooked at home and are appreciated only after enthusiastic Europeans adopt them, improve them, and reintroduce them to the United States. Blazing star became a staple of the florist industry abroad. Only recently have American gardeners embraced this sturdy plant that has been under their noses all along.

Bleeding Heart

Dicentra spectabilis

Other Names: Lyre Flower, Lady's Locket,
Valentine Flower

Mature Size: 2 to 3 feet tall

Bloom Time: April and May

Flower Color/Type: Deep pink or white; heart shaped

Features: Old-fashioned

Light Requirements:

Color photograph on page 206.

---

*T*his gentle woodland charmer evokes fascination and delight each spring
from even the most experienced gardener. It is impossible to take these
graceful, ephemeral plants for granted. Bleeding heart plants send up shiny,
reddish new shoots that become deeply cut, fragile, light bluish green foliage.
Then arching, leafless flower stems emerge, their tips drooping with the
weight of a row of exotic heart-shaped, deep-pink lockets. These namesake
flowers form pale, droplet-shaped petals at their lower tip, which look for all
the world like teardrops. Bleeding heart foliage browns, withers, and melts
away after flowering as temperatures rise, choosing to go dormant rather
than face our summers.

WHEN TO PLANT

Transplant containerized bleeding hearts in the garden in the spring . Plant
those sold as packaged roots when available at garden centers in either
spring or fall. Plant divisions of their roots after their leaves die back in late
summer or fall.

WHERE TO PLANT

Bleeding hearts are woodland dwellers and need a shady spot sheltered
from wind, such as among shrubs and trees, under a vine-covered pergola,
or near a wall. They can take some bright, indirect morning light, but the
more shade they get, the longer they last. They like acidic woodsy soil,
moist, rich in organic matter, and well-drained. When they die back, their
site will be empty, so be prepared with a filler plant.

HOW TO PLANT

Loosen the soil down 12 inches, simultaneously mixing in organic matter to
make it as rich and woodsy as possible. Add a bit of granular slow-acting
all-purpose fertilizer. Dig the planting hole about as deep as and slightly
wider than the rootball without its container. Handle the brittle roots carefully, setting the bleeding heart in the hole so that the soil at the top of the

rootball is level with the surrounding ground. Plant packaged roots at the depth suggested on its label. Fill in the hole with soil, firming it gently, and water well. Spread a 2- or 3-inch layer of organic mulch such as chopped leaves to keep the soil cool and moist. Space plants 2 feet apart.

CARE AND MAINTENANCE

Bleeding heart resents too much attention, needing only granular slow-acting fertilizer every spring. Cut back yellowed, ripened foliage when it collapses on the ground. If clumps become too large after several years, dig up the fleshy, brittle roots carefully when the plant is dormant. Divide them into chunks, each with a growing bud or "eye." Then replant them.

ADDITIONAL INFORMATION

Bleeding heart looks great with hostas and ferns, spring bulbs, and ground covers such as sweet woodruff that will obscure their dying foliage. Cut at peak bloom, they make wonderful bouquets with spring contemporaries such as lily of the valley, pansies, tulips, daffodils, and lilacs.

ADDITIONAL SPECIES, CULTIVARS, OR VARIETIES

'Alba' and 'Pantaloons' are less vigorous and have white flowers. Fringed bleeding heart (*Dicentra eximia*) is native to Pennsylvania and is a more compact, finer-textured plant. Only 12 to 18 inches tall, it blooms from May to September with red ('Luxuriant') or white ('Alba') flowers. It seeds readily and is tough and dependable.

 Did You Know?

Many plants are constitutionally unable to cope with heat and the droughtlike conditions that often accompany it. Paradoxically, they often come from regions where this climate is the norm, and they adapted to it by developing the capacity for storing moisture to tide them over until temperatures cooled. Common bleeding heart has deep tuberous roots, which soak up water and nutrients during the spring when its foliage is in full array. Then when harsh summer weather approaches, it dies back and rests underground until next spring.

Candytuft

Iberis sempervirens

Other Name: Evergreen Candytuft
Mature Size: 8 to 10 inches
Bloom Time: Late May
Flower Color/Type: White florets; flat clusters
Features: Evergreen foliage; old-fashioned; evening garden

Light Requirements:

Color photograph on page 206.

*I*t is often massed to serve ground cover duty, yet candytuft's tidy habit and tough constitution suit it equally well to be an element in a flower border or rock garden in its own right. It is amazingly low maintenance, its Mediterranean ancestry having accustomed it to heat and drought. Its soft, needled evergreen foliage lines its flexible stems, creating a dark-green backdrop for the domed clusters of white florets that bloom at their tips. Planted along walls and allowed to grow extended stems, candytuft will spill over the edges to soften them. Long-lived and slow-growing, these plants will brighten the yard for many seasons as long as there are no deer visitors.

WHEN TO PLANT

Plant rooted divisions from overlarge candytuft plants in either spring or fall. Transplant young plants in pots from the garden center anytime during the growing season.

WHERE TO PLANT

Candytuft flowers and overwinters best in full sun. It does fine in ordinary soil of any type as long as it is well-drained. It is not thrilled about being moved, so choose the site carefully.

HOW TO PLANT

Prepare the planting area by digging the soil down 8 to 10 inches. Mix in organic material such as compost or chopped leaves to improve drainage in heavy soil, and add a handful of a granular slow-acting all-purpose fertilizer per plant. Dig each planting hole about as deep as and slightly wider than the rootball without its container. Set the plant in the hole so that the surface of the rootball is level with, or slightly above, the surrounding soil. Fill in the hole with soil, firm it gently, and water well. Set plants about 1 foot apart to allow for their gradual spread.

CARE AND MAINTENANCE

Clip off only winter-damaged or semibare woody stems in early spring prior to flowering to groom the candytuft. After spring flowering, shear the stems and faded flowers back to about half their height to promote bushiness. Doing this limits candytuft stems' tendency to sprawl and get woody, and encourages possible repeat bloom toward fall. Once candytuft is established, there is no need to fertilize it routinely. A rich diet makes the stems limp and floppy. Because the Philadelphia area rarely accumulates snow cover, lay some evergreen boughs over candytuft to shield its evergreen foliage from winter sunburn. It is technically a woody plant, so its buds are above the soil and vulnerable to tip dieback.

ADDITIONAL INFORMATION

Use candytuft for edging or as fillers for container plantings. It is a good companion for bleeding heart, creeping phlox, minor bulbs, and other spring bloomers. Candytuft occasionally suffers from humidity and poor air circulation, which cause a fungal rot in the summer.

ADDITIONAL SPECIES, CULTIVARS, OR VARIETIES

'Alexander's White' blooms a bit earlier than most. 'Autumn Beauty' flowers in the fall, too. 'Snowflake' grows up to 10 inches tall with larger, brilliant-white flowers and larger leaves. 'Little Gem' is upright, bushy, and dwarf at 6 inches tall. Annual candytuft (*Iberis umbellata*) blooms in pink, white, or lilac all summer.

 Did You Know?

Gardeners of a certain age, those who went to high school when Latin and even Greek were still offered, have a real advantage in remembering plant names. Embedded in their formal or botanical names, and sometimes in their common names or nicknames, are all kinds of information useful in identifying plants. Often knowing these languages makes plants easier to remember, too. For instance, Iberis *means "Iberia," as in the Iberian Peninsula of Spain and Portugal whose classic Mediterranean climate is candytuft's favorite.* Sempervirens *means "always green," or "evergreen," referring to its foliage.*

Chrysanthemum, Garden

Dendranthema × morifolium

Other Names: Hardy Chrysanthemum, Hardy Mum, Cushion Mum

Mature Size: 1 to 3 feet tall; 1 to 3 feet wide

Bloom Time: August to November

Flower Color/Type: Shades of red and pink, white, yellow, lilac; single, double, novelty shapes

Features: Attracts butterflies; fall flower color

Light Requirements:

Color photograph on page 206.

---

*I*n the fall, gardeners have always been able to rely on chrysanthemums. The traditional backbone of the fall flower border, windowbox, and patio planter, they have only gotten better over the years. Choose from a rainbow of flower colors and wonderful flower shapes that belie their toughness. Daisy-, decorative-, pompom-, spoon-, or spider-shaped blooms top their familiar bushy, gray-green foliage with its distinctive scent when crushed. These plants are so tough that they transplant in full bloom without missing a beat. Visit the splendid annual display from late October through Thanksgiving at Longwood Gardens.

WHEN TO PLANT

Plant divisions or rooted cuttings in the spring. Transplant potted plants from the nursery anytime during the summer into fall.

WHERE TO PLANT

Choose a site in full sun for the best mum display. They can handle almost any type of soil as long as it is well-drained to prevent the winter soggies.

HOW TO PLANT

Loosen the soil down 8 to 10 inches. Mix in granular slow-acting all-purpose fertilizer, and add organic material to heavy soil for drainage. Dig planting holes for mums about as deep as and slightly wider than their rootballs so that they sit in the hole at the same depth that they were in their pots. Rooted cuttings can be shallower. Fill in the hole with soil, firm it gently, and water well. Mulch with 2 or 3 inches of an attractive organic material to discourage weeds and retain soil moisture. Set young plants about 2 feet apart to allow for their gradual spread. Fall-planted, mature, ready-to-bloom plants are full sized; you can space them as desired.

CARE AND MAINTENANCE

Pinch stem tips of young plants back by about half their new growth every few weeks after they reach 6 inches or so to delay blossoming and promote branching for a compact plant. Repeat this process until mid-July for early-fall bloom. Continue it until mid-August for late-fall bloom. Unpinched stems become tall and leggy and need staking. After hard frost, cut back browned stems and mulch their bed for winter, or treat the plants as annuals and pull them up. Divide large overwintered clumps in spring when their green foliage appears by digging up and separating rooted chunks, then replanting.

ADDITIONAL INFORMATION

Aphids may cluster at tender stem tips early in the season before their natural predators appear on the scene. Pinch them off, stem tips and all, and discard them in a plastic bag. Insecticidal soap will handle them and the occasional mite infestation, too. Florist mums, which are available as gift plants almost year-round, are not intended for garden use.

ADDITIONAL SPECIES, CULTIVARS, OR VARIETIES

Dendranthema zawadskii 'Clara Curtis', a current favorite of gardeners in our region, has salmon-pink daisy flowers with yellow centers. It is long blooming and tolerates more shade than most mums. Study the photographs on mum labels to choose your favorites from among the enormous number of choices.

Did You Know?

Mums were grown as early as 500 B.C. in China. Eventually their cultivation spread to Japan, and the Mikado adopted them as his personal emblem. They were exhibited there as early as A.D. 900. They were subsequently integrated into the art and culture of Japan as symbols of a long and happy life. The rising sun in the Japanese flag is actually a mum. When they were introduced into England in the late eighteenth century, mums entered the Victorian flower language, representing Cheerfulness in Adversity—no doubt because of their jaunty blooms in the face of autumn frost.

Columbine

Aquilegia hybrids

Other Names: Long-Spurred Columbine,
  Granny's Bonnet
Mature Size: 1 to 3 feet tall; 1 foot wide
Bloom Time: May
Flower Color/Type: Blue, violet, white, yellow, red, bicolored;
  spurred cups
Features: Attracts hummingbirds and hawk moths
Light Requirements: Sun to partial shade

Light Requirements:

Color photograph on page 206.

Columbines appear in a garden as a flurry of color—soft pastels or brighter, richer tones, such as yellow, red, or purple. Nodding at the tips of slim stems above pale-green or gray-green foliage, their flowers are uniquely shaped. They have 5 petals, each with a narrow spur, or extension, projecting from its base toward the back. There are both Eastern and Western native wildflower columbines, and others from Europe and Asia, larger flowered and more colorful, which grow well here, too. Columbines are short-lived but replace themselves constantly by reseeding, hybridizing freely into new colors and combinations. The overall effect is delicate and airy, qualifying columbine as a see-through plant as at home near the front of the border as in the middle.

WHEN TO PLANT

Plant young potted plants from the garden center in the spring. Columbines develop deep taproots and are difficult to transplant unless they are young or dormant in the fall or early spring.

WHERE TO PLANT

Columbines like sun, but flowering lasts longer in light shade. They are not fussy about soil as long as it is moist and well-drained. Soggy soil promotes rot. Expect that their site will become bare when columbine foliage gets ratty and dies or is cut back in midsummer. Plan for substitute plants to finish the season in their place.

HOW TO PLANT

Cultivate the soil down 8 to 10 inches to loosen and aerate it. Add organic matter such as compost or peat moss to heavy or clay soil to improve its drainage. Dig planting holes for young plants about as deep as and slightly wider than their pots. Remove the pots, and set each plant in its hole so that it is level with the surrounding soil. Fill in the hole with soil, firm it gently around plant stems, and water well. Set tall columbines about 1 foot apart, and dwarf types about half that distance. Sow seeds as directed on the seed packet.

CARE AND MAINTENANCE

Spread a layer of organic mulch around newly planted columbines to discourage weeds and keep soil moist. Tall types may need some support for best display of their flowers. Deadhead hybrid blooms before they can form and release seeds to forestall the appearance of unwelcome plants that are not the same color. Allow them to reseed at will if that is not a concern. Columbines have chronic problems with leaf miners that scar their leaves with white tracings. Sometimes they develop powdery mildew on the foliage. In both cases cut off infected leaves to stimulate new, healthy foliage.

ADDITIONAL INFORMATION

Dwarf columbines are great in rock gardens. Grow others with ferns, hosta, grasses, and sweet woodruff. Columbines make good, but fleeting, cut flowers.

ADDITIONAL SPECIES, CULTIVARS, OR VARIETIES

Hybrids include the following: Music Series Hybrids are about 18 inches tall with large, long-spurred, colorful flowers and 4 to 6 weeks of bloom; McKenna Hybrids grow more than 2 feet tall and are an All-America Selection; 'Nora Barlow' flowers are magenta and lime and are double; and many others are available by mail order. Species include the following: Wild columbine (*Aquilegia canadensis*) is native to our Northeastern part of the country and has red and yellow, small, dainty flowers. Japanese fan columbine (*Aquilegia flabellata*) Cameo Series offers dwarf plants that grow in 18-inch-tall mounds of white, lilac, or blue flowers and have fan-shaped bluish green leaves.

 Did You Know?

Columbine represents Folly in the Victorian language of flowers, probably because the nectaries within its flower structure resemble the pointed caps of medieval court jesters. Its common name also refers to its distinctive flower. In Latin columba *means "dove." Early fanciers saw the similarity between the arrangement of spurred petals of the flowers to a ring of doves, a common motif in ancient art.*

Coralbells

Heuchera species and hybrids

Other Names: Alumroot, Heuchera
Mature Size: 2 feet tall; 2 feet wide
Bloom Time: May and June
Flower Color/Type: Pink, red, coral, greenish,
   or white; bells
Features: Old-fashioned; attracts hummingbirds

Color photograph on page 206.

Light Requirements:

First, there were simply coralbells, charming plants from the West whose slender, dainty flower stalks branched into sprays of thready stems tipped with tiny bells. Their tidy mounds of evergreen foliage commonly bordered flower beds, the tall, airy, see-through flower stems permitting full view of the plants behind them. Cut stems of coralbells flowers filled in artful indoor bouquets of their more substantial garden companions. Then in the mid-1980s, there suddenly were heucheras from the East. They boasted strikingly improved foliage variously lobed or scalloped and marbled with green, bronze, purple, and silver. Now gardeners have the luxury of choosing from among an enormous number of variations of this tough, versatile plant that offers both charming flowers and stunning leaves. Modern coralbells have it all—disease resistance, hardiness, shade and drought tolerance, colorful foliage, and delicate but showy flowers.

WHEN TO PLANT

Plant divided sections of overlarge clumps or young plants in either spring or fall. Potted plants from the garden center transplant well anytime during the growing season.

WHERE TO PLANT

Coralbells prefer full sun for best flowering. Some foliage colors show best in partial shade. They like almost any soil as long as it is rich in organic matter and well-drained.

HOW TO PLANT

Prepare the soil by digging down 8 to 10 inches, mixing in a little granular slow-acting all-purpose fertilizer and organic material to improve drainage. Dig a planting hole large enough to accommodate the coralbells' root system. Set the plant in the hole so that its crown, where the roots meet the stems, is at soil level. Fill in the hole with soil, firm it gently, and water well. Spread 1 or 2 inches of organic mulch over the soil to discourage weeds and retain moisture. Set plants 12 to 18 inches apart to allow for their gradual spread, closer for edging.

CARE AND MAINTENANCE

Coralbells virtually take care of themselves. Cut off dying flower stems to neaten the plant and stimulate repeat bloom over the summer. Because they are shallow rooted, coralbells benefit from a year-round organic mulch. Divide plants in the fall every 3 or 4 years when the flower stems are sparser and the crowns of the plants grow woody. Discard the woodiest parts, then replant clumps that have some roots.

ADDITIONAL INFORMATION

Coralbells are good citizens in outdoor containers, surviving over several years as various annuals come and go. They are basically pest resistant except for black vine weevil that chews notches in leaf edges. In the spring drench the soil with a biological insecticide product containing beneficial (or predatory) nematodes to kill weevil larvae.

ADDITIONAL SPECIES, CULTIVARS, OR VARIETIES

Heuchera americana, our native species, has greenish silver foliage. 'Garnet' features deep-red-purple foliage. 'Pewter Veil' has silvery leaves with purple undersides. *Heuchera micrantha* 'Palace Purple', which has purplish bronze foliage, was selected by the Perennial Plant Association as its Plant of the Year in 1991. *Heuchera × brizoides* Bressingham Hybrids are heavy blooming. Consult mail-order nursery catalogs for hundreds of choices.

 Did You Know?

Pennsylvania nurseryman Dale Hendricks spotted a coralbells with interesting foliage growing wild in the mountains of North Carolina and brought it to the attention of Allen Bush at Holbrook Farm nursery in that state. Dubbed "Dale's Strain," this version of Heuchera americana *has distinctive silvery tracings on the foliage that form an attractive pattern. Eventually, Dale's Strain was crossed with the pioneering 'Palace Purple' to yield 'Montrose Ruby'. This plant set a new standard for complex coloration and elaborate, elegant venation in heuchera foliage.*

Coreopsis

Coreopsis grandiflora

Other Names: Bigflower Coreopsis,
  Lance Coreopsis
Mature Size: 6 to 24 inches tall
Bloom Time: June through September
Flower Color/Type: Yellow; daisy
Features: Attracts butterflies and beneficial insects; low water demand

Light Requirements:

Color photograph on page 206.

All the members of the coreopsis clan are native to the United States, having a prairie heritage of versatility and durability over the season. They feature cheerful daisylike flowers in various shades of gold and yellow at the tips of wiry stems with narrow, pointed leaves. Bigflower coreopsis is tall, relatively short-lived, and somewhat weedy. Its wide, fluted, fringed flower petals are standouts in many meadow wildflower mixes. It is best suited for informal, naturalized areas of the yard. The delightful, more domesticated cultivated varieties of this coreopsis are excellent garden plants. 'Early Sunrise', an All-America Selection winner in 1989, grows easily from seed and yields semidouble flowers that bloom dependably its first year. 'Sunray', a 1980 European Fleuroselect Award winner, is more compact with double blooms. All coreopsis are noted for their unusually long bloom season and resistance to disease and drought.

When to Plant

Plant root divisions from overlarge plants in either spring or fall. Transplant plants in pots from the garden center anytime during the growing season. Choose an overcast day or plant in the evening so that the newcomer is not stressed by the sun while it copes with transplant shock.

Where to Plant

Coreopsis do best in full sun and ordinary soil of any type as long as it is well-drained.

How to Plant

Dig the soil down 8 to 10 inches to prepare the planting bed. Improve the drainage of clay soil by mixing in organic material. If the soil is decent, do not add any fertilizer because most coreopsis do best in lean soil. Dig the planting hole about as deep as and slightly wider than the plant's pot. Remove the plant from the container, and set it in the hole so that the top of its soilball is level with the surrounding ground. Fill in the hole with soil,

168

firm it gently around plant stems, and water well. Set plants about 2 feet apart to allow for their gradual spread.

CARE AND MAINTENANCE

Cut off dead flowers and their stems to groom the plants, prevent reseeding, and stimulate continued bloom. To encourage reseeding, leave the last flowers in the fall. The goldfinches will thank you. Since self-sown plants cannot be depended upon to be true to type, divide oversized clumps of favorites to obtain plants that are identical. Some coreopsis are fast spreaders, so expect to have to divide them every 3 or 4 years. It may be necessary to stake taller types or those in very rich soil, which causes stems to flop.

ADDITIONAL INFORMATION

Coreopsis make good cut flowers. Dwarf types such as Goldfink' and 'Nana', which are about 9 inches tall, and 'Baby Sun' and 'Baby Gold', which are compact at about 15 inches tall, are ideal for rock gardens, containers, and edging. Coreopsis looks great with seasonal contemporaries such as blazing star, asters, goldenrod, purple coneflower, mallows, tithonia, black-eyed Susans, sneezeweed, and blanket flower.

ADDITIONAL SPECIES, CULTIVARS, OR VARIETIES

Threadleaf coreopsis (*Coreopsis verticillata*) varieties have thin, ferny foliage and daintier flowers. 'Moonbeam' and 'Golden Showers' grow to 2 feet tall; 'Zagreb' to only 12 inches. They are the most drought resistant of all. *Coreopsis rosea* has pink flowers and threadleaf foliage.

 Did You Know?

The distinctive seeds of coreopsis are responsible for both its botanical and its common names. Because they have two little protuberances, or horns, their shape suggests an insect. Thus the Greek koris, meaning "bedbug," and opsis, meaning "resemble," reflect the opinion of early horticulturists that the seeds looked like bedbugs. Prairie pioneers dubbed the plants tickseed because they thought the horned seeds looked like ticks.

Daylily

Hemerocallis hybrids

Other Name: Hybrid Daylily

Mature Size: 1 to 4 feet tall; 2 to 4 feet wide

Bloom Time: June through September

Flower Color/Type: Shades of red, yellow, orange, lilac, and cream; trumpets

Features: Edible flowers; fragrant (some); attracts butterflies; low water demand

Light Requirements:

Color photograph on page 206.

Wild roadside and meadow daylilies such as the orange tawny and yellow lemon lilies offer wonderful color in early summer plus great genes for toughness and drought and disease resistance. From them plant breeders have developed all kinds of domesticated hybrids for the garden, including rebloomers that perform all summer. These modern hybrids typically send up dozens of stems, each topped with multitudes of flower buds. Each flower blooms for only a day, those on a stem opening in succession over several days. Flowers may be single or double; they may have ruffled or crimped edges, rippled texture, iridescence, and fragrance. Their stems stretch above clumps of arching, narrow, green, straplike foliage, which mounds up from the soil. Deer seem to have a special fondness for daylilies; they have no other significant pest or disease problems.

WHEN TO PLANT

Traditional wisdom says to plant divisions in either spring or late summer and potted nursery stock anytime during the growing season, but growers concede that most daylilies can be planted and transplanted safely almost anytime the ground is not frozen. Cut back the foliage to about 4 inches, and choose a time when there is no sun to stress the transplants.

WHERE TO PLANT

Daylilies are at their best in full sun, but they can handle some shade if they must. Almost any type of soil is fine as long as it is well-drained and not very rich.

HOW TO PLANT

Cultivate the soil down 8 to 10 inches, digging in organic matter to improve drainage if necessary. Dig the planting hole slightly larger than the daylily roots or soilball. Remove its container or any wrappings, and set it in its hole so that the top of the rootball is at soil level. Fill the hole with soil, firm it gently, then water well. Space standard plants about 2 feet apart and dwarf types 1 foot apart.

CARE AND MAINTENANCE

Remove each stem after all its flowers have died to groom plants and stimulate repeat flowering in rebloomers. They respond to generous watering and feeding with more stems and blooms. Hybrid types flower best when divided every 3 or 4 years in the spring. Dig up the clump, and then slice through it with a sharp spade or knife to separate rooted chunks with at least one "fan" of leaves. When daylily foliage dies back after frost, clean it up and mulch the bed.

ADDITIONAL INFORMATION

Daylilies are team players, blending easily into flower borders or serving as ground covers to combat soil erosion. Individual specimens do star turns as focal points in the garden. Smaller types do well in containers. Some bloom at night for an evening garden.

ADDITIONAL SPECIES, CULTIVARS, OR VARIETIES

There are more than 40,000 named cultivars on record with the American Hemerocallis Society. Among the dependable rebloomers that do well in the Philadelphia region are 'Stella de Oro' (golden yellow), 'Happy Returns' (lemon yellow), and 'Hyperion' (canary yellow). Tetraploid types of daylilies have super-large blooms up to 6 inches wide on thick, sturdy stems. More weather resistant, they lack the grace of regular hybrids.

 Did You Know?

Daylilies have a place in the kitchen, too. Early spring shoots make tasty greens; fresh flower buds are delicious lightly battered and fried. Chinese cooks steam or dry the flowers (minus stamens) for use in soups and stews. Stuff the flowers with cream cheese, laced with smoked salmon. Sauté the seedpods in butter, or pickle them. High in vitamin A and C, they have almost as much protein as spinach. Flower flavors are influenced by scent and vary by color, so sample them first. Remember the basic rule of edible flowers: be sure they have not been exposed to pesticides.

Geranium, Hardy

Geranium species and hybrids

Other Names: Cranesbill, True Geranium

Mature Size: 6 inches to 4 feet tall;
1 to 2 feet wide

Bloom Time: May to July

Flower Color/Type: Magenta, pink, blue, violet, white; open cups

Features: Deer resistant

Light Requirements:

Color photograph on page 206.

The potential for confusion over names notwithstanding, hardy geraniums are easily distinguished from tender (or annual) geraniums, which are more properly called "Pelargoniums." Besides being perennial, the more than 500 kinds of hardy geraniums typically grow as mounds of low, multilobed or divided leaves in shades of dull green or gray-green. Their 1- or 2-inch-wide flowers appear at the tips of branching stems and have 5 rounded petals, sometimes streaked with color. Some types bloom lightly all season, but most put on a big show from May through June and then rebloom intermittently over the summer. They are endowed with tough constitutions and great adaptability. Many grow from rhizomes, which enable them to withstand harsh summers, but also help them spread vigorously. Some have scented foliage; others, fall color. Among these good garden plants, there is a variety to suit almost any landscape situation.

WHEN TO PLANT

Plant divisions from overlarge geranium clumps in the spring. Plant potted plants when they are available at the garden center.

WHERE TO PLANT

Geraniums like morning sun and afternoon shade. 'Ingwersen's Variety' can take dry shade under trees. Some do well in woodland settings; others, in full sun as ground covers. Most accept average, reasonably moist, well-drained soil of any type.

HOW TO PLANT

Cultivate the soil down 8 to 10 inches, digging in granular slow-acting all-purpose fertilizer while you are at it. Dig a planting hole about as deep as and slightly wider than the geranium rootball when it is removed from its container. Set the geranium in the hole so that the top of its rootball is level with the surrounding soil. Fill in the hole with soil, firm it gently, and water well. Plant geraniums in clusters of 3 for best effect, spaced about 1 foot apart to allow for their gradual spread. Plant small ones for edging in rows about 6 to 8 inches apart.

CARE AND MAINTENANCE

Water hardy geraniums when rainfall is scarce during the 2 years they take to become fully established. Mulch the soil around them to discourage weeds and keep soil moist. After their main bloom period, cut back flower stalks to groom the plant. Cut back ratty foliage of large geranium varieties to renew foliage and to encourage rebloom. When plants threaten to grow too large, divide them in early spring. Dig up the rootball, and separate rooted stems or groups of stems to replant elsewhere.

ADDITIONAL INFORMATION

Hardy geraniums have occasional problems with Japanese beetles in July. Handpick as many pests as possible. Cut back marred foliage at the end of July, and new will return. Sometimes mildew affects geranium foliage in late spring, disappearing later in the summer.

ADDITIONAL SPECIES, CULTIVARS, OR VARIETIES

Bigroot geranium (*Geranium macrorrhizum*) has magenta, pink, or white flowers, handles heat and drought, and is a vigorous spreader. Its evergreen foliage has a slight fragrance. Bloody cranesbill (*Geranium sanguineum*) has deep-rose, white, or pink flowers at 12 inches tall. 'Striatum' is only 6 inches tall with clear, pink flowers. *Geranium maculatum* is native to the Eastern United States; it is 2 feet tall, likes rich soil, and has lilac-pink flowers. Endress cranesbill (*Geranium endressii*) 'Wargrave Pink' bears salmon flowers all summer as a superb ground cover. 'Johnson's Blue' (*Geranium ibericum* 'Johnson's Blue') has pale-blue flowers in June, then sporadically. Hybrid 'Ann Folkard' trails with magenta flowers all summer with yellow-dotted lime-green foliage.

 Did You Know?

Hardy geranium appears on many lists of perennials to which deer are indifferent. Unless they are starving, deer show distinct preferences for certain plants, ignoring others. Some others on the list of relatively safe perennials are bellflower, black-eyed Susan, bleeding heart, columbine, fern, hellebore, poppy, and peony.

Goldenrod

Solidago species and hybrids

Other Name: Hybrid Goldenrod

Mature Size: 2 to 6 feet tall;
  2 to 4 feet wide

Bloom Time: Midsummer to fall

Flower Color/Type: Yellow florets on feathery spikes

Features: Attracts butterflies and beneficial insects; low water demand

Light Requirements:

Color photograph on page 206.

Goldenrod is another of our wonderful wild plants, high on the list of low-maintenance natives that are easy on the environment. After domestication by European breeders, many interesting versions of goldenrod are available for adoption into American gardens. They invariably earn their keep as heralds of the golden days of autumn. Goldenrod flowers bloom as tight groups of tiny, yellow florets at the tips of strong, flexible stems laddered with lance-shaped leaves. They are in plumed clusters or arrayed along narrow branchlets in horizontal tiers. Naturalize goldenrod in fields with asters and black-eyed Susans, or integrate it into a flower border.

When to Plant

Goldenrod can be transplanted just about anytime, even when it is in bloom. Plant rooted divisions from established plants in the spring. Fall planting gives plants plenty of time to develop strong root systems before they must put energy into foliage and flower production.

Where to Plant

Goldenrod's prairie heritage has accustomed it to full sun and ordinary soil of almost any type that is well-drained. Goldenrod can handle some shade at woodland edge. Tall types do best at the back of the flower border. Expect them to spread by both roots and self-sown seed.

How to Plant

Cultivate the soil down 8 to 10 inches to loosen and aerate it. Dig planting holes about as deep as and slightly wider than plant pots. Tip plants out of their pots, and loosen any matted roots. Set them in their holes, adjusted so that the top of the soilball is level with the surrounding ground. Fill in the hole with soil, firm it around plant stems, and water well. Set plants about 1 foot apart.

CARE AND MAINTENANCE

Water until goldenrod is established, then it is fairly drought resistant. Mulch to maintain soil moisture. For more compact plants and later bloom, cut stems back by half in early June. Tall types and those that grow in rich soil that causes softer stems may need staking. Hybrid goldenrod, as opposed to enthusiastically spreading wild ones, grows in fairly disciplined clumps. Even hybrids grow large, however, and need dividing every 3 or 4 years in the spring or fall immediately after flowering. Leave dried seedheads for winter interest, or cut them off to forestall self-seeding.

ADDITIONAL INFORMATION

Seeds of several types of goldenrod are often included in meadow mixes. Intended for the "wild" planting, they are typically more blowzy in habit and have stoloniferous roots that spread vigorously, making them more unruly than garden, or hybrid, varieties. Goldenrod makes a good cut flower fresh or dried.

ADDITIONAL SPECIES, CULTIVARS, OR VARIETIES

The golden florets of 'Crown of Rays' are arrayed along plume-like stems. 'Golden Dwarf' is only 12 inches tall. Golden fleece goldenrod (*Solidago sphacelata* 'Golden Fleece') grows to only 18 inches tall and spreads freely; it accepts shade. Rough-leafed goldenrod (*Solidago rugosa* 'Fireworks') can reach 4 feet tall. Unlike most, it can handle moist soil. Flower heads are flattened sprays of florets that form a loose web of golden stems. Canada goldenrod (*Solidago canadensis*) is the native weedy field version.

 Did You Know?

Goldenrod is not responsible for the annual hay-fever attacks that many people experience in late summer. The true culprit is ragweed, which blooms and produces pollen about the same time as wild goldenrod, its companion in open fields and along roadsides. Close observers will note that goldenrod is visited by zillions of tiny insects and butterflies, which are needed to assure that its sticky pollen is distributed to other flowers. Wind-pollinated plants, such as ragweed, cause allergies.

Hosta

Hosta species and hybrids

Other Names: Plantain Lily, Funkia
Mature Size: 6 to 24 inches tall;
  1 to 3 feet wide
Bloom Time: July or August
Flower Color/Type: White, lavender, purple; trumpets
Features: Foliage

Color photograph on page 206.

Light Requirements:

*K*ing of the shade garden, hosta is the ultimate foliage plant. Yes, hostas have flowers, quite lovely clusters of small trumpets arrayed along the upper part of stems that rise high above their mounds of leaves. It is hosta's regal, seemingly infinitely variable foliage that commands attention, however. Leaves may be any shade of green or even blue, plain, or with cream, yellow, or gold edges or streaks. Measuring from less than 1 inch to 22 inches long, they may be rippled, ruffled, or deeply textured with prominent ribs. Long-lived, they brighten dark corners, edge borders, and star as specimens all season until their leaves collapse with frost. In areas of Swarthmore, a town of towering street trees, hostas solve the problem of what to plant in their shade between the curb and the sidewalk.

WHEN TO PLANT
Plant rooted chunks from a divided larger plant in either spring or fall. Transplant potted hostas from the garden center anytime during the growing season.

WHERE TO PLANT
Yellow-foliaged hostas such as 'Sum and Substance' like more sun; blue-foliaged hostas prefer less sun. Most like some bright, indirect morning light, followed by mostly partial shade. Give them woodsy soil that is moist, slightly acidic, and rich in organic matter.

HOW TO PLANT
Dig the soil down 8 to 12 inches, and mix in granular slow-acting all-purpose fertilizer and compost, chopped leaves, or other organic matter to improve its moisture retention and drainage. Dig the planting hole as deep as the hosta rootball when removed from its container and a bit wider. Loosen any matted roots, then set the plant in the hole so that the top of the rootball is level with the surrounding ground. Fill in the hole with soil, firming it

gently, and water well. Allow plenty of space because hosta foliage splays a bit in midsummer heat.

CARE AND MAINTENANCE

Provide regular moisture over the first 2 seasons it takes for hostas to fully establish. Maintain a 2- or 3-inch layer of organic mulch to discourage weeds, and sprinkle slow-acting fertilizer on it each spring. Divide hostas in the spring when the circle of new buds appears, slice away a pie-shaped chunk of roots with a sharp spade or knife without disturbing the main plant. Then fill the space with soil.

ADDITIONAL INFORMATION

Unfortunately, deer love hostas! If necessary, grow them in pots out of deer reach. Hosta flowers work well in indoor arrangements. Use hostas to hide ripening bulb foliage, in woodland settings, around trees as a living mulch to protect their roots and trunk, or as substitutes for foundation shrubs around the house.

ADDITIONAL SPECIES, CULTIVARS, OR VARIETIES

August lily (*Hosta plantaginea*) has white, fragrant flowers in late summer. Siebold's hosta (*Hosta sieboldiana* 'Elegans') grows up to 4 feet tall and across with huge blue leaves and white flowers. Fortune's hostas (*Hosta fortunei*) have variegated foliage. Among them is 'Gold Standard', a 1988 Hosta Society pick. Venusta types, such as 'Tiny Tears', are only 6 inches tall. 'Guacamole' is the 1998 Hosta Growers Association Hosta of the Year with dark-green-edged, rounded gold leaves and fragrant lavender August flowers.

 Did You Know?

Slugs love hostas! They damage the smoother, more delicate, and lower-growing leaves. Leaves skeletonized by their feeding will be replaced by new leaves. Some slug controls include the following:

- *Spreading diatomaceous earth, sand, or ashes on the soil.*
- *Fastening copper strips to edges of boxed beds.*
- *Using spiky sweetgum balls for mulch.*
- *Setting beer or yeast traps.*
- *Handpicking early arrivals.*
- *Renting a toad.*

Lenten Rose

Helleborus hybridus

Other Name: Hellebore
Mature Size: 15 to 20 inches tall;
  15 to 20 inches wide
Bloom Time: March to April
Flower Color/Type: Cream, maroon, pink, purple, speckled; single or
  double open cups
Features: Winter interest

Light Requirements:

Color photograph on page 207.

---

*L*enten rose and its relatives have finally come into their own. Now recognized as a superior garden plant, it is all the more appreciated because
it sustains the garden during the bleak days of winter with its handsome
foliage and lovely blossoms. Its open mounds of glossy, leathery, deeply
divided leaves harbor slightly nodding flowers that seem shy about blooming
so early while it still seems like winter. Creamy, pink, and maroon-toned, the
5-petaled flowers rise from the crown of the plant, often acquiring a pinkish
tinge as they age over about 10 weeks. First sightings may be in February, thus
the Lenten name, but even after their peak, flowers persist as colorful sepals
with a swollen seedpod in the center. Long-lived, old clumps of Lenten rose
commonly produce up to 100 flowers.

WHEN TO PLANT

Plant Lenten rose sold in pots from the garden center in spring or early fall.
Transplant the seedlings from established plants in new sites in the spring.

WHERE TO PLANT

Lenten roses can handle sun or shade; however, in sun they require moister
soil. Locating them under deciduous trees permits some winter light on
them and the tree's leaf canopy protects them from hot sun in summer.
They prefer woodsy soil, rich in organic matter and well-drained. They can
handle dry shade. Soil can be a bit on the alkaline side.

HOW TO PLANT

Dig soil in the planting area down 1 foot or so to loosen and aerate it. Mix
in organic matter to enrich it and improve drainage. Dig the planting hole
deep enough to accommodate the plant rootball with the pot removed.
Loosen any matted roots, and set it so that its top is level with the surrounding ground. Fill in the hole with soil, firm it gently, and water well.
Maintain a 2- or 3-inch layer of organic mulch year-round to keep soil moist

and discourage weeds. Set plants 18 inches apart to allow for their temporary flattening in severe winter weather and gradual spread. They begin to flower in 3 years.

CARE AND MAINTENANCE

Clip off ratty leaves in the spring to improve Lenten rose's appearance. Heavy feeders, they appreciate fertilizing with a slow-acting product in the late spring. Deadhead spent flowers to prevent self-seeding. As a group, hellebores do not like to be disturbed, but Lenten rose will tolerate transplanting better than others in early spring before new foliage emerges. Avoid dividing if possible.

ADDITIONAL INFORMATION

Lenten rose makes a good ground cover, too. It combines well in a winter garden with snowdrops and other early bulbs, then later with ferns, hostas, and bleeding hearts. It will grow in containers—some are entered in the Philadelphia Flower Show every year.

ADDITIONAL SPECIES, CULTIVARS, OR VARIETIES

Helleborus hybridus (formerly *orientalis*) reseeds readily, producing unpredictable and varied flower colors. Christmas rose (*Helleborus niger*) blooms a bit earlier with greenish-tinged white flowers and prefers moister soil and a cooler site. Stinking or bearsfoot hellebore (*Helleborus foetidus*) is short-lived and bears tall stalks clustered with pale-green flowers with purple edges in December. Its foliage is narrow and medium green.

 Did You Know?

Hellebore is an unfortunate name for such a benign plant. The hell *syllable conveys the sense of darkness and witchery with which medieval society connected it. People strewed the flowers on the floor to drive out evil sprits. Actually, the botanical name is derived from the Greek words* helein *("to injure") and* bora *("food"). Perhaps "injurious food" is not such a misnomer after all, since hellebore roots contain toxic substances that are extremely irritating to internal and external tissues in humans. Wear gloves when handling this plant to avoid dermatitis.*

Peony

Paeonia hybrids

Other Names: Garden Peony, Chinese Peony

Mature Size: 2 to 3 feet tall; 3 feet wide

Bloom Time: May to June

Flower Color/Type: Yellow, rose, red, white, and shades of pink; single, double, or anemone

Features: Fragrance; old-fashioned; deer resistant

Light Requirements:

Color photograph on page 207.

*L*ush, fragrant peonies are one of the joys of late spring. Long-lived and relatively carefree, they are beloved through many generations. Some of these shrubby plants, more than 100 years old, are still blooming happily in fields that were once front yards of long-abandoned Pennsylvania farms. Peony flowers are 6 or more inches across, a flutter of tissue-paper petals around yellow centers. Sweetly fragrant, they bloom at the top of branched stems also holding dark-green, coarse, lobed foliage. Some peony blossoms are so top-heavy that the stems flop under their weight, especially when it rains. Blossoms typically last 4 to 7 days. Incorporate peonies into a mixed border, or use them in a row as an informal hedge.

WHEN TO PLANT

Plant chunks of rooted tubers divided from overlarge plants in the fall when the leaves have died back and they are dormant. Plant peonies sold in pots at the garden center in the spring or anytime during the growing season.

WHERE TO PLANT

Peonies appreciate full sun but will accept partial shade, which sometimes intensifies their flower color. Give them good garden soil rich in organic matter and well-drained. It can be slightly on the alkaline side. A somewhat sheltered spot with some leeway between them and other perennials or shrubs is ideal.

HOW TO PLANT

Loosen and aerate the soil thoroughly by digging down at least 12 inches and as widely as possible. Incorporate organic material such as compost, peat moss, or chopped leaves and also granular slow-acting all-purpose fertilizer. Proper planting depth is critical, or peonies will not bloom. Dig a hole just deep enough so that the pinkish, pointy-tipped growing buds end up just 1 inch below ground level when covered with soil. Set a plant that was in a pot in the hole so that the soil surface is exactly at ground level.

Fill in the hole with soil, firming it gently, and water well. Space plants as far apart as 3 feet to provide the roominess they like.

CARE AND MAINTENANCE

Water regularly and mulch around, but not on, peonies to discourage weeds during the 2 to 3 years it takes them to establish. Fertilize them with slow-acting fertilizer in late fall or early spring. Regularly mulched peonies eventually do not need annual fertilizing. The newer large-flowered types need supporting cages or stakes at bloom time. Cut off stems with spent flowers promptly to prevent fungal disease. Cut back discolored ripening foliage in early fall when it can no longer continue to soak up sunlight to support the new buds forming below ground. Peonies resent being disturbed, so dig up and divide clumps only if necessary. Do it toward fall and assure that each tuberous-rooted piece has 3 to 5 buds.

ADDITIONAL INFORMATION

Common reasons for no blooms are: receiving too much shade, being planted too deeply, enduring a cold spring, overfertilizing, competing with tree roots, being too young, getting waterlogged, and becoming too dry. Peonies get botrytis, a fungal infection, if plants are stressed by dampness and lack of air circulation. Clean up spent flowers and foliage promptly. Budded stems cut for bouquets store in the refrigerator for weeks in a plastic bag or in water.

ADDITIONAL SPECIES, CULTIVARS, OR VARIETIES

Peonies available for sale at local garden centers are likely to be suited to the Philadelphia area. Choose early-, mid-, and late-flowering types for a longer peony season. "Estate" labeled peonies have extra-large flowers.

 Did You Know?

Ants and big, fat peony buds seem to go together like ham and eggs. There is no need for alarm. In fact, the presence of ants is a sign that the peonies are in great health—so great that they are brimming with sweet juices. The ants are there for the sweet treat.

PERENNIALS

Phlox

Phlox paniculata

Other Names: Garden Phlox, Summer
  Phlox, Border Phlox

Light Requirements:

Mature Size: 3 to 4 feet tall; 2 feet wide

Bloom Time: July and August

Flower Color/Type: White, pink, rose, lilac-blue; florets in domed clusters

Features: Attracts butterflies; fragrance (some)

Color photograph on page 207.

A native wildflower that is at home along roadsides and streambeds, summer phlox has made the transition to residential yards and gardens without missing a beat. In its new, improved, hybrid incarnation it is slightly shorter with larger flowers. These domes of tightly clustered florets crown the straight stems for many summer weeks, and thanks to hybridizers, many colors are available. Some have contrasting colored "eyes," or centers; some even have maroon or variegated foliage. Protect them from deer; the butterflies will be grateful.

WHEN TO PLANT

Plant potted phlox from the garden center anytime during the growing season. Transplant clumps that have been split from larger plants in the spring or fall.

WHERE TO PLANT

Phlox require full sun, although blue- or lilac-flowered ones color best in light shade. Phlox are flexible about soil type as long as it is moist and well-drained. It can even be a bit on the alkaline side.

HOW TO PLANT

Dig and loosen the soil down 8 to 10 inches, and mix in granular slow-acting all-purpose fertilizer. Add organic material to improve the soil if it is clay, silty, or compacted. Make the planting hole about as deep as and slightly wider than the phlox rootball. Loosen any matted roots, then set it in the hole so that its top is level with the surrounding ground. Fill in the hole with soil, firm it gently, and water well. Set plants about 18 to 24 inches apart to provide good air circulation and allow them to spread gradually.

CARE AND MAINTENANCE

Phlox in a garden setting need some attention to look their best. A sprinkle of slow-acting fertilizer each spring will sustain them over the season.

Water them if rainfall is scarce, preferably at soil level so that foliage remains dry. A layer of organic mulch will help their soil stay moist. Stake phlox so that heavy flower heads do not flop in the rain, then cut off dead flowers promptly to promote rebloom and prevent seeding. Cut back stems entirely in the fall. Put them in the trash to minimize spread of mildew spores. Divide overlarge clumps every 4 or 5 years by digging them up and cutting off rooted chunks having 4 or 5 shoots. Replant them, liberally spaced.

ADDITIONAL INFORMATION

Garden phlox foliage has chronic and legendary problems with powdery mildew. It mars their appearance, but is not fatal. Seek out varieties reputed to be resistant. Site plants where there is good air circulation, and avoid overhead watering. Fungicide sprays will protect uninfected leaves if spraying is considered necessary. Phlox are delightfully fragrant, but short-lived, as cut flowers.

ADDITIONAL SPECIES, CULTIVARS, OR VARIETIES

Reputed to be mildew resistant are 'David' (fragrant, clear-white flowers on sturdy stems), 'Bright Eyes' (pink with red eyes), 'Eva Cullum' (pink), 'Franz Schubert' (lavender), and 'Sandra' (scarlet). 'Nora Leigh' grows to 3 feet with variegated, striped, gray-green-and-cream foliage with magenta flowers. 'Harlequin' has pinker flowers.

 Did You Know?

Phlox 'David' was discovered by F. M. Mooberry, former coordinator of horticulture at the Brandywine Conservancy and designer of the native plant garden at the Brandywine Museum in Chadds Ford. In her ongoing search for plants to be included in the garden she acquired some magenta-colored phlox from Thompson Palmer of Glen Mills. In 1987, after her volunteer corps planted the garden and the phlox had years to seed in, a lovely white one turned up among the many self-sown seedlings. Cuttings were taken, raised, and introduced by area nurseryman Dale Hendricks. When invited to name the new phlox, F. M. promptly pronounced it "David," her husband's name.

Pink, Cottage

Dianthus plumarius

Other Names: Grass Pink, Garden Pink

Mature Size: 10 to 12 inches tall;
  to 2 feet wide

Bloom Time: June

Flower Color/Type: White, red, pink, bicolored; single, double

Features: Evergreen foliage; fragrance; low water demand; old-fashioned;
  edible flowers

Color photograph on page 207.

Light Requirements:

Cottage pinks do well in the Philadelphia area, despite their reputation for sulking in hot, humid summers. Their soft mat of grassy, gray-green foliage softens rocky walls, stone pathways, rock gardens, and edges year-round. Then in early summer flower stems emerge and bear charming 1½-inch-wide blooms, more spritely than splashy, at their tips. Their trademark fringed petals and assorted colors and combinations are best appreciated close up. They are so modest that sometimes their arrival goes unnoticed until their spicy fragrance wafts across the yard. Long-lived, and drought resistant once established, pinks are garden stalwarts.

WHEN TO PLANT

Plant rooted clumps divided from larger plants in either spring or fall. Transplant potted plants from the garden center anytime during the growing season.

WHERE TO PLANT

Site pinks in full sun. They do fine in average soil that may be a bit alkaline. It must drain well to forestall stem rot. Plant in gravelly or sandy soil, raised beds, or containers to assure good drainage.

HOW TO PLANT

Prepare the soil by digging it down 8 to 10 inches, adding granular slow-acting all-purpose fertilizer and perhaps coarse sand to improve drainage. The planting hole should be about as deep as and slightly wider than the plant's rootball with the container removed. Set the pink in the hole so that its crown, where the roots meet the stems, is just slightly above soil level. Fill in the hole with soil, firm it gently over plant roots, and water well. Set plants about 2 feet apart to allow for their gradual spread.

CARE AND MAINTENANCE

Shear back the mat of foliage with scissors (or hedge clippers if the patch is large) after bloom to remove flower stems and rejuvenate foliage in the center, which tends to flatten. To neaten and control a large patch, lift the edges and trim a few inches off. Do not mulch pinks. Since they prefer lean soil, there is no need to fertilize once they are established. Every few years in the spring or fall divide large mats to improve air circulation and to acquire more plants. Dig down through the clump of foliage, and pry up and detach a section with its roots and soil attached.

ADDITIONAL INFORMATION

If soil is very acidic (the presence of moss is a clue), sprinkle lime in the fall in the area where pinks grow.

ADDITIONAL SPECIES, CULTIVARS, OR VARIETIES

'Kelsey' is sturdy with double, pink flowers and holds up to humidity. 'Spring Beauty' has double flowers in a variety of colors. Cheddar pinks (*Dianthus gratianopolitanus*) are good low-growing, petite, perennial pinks. 'Tiny Rubies' has deep-pink, double flowers and is 4 inches tall; it is ideal for rock gardens and edging. 'Bath's Pink' is 10 inches tall and especially tolerant of heat and humidity. Allwood Hybrids combine the best features of greenhouse carnations and cottage pinks. Flowers are showy in red, pink, white, yellow, cream, and bicolors. They are perennial, but short-lived. 'Alpinus' is good for rock gardens.

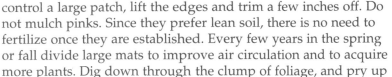

 Did You Know?

The common name "pinks" is not for their color. It is for the flower petals that have distinctively fringed or "pinked" tips as if they were trimmed by pinking shears. Most of the cousins in the Dianthus *family have this trademark petal. The color might have been named after the flower. The first known recorded use of the word "pink" to describe a color was in 1720. Prior to that, what we call pink was labeled blush, flesh, or carnation.*

Primrose

Primula × polyantha

Other Name: Polyantha Primrose
Mature Size: 6 to 12 inches tall;
  8 to 10 inches wide
Bloom Time: April into May
Flower Color/Type: Pastels and crayon colors with yellow centers
Features: Will grow in clay; edible flowers

Color photograph on page 207.

Light Requirements:

*In return for their welcome spring show of extraordinary colors, primroses demand specific garden conditions. Humidity is easy—that is plentiful in the Philadelphia area—but the constantly moist soil may be harder to provide. Our hot summers challenge them after their flowering is finished. It is worth the trouble to try primroses, however, and the polyantha types are a good place to begin. Their colorful, perky, 1-inch-wide blooms boast some of the brightest, richest colors in the floral world. They cluster at the ends of straight stems that rise above whorled clumps of paddle-shaped, often crinkly textured, yellow-green leaves. Group them at the edge of a bed of spring flowers, beside a pond, in the light shade of a spring woodland garden, or in decorative containers.

WHEN TO PLANT

Transplant plants from pots into the garden in the spring when they are available at the garden center. Plant rooted divisions from larger clumps after bloom is finished.

WHERE TO PLANT

An ideal primrose site gets little wind, some morning sun, and bright light or partial shade in the afternoon. Any soil (even clay) enriched with lots of organic matter to hold moisture will do. It can be toward neutral or even slightly alkaline.

HOW TO PLANT

Prepare the planting area thoroughly by digging in lots of organic material (avoid peat moss, which tends to increase soil acidity) into the top 12 inches of the soil to bolster its moisture retention. Add gravel or sand to improve drainage and granular slow-acting all-purpose fertilizer. Dig a planting hole large enough to accommodate its rootball, then set the plant in the hole so that its crown, where the roots meet the stems, is exactly at soil level. Fill in the hole with soil, and water well. Set plants about 6 to 8 inches apart.

CARE AND MAINTENANCE

Primroses need constant moisture, or buds may drop off before opening. Maintain rich soil by mulching primrose beds. A thin layer of organic mulch improves soil texture as it decomposes over time. In truly boggy areas, a gravel mulch will drain excess water away from plant crowns to prevent rot. Fertilize primroses each spring with a sprinkle of granular slow-acting fertilizer. To forestall fungal disease, remove dead leaves before new growth begins. Deadhead spent flowers to groom the plants and to prevent self-seeding. Divide plants when crowding causes their leaves to overlap. In the spring just after they bloom dig up clumps and tease rooted sections apart. Replant the sections promptly.

ADDITIONAL INFORMATION

Slugs may chew holes in primrose leaves. They hide under garden debris during the daytime. Bait a shallow plate or commercial slug trap with beer or yeast, and set it in the area, but not near primroses. Or sprinkle diatomaceous earth (DE) on the soil around primroses. The sharp particles cut slugs when they crawl over them.

ADDITIONAL SPECIES, CULTIVARS, OR VARIETIES

The 'Pacific Giants' strain of polyanthus primrose is widely available with flowers up to 2 inches wide in many colors, but the plants are not long-lived perennials. Look for the following: Siebold's primrose (*Primula sieboldii*) is reputed to be the easiest to grow; 'Mikado' has 10 to 15 rosy-purple flowers, each with white eyes, atop every 6-inch stem, and it goes dormant after bloom; and Japanese primroses (*Primula japonica*) hold their flowers candelabra style, tiered at points along a tall stem, and they especially love boggy areas in partial shade.

 Did You Know?

It is easy to confuse common names. Primrose is also the common name of certain plants in the Oenothera *genus. When in doubt, always check Latin botanical names.*

Purple Coneflower

Echinacea purpurea

Other Name: Purple Echinacea

Mature Size: 4 feet tall

Bloom Time: July to August

Flower Color/Type: Deep pink, white; daisy

Features: Low water demand; attracts butterflies and goldfinches

Light Requirements:

Color photograph on page 207.

*P*urple coneflower, a sturdy native of the midwestern United States, is a welcome addition to informal yards and gardens in the Philadelphia area. Essentially a wildflower that has been tamed, it is low maintenance and attractive as a substantial presence in the middle of the flower border, in meadow areas, or front and center as a specimen. Its jaunty, colorful purple, droopy-petaled midsummer daisies persist over many, many weeks when most other perennials are idle. Once established, it is very self-reliant, spreading slowly, cheerfully accommodating the vagaries of soil, light, and weather. Purple coneflower is truly a great plant for the support of wildlife. Like most daisy-flowered plants, it hosts all kinds of beneficial insects. It is notably heat and drought tolerant, has virtually no pest or disease problems, and lasts for years.

WHEN TO PLANT

Plant divisions from overlarge clumps of purple coneflower in either spring or fall. Transplant potted plants from the garden center anytime during the growing season.

WHERE TO PLANT

Purple coneflowers prefer full sun. They are not particular about soil type as long as it is reasonably well-drained. Average garden soil is preferable to rich soil, which makes their stems floppy.

HOW TO PLANT

Loosen and aerate the soil down about 12 inches. Dig a planting hole about as deep as and slightly wider than the plant's rootball when it is removed from its container. Loosen any roots matted by confinement in the pot. Then set the purple coneflower in the hole, positioned so that the top of its rootball is level with the surrounding ground. Fill in the hole with soil, firming it gently around plant stems, and water well. Spread a 2-inch layer of chopped leaves or other organic material as a mulch to keep soil moist and discourage weeds. Set plants about 2 feet apart to allow for their gradual spread.

CARE AND MAINTENANCE

Once established, purple coneflowers need very little attention. In a more formal garden setting they look best if they are staked. Deadhead the early blossoms to promote repeat bloom and to discourage weeds and self-seeding. As the season wanes, allow the last flush of blooms to remain and develop into their namesake bristly raised cones. Left to ripen on the plant, the seeds that form within the cones attract delighted finches. Harvested, they are useful for flower crafts. Divide purple coneflowers in either spring or fall if they exceed their allotted space. Otherwise, just let them continue to do their thing.

ADDITIONAL INFORMATION

The foliage of purple coneflowers may develop powdery mildew late in the season. It mars their appearance, but it does not seriously harm the plants. Thinning plants to improve air circulation will discourage this fungus.

ADDITIONAL SPECIES, CULTIVARS, OR VARIETIES

'Magnus', a deep-rose color, earned the Perennial Plant Association's Plant of the Year award for 1998. 'Crimson Star' is a truer red. Among the more recently developed white versions, 'Alba', 'White Swan', and 'White Lustre' are generally available at garden centers. White types are not as sturdy as the purplish-red ones.

 Did You Know?

Purple coneflower has attracted the attention of doctors as well as gardeners. Extracts from the roots and flowering tops of Echinacea *have become one of the best-selling herbal remedies in U.S. health food stores and drugstores. Reputed to stimulate the body's immune system to ward off colds and speed healing of infections, it is a common over-the-counter medicine in Germany and, increasingly, in the United States.*

Sedum 'Autumn Joy'

Sedum 'Autumn Joy'

Other Names: Autumn Joy Sedum, Showy Stonecrop

Light Requirements:

Mature Size: 2 feet tall; 2 feet wide

Bloom Time: August to October

Flower Color/Type: Greenish white to russet; flat cluster

Features: Winter interest; low water demand; attracts butterflies and larvae, bees, and beneficial insects

Color photograph on page 207.

Many gardeners regard 'Autumn Joy' as one of the 10 best perennials grown in the United States today. It is a tall sedum, or showy stonecrop, as distinguished from ground-hugging, ground cover sedums. Virtually foolproof to grow, it takes in stride all the misfortunes to which plants in the Philadelphia area are heir. Its succulent, light-green foliage stores moisture to withstand humid summer heat and drought without complaint. Its latesummer, flat flower heads of tightly clustered, tiny, star-shaped florets age from a pale greenish white "broccoli" stage to light pink to rich salmon-rose, then burgundy as the season progresses. Up to 6 inches across, they dry to a rusty maroon, persisting to spark the bleak winter landscape. Plant 'Autumn Joy' alone or with black-eyed Susans, mums, asters, and ornamental grasses.

WHEN TO PLANT

Plant chunks divided from a larger plant in the spring. Plant potted sedums from the garden center anytime during the season. Longer stems wilted from transplant shock retain that posture all season even when the sedum is watered. Stems are okay the following season.

WHERE TO PLANT

'Autumn Joy' prefers full sun, at least 5 hours daily. Even hot spots near walls and pavement, where reflected sun and heat are severe, are fine. Any type of soil will do, including clay, as long as it drains well. Average or lean soil assures that the stems do not flop.

HOW TO PLANT

Dig the soil down 8 to 10 inches, and mix in gravel or coarse sand to improve its drainage if necessary. Although established plants do not need feeding, a handful of a granular slow-acting all-purpose fertilizer mixed into the soil at this point will get transplants off to a good start. Dig a planting hole about as deep as and slightly wider than the sedum rootball, then set it in the hole so that its surface is level with the surrounding ground. Fill in the hole with soil, firm it gently, and water well. Set plants 1 to 2 feet apart.

CARE AND MAINTENANCE

There is no need to fertilize 'Autumn Joy'. It may be necessary to support flower stems at bloom time to prevent their splaying outward. Pinching stems back by half when they are about 8 inches tall (in June) makes a denser, more compact clump. Flowers will be more numerous, but later blooming. Cut back dried stems in the spring when the green nubs of new stems show at the base of the plant. Divide large sedums when their center buds get woody and flower stems are spindly and weak. In the spring dig up the clump, and cut off rooted chunks having 4 to 6 buds from its edges. Discard the woody center, and replant the pieces.

ADDITIONAL INFORMATION

Sedums do well in outdoor containers. As cut flowers 'Autumn Joy' stems may root in the water. Allow flowers to dry on the plant, or bring them indoors at their peak to air dry in an empty vase for use in floral crafts.

ADDITIONAL SPECIES, CULTIVARS, OR VARIETIES

Showy stonecrop (*Sedum spectabile*), one of the parents of 'Autumn Joy', has bluish green leaves. 'Brilliant' has raspberry-red flowers and blooms before 'Autumn Joy'. 'Album' has white ones. 'Variegatum' has yellow-and-green foliage and pink flowers. Others have purple leaves. 'Matrona' is the hottest new sedum among perennial gardeners.

 Did You Know?

Sedums such as 'Autumn Joy' host hoards of tiny beneficial insects that covet the nectar in the tiny flowers in their flower heads. Encouraged by the availability of this food, they stay in the area to prey on pest insects, the other part of their diet.

Shasta Daisy

Leucanthemum × superbum

Other Name: *Chrysanthemum superbum*
Mature Size: 1 to 3 feet tall; 2 feet wide
Bloom Time: June and July
Flower Color/Type: White; single, double,
   frilled; daisy
Features: Attracts butterflies and beneficial insects; evening garden

Light Requirements:

Color photograph on page 207.

*E*veryone loves daisies. In fact, they are often the first flower that children learn to recognize. They are called composite flowers because they are composed of many individual flowers, and they have two types of flowers. White ray flowers, or petals, ring clusters of tiny yellow disk flowers, the center of the daisy. These 2-inch blossoms grow singly at the tips of wiry stems above dull-green, coarse, toothed, narrow leaves. A classic, the shasta daisy is beloved for easygoing egalitarianism and generosity of bloom. Naturalize these flowers in informal meadow areas, or include them in a flower border or cutting garden.

WHEN TO PLANT

Plant shasta daisies in the spring, if possible, to enjoy the current season of flowers. Plants in pots from the garden center can be planted anytime during the growing season.

WHERE TO PLANT

Most shasta daisies love full sun; however, double-flowering ones appreciate some shade. Any good garden soil that is moist, but well-drained, is fine.

HOW TO PLANT

Prepare the soil by digging down at least 12 inches, simultaneously incorporating granular slow-acting fertilizer and organic material such as compost into it. Dig the planting hole deep enough to accommodate the plant rootball when it is removed from the pot. Loosen any matted roots, then set the rootball in the hole so that it is level with the surrounding soil. Fill in the hole with soil, firm it gently, and water well. Plant daisies in groups of 3 for best effect, spacing them about 2 feet apart to allow for spreading.

CARE AND MAINTENANCE

A year-round, 2- or 3-inch layer of organic mulch keeps soil moist, weeds down, and winter soil temperatures even. Water shasta daisies in the absence of rain because they are somewhat shallow rooted. Sprinkle slow-acting fertilizer on their soil every spring before flowering. Pinch back their emerging flower stems to force them to branch and to make plants more compact. Taller stems may need support to prevent flopping in rainstorms and wind. Cut back the stems after flowering to generate renewed foliage at their base, which will continue to look good. They may even rebloom sporadically over the summer. Shastas spread and are short-lived if not divided every 2 or 3 years. Dig up the main plant, and separate rooted pieces from the edges of the large rootball. If the center seems woody, throw it away. Replant the smaller chunks.

ADDITIONAL INFORMATION

Shasta daisies are the right height for the middle of the flower border. They are particularly useful with foliage plants and those with hot-colored flowers. Lower plants in front will screen their ragged lower stems. The dwarf shastas do well as edging and in containers. Shasta daisies make good cut flowers, but do not dry well.

ADDITIONAL SPECIES, CULTIVARS, OR VARIETIES

'Alaska' and 'Polaris' have very large single flowers. 'Snow Lady' is a 1988 All-America Selection winner. 'White Knight Hybrid' has 4-inch-wide flowers on sturdy 20-inch stems; the W. Atlee Burpee Seed Company headquartered in Bucks County bred it. 'Thomas Killen' has thick stems for cutting. 'Aglaya' has frilled double flowers. 'Becky' has very strong stems and blooms later.

Did You Know?

Daisies were prominent in the floral lexicon of Victorian times, communicating Secret Love and coy courtship. We still acknowledge their power to convey sentiment when we stop to pull petals from a daisy in rhythm to "he loves me; he loves me not." A white daisy has always signified innocence, perhaps because of its traditional association with newborns. A double-flowered one signifies Participation. Think about the implications when tempted to give a bouquet of shasta daisies to someone!

Veronica

Veronica spicata

Other Name: Spike Speedwell
Mature Size: 1½ to 3 feet tall;
　1½ to 2 feet wide
Bloom Time: June and July
Flower Color/Type: Blue, pink, white; spikes
Features: Attracts butterflies

Color photograph on page 207.

Light Requirements:

This plant is a garden standby if ever there was one. Respected for their self-reliance and long bloom period, veronicas are attractive, versatile, and adaptable. First, there are the narrow, rich-green, sometimes grayish green, leaves. Then for 4 to 8 weeks, there are the slim, unassuming flower spikes loaded with tiny florets of shades of blue or pink. They just keep coming, punctuating the flower border or rock garden with low- or medium-height, colorful, vertical interest. Pinching off the spent ones encourages more and more. Because they have no pests or diseases, veronicas can be depended upon to carry on without any fuss.

WHEN TO PLANT

Plant rooted divisions from larger clumps of veronicas in either spring or fall. Transplant potted plants from the garden center anytime during the growing season.

WHERE TO PLANT

Veronicas like full sun best. They will take some shade, but their stems may flop. Easygoing, they accept any type of average garden soil as long as it is well-drained, especially in the winter.

HOW TO PLANT

Loosen the soil down 8 inches, and mix in a little granular slow-acting fertilizer. Add organic matter to improve soil drainage if necessary. Dig a planting hole about as deep as and slightly wider than the plant rootball when removed from the pot. Loosen any matted roots. Be sure the top of the rootball is level with the surrounding soil when it is set in the hole. Fill in the hole with soil, firm it gently around plant stems, and water well. Set veronicas about 1 to 2 feet apart to allow for their gradual spread.

CARE AND MAINTENANCE

Spread a 2- or 3-inch layer of mulch over the soil around newly planted veronicas to discourage weeds and maintain soil moisture. Water them well if rain is sparse while they are getting established. After they bloom, cut off spent flower spikes to stimulate plants to produce more. Young plants may bloom all summer with faithful deadheading. Shear low-growing, or prostrate, veronicas down to their foliage at the soil after their second flush of bloom. Cut the stems of taller veronicas back by about 6 inches in June so that plants become more compact. Bloom time is delayed a bit, but plants may not need staking. Divide veronicas that have outgrown their allotted space after 3 or 4 years in the spring or fall by digging up the rootball and cutting or pulling apart rooted chunks for replanting elsewhere.

ADDITIONAL INFORMATION

Veronicas make good cut flowers. Dry them for floral crafts when flower spikes are half bloom and half buds. Air dry, or use sand or silica methods. Sometimes veronica foliage develops a coating of mildew during wet weather. Cut back any blackened stems, and wait for dry weather.

ADDITIONAL SPECIES, CULTIVARS, OR VARIETIES

'Blue Fox', 'Blue Peter', and 'Blue Spires' have flowers in various shades of blue. 'Red Fox' has long-blooming, rosy-pink flowers. 'Icicle' has white flowers. Hybrids of different veronica parents have produced the following: 'Sunny Border Blue' was the 1993 Perennial Plant Association Plant of the Year, and it boasts long-blooming, deep-blue-violet flowers; and 'Goodness Grows' is low growing with violet-blue flowers until November.

 Did You Know?

The second part of a plant's botanical two-word name (binomial) is descriptive. It usually reveals an important fact about the plant. Sometimes it is a person's name, such as douglasii, *which indicates that the plant was discovered by someone named Douglas. Often the second word describes a prominent physical trait of the plant. For instance,* macrophylla *means "large leafed." Several plants have* spicata *in their names; it refers to the fact that their flowers grow as spikes.*

195

Yarrow

Achillea species and hybrids

Other Name: Milfoil

Mature Size: 1 to 4 feet tall;
up to 3 feet wide

Bloom Time: June through August

Flower Color/Type: Yellow, gold, white, red, pink, rust, salmon;
flat floret cluster

Features: Attracts butterflies and beneficial insects; low water demand;
deer resistant

Light Requirements:

Color photograph on page 207.

*I*n all its forms yarrow is easy to take for granted. Because it is so easy to grow and has attractive green or grayish green, aromatic foliage that blends well with so many other plants, nearly everyone seems to include its excellent hybrids in the flower border. Whereas common yarrow, found naturally along roadsides and in fields, is best suited for areas that are more informal and meadowlike, the new hybrids have neater, more compact shapes and more interesting flower colors. They bloom almost all season long if their spent blossoms are cut off. In between flushes of bloom their foliage adds texture and variety to the garden. Best of all, deer ignore them.

WHEN TO PLANT

Plant small yarrow plants divided from larger clumps in either spring or fall. Plants purchased in pots from the garden center can go in the garden anytime during the growing season.

WHERE TO PLANT

Plant yarrow in full sun. It is not particular about soil as long as it drains well. Average garden soil is fine; even thin, poor soil is tolerable.

HOW TO PLANT

Loosen the soil down 8 to 10 inches, and add coarse sand or gravel to improve drainage if necessary. Make the planting hole about as deep as and slightly wider than the yarrow's rootball when removed from its pot. Loosen any matted roots, then set it in the hole so that its top is level with the surrounding ground. Fill the hole with soil, firm it gently, and water well. Yarrow looks good in groups of 3 plants, set 1 foot apart.

CARE AND MAINTENANCE

Water yarrow until it is established. Then it rarely needs watering unless there is a particularly severe drought. The plants that get more water tend to bloom more prolifically, especially if they are deadheaded faithfully. Tall types need staking if they are in some shade or are overfertilized, which make their stems limp. Cut off the first flush of flowers when they fade to encourage repeat bloom and to control self-sowing and stem height. In the fall, cut all stems to the soil. Clumps of foliage will remain. Expect to divide rapidly spreading common yarrow every year or two.

ADDITIONAL INFORMATION

Yarrow is basically pest free but may develop mildew on its foliage if it is overcrowded or the summer is particularly damp and humid. Thin out plants, and remove affected stems, then place them in the trash. Be sure soil drains well. Cut yarrow for fresh and dried arrangements. Air-dried flowers hold their color and are wonderful for flower crafts. Cut blooms when they are newly, but fully opened, before pollen development.

ADDITIONAL SPECIES, CULTIVARS, OR VARIETIES

Common yarrow (*Achillea millefolium*) is a spreader with off-white flowers atop tall stems that tend to flop. 'Cerise Queen' has reddish pink flowers. 'Paprika' is salmony. Galaxy Hybrid yarrows offer great colors. 'Summer Pastel' is a 1990 All-America Selection winner; its flowers are mixed colors. Fernleaf yarrow (*Achillea filipendulina*) has flowers in shades of yellow, which are favorites for drying. An excellent hybrid is 'Coronation Gold'. Another is 'Anthea' with pale-yellow flowers, deeply cut gray leaves, and a compact 24-inch height. Woolly yarrow (*Achillea tomentosa*) is only 6 inches tall, good for a rock garden situation.

 Did You Know?

Achillea is a healing herb. Its foliage has antiseptic and astringent qualities. It is named after the Greek hero Achilles, who used it to staunch the wounds of his soldiers at the siege of Troy. It has since acquired common names such as soldier's woundwort, carpenter's weed, and nosebleed for its medicinal properties. It is still used in modern-day homeopathic practice.

Yucca

Yucca filamentosa

Other Names: Adam's Needle,
Spanish Bayonet

Light Requirements:

☀

Mature Size: 3 to 5 feet

Bloom Time: June to August

Flower Color/Type: Cream; nodding bells

Features: Evergreen foliage; attracts hummingbirds and moths; fragrance;
evening garden; edible flowers; low water demand; barrier plant

Color photograph on page 207.

Yuccas are an acquired taste. For some people, they are exciting specimens; for others, they are visitors from an alien climate. With their sharp-tipped, stiff, swordlike leaves and no-nonsense flower spikes, they have a coarse toughness that suggests desert survival. The thin, wispy threads that split from the edges of their leaves hardly soften their profile. Yet yuccas are perfectly at home in our region, contributing a strong sculptural element to the landscape and holding soil on slopes with their thick roots. Their sturdy rosettes of gray-green or green, 1-inch-wide leaves are attractive. The bonus is the flower stalk that resembles a giant 8- to 10-foot-tall asparagus prior to flowering. Yucca takes on a whole new personality when it bears its waxy, creamy, fragrant bells that nod demurely in the sun and then tilt upward when night falls to await visits by moths. Use yuccas as accents in mixed borders or as specimens or focal points. They are on prominent display at the Theater Garden at Longwood Gardens.

WHEN TO PLANT

Plant rooted offshoots from the base of older established plants in the spring. Transplant containerized nursery stock anytime during the growing season. Wear protective clothing and glasses to avoid injury from sharp foliage.

WHERE TO PLANT

Yuccas love full sun, but they will take some shade. Any type of decent soil, even sandy or clay is fine, as long as it is well-drained year-round. They do well on slopes or flat ground.

HOW TO PLANT

Loosen the soil down 8 to 10 inches, and mix in gravel or coarse sand to improve its drainage if necessary. Although established plants do not need any special feeding, a handful of a granular slow-acting all-purpose fertilizer mixed into the soil at this point will give new transplants a boost in their first season. Dig a planting hole about as deep as and slightly wider than the yucca rootball when removed from its container. Set it in the hole so that its top is level with, or just slightly above, the surrounding ground. Fill in the hole with soil, firm it gently, then water well. Set plants about 2 to 3 feet apart.

CARE AND MAINTENANCE

Yuccas take 2 or 3 seasons to settle in and start blooming. During this time water them during dry periods. Once established, they are extremely drought resistant. Sprinkle slow-acting fertilizer on the soil the first spring or two. Cut back flower stalks after flowers have faded to groom the plant. Divide overlarge clumps of yucca into new plants in the spring by removing the rooted offsets they develop at the edges of the clump and replanting them. Established yuccas are too tough to try to dig up.

ADDITIONAL INFORMATION

Each crown, or rosette, of yucca leaves produces 1 flower stalk. As new offshoot crowns form and clumps expand, the number of stalks increases, creating a stunning stand of flowers.

ADDITIONAL SPECIES, CULTIVARS, OR VARIETIES

'Golden Sword' has variegated yellow leaves with green edges; 'Bright Edge' foliage is the reverse. Soapweed (*Yucca glauca*) is less coarse, its leaves narrower and flower stems shorter. Its foliage is green with white edges and wispy threads along their sides. Its flowers are greenish white.

 Did You Know?

Butterflies seem to get all the attention. Moths deserve some attention, too. Because most are nocturnal, their beauty and contribution to plant pollination are overlooked. Moths are easily distinguished from butterflies by their plumper, furrier bodies and feathery antennae. When at rest, their wings lie flat or folded like roofs over their backs. Their attraction to light is legendary and explains why they visit pale and white nighttime flowers such as yucca for nectar.

The towering trees that sheltered the Lenni Lenape for thousands of years greeted William Penn when he arrived to survey the 45,000 square miles of forested land granted to him by King Charles II as payment for a debt he owed Penn's father. The great forest inspired William Penn to call his colony Pennsylvania, or Penn's Woods. As fundamental to his vision of this colony as a place of religious freedom was Penn's desire to have it be a "greene countrie towne" where trees continued to dominate the landscape.

Alyssum
Lobularia maritima

Begonia, Wax
Begonia semperflorens-cultorum hybrids

Coleus
Coleus × hybridus;
Solenostemon scutellarioides

Corn Poppy
Papaver rhoeas

Cosmos
Cosmos bipinnatus

Four O'Clock
Mirabilis jalapa

Geranium
Pelargonium × hortorum

Impatiens
Impatiens wallerana

Larkspur
Consolida ambigua

Marigold
Tagetes species and hybrids

Nasturtium
Tropaeolum majus

Nicotiana
Nicotiana species and hybrids

Pansy
Viola × wittrockiana

Petunia
Petunia × hybrida

Portulaca
Portulaca grandiflora

Red Salvia
Salvia splendens

Snapdragon
Antirrhinum majus

Spider Flower
Cleome hasslerana

Sunflower
Helianthus annum

Zinnia
Zinnia elegans

Begonia, Tuberous
Begonia × tuberhybrida

Canna
Canna × generalis

Crocus
Crocus vernus

Daffodil
Narcissus species and hybrids

Dahlia
Dahlia species and hybrids

Gladiolus
Gladiolus × hortulanus

Iris, Bearded
Iris germanica hybrids

Lily
Lilium species and hybrids

Onion, Ornamental
Allium 'Purple Sensation'

Tulip
Tulipa gesneriana

Blue Fescue
Festuca glauca

Fountaingrass, Red
Pennisetum setaceum 'Rubrum'

Hakonechloa
Hakonechloa macra 'Aureola'

Maiden Grass
Miscanthus sinensis

Switch Grass
Panicum virgatum

Ajuga
Ajuga reptans

Barrenwort
Epimedium species and hybrids

Bellflower
Campanula poscharskyana

Creeping Juniper
Juniperus horizontalis

Creeping Phlox
Phlox stolonifera

Deadnettle
Lamium maculatum

English Ivy
Hedera helix

Flower Carpet® Pink Rose
Rosa 'Noatraum'

Foamflower
Tiarella wherryi

Ginger
Asarum europaeum

Japanese Painted Fern
Athyrium nipponicum 'Pictum'

Lamb's Ears
Stachys byzantina

Lily-of-the-Valley
Convallaria majalis

Lilyturf
Liriope spicata

Moneywort
Lysimachia nummularia 'Aurea'

Ostrich Fern
Matteuccia struthiopteris

Pachysandra
Pachysandra terminalis

Sweet Woodruff
Galium odoratum

Vinca
Vinca minor

Wintercreeper
Euonymus fortunei

Artemisia
Artemisia species and hybrids

Aster, Native
Aster novi-belgii; Aster novae-angliae

Astilbe
Astilbe × arendsii

Baby's Breath
Gypsophila paniculata

Bee Balm
Monarda didyma

Black-Eyed Susan
Rudbeckia fulgida var. *sullivantii* 'Goldsturm'

Blazing Star
Liatris spicata

Bleeding Heart
Dicentra spectabilis

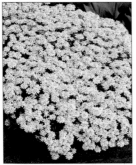

Candytuft
Iberis sempervirens

Chrysanthemum, Garden
Dendranthema × *morifolium*

Columbine
Aquilegia hybrids

Coralbells
Heuchera species and hybrids

Coreopsis
Coreopsis grandiflora

Daylily
Hemerocallis hybrids

Geranium, Hardy
Geranium species and hybrids

Goldenrod
Solidago species and hybrids

Hosta
Hosta species and hybrids

Lenten Rose
Helleborus hybridus

Peony
Paeonia hybrids

Phlox
Phlox paniculata

Pink, Cottage
Dianthus plumarius

Primrose
Primula × polyantha

Purple Coneflower
Echinacea purpurea

Sedum 'Autumn Joy'
Sedum 'Autumn Joy'

Shasta Daisy
Leucanthemum × superbum

Veronica
Veronica spicata

Yarrow
Achillea species and hybrids

Yucca
Yucca filamentosa

American Arborvitae
Thuja occidentalis

Azalea, Evergreen
Rhododendron species and hybrids

Barberry, Japanese
Berberis thunbergii 'Atropurpurea'

Beautyberry
Callicarpa dichotoma

Boxwood
Buxus hybrids

Butterfly Bush
Buddleia davidii

Cherrylaurel, Dwarf
Prunus laurocerasus 'Otto Luyken'

Cotoneaster, Willowleaf
Cotoneaster salicifolious

Crapemyrtle
Lagerstroemia indica

Daphne, 'Carol Mackie'
Daphne × *burkwoodii* 'Carol Mackie'

Firethorn
Pyracantha coccinea

Forsythia
Forsythia × *intermedia*

Fothergilla
Fothergilla gardenii

Hybrid Tea Rose
Rosa × hybrida

Hydrangea, Oakleaf
Hydrangea quercifolia

Juniper, Pfitzer
Juniperus chinensis 'Pfitzeriana'

Landscape Rose
Rosa species and hybrids

Lilac, Common
Syringa vulgaris hybrids

Mahonia
Mahonia aquifolium

Mockorange
Philadelphus coronarius

Mountain Laurel
Kalmia latifolia

Mugo Pine, Dwarf
Pinus mugo compact selections

Nandina
Nandina domestica

Pieris, Japanese
Pieris species and hybrids

Privet, Common
Ligustrum vulgare

Rhododendron
Rhododendron species and hybrids

Rose of Sharon
Hibiscus syriacus

Shadblow
Amelanchier species and hybrids

Smokebush
Cotinus coggygria

Spirea, Vanhoutte
Spiraea × vanhouttei

Summersweet
Clethra alnifolia

Viburnum, Doublefile
Viburnum plicatum tomentosum

Virginia Sweetspire
Itea virginica

Weigela
Weigela florida

Winged Euonymus
Euonymus alatus

Winterberry Holly
Ilex verticillata

Witchhazel
Hamamelis mollis

Yew
Taxus × media

Atlas Cedar, Blue
Cedrus atlantica 'Glauca'

Bald Cypress
Taxodium distichum

Beech, European
Fagus sylvatica

Birch, River
Betula nigra 'Heritage'

Catalpa, Northern
Catalpa speciosa

Cherry, Ornamental
Prunus species and hybrids

Crabapple, Flowering
Malus species and hybrids

Dogwood, Flowering
Cornus florida

Falsecypress, Hinoki
Chamaecyparis obtusa 'Nana Gracilis'

Fringe Tree
Chionanthus virginicus

Ginkgo
Ginkgo biloba

Goldenrain Tree
Koelreuteria paniculata

Hawthorn, Green
Crataegus viridis 'Winter King'

Holly, American
Ilex opaca

Honeylocust, Thornless
Gleditsia tricanthos 'Inermis'

Linden, Littleleaf
Tilia cordata

Magnolia, Saucer
Magnolia × soulangiana

Maple, Japanese
Acer palmatum

Maple, Red
Acer rubrum

Oak
Quercus species

Pear, Ornamental
Pyrus calleryana

Pine, Eastern White
Pinus strobus

Redbud, Eastern
Cercis canadensis

Sourwood
Oxydendrum arboreum

Spruce, Colorado Blue
Picea pungens 'Glauca'

Sweetgum
Liquidambar styraciflua

Sycamore, American
Platanus occidentalis

Tuliptree
Liriodendron tulipifera

Willow, Weeping
Salix species

Zelkova, Japanese
Zelkova serrata

Boston Ivy
Parthenocissus tricuspidata

Clematis
Clematis hybrids

Climbing Hydrangea
Hydrangea anomala var. *petiolaris*

Hardy Kiwi
Actinidia kolomikta

Hyacinth Bean
Dolichos lablab (Lablab purpureus)

Moonflower
Ipomea alba

Rose, Climbing
Rosa × hybrida

Scarlet Honeysuckle
Lonicera sempervirens

Wisteria
Wisteria species and hybrids

Anacharis
Egeria densa

Cattail
Typha angustifolia

Lotus
Nelumbo nucifera

Papyrus
Cyperus isocladus

Parrot's Feather
Myriophyllum aquaticum

Pickerel Rush
Pontederia cordata

Taro
Colocasia esculenta

Water Hyacinth
Eichhornia crassipes

Water Lily
Nymphaea species

Yellow Flag
Iris pseudacorus

USDA PLANT
HARDINESS MAP

*Greater Philadelphia
Counties*

Bucks

Montgomery

Philadelphia

Chester

Delaware

ZONE | 6B
ZONE | 7A

The Philadelphia area is home to some of the most beautiful gardens in the world.

Philadelphia Area Gardens

PENNSYLVANIA

DELAWARE

CHESTER

NEW JERSEY

PHILADELPHIA

Winterthur Museum Garden and Library

Longwood Gardens

Hagley Museum and Library

Rockwood Museum

Brandywine Conservancy/ Brandywine River Museum

Tyler Arboretum

Jenkins Arboretum

Welkinweir

Chanticleer

Scott Arboretum of Swarthmore College

Arboretum Villanova

The Grange Estate

The American College Arboretum

Historic Bartram's Garden

The Japanese House and Garden (Shofuso, the Pine Breeze Villa)

Wyck

Awbury Arboretum

Morris Arboretum of the Univ. of Penn.

The Mansion Highlands of Gardens

The Henry Schmieder Arboretum of Delaware Valley College

Historic Fallsington

Bowman's Hill Wildflower Preserve

Medford Leas The Lewis W. Barton Arboretum and Nature Preserve

PENNSYLVANIA TURNPIKE

SCHUYLKILL RIVER

GERMANTOWN PIKE

DELAWARE RIVER

NEW JERSEY TURNPIKE

N

Map courtesy of The Gardens Collaborative

© JOANNE D'HOLBY 1998

Those of us who already garden or are starting to garden here in the Philadelphia area are heirs to this rich horticultural tradition. Rather than be intimidated by it, be inspired by it. Almost nowhere else in this country are conditions so favorable and information so available. While gardening here is a healthy pastime, a source of creative expression and personal pleasure, it is simultaneously a contribution you can make to the preservation of the legacy of the "greene countrie towne."

Shrubs

S HRUBS ARE THE GLUE that holds a home landscape together, giving it coherence. Builders put them next to new homes even before there is a lawn to announce that "this is a livable place." From the beginning we take shrubs for granted, often to the point that we do not notice that the original low foundation shrubs now cover the second-floor windows!

SHRUBS IN THE LANDSCAPE

Of course, in addition to their design role as a landscape's vegetation infrastructure, shrubs play a decorative role. As the understory layer in the landscape—the transition between the taller trees and the low-growing ground cover plants—they provide variety with their different heights, shapes, and textures. Collectively, shrubs offer flower color, fragrance, cones or berries, wonderful bark, needled or broadleaf foliage, and bare stems and branching silhouettes against sheltering walls or the open winter sky. As ornamental as any herbaceous perennial, flowering shrubs extend these smaller plants' scale, magnifying their impact with their *gravitas*. Shrub foliage also provides a rich, textural backdrop to showcase perennial and annual flowering plants.

Shrubs of all kinds are extremely versatile. In the ground or in containers they decorate doorways, pools and patios, property lines, and flower beds. They are also functional, solving a landscape's problems as they contribute to its beauty. Use them to obscure unsightly utilities, to hold soil on stream banks or on slopes, or to form a screen to assure privacy and quiet, and block wind and sun. As hedges, especially thorny ones that discourage trespassers, they control foot traffic. A grove of mulched shrubs reduces lawn size considerably.

SHRUB TRENDS

Renewed interest in shrubs is reflected in the recent increasing availability of a wider variety of them and the numerous shrub trends that are evident lately. The concept of foundation shrubs is falling by the wayside. Contemporary homes are less likely to have visible ugly cement foundations, so there is no need to automatically plant shrubs next to the house. Dwarf shrubs, especially conifers, are very popular because they are a more appropriate scale for the typical smaller home landscape. Shrubs with purple, gold, and blue foliage are perceived as more interesting and useful. Native

Chapter Six

shrubs are gaining long overdue respect for their beauty, adaptability, and low maintenance. Finally, as the relentless exurban sprawl in Chester and Bucks Counties reduces wildlife habitat even more, shrubs are increasingly valued as key elements in creating a backyard habitat that supports songbirds, honeybees, beneficial insects, and other creatures. Because deer are not usually invited, shrubs that they ignore are becoming popular.

BUYING SHRUBS

Shrubs are commercially available in three ways. Mail-order plants and many hybrid tea roses usually come with their roots bare of soil and wrapped in damp moss, sawdust, or the like. They tend to be dormant and quite small, and they should be planted as soon as possible. Since larger shrubs, or ones that are to be moved to a new site in the yard, are recently dug from the soil where they grew, their ball of roots and soil are wrapped in burlap or similar material to hold them together. Shrubs raised in containers are most prevalent in garden centers. Planting them is easiest on both home owner and plant because they are manageable and their roots are well developed and minimally disturbed in the process.

PLANTING PRACTICES

Current shrub-planting practices deviate from tradition—a result of new knowledge and technology relating to shrub production. Planting holes with sloping sides encourage shrub roots to grow outward rather than sulk in a straight-sided "container" hole. Because the fill soil is not specially amended, roots are forced to adjust quickly to the local soil. Since burlap these days may, in fact, be synthetic and not biodegradable, cutting it all away is advisable. Delayed fertilizing prevents stimulation of more top growth on the shrub than roots struggling to establish can support. Sprinkling granular fertilizer on the soil surface provides more uniform distribution of nutrients than do root-feeding techniques. Also, slow-acting fertilizer offers more consistent nutrition over an extended period, minimizing plant stress and home-owner effort. Finally, a layer of mulch over the root zones of newly planted shrubs discourages weeds and grass, which compete for moisture and nutrients and give lawn mowers and weed trimmers an excuse to get too close.

American Arborvitae

Thuja occidentalis

Other Names: Eastern Arborvitae,
 Northern Whitecedar
Type: Evergreen, conifer
Mature Size: Dwarf to 4 feet tall, others 20 to
 60 feet tall; variable widths
Foliage: Green, yellow-green; flattened sprays
Features: Colorful foliage; cones for wildlife

Light Requirements:

Color photograph on page 207.

Arborvitae are relatively slow-growing evergreens, valued for their
dense foliage, which grows down to the ground, and their adaptability
to heat, cold, and air pollution. Their versatility and variety of handsome
forms make them very useful in residential landscapes. Unfortunately, these
Eastern natives also top the list of deer favorites. Soft and scalelike, rather than
sharp-needled, arborvitae leaves are arranged on the branches in flattened,
parallel sprays. These shrubs bear male and female flowers (cones) in the
spring, which turn brown by late summer. Use arborvitae as specimens, as
foundation shrubs, and in rows as windbreaks, screens, and hedges. They
provide wonderful background for more colorful plants.

WHEN TO PLANT

Plant arborvitae with roots and soil wrapped in burlap in either spring or
fall. Plant those grown in containers anytime during the growing season,
except the hottest and driest part of the summer. Buy plants that were
grown from seed or cuttings of plants from our region.

WHERE TO PLANT

Arborvitae, especially the yellow-foliaged ones, do best in full sun but
accept some shade. Too much shade makes their branching looser and more
open. They prefer soils that are moist, rich in organic matter, slightly acid,
and well-drained. They can cope with wet or dry soil if they must. If the
site is exposed to winter sun and wind, shrubs may need a temporary
screen of burlap or garden fleece. Do not plant them under roof lines where
sliding snow may cause branches to break off.

HOW TO PLANT

Arborvitae root easily and grow quickly. If the soil is poor, loosen it over a
wide area, and dig in organic material such as peat moss or chopped leaves.
Then in the center of the prepared area dig a planting hole with sloping

sides as deep as the rootball is high and about twice as wide. Remove the arborvitae from its container, and untangle or clip any circling roots. Set the plant in the hole so that the top of its rootball is exactly level with the surrounding soil. If the rootball is wrapped in burlap, cut as much of it away as possible. Then fill in the hole with soil, firming it gently, and water well.

CARE AND MAINTENANCE

Narrow, columnar arborvitae may need temporary staking over their first winter. Maintain a year-round layer of organic mulch over their root zone. Water them regularly if rainfall is unreliable the first year and during the hot, dry periods every summer. In the spring sprinkle slow-acting granular fertilizer formulated for conifers on the mulch for the rain to soak in. After a few years, annual fertilization will not be necessary. Prune out dead or broken branches promptly. Correctly sited shrubs do not need pruning to control their size. Shear only to form a hedge. Never cut back to bare wood on branches because new growth and foliage may not regenerate there.

ADDITIONAL INFORMATION

Smaller arborvitae do well in containers that are at least 2 feet deep. Arborvitae that are stressed will develop mite problems. Spray mites with forceful water from a hose several times over a week.

ADDITIONAL SPECIES, CULTIVARS, OR VARIETIES

Although some arborvitae are virtually trees, there are many good shrubby choices. 'Emerald Green' has good color all winter. 'Green Giant' won the Pennsylvania Horticultural Society's Gold Medal Award in 1998. 'Hetz's Midget' is dwarf. 'Aurea' and others have yellow foliage.

 Did You Know?

*Bagworm caterpillars build spindle-shaped bags, or cocoons, that dangle from conifer branch tips. They protect overwintering eggs laid by a moth in the fall, then shelter young caterpillars that emerge periodically to feed on shrub foliage. Pick off all the bags within reach. Spray foliage of large shrubs with Bt (*Bacillus thuringiensis*) while the caterpillars are feeding so they will ingest it, sicken, and die.*

Azalea, Evergreen

Rhododendron species and hybrids

Type: Broadleaf evergreen
Mature Size: 3 to 8 feet tall;
   4 to 10 feet wide
Bloom Time: Early May
Flower Color/Type: Shades of red and pink, white; funnels
Features: Flowers; attracts butterflies and hummingbirds

Color photograph on page 208.

Light Requirements:

The first weekend in May, the Philadelphia area is abloom with azaleas. Suddenly, nondescript, little green shrubs come alive with color and the wildlife they attract. From the Azalea Garden behind the Philadelphia Art Museum to the Jenkins Arboretum in Devon and in practically every yard in between, azaleas rule for 2 or 3 wonderful weeks. Among the standouts are the Asian azaleas and the hybrids bred from them. Compact and bushy, they bear a profusion of flowers, sometimes double and semidouble, along their stems among rich, green, lustrous foliage. In the fall they take a curtain call as their evergreen leaves turn reddish or bronze with the approach of winter. Use them as specimens, as focal points, as anchors for a mixed border, as hedges, and in woodland settings.

WHEN TO PLANT

Plant burlap-wrapped azaleas in either early spring or fall. Transplant those raised in containers anytime during the growing season, but spring is best.

WHERE TO PLANT

Most azaleas prefer sunny sites, but they also enjoy some afternoon shade in the summer. Dappled light in woodland settings is ideal as long as they are not under shallow-rooted trees such as elms and maples, which compete with them for moisture. Azaleas like moist, woodsy soil that is acidic and rich in organic matter. Choose a site that offers shelter from harsh winter wind and sun.

HOW TO PLANT

If the soil is primarily clay, mix organic material such as compost or peat moss into it, or build a raised bed above it to improve drainage. Dig a saucer-shaped planting hole as deep as the rootball is high and about twice as wide. Remove the azalea from its container, and untangle or clip any circling roots. Set the rootball in the hole so that the top of its rootball is exactly level with the surrounding soil. If the rootball is wrapped in burlap, cut as much of it away as possible. Then fill in the hole with soil, firming it gently, and water well.

CARE AND MAINTENANCE

Mulch azalea root zones year-round with 2 or 3 inches of organic material such as chopped leaves to keep the soil moist. If rainfall is unreliable, water the shrub regularly until it is well established. In the spring, sprinkle slow-acting granular fertilizer formulated for acid-loving plants on the mulch for the rain to soak in. Renew old shrubs by cutting back dead or tired branches to within 6 inches of the ground to stimulate new, dense growth.

ADDITIONAL INFORMATION

Lacebugs attack azaleas that are stressed by too much reflected sun or dry, compacted soil; they cause pale stippling on foliage. Deer and rabbits also have a taste for azaleas.

ADDITIONAL SPECIES, CULTIVARS, OR VARIETIES

Azaleas are often listed as groups of hybrids developed by a particular person. An example is Polly Hill Hybrids. Tough and low-growing, they make excellent ground covers, blooming a month after the common ones. Deciduous azaleas are often fragrant, and they offer a range of colors (including orange and yellow) and bloom times. Native ones do not get mildew on the foliage in summer. Pinxterbloom (*R. periclymenoides*) is native and blooms in May. Florida azalea (*R. austrinum*) is yellow and orange. Plumleaf azalea (*R. prunifolia*) blooms orange-red in July/August.

 Did You Know?

Azaleas are technically rhododendrons. Botanists distinguish between them because azaleas have only five stamens in the center of their flowers, while rhododendrons have ten or more. With some exceptions, azaleas are also smaller shrubs with smaller leaves, flowers, and flower clusters. Their leaves have hairy surfaces, whereas rhododendron leaf surfaces are smooth. Both azaleas and rhododendrons share similar soil and care preferences, although azaleas can take more heat and drier, even dry shade, conditions.

Barberry, Japanese

Berberis thunbergii 'Atropurpurea'

Other Name: Red Barberry
Type: Deciduous
Mature Size: 2 to 5 feet tall; 2 to 5 feet wide
Bloom Time: Spring
Foliage: Maroon, mottled pink, or yellow
Features: Fall foliage color; berries; thorns; deer resistant

Color photograph on page 208.

Light Requirements:

*B*arberries have always been a landscape standby, tough, long-lived, and accommodating of prevailing conditions. Japanese barberries add a truly ornamental element to the scene with their colorful foliage. All barberries have yellow wood beneath their bark, and the twigs of Japanese types bear tufts of neat little ovoid leaves, single thorns, and inconspicuous yellow flowers in the spring. They become tiny red berries dangling singly or in pairs among the foliage in late summer and fall. Japanese barberries are preferable to common or European barberries because they are not alternate hosts for a rust disease that infects grain crops in farming regions. Because of their thorns, barberries are good barrier plants under windows to thwart intruders and in areas where foot traffic is to be discouraged. They take shearing for hedges, and dwarf types look wonderful massed as a ground cover with contrasting plants or as edging for planted beds.

WHEN TO PLANT

Plant barberries in the spring or, if raised in containers, anytime the ground is not frozen.

WHERE TO PLANT

For best foliage color, plant barberries in full sun. In too much shade, their purple foliage turns green. They like well-drained, decent, even poor, soil of any type and can handle urban conditions. They will grow uncomplainingly in bare spots that other plants reject.

HOW TO PLANT

Dig a saucer-shaped planting hole as deep as the barberry rootball and about twice as wide. For a hedge dig holes 4 feet apart for standard-size shrubs, 2½ feet for dwarf types. Setting them in a long trench of the correct depth works, too. Although established plants do not need feeding, a handful of a granular all-purpose slow-acting fertilizer mixed into the soil at planting time gives transplants a boost their first season. Set the rootball in the hole so that its top is level with the surrounding soil. Fill in the hole with soil, firming it gently around plant stems, and water well.

CARE AND MAINTENANCE

Barberries are very self-reliant. Mulch them year-round with 2 or 3 inches of chopped leaves or wood chips to retain soil moisture and discourage weeds. Once established, they do not need watering unless there is severe drought. They are light feeders, so follow-up fertilizing is not necessary. Prune or shear them for a hedge in late spring. Rejuvenate old or neglected shrubs by cutting them back to the ground in the spring.

ADDITIONAL INFORMATION

Japanese barberries do nicely in containers on the deck or patio. Verticillium wilt is their primary nemesis, causing their foliage to turn brown and fall off during the season. Promptly remove infected plants and the soil in the area to limit the spread of the infection, especially if they are part of a hedge or mass planting. Sterilize shovels and pruners by dipping them in a solution of hot water and household bleach.

ADDITIONAL SPECIES, CULTIVARS, OR VARIETIES

Popular purple-leafed barberries are 'Crimson Pygmy' at 2 feet tall with deep-red leaves, and 'Rosy Glow' at 5 feet with burgundy foliage marbled with pink. A barberry with yellow foliage is 'Aurea', which also has red berries and grows to 2 feet.

 Did You Know?

Barberries head most lists of deer-resistant plants. Others on the lists are usually thorned or spined or have fuzzy foliage, such as lamb's ears, or strong, resinous odors, such as artemisias. It is always risky, however, to try to list deer-resistant plants because deer appetites vary from neighborhood to neighborhood. Also, while casual visitors may pick and choose among plants, deer under serious population pressure will eat almost anything.

Beautyberry

Callicarpa dichotoma

Other Name: Purple Beautyberry
Type: Deciduous
Mature Size: 4 to 6 feet tall; 4 to 5 feet wide
Bloom Time: August
Flower Color/Type: Shades of purple, magenta, and white
Features: Fall color; berries; attracts songbirds

Light Requirements:

Color photograph on page 208.

*B*eautyberries are unprepossessing shrubs, content to coexist with more assertive ones and wait for their magic moment at the end of the season. Multistemmed and upright to horizontal, they develop pairs of dull, medium-green leaves neatly arrayed along pale-gray stems in the spring. By midsummer their tiny, inconspicuous pinkish flowers appear, giving way to showy ¼-inch berries clustered intermittently around the slender, layered, arching stems by early fall. As the leaves turn purplish and drop, the intense, luminously colored (some might say gaudy) berries become more obvious on the bare stems, lasting until Christmas. These shrubs have excellent drought resistance and are suitable for hedgerows, in front of evergreens, or in a shrub border. They can also be massed for a ground cover. Purple beautyberry is a 1989 winner of the Pennsylvania Horticultural Society's Gold Medal Award (Styer Award) for superior performance in the Philadelphia area.

WHEN TO PLANT

Plant in either spring or fall. Beautyberries raised in containers transplant well anytime during the growing season. They root easily and are vigorous growers in the spring.

WHERE TO PLANT

Beautyberry does best in full sun, but partial shade is okay. Plants will take any decent soil as long as it is well-drained. Once established, they can handle dry or moist soil, if they must, as well as salt and urban conditions. Plant them in view of the house to enjoy the berries and the mockingbirds, catbirds, and robins that come for them.

HOW TO PLANT

No special soil preparation is necessary for beautyberries. Dig a saucer-shaped planting hole as deep as the rootball is high and about twice as wide. Remove the shrub from its container, and untangle or clip any circling roots. Set the beautyberry in the hole so that the top of its rootball is exactly level with the surrounding soil. If the plant is wrapped, cut as much of the burlap and twine away as possible. Then fill in the hole with soil, firming it gently around plant stems to remove air pockets, and water well. Set plants at least 4 feet apart from each other or away from buildings.

CARE AND MAINTENANCE

Spread a 2- or 3-inch layer of organic material such as chopped leaves over the shrub's root zone to conserve soil moisture and discourage weeds. Although established beautyberries are fairly drought resistant, they are grateful for water during extended dry periods. There is no need to fertilize them if their soil is half decent; too rich a diet promotes excess vegetative growth at the expense of flower/fruit production. Prune stems back to within a few inches of soil level each spring to cut off any winter dieback. Prune to keep the shrub at a compact 3 to 5 feet and stimulate heavy fruiting.

ADDITIONAL INFORMATION

Use fruit-laden beautyberry stems in fresh or dried autumn flower arrangements. These shrubs are virtually pest free except possibly for rabbits, which take an interest in their tender new stems in the spring until they harden with age. To enhance fruit production, plant shrubs in groups.

ADDITIONAL SPECIES, CULTIVARS, OR VARIETIES

Japanese beautyberry (*Callicarpa japonica* 'Leucocarpa') has white flowers and white berries. Native beautyberry (*Callicarpa americana*) grows wild all over the South. Its larger berries were noted by William Bartram in his travels in 1773. 'Alba' has white berries. Bodinier beautyberry (*Callicarpa bodinieri*) 'Profusion' has clusters of deep-lilac berries numbering 30 to 40 per cluster, and it has slightly purple fall leaf color.

 Did You Know?

Berry-laden shrubs are the backbone of a National Wildlife Federation Backyard Wildlife Habitat. The program began in 1973 to encourage home owners to provide shelter, food, and water for birds and other wildlife. For an information packet on how to develop your landscape and have it certified, call 410-516-6583.

Boxwood

Buxus hybrids

Other Names: Common Box,
   American Boxwood
Type: Broadleaf evergreen
Mature Size: 3 to 15 feet tall; 3 to 10 feet wide
Foliage: Small, oval, dark green
Features: Fine texture

Color photograph on page 208.

Light Requirements:

Elegant but utilitarian boxwood has often been avoided in favor of sturdy Japanese holly in the Philadelphia area because it was thought to be only marginally hardy here. However, there are now excellent boxwood hybrids suitable for the Delaware Valley. Their branching clouds of small, fine-textured foliage and naturally rounded, formal-looking habit are boxwood trademarks. So is the odor, redolent of used cat litter, that some boxwoods exude. This may be the reason deer tend to overlook box in many landscapes. Their longevity is legendary; some at Mount Vernon are more than 200 years old. Because it is dense and slow growing, boxwood is great for edging walks and beds, especially herb gardens. It shears beautifully for topiary, hedges, and mazes.

WHEN TO PLANT

Plant shrubs with roots wrapped in burlap in spring or fall. Transplant boxwoods raised in containers anytime during the growing season when it is not very hot and dry. Those that are at least 3 years old transplant best.

WHERE TO PLANT

Boxwoods prefer full sun and soil that is moist, rich in organic matter, toward neutral, and well-drained. Do not crowd boxwoods because their shallow and invasive roots compete vigorously with neighboring plants.

HOW TO PLANT

Improve the drainage of clayey soil by digging in organic material. Dig a saucer-shaped planting hole as deep as the boxwood's rootball is high and about twice as wide. Remove the shrub from its container, and untangle or clip any circling roots. Set it in the hole so that the top of its rootball is exactly at, or a bit above, ground level. Cut as much burlap as possible away from a wrapped rootball. Then fill in the hole with soil, firming it gently around plant stems, and water well.

CARE AND MAINTENANCE

Mulch the boxwood's root zone with a 2- or 3-inch layer of organic material to conserve soil moisture and discourage weeds. Water the shrub regularly if rainfall is scarce over the year that it will take to get established and during periods of drought thereafter. About 6 months after planting, sprinkle granular slow-acting fertilizer on the mulch for the rain to soak in. Erect a screen of burlap or garden fleece to protect older shrubs that are exposed to drying winter wind and sun. Never use plastic, and do not wrap the shrub, because air circulation is important.

ADDITIONAL INFORMATION

Boxwoods do very well in outdoor containers. Prune out any browned twigs or branches from winterkill. Thin dense twigginess within the shrub to improve air circulation. Renovate an old specimen gradually, cutting back only ⅓ of its height or breadth per year. Mites and scale are occasional nuisances treatable with horticultural oil. Dig up and discard shrubs infected with root rot from poor soil drainage. Identify and correct any stress factors that may predispose boxwood to these problems.

ADDITIONAL SPECIES, CULTIVARS, OR VARIETIES

Some dependable hybrids of Korean and English boxwoods include the following: 'Green Gem' is 2 feet tall and wide and ball shaped; 'Green Mountain' is 5 feet tall and somewhat narrower; 'Green Velvet' is about 3 feet wide and tall and a Pennsylvania Horticultural Society's Gold Medal Award winner; 'Suffruticosa' is great for edging; and 'Northern Find' and 'Varder Valley' are extra hardy, good for Pennsylvania.

 Did You Know?

*Parterre gardens are popular again for more formal yards and gardens. Originally French (*parterre *means "along the ground"), this garden style was enthusiastically adopted by the English in the 17th century. Gardens are laid out as large flat squares or rectangles, which are then subdivided by means of low, tidy boxwood hedges into geometrically pleasing flower or vegetable beds. Sometimes a fountain, sculpture, or planted container is placed at the center of the design. Knot gardens are similar, usually limited to herbs and/or flowers, with a curved edging of boxwood or something similar.*

Butterfly Bush

Buddleia davidii

Other Name: Summer Lilac
Type: Deciduous, flowering
Mature Size: 6 to 8 feet tall; 8 to 10 feet wide
Bloom Time: June through October
Flower Color/Type: Lavender, purple, white, pink
Features: Showy flowers; fragrance; attracts butterflies, hummingbirds, beneficial insects

Light Requirements:

Color photograph on page 208.

Butterfly bush tops every list of plants that attract butterflies. Actually, it should top any list of totally delightful landscape plants. It deserves its reputation for vigorous growth, easy care, and reliable season-long bloom. Its slightly coarse, pale gray-green or bluish green foliage provides contrast for the green in the garden, and its upright, sometimes unruly arching branches add informality. Butterfly bush flowers grow at the branch tips as 4- to 8-inch-long tubes of tightly packed, tiny florets that resemble narrow lilac blossoms. Usually in shades of lilac or purple, but also yellow, white, and pink, the florets sometimes have orange centers, or "eyes." While often used as specimens or focal points in the yard, butterfly bushes make good summer hedges and can also be integrated into a mixed flower border. They do not seem to appeal to deer.

WHEN TO PLANT

Most butterfly bushes are sold in containers. They can be planted anytime during the growing season, but spring is best so that they have time to grow full-sized and bloom by the end of the season.

WHERE TO PLANT

Put butterfly bushes in full sun; too much shade makes them gangly with fewer flowers. They like good garden soil that is well-drained. It can be on the sandy side. To please butterflies, plant these shrubs out of wind in a sheltered area.

HOW TO PLANT

Dig a saucer-shaped planting hole in average garden soil as deep as the rootball is high and about twice as wide. Remove the butterfly bush from its container, and untangle or clip any circling roots. Set the plant in the hole so that the top of its rootball is exactly level with the surrounding soil; a bit higher is fine, too. Then fill in the hole with soil, firming it gently around plant stems to remove air pockets, and water well. Set plants at least 4 feet apart from each other or away from buildings.

CARE AND MAINTENANCE

Mulch the root zone of the butterfly bush with a 2- or 3-inch layer of organic material such as chopped leaves or wood chips. If rainfall is unreliable, water the shrub regularly until it is well established. Although it is not essential, trimming off spent flowers during the season will keep the shrub shaped, groomed, and productive. It also discourages self-seeding around the property. Every spring sprinkle slow-acting granular fertilizer formulated for trees and shrubs on the mulch for the rain or snow to soak in. Prune the previous year's branches to within 6 inches of the ground to stimulate new and dense growth that will produce lots of flowers.

ADDITIONAL INFORMATION

Butterfly bush flowers make good cut flowers for arrangements. They tend to self-sow, so there may be bonus seedlings to share next season.

ADDITIONAL SPECIES, CULTIVARS, OR VARIETIES

Readily available butterfly bushes are 'Black Knight' (dark purple); 'White Profusion' (white); 'Charming' (pink); and 'Harlequin' with variegated foliage and magenta flowers. 'Nanho Purple' is a dwarf, 3 or 4 feet tall. Fountain butterfly bush (*Buddleia alternifolia*) produces blooms on old wood, so it is not cut back annually until after it blooms. It has paler bark and foliage, and a shorter bloom period.

 Did You Know?

Attracting butterflies begins with providing food for their larvae, caterpillars. Each species requires a favorite plant on which female butterflies lay eggs. Newly hatched larvae eat its leaves and sometimes its flowers. Larval host plants tend to be wildflowers, weeds, and grasses that are not usually part of a backyard. Host plants for adult butterflies have brightly colored, daisylike flowers that produce nectar over the entire season. Concentrations of these plants with different bloom times and heights lure the greatest number of butterflies.

Cherrylaurel, Dwarf

Prunus laurocerasus 'Otto Luyken'

Other Name: Dwarf English Laurel
Type: Broadleaf evergreen
Mature Size: 5 feet tall; 5 feet wide
Bloom Time: Late spring
Flower Color/Type: Cream-white; cylindrical
Features: Flowers; fragrance; deer resistance

Light Requirements:

Color photograph on page 208.

If this shrub did not exist, someone would have to invent it. It is a landscape special—growing happily in shade with virtually no care. While some cherrylaurels are full-sized trees and others are large shrubs, the dwarf 'Otto Luyken' is the perfect size for residential yards. A fast-growing, versatile compact shrub, it boasts attractive lustrous, dark-green foliage year-round. In the spring it bears narrow 2- to 5-inch-long upright clusters of fuzzy, musky-smelling white florets, followed by purplish-black fruits that nestle inconspicuously among the foliage. Both the fruit and the foliage are reputed to be poisonous, which may explain why deer ignore cherrylaurel. Cherrylaurel makes great hedges and foundation plantings where sun is in short supply.

WHEN TO PLANT

Plant shrubs raised in containers at the nursery anytime during the growing season; however, spring and fall are more desirable times.

WHERE TO PLANT

Cherrylaurel prefers partial shade. In fact, exposure to sun reduces its vigor. It appreciates bright, indirect light for a few hours a day, but not full sun. Cherrylaurels are not fussy about soil as long as it is reasonably fertile, not too acid, and well-drained.

HOW TO PLANT

Dig a saucer-shaped planting hole as deep as the rootball is high and about twice as wide. Remove the cherrylaurel from its container, and untangle or clip any circling roots. Set the plant in the hole so that the top of its rootball is exactly level with the surrounding soil; a bit higher is fine too, especially if the soil is heavy. Then fill in the hole with soil, firming it gently around plant stems to remove air pockets, and water well. Set plants at least 4 feet apart from each other or away from buildings.

CARE AND MAINTENANCE

Maintaining a 2- or 3-inch layer of organic mulch, such as chopped leaves or wood chips, on the soil over the cherrylaurel's root zone will conserve soil moisture, discourage weeds, and enrich the soil as it decomposes. Keep it away from shrub stems to prevent rot problems and deny rodents a winter nesting site. Water regularly in the absence of rain over the first year while the shrub gets established, then only during periods of drought. For the first year or two in the fall, sprinkle slow-acting fertilizer formulated for trees and shrubs over the mulch for the rain to soak in. Then the continuously decomposing mulch will add organic material to the soil, and regular fertilization will not be necessary.

ADDITIONAL INFORMATION

Cherrylaurels take shearing for hedges well, although clipping individual branches in the spring after they flower creates a more natural look. 'Otto Luyken' has such a nice, compact shape that the only pruning needed is to cut out the occasional broken branch. Neglected, larger forms of cherrylaurel can be renewed by cutting back their stems to ground level and fertilizing.

ADDITIONAL SPECIES, CULTIVARS, OR VARIETIES

Of the many types of cherrylaurel, none is as commercially available and as suitable a shrub for residential landscapes as 'Otto Luyken'.

 Did You Know?

Cherrylaurels are not really laurels; they are cherries. Their name alludes to the resemblance of their foliage to that of true laurel. Bay laurel (Lauris nobilis) is the true laurel—its botanical name derived from the Latin words for "praise" and "famous" (thus the practice of crowning victorious Roman athletes and generals with wreaths made of laurel leaves). True laurel is in contemporary kitchens under the name of sweet bay (not to be confused with sweet bay magnolia, Magnolia virginiana) or bay laurel as dried leaves to flavor soups and stews. It is found in little jars labeled "Bay Leaf."

Cotoneaster, Willowleaf

Cotoneaster salicifolious

Other Name: Tall Cotoneaster
Type: Broadleaf evergreen
Mature Size: 10 to 15 feet tall
Bloom Time: May/June
Flower Color/Type: Off-white; flat clusters
Features: Berries; attracts beneficial insects

Light Requirements:

Color photograph on page 208.

There is a cotoneaster for just about every landscape situation. The tall ones, such as the willowleaf, are large and open, some to the point of being rangy. Their narrow, leathery, textured dark evergreen leaves provide winter interest, even though their purplish fall tinge is not very dramatic. Willow-leaf's flexible arching branches droop gracefully when covered with its musky-smelling flowers and later when its bright-red berries form along them. Relatively fast growers, these plants make good screens and hedges. They are easily trained through pruning and can be espaliered against a wall for a wonderful effect.

WHEN TO PLANT
Choose containerized nursery stock because cotoneaster roots are sparse and stringy and shrubs accustomed to containers transplant better. Plant anytime during the growing season, but spring is best.

WHERE TO PLANT
Cotoneaster does best in full sun, but some shade is fine. The plant is not fussy about soil; in fact, the drier and poorer the soils, the more richly colored the berries seem to be. The soil must be well-drained, however.

HOW TO PLANT
Dig a saucer-shaped planting hole as deep as the rootball is high and about twice as wide. Remove the cotoneaster from its container, and gently untangle or clip any circling roots. Set the plant in the hole so that the top of its rootball is exactly level with, or even slightly above, the level of the surrounding ground. Then fill in the hole with soil, firming it gently around plant stems, and water well.

CARE AND MAINTENANCE
Mulching newly planted cotoneasters assures that the soil around their roots stays moist while they struggle to become established. Spread a 2- or

3-inch layer of organic material such as chopped leaves or wood chips over the root zone, but do not pile it against shrub stems. If rainfall is unreliable, water cotoneaster regularly until it is well established. These shrubs are extremely low maintenance and will need watering only in severe drought. They do not need fertilizing. Prune only to remove brown and damaged branches and to control their shape. Cut branches at their base, where they join another, rather than at their tips, which causes browning and dieback at the cut end.

ADDITIONAL INFORMATION

Lacebugs or mites may infest stressed cotoneasters. Spray them with horticultural oil as directed on the product label, and address the cause of the shrub's stress. Occasionally, fireblight blackens stems and leaves as if they were scorched by fire. Prune out affected parts immediately, and burn the debris or wrap it in plastic and discard it in the trash. Disinfect tools **after every cut** to avoid spreading the infection by dipping them into a solution of hot water and household bleach. In serious cases dig up and throw away the shrub.

ADDITIONAL SPECIES, CULTIVARS, OR VARIETIES

Cotoneaster salicifolius var. *floccosus* has larger flowers; it may be semievergreen in severe winters. Spreading cotoneaster (*Cotoneaster divaricatus*) has arching branches, red berries, and wonderful reddish purplish yellow fall foliage. Some cotoneasters make good ground covers: *Cotoneaster dammeri* 'Coral Beauty' and 'Lowfast' are only 1 to 2 feet tall and spread as far as 6 feet. Rock spray cotoneaster (*Cotoneaster horizontalis*), which has pink flowers that become red berries on stiffly splayed low branches, is ideal for rock walls, banks, and similar situations.

 Did You Know?

Sometimes distinguishing between a cotoneaster and a firethorn is difficult. The presence of thorns confirms a firethorn's identity. Other indications are that firethorn berries are typically orange and tightly bunched. Both bear whitish, smelly flowers about the same time in the spring, but firethorn flowers are more abundant and ornamental, and they grow along the stems.

Crapemyrtle

Lagerstroemia indica

Type: Deciduous, flowering

Mature Size: 3 (dwarf) to 30 feet tall;
3 to 15 feet wide

Bloom Time: Late July to October

Flower Color/Type: Shades of pink, lavender, white, red; clusters

Features: Mottled bark; fall color; 4-season interest

Light Requirements:

Color photograph on page 208.

Crapemyrtles are traditional Southern plants, but fortunately, the National Arboretum has developed cold-hardy hybrids that make it possible for Philadelphia area home owners to enjoy their considerable virtues. Rugged and versatile, these summer bloomers bear 6- to 15-inch-long clusters of flowers with crimped edges on their petals at the ends of upright, arching branches. Their foliage, which appears late in the spring as a glossy yellowish bronze and then becomes bright green, changes again to yellow, orange, or reddish fall color. For the winter season there remains handsome bark mottled with brownish and gray patches. Use crapemyrtles as hedges, background screening, specimen, or foundation shrubs. Pruned low, they make a good accent or anchor for a flower bed. Look for the massed grouping along Kelly Drive planted as part of the Pennsylvania Horticultural Society's renovation of the Azalea Garden.

WHEN TO PLANT

Crapemyrtles tend to arrive at local nurseries a bit later in the spring than most shrubs. Purchase specifically named shrubs, not just generically labeled "pink" or "white" ones. Plant them immediately after purchase, although container-grown ones can be planted anytime during the growing season.

WHERE TO PLANT

Site crapemyrtles in full sun in any soil that is rich in organic matter, acidic, moist, and well-drained. Shrubs with some shelter, such as on a south-facing wall, on a drained slope, or in front of a building, are less likely to get dieback in severe winters. Be sure they have good air circulation to avoid powdery mildew on their foliage.

HOW TO PLANT

Dig a saucer-shaped planting hole as deep as the rootball is high and about twice as wide. Remove the crapemyrtle from its container, and untangle or clip any circling roots. Set the plant in the hole so that the top of its rootball is exactly level with the surrounding ground, although a bit higher is fine, too. Then fill in the hole with soil, firming it gently around plant stems, and water well. Set shrubs at least 5 feet apart from each other or away from buildings.

CARE AND MAINTENANCE

Maintain a year-round, 2- or 3-inch layer of organic mulch over the shrub's root zone to protect the tender bark on crapemyrtle stems from injury by mower or weed trimmer. It will also conserve soil moisture and discourage weeds. Water well the first year until it is established, then during periods of drought. Fertilize lightly, if at all, because rich diets reduce flowering. Decomposing mulch will aid soil fertility. Prune while dormant in late winter or very early spring to establish the strongest stems and remove weak or winter-killed ones. Thin dense foliage canopies for good air circulation and discourage powdery mildew.

ADDITIONAL INFORMATION

Several semidwarf crapemyrtles, such as 'Hopi' and 'Zuni', do well in outdoor containers. Wrap containers with bubble wrap, or something similar for winter insulation. Better yet, sink their pots in a hole in the ground or mulch pile for the winter.

ADDITIONAL SPECIES, CULTIVARS, OR VARIETIES

'Acoma' (white) grows 6 to 8 feet. Others include 'Muskogee' (lilac pink); 'Natchez' (white), which is a best-seller and makes a good small tree; 'Powhatan' (purple); and 'Tuskegee' (deep rose).

 Did You Know?

Summer-blooming shrubs bridge the landscape color gap between spring dogwood and azaleas and fall foliage color. Here are good choices:

- *Bluebeard (*Caryopteris × clandonensis*)*
- *Butterfly bush (*Buddleia davidii*)*
- *Chaste tree (*Vitex agnus-castus*)*
- *Glossy abelia (*Abelia × grandiflora*)*
- *Big leaf hydrangea (*Hydrangea macrophylla*)*
- *Plumleaf azalea (*Rhododendron prunifolium*)*
- *Rose of Sharon (*Hibiscus syriacus*)*
- *Summersweet (*Clethra alnifolia*)*

Daphne, 'Carol Mackie'

Daphne × burkwoodii 'Carol Mackie'

Other Name: Burkwood Daphne
Type: Semievergreen, flowering
Mature Size: 3 to 5 feet tall; 3 to 6 feet wide
Bloom Time: Late spring
Flower Color/Type: White; rounded clusters
Features: Fragrance; variegated foliage

Color photograph on page 208.

Light Requirements:

Daphne is another plant that is more associated with the South than with the Philadelphia area. The very name suggests a delicate Southern belle, and many of them have a reputation for being relatively short-lived and fussy. An exception to this stereotype, one that copes with our winters and represents the best that daphnes have to offer anywhere, is 'Carol Mackie'. This low-growing, densely twiggy shrub offers eye-catching variegated foliage of green margined in yellow, which fades to white with age. Poised along its branches are charming flowers, their waxy, pinkish-tinged white clusters of up to 16 individual florets of renowned fragrance. Fortunate is the home owner whose daphne repeat blooms a bit in the early fall. Any fall berries and all parts of all daphnes are poisonous, which may explain why deer pass up such charming shrubs.

WHEN TO PLANT

Plant daphnes with roots wrapped in burlap in early spring. Plant those raised in containers anytime during the growing season, except when it is extremely hot and dry.

WHERE TO PLANT

Judicious placement assures that daphnes thrive. Site them where they can enjoy full sun in the spring and perhaps some afternoon shade in midsummer. 'Carol Mackie' does fine in most good garden soils, especially those on the sandy side, that are rich in organic matter and very well-drained. Plant daphnes near a walk or doorway so that passersby can enjoy the fragrance when they are in bloom. Keep shrubs away from roof overhangs from which snow may fall and split their soft wood.

HOW TO PLANT

Dig a planting hole with sloping sides as deep as the rootball is high and about twice as wide. Remove the daphne from its container, and untangle or clip any circling roots. Orient them to grow outward when setting the plant in the hole. Daphne roots tend to wrap around themselves even under the best of conditions. Position the shrub so that the top of its rootball is at, or slightly above, the level of the surrounding soil for good drainage. Cut as much burlap as possible away from wrapped rootballs. Then fill in the hole with soil, firming it gently, and water well. Set plants at least 4 feet apart or away from buildings. Balled and burlap-wrapped daphnes may take longer to establish.

CARE AND MAINTENANCE

A year-round, 2- or 3-inch layer of organic mulch conserves soil moisture and discourages weeds. Do not pile it against daphne stems, but be sure the roots are lightly covered. Decomposing mulch is all the fertilizer they need. Daphnes rarely need pruning, except to remove broken or rubbing branches. Do any other shaping in the spring, immediately after the plant flowers.

ADDITIONAL INFORMATION

Daphnes do not like to have their roots disturbed, so do not move them. The flowering of 'Carol Mackie' is sparse the first year, but it musters a full show by its second or third year. Beware of the mysterious "daphne death," which sometimes causes a shrub to die unexpectedly.

ADDITIONAL SPECIES, CULTIVARS, OR VARIETIES

Caucasian daphne (*Daphne caucasica*) also does very well in the Delaware Valley. It is a 1990 winner of the Pennsylvania Horticultural Society's Gold Medal Award for its adaptability and pest and disease resistance. Rose daphne (*Daphne cneorum*) is dwarf, grows to 12 inches, and is suitable for rock gardens or as a ground cover in similar conditions. It has fragrant rose-colored flowers.

 Did You Know?

In Greek mythology Daphne was a river nymph whose beauty attracted Apollo. When he pursued her, she rejected him and prayed to the gods for help. Unable to deter Apollo, who was apparently accustomed to getting his way, the gods turned Daphne into a lushly fragrant shrub. Henceforth the shrub was sacred to Apollo.

Firethorn

Pyracantha coccinea

Other Name: Scarlet Firethorn
Type: Broadleaf evergreen
Mature Size: 8 to 10 feet tall;
   3 to 12 feet wide
Bloom Time: June
Flower Color/Type: White; open
Features: Berries; thorns; attracts honeybees; provides food and shelter
   for songbirds

Color photograph on page 208.

Light Requirements:

Firethorns are aptly named, their upright or sprawling stems covered with thorns and bright-red or orange fall berries that seem to set them afire. These tough plants have a softer side in spring when they are covered with white flowers clustered among lustrous, leathery, dark-green pointed leaves. Firethorns are well suited to guard duty as barrier plants under windows and around porches, and as hedges along property lines; they are also strongly ornamental, especially when trained as espalier to a trellis or wall. Once established, they are very self-reliant and drought tolerant. Also, it is a desperate deer that nibbles on firethorn.

When to Plant

In spring or fall choose container-grown firethorns that have healthy foliage. They are easier to handle and establish faster. They can be planted anytime during the growing season, but spring is best.

Where to Plant

For best flower and fruit production, plant firethorns in full sun. Although they can manage in poor soil, they are healthier and do best in good garden soil that is rich in organic matter and drains well. Locate them in view of a window to enjoy their seasonal beauty and the birds that visit them. Be sure of the location because the thorny large plants are difficult to move. Leave enough room around the shrub to permit access for pruning, even after it grows larger.

How to Plant

Add peat moss or compost to heavy clay soil in the planting area to improve its drainage. Dig a saucer-shaped planting hole in the center of the prepared bed as deep as the firethorn rootball is high and about twice as wide. Remove the shrub from its container, and untangle or clip any roots that may be circling themselves from confinement in the pot too long. It may be necessary to actually slice partway through the rootball in several places if the shrub is terribly rootbound. Set it in the hole so that its top is exactly level with, or slightly higher than, the surrounding soil. Then fill in the hole with soil, firming it gently, and water well. Set plants at least 6 feet apart from each other, a bit closer to establish a hedge.

CARE AND MAINTENANCE

Maintain a 2- to 3-inch layer of organic mulch over the firethorn root zone to retain soil moisture and discourage weeds so there will be no need to work under or near this thorny plant. Water regularly in the absence of rain for the first year to assure that its roots are well established. After 6 months or so, sprinkle granular slow-acting fertilizer for shrubs and trees on the mulch for the rain to soak in. Prune away dead or damaged branches as they occur. Prune the longest berry-laden branches to shape the shrub and control its size to enjoy at Christmas or in the spring after firethorn blooms.

ADDITIONAL INFORMATION

Fireblight is a bacterial disease that sometimes infects firethorn. Prune out the blackened, dead stems, clean up all leaf debris, and disinfect tools in a solution of hot water and household bleach. Berry-laden branches of firethorn are wonderful additions to fall dried or fresh floral arrangements.

ADDITIONAL SPECIES, CULTIVARS, OR VARIETIES

'Fiery Cascade' is noted for its cold hardiness and disease resistance. 'Lalandei' has large leaves and orange-red fruit, and it grows tall for espalier. 'Mohave', a hybrid, has prolific berries; see it espaliered at the Morris Arboretum.

Did You Know?

Shrubs with fall berries for wildlife are:

Barberry	*Euonymus*
Beautyberry	*Firethorn*
Cotoneaster	*Holly*
Dogwood	*Viburnum*

Forsythia

Forsythia × intermedia

Other Names: Border Forsythia,
  Golden Bells
Type: Deciduous, flowering
Mature Size: 8 to 10 feet tall; 10 to 12 feet
  wide or wider
Bloom Time: April
Flower Color/Type: Bright yellow; trumpet
Features: Flowers; old-fashioned plant

Color photograph on page 208.

Light Requirements:

Originally from Asia, forsythias have had 100 years in this country to win their way into our hearts each year as heralds of a new spring. When their graceful, arching branches are loaded with bright-yellow flowers, who cares if they are ordinary the rest of the year? After they flower, bright-green leaves appear and age over the summer to darker green and then yellow-green and, sometimes, purplish-red before dropping. Because forsythias bloom on the previous year's wood, the buds for the next season form by midsummer. Branches that dip to the ground may root there and can be cut from the mother plant and transplanted to a new site. Forsythias tolerate city conditions and benign neglect. They have virtually no pests and diseases. Use them individually as specimens, as foundation plants, or as part of a larger shrub border where they can blend in during the summer. They make good hedges if not overpruned. With a little attention these shrubs can live more than 50 years.

WHEN TO PLANT

Plant forsythias in either spring or fall. Plant young shrubs in containers from the nursery or garden center anytime during the growing season.

WHERE TO PLANT

Full sun is essential for best forsythia bloom and compact growth. They adapt to a wide range of soil types, including that of abandoned city housing sites but, of course, do their best in rich, well-drained garden soil. Site forsythias where they can billow and show off.

HOW TO PLANT

Dig a saucer-shaped planting hole as deep as the forsythia rootball is high and about twice as wide. Remove the shrub from its container, and untangle or clip any circling roots. Set the plant in its hole so that the top of its rootball is exactly level with the surrounding soil, no lower. If the rootball is wrapped in burlap, cut as much of it away as possible. Then fill in the hole with soil, firming it gently around plant stems, and water well. Set plants at least 10 feet apart from each other or away from buildings, 8 feet for hedges.

CARE AND MAINTENANCE

Mulch forsythia root zones all year long with a 2- or 3-inch layer of organic matter such as chopped leaves or wood chips. Water these shrubs regularly if rainfall is unreliable until they are well established. In the spring sprinkle slow-acting granular fertilizer formulated for trees and shrubs on the mulch for the rain to soak in. Forsythias are not heavy feeders, so after a year or two, the soil, enriched by continuously decomposing mulch, will provide for the shrub.

ADDITIONAL INFORMATION

Prune the single stem of spring-planted bare-root shrubs back to 18 inches when planting to encourage side branching. Renovate scraggly older shrubs by cutting ⅓ of the old woody canes back to the ground each spring after they flower to stimulate new shoots. Frequent cutting back of unruly growth creates a dense twiggy, unattractive shape and few flowers. Never shear forsythias.

ADDITIONAL SPECIES, CULTIVARS, OR VARIETIES

'Lynwood Gold' has pale-yellow flowers. 'Spectabilis' is the old faithful, still a good choice. 'Bronxensis' makes a good ground cover. Weeping forsythia (*Forsythia suspensa* var. *sieboldii*) trails over walls or other supports; pruning ruins the weeping effect.

Did You Know?

Enjoy spring early by forcing forsythia, quince, dogwood, magnolia, witchhazel, and others to bloom indoors. Cut branches showing flower buds, and put them in lukewarm water in a cool room while the buds swell. Change the water every few days if it becomes cloudy. When the buds swell, recut the branch ends, arrange them in a vase with fresh water, and bring them into a heated room to show their stuff.

Fothergilla

Fothergilla gardenii

Other Name: Dwarf Fothergilla
Type: Deciduous, flowering
Mature Size: 3 to 4 feet tall; 2 to 3 feet wide
Bloom Time: April
Flower Color/Type: White; bottlebrushes
Features: Flowers; fragrance; fall color

Color photograph on page 208.

Light Requirements:

*I*n the wild, fothergillas are found in woodlands and swamps in the South. Increasingly, they are found in yards and gardens in the North because they are sturdy shrubs with lots of appeal. Like so many natives, they have few pest or disease problems and many assets. The first asset is their flowers, stubby spikes of many petal-less flowers that look like fuzzy bottlebrushes at the tips of their stems. A close second is their foliage, which usually appears after they bloom. It is toothed and a dull dark green or blue-green, which turns bright red, orange, and yellow in the fall. Fothergillas are attractive grouped for a landscape accent or massed on a hillside to hold the soil. Use them individually to anchor a mixed border or to become a foundation planting. They are slightly small and a bit drab between spring and fall to be front and center as specimen shrubs.

WHEN TO PLANT

Fothergillas are usually grown and sold in containers and can be planted anytime during the growing season. Spring is the best time, however.

WHERE TO PLANT

For best flowering and fall color, plant fothergillas where they get mostly sun in the spring, but perhaps some shade as fall approaches, which reportedly improves their yellow-orange foliage color. They are adaptable to most garden soils that are moist, on the acidic side, and well-drained.

HOW TO PLANT

Dig a saucer-shaped planting hole as deep as the fothergilla rootball is high and a bit wider. Remove the shrub from its container, and untangle or clip any circling roots. Set it in the hole so that the top of its rootball is exactly level with the surrounding soil. Then fill in the hole with soil, firming it gently around plant stems to remove air pockets, and water well. Set plants at least 4 feet apart from each other or from buildings.

CARE AND MAINTENANCE

Spread a 2- or 3-inch layer of organic material as a mulch over the root zone of the fothergilla. Chopped leaves or wood chips are fine. Water it regularly if rainfall is unreliable until it is well established. In the spring sprinkle slow-acting granular fertilizer formulated for trees and shrubs on the mulch for the rain or snow to soak in. Eventually, the decomposing mulch will enrich the soil, and annual fertilizer will not be necessary.

ADDITIONAL INFORMATION

Fothergillas do not need routine pruning. Clip off the occasional broken branch. If after several years it becomes thin and lanky, cut back the entire shrub to ground level in the spring to renew it. Its spreading roots will sprout new shoots. Clipped off the main shrub, these rooted pieces can be planted to produce a new shrub. Otherwise, the shrub will gradually widen in its spot.

ADDITIONAL SPECIES, CULTIVARS, OR VARIETIES

'Blue Mist' is a winner of the 1990 Pennsylvania Horticultural Society's Gold Medal Award. It has blue-green foliage and requires partial shade in the summer. Its fall color is less showy. 'Mt. Airy' is a superior selection. Upright, more rounded, it has great fall color. Large fothergilla (*Fothergilla major* or *F. monticola*) grows to 10 feet tall.

Did You Know?

Ironically, our native fothergillas were named after a British physician, John Fothergill (1712-80), who grew American plants in England. The dwarf one was named for Dr. Garden who discovered this smaller version.

Hybrid Tea Rose

Rosa × hybrida

Roses have been considered the "queen of flowers" for 2,000 years, and hybrid tea roses certainly require the dutiful attention usually lavished on royalty. They are the classic high-maintenance plant because they are susceptible to so many environmental, pest, and disease problems. They require solicitous attention and seemingly constant spraying to foster healthy foliage and the classic single flower at the tip of a straight stem. Sometimes other bush roses, such as grandifloras and floribundas, are included in discussions of hybrid teas because they have similar, although not quite so strict, cultivation requirements. They produce more than one flower per stem and are not necessarily grafted.

WHEN TO PLANT

Plant bare-root or balled and burlapped hybrid teas while they are dormant in spring. Plant those in containers anytime during the growing season, but spring is best.

WHERE TO PLANT

Give tea roses the best sun and soil on your property. Concentrating them in a rose garden is most practical for efficient spraying and pruning. They do not blend well with other plants because of their stiff, formal habit. Soil must be extremely well-drained. Lay drainage gravel and piping to assure excellent drainage under heavy soil, or double dig it with organic matter. Allow plenty of air circulation around roses to discourage fungal disease.

HOW TO PLANT

Keep rose roots moist until planting time. Dig a planting hole with sloping sides as deep as the rootball is high and wide enough to accommodate the entire root system with room to spare. Remove the rose from its container, and untangle or clip any circling roots. Set the rootball in the hole exactly level with the surrounding soil. Set rootballs wrapped in burlap so that the graft—the swollen knob where the elegant flower stock was joined to the sturdy root stock—is 2 inches below the soil surface. Then cut away as much of the wrapping as possible. Position bare-root roses over a cone of packed soil in the middle of the hole so that the roots splay down its sides and the graft is 2 inches below soil level. Then fill in the hole with soil, firming it gently around plant stems, and water well.

CARE AND MAINTENANCE

Mulch rose root zones with aged wood chips to help the soil retain moisture and discourage weeds. After the ground freezes, pile them up around bush stems. Water regularly in the absence of rain. Hybrid teas are heavy feeders. Follow label instructions on slow-acting granular fertilizer formulated especially for roses. Prune away winter-killed canes in the spring. Establish 3 to 5 healthy canes 12 to 18 inches tall. Snip them at a 45-degree angle just above a leaf bud on the outside of the cane to direct the growth outward. Cut off faded flowers promptly.

ADDITIONAL INFORMATION

Black spot on foliage and Japanese beetles are the most obvious and ubiquitous hybrid tea pests. Consult a book on rose care for specifics on treating these and other problems. Cut fresh flowers for indoor display as swelling buds. Dry roses for floral crafts, their stems wired, and set upright in a box of sand or borax.

ADDITIONAL SPECIES, CULTIVARS, OR VARIETIES

Dozens of hybrid tea roses are available. Those having the All-American Rose Society (AARS) label have been trialed under various conditions and found superior. Judy McKeon at the Morris Arboretum recommends 'Love' and 'Gold Medal' for Philadelphia area rose gardens.

 Did You Know?

The most famous, most planted hybrid tea rose is 'Peace', introduced by Conard-Pyle in Chester County. Its fate intertwined with dramatic events of World War II, it was smuggled out of France in Robert Pyle's diplomatic pouch on the last plane from Lyons before France fell to the Germans. Christened the day Berlin fell to the Allies, it won the AARS medal on V-E day in 1945.

Hydrangea, Oakleaf

Hydrangea quercifolia

Type: Deciduous, flowering
Mature Size: 6 to 8 feet or more tall;
  6 to 8 feet wide
Bloom Time: July
Flower Color/Type: White florets in upright "cone"
Features: Flowers; fall color; bark; 4 seasons of interest

Light Requirements:

Color photograph on page 209.

Fortunately, oakleaf hydrangea, which is native to the Deep South, thrives here as well. As its name suggests, its lobed leaves resemble those of oaks. Coarse-textured, they emerge gray-green with felty undersides in the spring. Their summer dark green turns a striking reddish purple before they fall in November to reveal richly colored, peeling tan bark on thick stems. Their flowers captivate. Cone-shaped, lacy clusters of both sterile (with "petals") and fertile (tiny and round) white florets, they grow up to 12 inches long at stem tips. With age they turn creamy beige and increasingly pink tinged. Use oakleaf hydrangeas to brighten shady woodland areas, as specimens, as foundation plants, or in a shrub border.

WHEN TO PLANT

Plant in spring to assure plenty of time for hydrangea roots to get established before their first winter. Those raised in containers can be planted anytime during the growing season. Because of their shallow, fibrous roots, they transplant without difficulty.

WHERE TO PLANT

Although they are used to some shade as woodland understory plants in the South, oakleafs can take some sun in the North as long as their soil is woodsy—acidic, moist, rich in organic matter, and well-drained.

HOW TO PLANT

If soil is clay, dig and loosen it over a large area, and dig in organic matter to improve its drainage and water-holding capacity. In its center dig a saucer-shaped planting hole as deep as the rootball is high and about twice as wide. Remove the hydrangea from its container, and untangle or clip any circling roots. Set the plant in the hole so that the top of its rootball is roughly level with the surrounding soil. Unlike most shrubs, hydrangeas can be planted a bit deeper than grade level. If its rootball is wrapped, cut as much of the burlap away as possible. Then fill in the hole with soil, firming it gently around plant stems, and water well. Since oakleafs spread by means of root runners, allow at least 6 feet between them or away from buildings.

CARE AND MAINTENANCE

Mulch the bare soil over the shrub root zone with 2 to 3 inches of organic material to help the soil retain moisture, discourage weeds, and improve the soil as it decomposes. Renew it to maintain year-round protection. Water when rainfall is scarce. After 6 months or so, sprinkle slow-acting granular fertilizer for acid-loving plants on the mulch for the rain to soak in. If the soil is good, there is no need for subsequent annual feedings. Leave spent blossoms not harvested for indoor decoration on the shrub until late winter to protect the growing tips.

ADDITIONAL INFORMATION

Prune gangly branches to control shrub width, if necessary, just after flowering. Do not wait too long because flower buds for next year's bloom begin to form shortly thereafter. Renew neglected shrubs by cutting stems virtually to the ground in early spring or just after flowering to stimulate denser new growth. They may not produce flowers that season.

ADDITIONAL SPECIES, CULTIVARS, OR VARIETIES

'Snow Queen', a 1989 Pennsylvania Horticultural Society's Gold Medal Award winner, has more upright flower clusters. PeeGee hydrangea (*Hydrangea paniculata* 'Grandiflora') has similar flowers, but blooms in August.

 Did You Know?

Dried hydrangea blossoms are wonderful for floral crafts. Allow them to dry on the shrub for a while. Then pick oakleaf hydrangea blossoms over several weeks to get a range of colors—pinker as they get drier. Let them air dry indoors in an empty vase. Hairspray will preserve them longer. After a year or two, when their color fades, spray them with metallic paint for December holiday decorations.

Juniper, Pfitzer

Juniperus chinensis 'Pfitzeriana'

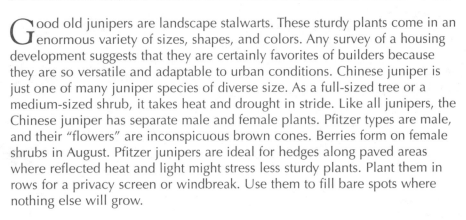

Other Name: Chinese Juniper
Type: Evergreen; conifer
Mature Size: 5 to 10 feet tall; 5 to
  10 feet wide
Foliage: Immature prickly needles; mature flat scales
Features: Berries; attracts songbirds

Light Requirements:

Color photograph on page 209.

Good old junipers are landscape stalwarts. These sturdy plants come in an enormous variety of sizes, shapes, and colors. Any survey of a housing development suggests that they are certainly favorites of builders because they are so versatile and adaptable to urban conditions. Chinese juniper is just one of many juniper species of diverse size. As a full-sized tree or a medium-sized shrub, it takes heat and drought in stride. Like all junipers, the Chinese juniper has separate male and female plants. Pfitzer types are male, and their "flowers" are inconspicuous brown cones. Berries form on female shrubs in August. Pfitzer junipers are ideal for hedges along paved areas where reflected heat and light might stress less sturdy plants. Plant them in rows for a privacy screen or windbreak. Use them to fill bare spots where nothing else will grow.

WHEN TO PLANT

Plant balled and burlapped juniper shrubs in either spring or fall. Transplant those raised in containers anytime during the growing season. Shade new transplants their first day or two from strong sun.

WHERE TO PLANT

Junipers love full sun and adapt to almost any kind of soil pH and type as long as it is not soggy. Their branches grow loose and spindly in shade. Because they can handle salt, they are ideal for the house at the Shore.

HOW TO PLANT

Choose containerized plants. Take this opportunity to improve soil drainage in the entire bed by breaking up the soil and digging in organic material. Dig a saucer-shaped planting hole in the center of the prepared area exactly as deep as and slightly wider than the juniper's rootball when it is removed from the container. If roots are circling the rootball, cut or loosen them so they can spread outward. Set the shrub in its hole so that it is at, or slightly above, soil level. Then fill in the hole with soil, firming it gently around the stems, and water well. Set junipers at least 6 feet apart from each other or from a wall, or somewhat closer to hurry their blending into a hedge.

CARE AND MAINTENANCE

Mulch the bare soil under junipers with 2 or 3 inches of organic material to keep it moist and discourage weeds. Keep it at least 6 inches away from the juniper stems to avoid stem rot and rodent damage. While they establish themselves over the first year or two, junipers need regular watering. Fertilize in the fall with a granular slow-acting product formulated for evergreens. After a couple of years the constantly decomposing mulch will improve the soil, and annual fertilization will not be necessary. Routine pruning is not needed, but be sure to clip off damaged branches promptly.

ADDITIONAL INFORMATION

Junipers under 5 years old occasionally develop a tip blight called *Phomopsis*. Prune out the browned, dying twigs. Mites attack when shrubs are stressed by unusually wet, dry, or hot weather. If a water spray does not dislodge them, spray horticultural oil as directed on the product label. Junipers under stress may also develop bagworms, whose bags hang like ornaments from the branches. Pick them off, and trash them.

ADDITIONAL SPECIES, CULTIVARS, OR VARIETIES

Chinese juniper (*Juniperus chinensis*) 'Old Gold' resembles a dwarf golden Pfitzer. 'Torulosa' (Hollywood juniper) is upright with deep-green foliage and twisted branches. 'Mint Julep' resembles a dwarf Pfitzer.

 Did You Know?

*The berries of Chinese juniper are celebrated in song and story as the key ingredient in gin. The Dutch developed the recipe, and the British perfected it. After male junipers pollinate the female shrubs and berries form, it takes 2 years for them to ripen from green to bluish purple. Then they are ready for the distillation process. Do **not** try this at home!*

Landscape Rose

Rosa species and hybrids

Other Name: Shrub Rose
Type: Deciduous, flowering
Mature Size: 3 to 8 feet tall; 4 to 6 feet wide
Bloom Time: June through October
Flower Color/Type: Mostly white, shades of pink, red
Features: Fragrance (some); hips; fall color

Light Requirements:

Color photograph on page 209.

Although everyone loves roses, not everyone is willing to devote the time and effort necessary to grow hybrid tea roses. In response to a rising interest in low-maintenance roses that integrate well into residential landscapes, breeders have produced many sturdy, colorful, self-reliant roses that are called landscape, or shrub, roses. These roses do not just sit and look pretty. Their easygoing, informal habits assure their versatility. They function in the landscape as ground covers, barrier plants, focal points, hedges, edges, and accents. Many have the "cottage garden" look; some do well in containers. Many have multiseason interest, offering season-long bloom, then colorful seedpods, or hips, and fall foliage color. They do not produce the classic single blooms at the end of long stems that hybrid teas do, but their flowers are lovely, abundant, and often fragrant. Large plantings of landscape roses are on view at the approach to the Philadelphia International Airport.

WHEN TO PLANT

Shrub roses usually come in containers. Plant them anytime, but spring planting assures some bloom over their first season.

WHERE TO PLANT

Like most flowering shrubs, landscape roses do best in full sun, at least 6 hours daily, but can handle some shade. They like well-drained soil, rich in organic matter, but accept almost any kind. Rugosa-type roses positively thrive on thin, poor soils.

HOW TO PLANT

Dig a saucer-shaped planting hole as deep as the shrub rose rootball is high and about twice as wide. Remove it from its container, and untangle or clip any circling roots. Set it in its hole so that the top of its rootball is exactly level with the surrounding soil, no lower. There is no graft to worry about. Then fill in the hole with soil, firming it gently around plant stems to

remove air pockets, and water well. Set plants about 5 feet apart from each other, slightly less for hedges.

CARE AND MAINTENANCE

Mulch landscape roses all year long with a 2- or 3-inch layer of organic matter such as chopped leaves or wood chips. Water them well while they become established. Many are amazingly drought tolerant, but appreciate water when rainfall is sparse. In the spring sprinkle slow-acting granular fertilizer formulated for trees and shrubs, or specifically for roses, on the mulch for the rain to soak in. Shrub roses are not, as a group, as heavy feeders as hybrid teas; once a year is fine. Most are self-cleaning, dropping their petals after blooming and forming bright-red or orange hips, so deadheading is not necessary. They need no special winter protection other than their usual mulch. Cut stems back in the spring to promote dense, new growth.

ADDITIONAL INFORMATION

Shrub roses have very few problems. Occasionally, Japanese beetles sample their foliage. 'Fairy' shows some fungal disease on the foliage in extremely humid periods, but does not tolerate spraying well. Let the plant handle it.

ADDITIONAL SPECIES, CULTIVARS, OR VARIETIES

'Carefree Delight'™, 'Ice and Fire', and 'The Fairy' make great hedges. Meidiland™ hybrids include 'Bonica'™, which was the first rose to win the Pennsylvania Horticultural Society's Gold Medal Award. It has double, pink flowers. Many others in this series are also tough and attractive for hedges, ground covers, or massing. Rugosa hybrids do well in coastal areas and tough conditions such as along the Blue Route. They have simple flowers, wonderful hips, and leathery foliage, especially 'Frau Dagmar Hartopp'.

 Did You Know?

A good landscape rose has the following:
- *All-season bloom*
- *No special pruning needs*
- *Drought resistance*
- *Winter sturdiness*
- *No foliage diseases*
- *Self-cleaning flowers*

Lilac, Common

Syringa vulgaris hybrids

Type: Deciduous, flowering

Mature Size: 8 to 15 feet tall;
6 to 10 feet wide

Bloom Time: Late April through May

Flower Color/Type: Shades of purple, white, pink, rose; double or
bicolor; tubular clusters

Features: Fragrance; attracts butterflies; old-fashioned

Light Requirements:

Color photograph on page 209.

Since 1700, lilacs have enjoyed enormous popularity in America. The introduction of many hybrids from France has only increased their appeal. The focus is on the flowers, of course, since the plant is an unremarkable, leggy shrub 11 months of the year. Its smooth, plain green, and heart-shaped foliage sets off the gorgeous blooms. Lilac blossoms are composed of many tiny, tubular florets, clustered in 4- to 6-inch-long sprays that feature the classic lilac fragrance. Different lilac varieties bloom at different times over 5 or 6 weeks each spring. Typical bloom periods are 2 weeks; the lilacs that bloom later tend to be less fragrant. Properly cared for, lilac shrubs live for many decades. On the farms of Chester County they grow near barns and front porches and along fence rows; they also anchor flower beds. They blend well into a mixed shrub border when they are not blooming.

WHEN TO PLANT

Buy plants grown on their own roots, rather than grafted, if possible. Plant bare-rooted shrubs in early spring. Plant lilacs raised in containers anytime during the growing season.

WHERE TO PLANT

For best flowering, site lilacs in full sun. They are not terribly fussy about soil as long as it is closer to neutral than acidic. Make sure there is ample space around lilacs for good air circulation to discourage fungal mildews on leaves.

HOW TO PLANT

Remove the lilac from its container, and untangle or clip any circling roots. Then dig a saucer-shaped planting hole as deep as the rootball is high and about twice as wide. Set the shrub in the hole so that the top of its rootball is exactly level with the surrounding soil. If it is bare root, pack a cone of soil at the bottom of the hole, and set the plant over it so that the roots drape down its sides and the crown of the plant, where they join the stem, is level with the surrounding soil. Then fill in the hole with soil, firming it gently around plant stems, and water well.

CARE AND MAINTENANCE

Mulch the root zone of the lilac year-round with a 2- or 3-inch layer of organic matter. Water the shrub regularly if rainfall is unreliable until it is well established. Every spring sprinkle slow-acting granular fertilizer formulated for trees and shrubs on the mulch for the rain to soak in. Prune shrubs while in flower to enjoy some indoors, or immediately after flowers die to prevent seed formation and to stimulate new growth. Renew an aging lilac by cutting back the thickest, oldest stems to within 6 inches of the ground to stimulate new shoots. Thin them to a few strong ones. Periodically cut off the suckers that form along some stems.

ADDITIONAL INFORMATION

Chronic mildew problems turn lilac foliage gray in late summer. It mars their appearance, but does not harm established shrubs. Borers leave small holes in bark with sawdust clinging to the outside. Prune off branches below the holes.

ADDITIONAL SPECIES, CULTIVARS, OR VARIETIES

Hundreds of hybrids of a variety of colors are available. Japanese tree lilac (*Syringa reticulata*) grows to about 30 feet with mal-odorous white flowers in June. 'Ivory Silk' is a winner of the Pennsylvania Horticultural Society's Gold Medal Award.

 Did You Know?

In the tradition of the language of flowers, lilacs have communicated volumes. Lore has it that an English nobleman abandoned an innocent girl whom he had seduced and she died of a broken heart. Because a wreath of purple lilacs left on her grave turned white, white lilacs have come to denote Youthful Innocence. Lilacs tend to be associated with death, never more poignantly than when Walt Whitman mourned the death of Lincoln in his classic poem "When Lilacs Last in the Dooryard Bloom'd."

Mahonia

Mahonia aquifolium

Other Name: Oregon Grapeholly
Type: Broadleaf evergreen
Mature Size: 6 to 8 feet tall;
  3 to 5 feet wide
Bloom Time: Early spring
Flower Color/Type: Yellow; urn-shaped florets
Features: Fragrance; berries; attracts wildlife

Color photograph on page 209.

Light Requirements:

Resembling in its particulars both holly and grapes, this Pacific Northwest native is an acquired taste. Its in-your-face, two-ranked, glossy, leathery, dark-green spined leaflets resemble giant holly leaves. They form a dark backdrop for the multiple, upright, elongated clusters of tiny yellow bells that fountain out of the stem-growing tips in April. By midsummer these flowers give way to grapelike, purplish edible berries that decorate the shrub as fall chill turns the foliage a rich maroon. Spreading gradually by underground roots into ever larger clumps, mahonias maintain a strong profile in the landscape. Deer show them considerable respect by avoiding them. Use them as specimens or in a shrub border.

WHEN TO PLANT

Plant easier-to-handle container-grown mahonias anytime during the growing season, although spring is best. Water well if planting during hot weather.

WHERE TO PLANT

Mahonia grows shorter and fuller in sun, but appreciates some shade during Philadelphia summers to prevent leaf scorch. It accepts almost any kind of soil, including clay, as long as it is acidic and reasonably well-drained. The best site offers some shelter from harsh winter sun and winds to protect foliage from desiccation and puncturing.

HOW TO PLANT

Dig a saucer-shaped planting hole as deep as the rootball is high and about twice as wide. Remove the mahonia from its container, and untangle or clip any circling roots. Set the plant in the hole so that the top of its rootball is exactly level with the surrounding soil; a bit higher is fine, too. Then fill in the hole with soil, firming it gently around plant stems to remove air pockets. Water well. Set plants at least 5 feet from neighboring shrubs or walls.

CARE AND MAINTENANCE

Maintain a year-round, 2- or 3-inch layer of organic mulch over the root zone of the mahonia. Water the shrub regularly if rainfall is unreliable until it is well established. Then it will be extremely drought tolerant. In its first spring, sprinkle slow-acting granular fertilizer formulated for acid-loving trees and shrubs on the mulch for the rain or snow to soak in. In the future constantly decomposing mulch will maintain good soil, and routine fertilization will not be necessary. To reduce clump size and/or gain more mahonias, cut off and dig up rooted side shoots. In the spring cut back dead and/or the tallest branches to within 6 inches of the ground to stimulate new and dense growth. Trimming off spent flowers during the season will stimulate more flower growth and prevent reseeding, but it will also reduce berry production.

ADDITIONAL INFORMATION

Mahonias are remarkably pest and disease free.

ADDITIONAL SPECIES, CULTIVARS, OR VARIETIES

Oregon grapeholly (*Mahonia aquifolium*) 'Compactum' grows to 30 inches tall. Leatherleaf mahonia (*Mahonia bealei*) is more heat tolerant and more fragrant but coarser. In 1860 a plant from the Joseph Hoops Nursery in West Chester ended up at Tyler Arboretum where it still grows.

 Did You Know?

It was most likely mahonia that Lewis and Clark found on their trip west in 1804-6. Their description strongly resembled these shrubs, which were eventually discovered growing wild all over Oregon. They were named for a Pennsylvania nurseryman, Bernard McMahon (1775-1816) from Germantown. He is known also for producing The American Gardener's Calendar, *one of the earliest gardening guides.*

Mockorange

Philadelphus coronarius

Other Name: Sweet Mockorange
Type: Deciduous, flowering
Mature Size: 5 to 10 feet tall; 5 to 8 feet wide
Bloom Time: June
Flower Color/Type: White; single or double
Features: Fragrance; old-fashioned

Color photograph on page 209.

Light Requirements:

This shrub evokes a bygone era, and like others of its time, weigela and kolkwitzia, it tends to be underrated in this day of designer plants and highly hybridized "stars" of the landscape. Truth to tell, mockorange boasts only modest assets, among them lovely white flowers—their citrus fragrance reminiscent of the orange blossoms that traditionally accompanied June weddings—and a sturdy constitution. Mockorange is reliably drought resistant, too. Newer hybrids have extra-large flowers, some with showy double petals. Mockoranges serve basic green background duty most of the summer, fitting in companionably with other shrubs in a border or alone near a wall or corner of a building. Carefully pruned and groomed, they have sufficient grace and form to stand alone as specimens. They are essentially pest and disease free.

WHEN TO PLANT

Plant shrubs with roots wrapped in burlap in either spring or fall. Those raised in containers at the nursery can be planted anytime during the growing season.

WHERE TO PLANT

Mockorange accepts either full sun or partial shade in any decent garden soil that is well-drained. The richer the soil, the better the flowering.

HOW TO PLANT

Dig a saucer-shaped planting hole as deep as the rootball is high and about twice as wide. Remove the mockorange from its container, and untangle or clip any circling roots. Set the shrub in the hole so that the top of its rootball is exactly level with the surrounding soil. If the roots are wrapped in burlap, cut as much of it away as possible. Then fill in the hole with soil, firming it gently around plant stems, and water well. It may take 2 or 3 years for mockorange to completely establish and bloom profusely. Set plants at least 6 feet apart from each other or from buildings.

CARE AND MAINTENANCE

Mulch the root zone of the mockorange year-round with a 2- or 3-inch layer of organic material such as chopped leaves or wood chips. Do not let it touch shrub stems. Water the shrub regularly if rainfall is unreliable until it is well established. In the spring sprinkle slow-acting granular fertilizer formulated for trees and shrubs on the mulch. Subsequently, the constantly decomposing mulch will maintain soil fertility. Prune to shape mockorange just after it blooms. When it is 2 feet tall, cut ⅓ off the new growth, and do this again when it is 4 feet tall. This forces the shrub to branch, making it more compact. As the mockorange ages, each spring cut back about ¼ of its oldest, thickest branches to the ground to stimulate new shoots and dense growth. To renew neglected, ragged shrubs, cut all the stems back to the ground. The shrub will regrow within about 3 years.

ADDITIONAL INFORMATION

Boughs of mockorange flowers are lovely alone or in arrangements with other flowers picked for indoor display.

ADDITIONAL SPECIES, CULTIVARS, OR VARIETIES

Philadelphus × 'Miniature Snowflake' is compact and has double flowers and dark-green leaves. *Philadelphus* × 'Buckley's Quill' is compact with double, white flowers, which have narrow "quill-like" petals. 'Aureus' has golden foliage. Shade promotes the best color.

 Did You Know?

Mockorange is one of a handful of deciduous ornamental shrubs that do not insist on full sun. The adaptability of mockoranges to indirect light and partial shade makes them extremely useful in a landscape. Others include the following:

Burkwood daphne (Daphne × burkwoodii)
Doublefile virburnum (Virburnum plicatum tomentosum)
Dwarf fothergilla (Fothergilla gardenii)
Glossy abelia (Abelia × grandiflora)
Oakleaf hydrangea (Hydrangea quercifolia)
Old-fashioned weigela (Weigela florida)
Rhododendron species and hybrids
Summersweet (Clethra alnifolia)
Winged euonymus (Euonymus alata)
Winterberry (Ilex verticillata)
Witchhazel (Hamemelis sp.)

Mountain Laurel

Kalmia latifolia

Type: Broadleaf evergreen
Mature Size: 8 to 15 feet tall;
  6 to 20 feet wide
Bloom Time: Late May or June, depending
  on the variety
Flower Color/Type: White, pink, rose, bicolor; starlike cup
Features: Flowers; Pennsylvania's state flower

Light Requirements:

Color photograph on page 209.

Mountain laurel, the lovely native shrub of our Pennsylvania forests, is our state flower. It has always been valued for its wonderful glossy, dense, dark-green foliage, its large round clusters of white flowers, and its vigor. Over the last 40 years or so this wild beauty has undergone a transformation at the hands of plant breeders and now ranks high on every list of first-rate ornamental shrubs. Its globes of intricately formed florets come in many rich colors, the florets sometimes fancifully marked with brownish bands or splotches. Reportedly resistant to the attentions of deer, it is slow growing and long lived. Use mountain laurel as specimens, as foundation plants, or naturalized in woodland settings.

WHEN TO PLANT

Mountain laurel is available in containers and does best planted in early spring or early fall. Its dense, fibrous roots are shallow and transplant easily.

WHERE TO PLANT

Mountain laurel prefers the woodland conditions of its wild habitat, similar to those favored by rhododendrons. An understory plant, it likes dappled sun or partial shade and moist, well-drained, acidic soil that is rich in organic matter. Newer varieties can handle more sun, especially in the morning, but still appreciate some shade during hot summer afternoons.

HOW TO PLANT

Improve heavy clay or very sandy soil prior to planting by digging it over the entire planting area and mixing in organic matter such as peat moss or compost. Remove the mountain laurel from its container, and untangle or clip any circling roots. Dig a planting hole with sloping sides just as deep as the rootball is high and about twice as wide. Set the plant in the hole so that the top of its rootball is exactly level with the surrounding soil, or a

bit higher. Then fill in the hole with soil, firming it gently, and water well. Set plants at least 5 feet apart from each other or from buildings.

CARE AND MAINTENANCE

Mulch the root zone of the mountain laurel year-round with a 2- or 3-inch layer of organic matter such as chopped leaves or wood chips. Water the shrub regularly if rainfall is unreliable until it is well established. In the spring sprinkle slow-acting granular fertilizer formulated for acid-loving shrubs on the mulch for the rain to soak in. Over the years the decomposing mulch will maintain soil fertility and eliminate the need for routine fertilizing. In the spring cut back any broken or winter-killed branches to live wood. Otherwise, allow the branching to remain natural and free form. After bloom, trim off spent flowers. If shrubs are old and gangly, renew them by cutting the stems back to within 6 inches of the ground to stimulate new and dense growth.

ADDITIONAL INFORMATION

Cut branches of mountain laurel for indoor display when the flowers are mostly swelling buds. Strip off any leaves that will be below the water in their container, recut the woody stem ends, and put them immediately into a container filled with lukewarm water.

ADDITIONAL SPECIES, CULTIVARS, OR VARIETIES

'Ostsbo Red' has red buds and light-pink flowers. 'Bullseye' flowers have a cinnamon-red band on the petals. 'Elf' is dwarf, averages half the size of standard mountain laurels.

 Did You Know?

Sometimes the leaves of plants that love acid soil, such as mountain laurel, rhododendron, and pieris, turn yellowish, their veins remaining green. This condition is called chlorosis, and it signals an iron deficiency in the plant. Because of insufficient soil acidity (high pH), they cannot access the iron in the soil. To correct the chlorotic condition, acidify the soil by adding powdered garden sulfur to the soil as directed on the product label. (Used coffee grounds are a good soil conditioner and acidifier, too.)

Mugo Pine, Dwarf

Pinus mugo compact selections

Other Name: Dwarf Swiss Mountain Pine
Type: Evergreen conifer
Mature Size: 3 to 5 feet tall; 6 to 12 feet wide
Foliage: Dark-green needles
Features: Cones; aromatic foliage

Light Requirements:

Color photograph on page 209.

Dwarf mugo pines are popular ornamental conifers and with good reason. They have all the virtues of pines—fine needles, aromatic foliage, plump cones, and sturdy constitutions—plus a compact form. Their irregular, rounded cushions of dense needles provide contrasting texture to broadleaf plant neighbors near the front of the border. They are eminently adaptable to home landscapes, serving equally effectively as foundation plants, focal points, rock garden or container specimens, and ground covers. They are likely to be bypassed by deer that may venture into the yard.

WHEN TO PLANT

Plant shrubs with their roots wrapped in burlap in either spring or fall. Those raised in containers at the nursery can be planted anytime during the growing season. Container-grown mugos accept transplanting well.

WHERE TO PLANT

Pines need full sun for best vigor. Since Philadelphia summer heat may stress them, a site with some afternoon light shade is good. They accept just about any type of decent garden soil, even if it is a bit on the alkaline side, as long as it is well-drained. Add organic matter to heavy, clay soil to improve drainage before planting. Keep mugos away from turfgrasses, which release a growth-inhibiting substance into their soil.

HOW TO PLANT

Dig a saucer-shaped planting hole as deep as the rootball is high and a bit wider. Remove the mugo pine from its container, and untangle or clip any circling roots. Set it in the hole so that the top of its rootball is exactly level with the surrounding soil; a bit higher is fine, too. If the rootball is wrapped in burlap, cut as much of it away as possible. Then fill in the hole with soil, firming it gently to remove air pockets, and water well. Mugo pines are very slow growing, so will stay within their allotted space for years.

CARE AND MAINTENANCE

Mulch the mugo's root zone with a 2- or 3-inch layer of organic matter such as chopped leaves, pine needles, or wood chips. Water it regularly for a year or more if rainfall is unreliable until it is well established. In the spring sprinkle slow-acting granular fertilizer formulated for evergreen shrubs on the mulch for the rain to soak in. Clip out any brown or broken branches anytime. Their natural shapes are part of their charm, so mugos do not really need pruning for shape.

ADDITIONAL INFORMATION

Pine sawfly larvae are caterpillars about the same color as pine needles. When disturbed, they sort of stand erect, as if to scare off the intruder. Pick them off infested shrubs, place them in a plastic bag, and discard it in the trash. Treat heavy infestations by spraying the needles with a product containing Bt (*Bacillus thuringiensis*) while caterpillars are actively eating them. They will sicken and die within days. Thwart scale problems by spraying foliage with light horticultural oil. Always follow label instructions.

ADDITIONAL SPECIES, CULTIVARS, OR VARIETIES

Pinus mugo 'Mops' is very dense and globe shaped; it grows to 4 feet. *Pinus mugo* var. *mugo* has medium-green foliage in summer, lighter in summer; it tends to be twice as wide as tall. *Pinus mugo* var. *pumilio* is low growing, up to 10 feet wide.

Did You Know?

Buyer beware: Plants are not always what they are labeled. Sometimes growers or retailers get labels confused, and because many plants do not mature enough to be easily identified before sale, they are not able to correct the error. Sometimes male and female plants are difficult to tell apart for many years. Sometimes plants grown from seed are unpredictable. Thus it occasionally happens that dwarf mugo pines turn out not to be dwarf. Purchasing grafted nursery stock of known parentage usually avoids this problem.

Nandina

Nandina domestica

Other Names: Heavenly Bamboo,
  Sacred Bamboo
Type: Variably evergreen
Mature Size: 2 (dwarf) to 18 feet tall;
  2 to 5 feet wide
Bloom Time: Late June/early July
Flower Color/Type: White florets in loose clusters
Features: Berries; fall and winter color; interesting stems

Light Requirements:

Color photograph on page 209.

Nandina is often labeled as overused in the South, but definitely not here where it provides interesting, unusual texture and form to residential landscapes. The stiff, upright, unbranched stems of full-sized nandinas are reminiscent of bamboo. They are softened by intricately divided foliage made up of pointed leaflets, creating an airy look. Their foliage progresses from its young, glossy, bronzy red stage to summer green, acquiring a handsome red or purplish tint in autumn. It backdrops nandina's very large, 6- to 12-inch upright clusters of creamy-white flowers at the tips of its branches in the spring. It remains to showcase the subsequent large clusters of red berries that develop by fall and droop heavily on the shrub through the winter. Dwarf versions of nandina offer wonderful glowing reddish winter foliage, but less spectacular flowers and berries. A Japanese symbol of hospitality, nandinas are a welcome, virtually problem-free addition to any yard as specimens, foundation plants, or ground covers.

WHEN TO PLANT

Nandinas are usually available in containers, so they can be planted almost anytime during the growing season. Because they are not thrilled about being moved, pick a good site.

WHERE TO PLANT

Full sun brings out the best in nandina flowers and foliage, especially the foliage of the red-leafed dwarf ones, although all will grow fine in some shade. They prefer good soil, rich in organic matter, but they tolerate clay or even thin, sandy soils if they get enough water during the summer. Generally, nandinas are quite drought tolerant.

How to Plant

Dig a saucer-shaped planting hole as deep as the rootball is high and about twice as wide. Remove the nandina from its container, and untangle or clip any circling roots. Set the plant in the hole so that the top of its rootball is exactly level with the surrounding soil. Then fill in the hole with soil, firming it gently to remove air pockets, and water well.

Care and Maintenance

Mulch the root zone of the nandina year-round with a 2- or 3-inch layer of organic matter to retain soil moisture and discourage weeds. Water the shrub when rainfall is unreliable until it is well established. In the spring sprinkle slow-acting granular fertilizer formulated for trees and shrubs on the mulch for the rain to soak in. To maintain bushiness, cut back the tallest stems annually to various heights. Renew a longtime planting of nandina by cutting out dead wood and pruning back to ground level about ⅓ of the oldest, thickest stems.

Additional Information

Their notable environmental toughness notwithstanding, in the North some nandinas lose their leaves during the winter. Both foliage and berries are great additions to indoor flower arrangements and holiday decorations. Birds do not eat the berries.

Additional Species, Cultivars, or Varieties

Some full-sized (old-fashioned) nandinas include 'Alba', which has cream-colored berries and new foliage green without red tints, and needs shade; and 'Moyers Red', which is slow growing to 5 or 6 feet. Some dwarf (new) nandinas generally have fewer flowers and fruit; they include 'Gulf Stream', which has red leaves in winter, and 'Harbour Dwarf', which grows to 3 feet tall and is wide spreading.

 Did You Know?

Heavenly bamboo is a lovely common name, but it may do a disservice to this fine shrub. The reputation of true bamboos as invasive thugs whose spreading roots run rampant through yards predisposes some home owners and gardeners to shy away from the similarly named nandina, which is a well-mannered clumping shrub.

Pieris, Japanese

Pieris japonica

Other Name: Lily of the Valley Shrub
Type: Broadleaf evergreen
Mature Size: 4 to 12 feet tall; 4 to 8 feet wide
Bloom Time: Early April
Flower Color/Type: White; urn shaped
Features: Fragrance; evergreen

Light Requirements:

Color photograph on page 209.

The elegance of pieris enhances any residential landscape. Its compact, yet free-form, open branching becomes more interesting with age. As it presides over the seasons, its rosettes of narrow, finely toothed, lustrous evergreen foliage mature from bright lime-green or reddish green to dark green just in time to showcase its flowers. The buds that it has carried all winter develop into stunning, waxy, urn-shaped florets arrayed in 3- to 5-inch pendulous, fragrant clusters that bloom for 3 weeks or more. Slow-growing, pieris is at home in woodland settings or front and center as foundation, accent, or specimen plantings in shady yards.

WHEN TO PLANT

Pieris is available as container-grown shrubs and can be planted anytime during the growing season.

WHERE TO PLANT

Light is a critical consideration when siting pieris. They do best in some degree of shade because the stress of hot sun invites pest problems. They like woodland conditions similar to those preferred by azaleas, mountain laurel, and rhododendron. Wherever you plant them, give them moist, acidic soil rich in organic matter that drains really well. If they are near a brick or stone wall, check the soil's pH to be sure its acidity is not being neutralized by the lime from leaching mortar.

HOW TO PLANT

Improve heavy clay or thin, sandy soil in the planting area by digging in organic matter. Dig a saucer-shaped planting hole as deep as the rootball is high and somewhat wider. Remove the pieris from its container, and untangle or clip any circling roots. Set it in the hole so that the top of its rootball is exactly level with the surrounding soil; a bit higher is fine, too. Then fill in the hole, firm the soil gently, and water well. Distance shrubs at least 5 feet from each other or from buildings.

CARE AND MAINTENANCE

Mulch pieris root zones with a 2- or 3-inch layer of organic matter such as chopped leaves or wood chips. Water the shrub regularly if rainfall is unreliable until it is well established. It likes moist soil and does best if the soil does not dry out in the summer. In the spring sprinkle slow-acting granular fertilizer formulated for acid-loving shrubs and trees on the mulch for the rain or snow to soak in. Also, cut back any dead branches then to within 6 inches of the ground to stimulate new, dense growth. Pieris in exposed sites may need screening from harsh winter wind and sun.

ADDITIONAL INFORMATION

Like all broadleaf evergreens, pieris continues to transpire moisture from its leaves during the winter. If the ground is frozen, it cannot take up replacement moisture from the soil over the cold weeks. Water the ground deeply before it freezes to prevent its leaves from drying out. Spray foliage with an anti-dessicant in late autumn.

ADDITIONAL SPECIES, CULTIVARS, OR VARIETIES

Many Japanese pieris varieties have colored flowers, such as 'Flamingo' (rose-red), 'Dorothy Wycoff' (pink), and 'White Cascade' (white), very floriforous. The new foliage of 'Mountain Fire' is particularly red. 'Variegata' foliage is edged with white. Mountain pieris (*Pieris floribunda*) blooms in April with smaller, upright flower clusters; native to the South, it is resistant to lacebugs. 'Brouwer's Beauty' is a hybrid of the two pieris species.

 Did You Know?

Lacebugs are a pieris nemesis. Their feeding on foliage covers it with pale stippling above and brown specks of excrement underneath. They target pieris (and azaleas) stressed by drought and too much sun. Identify and treat infestations early because lacebugs have many generations over a single season. Their damage to foliage remains visible even after they have been eliminated by repeated sprays of an insecticidal soap or encapsulated pyrethrum product applied according to label instructions.

Privet, Common

Ligustrum vulgare

Other Name: European Privet
Type: Semievergreen
Mature Size: 5 to 15 feet tall; about as wide
Bloom Time: May and June
Flower Color/Type: White
Features: Flowers support honeybees

Light Requirements:

Color photograph on page 209.

Not every shrub can be a landscape star. Privet plays in the chorus line, contributing enormously to the structure and functionality of the home landscapes it graces. Its primary role is as hedging, its reliable toughness, pollution tolerance, and environmental adaptability assuring that it will be around for many years. It takes shearing in stride, holds its leaves, which turn purplish in all but severest winters, manages drought, and accepts shade. Left unpruned, privet bears clusters of musky-scented, off-white flowers that attract lots of honeybees. The small black berries that follow persist into winter if the birds do not get them first.

WHEN TO PLANT

Plant container-grown privets anytime during the growing season. Spring or fall is preferred to avoid stressing these or bare-root transplants with summer heat and drought.

WHERE TO PLANT

Privet thrives in full sun or partial shade. It takes virtually any kind of soil with almost any pH. Its adaptability is so legendary that many people regard it as an indicator plant. If it does not grow on a particular site, nothing will. Plant privets as hedges along walks and property lines and in the lawn to divide the yard into rooms.

HOW TO PLANT

Dig individual saucer-shaped planting holes or dig a trench with sloping sides the length of the intended hedge as deep as privet rootballs are high and about twice as wide. Remove the privets from their containers, and untangle or clip any circling roots. Set the plants so that the tops of their rootballs are exactly level with the surrounding soil. Then fill in the holes or trench with soil, firm it gently, and water well. Space shrubs for a hedge about 3 feet apart.

CARE AND MAINTENANCE

Mulch privet root zones year-round with a 2- or 3-inch layer of organic matter. It will discourage weeds, hold soil moisture, and improve the soil as it constantly decomposes. Water the shrubs regularly if rainfall is unreliable until they are established. In the spring sprinkle slow-acting granular fertilizer formulated for trees and shrubs on the mulch for the rain to soak in. Prune out the occasional dead or damaged stem promptly. To establish the hedge, shear for uniform growth when privets are about 18 inches tall. Maintain the lower branches as wide or wider than the upper so that the sun can reach them. In spring shear back below the intended maintenance height to allow for a gradual height increase over the season. Then shear back only some of the new growth each pruning time during the season to assure that some new leaves remain at all times.

ADDITIONAL INFORMATION

To renew an old, ratty hedge, cut back all stems to within 6 inches of the ground in the spring. Cut out old and dead ones. Fertilize and water well, and spread new mulch. In no time new, dense growth will appear. Young, tender privet stems will often root on their own when stuck into good, moist, well-drained soil.

ADDITIONAL SPECIES, CULTIVARS, OR VARIETIES

'Lodense' is a dwarf form that needs less pruning but is deciduous. Noble privet (*Ligustrum japonicum* 'Nobilis') has a narrow habit.

 Did You Know?

Hedges are barriers; however, because they are plants, they are less intimidating than fences. They mediate the contrast between the structural hardscape of buildings and walls and the natural softscape of plants in a yard. As they do their job of defining and enclosing space, they are more welcoming than rejecting. Certainly, that is why mazes appeal rather than intimidate. A good hedge plant branches low to the ground, has fairly small leaves, withstands shearing well, and is at right angles rather than parallel to a building.

Rhododendron

Rhododendron species and hybrids

Other Name: Rhody
Type: Broadleaf evergreen
Mature Size: Dwarf to 3 feet; others to
  15 feet tall and as wide
Bloom Time: Early April through May to June
Flower Color/Type: Shades of red, pink, purple, white; bell shaped
Features: Flowers; attracts butterflies and hummingbirds

Light Requirements:

Color photograph on page 210.

*R*hododendron means "rose tree," and it is easy to see the connection. Rhodendrons' huge clusters of showy bell-shaped flowers framed by large, smooth, dark-green leaves add an elegant note to the landscape. They grow all over the world, including the United States, and have been cultivated for more than a century. Hybrids bred from native species were introduced in 1876 at the Centennial Exhibition in Philadelphia and represent the majority of the rhododendrons sold in our part of the country. New types from Asia are proving to be popular as well. In the wild, rhododendrons are understory shrubs in woodland settings, but many make fine specimens, informal hedges and screens, and foundation plantings. Unfortunately, the deer appreciate them almost as much as we do.

WHEN TO PLANT

Plant burlap-wrapped rhododendrons in either early spring or fall. Transplant those raised in containers anytime during the growing season, but spring is best. Their shallow, fibrous roots establish easily.

WHERE TO PLANT

Most rhododendrons prefer sunny sites with afternoon shade in the summer and winter. Dappled light in woodland settings suits many if they are not under shallow-rooted trees such as beeches and maples, which compete with them for moisture. Rhododendrons dry out quickly anyway. They like woodsy soil, acidic, rich in organic matter, and well-drained. The best sites are sheltered from harsh winter wind and sun.

HOW TO PLANT

Improve clay soil drainage by mixing organic material into it. Dig a saucer-shaped planting hole as deep as the rootball is high and about twice as wide. Remove the rhody from its container, and untangle or clip any cir-cling roots. Set the plant in the hole so that the top of its rootball is exactly level with the surrounding soil. Cut as much burlap away as possible from wrapped rootballs. Then fill in the hole, firm the soil gently, and water well. Plants raised locally are best because the soil around their rootball is more likely to be similar to the soil in your yard and they are acclimated to our winters.

CARE AND MAINTENANCE

Mulch rhododendron root zones year-round with 2 or 3 inches of organic matter to keep the soil moist and their roots cool. Water shrubs regularly if rainfall is unreliable until they are established and then during hot, dry summers. In the spring fertilize with slow-acting granular fertilizer formulated for acid-loving plans. Pinch or clip off faded flowers to enhance appearance and to prevent seed formation. Renewal of old shrubs by cutting back their stems to within 6 inches of the ground to stimulate new, dense growth is usually successful, but not guaranteed.

ADDITIONAL INFORMATION

Glossy, leathery rhody leaves are good for indoor arrangements, holiday decorations, and crafts. Watch for borer holes in older stems, and prune them off below the hole.

ADDITIONAL SPECIES, CULTIVARS, OR VARIETIES

Rosebay rhododendron (*R. maximum*) is locally native and can handle drier soil. Flowers are white with pink buds, blooming late June to July. Rugged hybrids for sunny spots are Catawba Hybrids. 'Catwbiense Album' blooms late May to June. Fortunei Hybrids bloom in early May with the largest flowers. 'Scintillation' is pink; 'Janet Blair' is soft pink. Yakushimanum Hybrids are dwarf and compact with brown fuzzy undersides on leaves. They bloom in May and do best in partial sun.

 Did You Know?

Dr. John Wister, former director of both Tyler Arboretum in Media and Scott Arboretum at Swarthmore College, was instrumental in bringing to prominence the Dexter hybrids, some of the best rhododendrons we have. An enthusiastic promoter of rhodys, he bred them during the 1950s. Shrubs from the many seedlings these efforts produced still bloom in gardens and along streets all over Swarthmore.

Rose of Sharon

Hibiscus syriacus

Other Name: Shrub Althea
Type: Deciduous, flowering
Mature Size: 8 to 12 feet tall;
  6 to 10 feet wide
Bloom Time: July into September
Flower Color/Type: White, red, lavender, pink, bicolor; double; open cups
Features: Old-fashioned; evening garden ('Diana'); attracts hummingbirds

Light Requirements:

Color photograph on page 210.

Owners of older or homes may have discovered old-fashioned rose of Sharon along fence lines and in overgrown shrub borders somewhere on the property. A survivor from the old days, her pinkish purple flowers produce copious seeds that self-sow to assure new generations of shrubs over the decades. These tough, upright shrubs offer welcome summer flowers, adaptability to virtually any soil and temperature, and resistance to pollution and road salt. Now more civilized hybrids that do not seed promiscuously have endowed rose of Sharon with a new respectability. Their long-lasting flowers are bigger and are available in more colors, yet they retain all their toughness. Use them along fences, at the edge of lawns, along drives, or in shrub borders. They are ideal for cottage-type gardens, screening, and even sheared hedges (usually at the sacrifice of their flowers).

WHEN TO PLANT

Rose of Sharon is usually container grown and can be planted anytime. As a summer bloomer, however, it is better to plant in spring or fall.

WHERE TO PLANT

Rose of Sharon thrives in full sun. Although it prefers moist soil, once established, it copes with almost any type except boggy. Ordinary garden soil that is well-drained is fine. Of course, the richer the soil in organic matter, the happier the shrub.

HOW TO PLANT

There is no need to take extra measures to prepare the soil. Dig a saucer-shaped planting hole as deep as the rose of Sharon rootball is high and about twice as wide. Remove it from its container, and untangle or clip any circling roots. Set it in the hole so that its top is exactly level with the surrounding soil. Then fill in the hole with soil, firm it gently, and water well.

CARE AND MAINTENANCE

Mulch the root zone of the rose of Sharon with a 2- or 3-inch layer of organic matter such as chopped leaves or wood chips. Water the shrub regularly if rainfall is unreliable until it is well established. Otherwise, it needs no special care. Cut off spent flowers of old types before they become dried seed capsules to prevent reseeding. To control size and keep flowers at eye level, cut back branches by several feet during the late winter when it is dormant. To renew old, tired shrubs, in the spring cut back dead or old, thick branches to within 6 inches of the ground to stimulate new and dense growth.

ADDITIONAL INFORMATION

Rose of Sharon grows well in containers. It can also be trained as a standard with a single stem. Keep an eye out for Japanese beetles on the foliage.

ADDITIONAL SPECIES, CULTIVARS, OR VARIETIES

'Diana' is a hybrid with clear-white flowers. Because it does not seed itself all over, it is recommended for landscape use. It stays open at night. It is a winner of the Pennsylvania Horticultural Society's Gold Medal Award. Other hybrids offering a variety of colors are 'Aphrodite' (dark pink), 'Minerva' (lilac with a red center), and 'Blue Bird' (blue with purple eye).

 Did You Know?

In the Philadelphia area Japanese beetles emerge from lawns, where they spend their white grub stage, around the Fourth of July weekend. They zero in on foliage food favorites where they can be found eating and mating with abandon. Because they are so predictable, it is easy to start dealing with them within hours of their arrival. Check rose of Sharon, raspberries, roses, four o'clocks, or other known favorites in the yard, and immediately begin control. Handpick them or spray them with encapsulated pyrethrum as directed on the product label. (Do not use bag beetle traps, which only attract more to the area.) Treat the lawn for white grubs for next year.

Shadblow

Amelanchier species and hybrids

Other Name: Serviceberry
Type: Deciduous, flowering
Mature Size: 6 to 20 feet tall; variable width
Bloom Time: Late March, early April
Flower Color/Type: White
Features: Edible fruit; attracts songbirds; fall color

Light Requirements:

Color photograph on page 210.

This native woodland gem has many names, but in the Philadelphia area it is mostly called shadblow because it blooms very early, when the shad are running in the Delaware River. Its cloud of small, delicate white flowers clustered at its branch tips above its upright stems is visible from the highway through the still leafless forest. Just behind them the down-covered new leaves arrive, maturing over 3 or 4 weeks to medium green. By June shadblow bears edible, juicy black fruit, which the birds grab immediately. Its season finale is yellowish or gold foliage, sometimes tinged orange-red. In addition to its multiseason beauty, shadblow is tough and adaptable. Use it in a natural woodland or streamside planting. It is also effective as a foundation or patio plant.

WHEN TO PLANT

Plant shadblow in either spring or fall. Shrubs in containers can be planted anytime during the growing season. They transplant uncomplainingly.

WHERE TO PLANT

Shadblow can handle a range of light situations from full sun to real shade. It produces more flowers and better fall foliage color where it gets more sun. It is not fussy about soil, so any well-drained ordinary garden soil on the acidic side will do. Give it room because some types expand their clumps by means of suckering roots.

HOW TO PLANT

Remove the shadblow from its container, and untangle or clip any circling roots. Dig a saucer-shaped planting hole as deep as the rootball is high and about twice as wide. Set it in the hole so that its top is exactly level with the surrounding soil. If the plant's rootball is wrapped, cut as much of the burlap away as possible. Then fill in the hole with soil, firm it gently to remove air pockets, and water well.

CARE AND MAINTENANCE

Mulch the root zone of the shadblow with a 2- or 3-inch layer of organic matter such as chopped leaves or wood chips. Water it regularly if rainfall is unreliable until it is well established. If it gets a fair amount of sun, be sure it does not dry out during summer hot spells. If the soil is decent, there is no need to fertilize. The constant decomposition of the organic mulch will maintain soil fertility. Pruning is not necessary except to remove old or damaged stems or reduce height.

ADDITIONAL INFORMATION

Shadblows are related to apple trees and sometimes fall victim to their diseases. Fireblight causes twig dieback in the middle of the summer. Affected shoots look as if they were scorched by fire and develop distinctive curved ends. Prune out infected plant parts promptly, and put them in the trash to control the spread of the infection. Disinfect tools by dipping them into a solution of hot water and household bleach.

ADDITIONAL SPECIES, CULTIVARS, OR VARIETIES

Juneberry or downy serviceberry (*Amelanchier arborea*) is more treelike at 30 or more feet tall with all the shadblow assets. While experts have some trouble keeping track of the many types of shadblows, they have produced hybrids that make excellent landscape plants. Some examples are 'Autumn Brilliance', 'Cole's Select', 'Cumulus', 'Forest Prince', 'Spring Glory', and 'Tradition'.

Did You Know?

Traditionally, early-blooming shadblow has signaled that spring is about to arrive in Pennsylvania. For early settlers it also meant that the ground was due to thaw enough that graves could be dug for those who had died during the winter. "Serviceberry" flowers marked the time to hold services for the departed and give them a proper burial. Both Native Americans and settlers cultivated these shrubs for their edible berries, which resemble blueberries.

Smokebush

Cotinus coggygria

Other Name: Smoketree
Type: Deciduous, flowering
Mature Size: Up to 15 feet tall;
  10 to 12 feet wide
Bloom Time: June
Flower Color/Type: Yellowish; tiny
Features: Old-fashioned; fall foliage; "smoke" seedheads; attracts bees

Light Requirements:

Color photograph on page 210.

The heyday of smokebushes was the Victorian era, but their unique flowers and accommodating nature are winning them renewed interest. The attraction, of course, is the distinctive puffy flower clusters. Actually, the hairy stalks that hold the flowers elongate as they fade and form plumes of "smoke." They turn pinkish gray and persist over the summer, casting a haze at tips of shrub branches, upstaging the wonderful leaves. Foliage is broadly oval and usually a bluish green, but some versions of smokebush have deep-purple leaves changing to reddish or orange-yellow with the approach of fall. Large enough to often be called smoketrees, these shrubs need pruning to maintain a good size for the typical residential landscape where they are useful as foundation and mixed border plants. The purple-foliaged ones contrast dramatically with silver or gray plants such as artemisias, or lamb's ears. They also make a stunning hedge. Mercifully, deer seem to leave them alone.

WHEN TO PLANT

Plant shrubs raised in containers anytime over the growing season. Smokebush transplants easily.

WHERE TO PLANT

Full sun encourages smokebush flowers and foliage color. Shrubs are flexible about soil type, accepting everything from dry and rocky to moist and clayey. They can handle soils that are on the alkaline side or even compacted. A site somewhat sheltered from the wind protects their brittle branches.

HOW TO PLANT

Remove the smokebush from its container, and untangle or clip any circling roots. Dig a saucer-shaped planting hole as deep as its rootball is high and about twice as wide. Set the shrub in the hole so that the top of its rootball is even with the surrounding soil. Then fill in the hole with soil, firm it gently, and water well.

CARE AND MAINTENANCE

Mulch the root zone of the smokebush with a 2- or 3-inch layer of organic matter such as chopped leaves or wood chips. Water it regularly if rainfall is unreliable until it is well established, then it can cope with drought if it must. A slow-acting granular fertilizer formulated for trees and shrubs sprinkled on the mulch in the spring the first year gives it a good start, but is not essential. To maintain the smokebush as a smallish shrub, cut back its stems to the ground in late winter. This stimulates the production of new shoots that will have larger, more intensely colored leaves, but no flowers, since they bloom on the previous year's wood that is cut off. The pruning also controls its size and prevents any scale insects, which sometimes attack smokebush, from overwintering on the shrubs.

ADDITIONAL INFORMATION

Smokebush has few problems, but it may be pestered by rodents, which gnaw on tender bark of young transplants in the winter. Delay spreading winter mulch until the ground freezes hard to deny them a nesting place. Wrap stem bases in hardware cloth or commercial tree guards.

ADDITIONAL SPECIES, CULTIVARS, OR VARIETIES

'Royal Purple' has deep-purple foliage, purplish red "smoke," then red-orange-yellow fall foliage. 'Velvet Cloak' has rich, reddish purple foliage. 'Daydream' has green leaves and pale pinkish beige smoke. American Smoketree (*Cotinus obovatus*) is native. It grows to 30 feet with a rounded canopy of blue-green foliage, small flowers, and interesting winter bark. Its lovely fall foliage is apricot to red and purple in color.

 Did You Know?

Coppicing (also called stooling) is a pruning technique that seems drastic but often improves plant health. It means cutting woody plants back to ground level. It prompts trees and shrubs to send up multiple stems from the base of their former trunks. A way to renew old tired plants, it also forces them to grow foliage on new, tender wood, which is less brittle and possibly more colorful.

Spirea, Vanhoutte

Spiraea × vanhouttei

Other Name: Bridalwreath Spirea
Type: Deciduous, flowering
Mature Size: 6 to 10 feet tall;
  8 to 12 feet wide
Bloom Time: Late May
Flower Color/Type: White; clusters of florets
Features: Old-fashioned

Light Requirements:

Color photograph on page 210.

There are all kinds of spireas these days, but the classic Vanhoutte is still the sentimental favorite. Featuring upright, arching branches that dip to the ground under the weight of its rows of flat, round clusters of tiny white florets, it has graced American yards since the 1850s. After this spirea's brief bloom period, its small, oval blue-green leaves are more visible, blending in with other greenery in a shrub border until they turn yellowish and drop in the fall. Vanhoutte spirea is fast growing, easy to care for, and drought tolerant.

WHEN TO PLANT

Plant in either early spring or fall. Plant container-grown Vanhoutte spireas anytime during the growing season. Avoid periods of intense summer heat and drought if possible.

WHERE TO PLANT

Vanhoutte spireas like full sun best. Although they prefer good garden soil rich in organic matter that is moist and well-drained, they accept considerably less.

HOW TO PLANT

Improve the soil in the planting area by digging in organic material such as peat moss or compost. Remove the spirea from its container, and untangle or clip any circling roots. Dig a saucer-shaped planting hole as deep as the rootball is high and about twice as wide. Set the plant in the hole so that the top of its rootball is exactly level with the surrounding soil. Then fill in the hole with soil, firm it gently to remove air pockets, and water well. Set plants at least 6 feet apart from each other for hedges.

CARE AND MAINTENANCE

Spread a 2- or 3-inch layer of organic material over the root zone of the spirea to keep the soil moist and discourage weeds. The chopped leaves, wood chips, or shredded bark will decompose over time, adding valuable organic matter to the soil. Renew the mulch when the layer is thin. Water the shrub regularly if rainfall is unreliable until it is well established. Every spring sprinkle slow-acting granular fertilizer formulated for trees and shrubs on the mulch for the rain to soak in. To revitalize older shrubs, yet maintain their fountainlike branching habit, prune out thicker, woody stems by cutting them back to ground level. To totally renovate them, cut all the stems back to near ground level. Clip stem tips off individually just after they flower for light natural shaping. **Never shear spireas.**

ADDITIONAL INFORMATION

Except for rust, a fungal disease on the foliage, spireas are pest and disease free.

ADDITIONAL SPECIES, CULTIVARS, OR VARIETIES

Snowmound spirea (*Spiraea nipponica* 'Snowmound') is denser and shorter. Double pink bridal wreath (*Spiraea × bumalda* 'Anthony Waterer') has flat-topped rosy-pink flowers and grows only 2 to 3 feet tall. Goldflame spirea (*Spiraea × bumalda* 'Goldflame') has yellow-green foliage and rose flowers and fall foliage color, and it grows to 4 feet tall. Varieties and hybrids of Japanese Spirea (*Spiraea japonica*) are commonly grown in gardens today. They tend to be only 4 or 5 feet tall and wide, with narrow, pointed foliage and individual flat clusters of flowers in shades of pink, or pink and white. Some types have chartreuse or reddish foliage. They are drought tolerant, disease resistant, and virtually pest free. They take shearing well. Examples are 'Little Princess' and 'Shirobana'.

 Did You Know?

In March of 1850 The Horticulturist, *an early gardening magazine, responded to a reader's request for "the best and simplest directions for cultivating the finest of our common flowers." Among the shrubs on the list of easy-to-grow plants that the magazine printed were forsythia, althea, spirea, and lilac. Obviously, spirea was much loved many decades ago!*

Summersweet

Clethra alnifolia

Other Name: Sweetpepper Bush
Type: Deciduous, flowering
Mature Size: 5 to 10 feet tall;
  6 to 12 feet wide
Bloom Time: July into August
Flower Color/Type: White, rose, pink; florets on spikes
Features: Flowers; fragrance; attractive bark; attracts honeybees,
  butterflies, and beneficial insects

Light Requirements:

Color photograph on page 210.

Summersweet is a name that truly conveys the virtues and beauty of this wonderful native shrub. After its glossy, green foliage backdrops all the riotously flowering plants through the spring and early summer, it is summersweet's turn. Its midsummer flowers are upright 6-inch spikes, fuzzy with tiny florets, at branch tips. They fill the heavy summer air with a spicy fragrance that attracts insects galore. They bloom for more than a month, finally giving way to seed capsules that persist through the winter, long after the foliage has turned yellow and dropped. Summersweet's handsome, upright stems form an oval profile, even as the shrub slowly widens by means of underground roots. This tendency to colonize makes summersweet shrubs good soil holders on berms or hillsides and at the Shore. Individual shrubs make good specimens, anchors for a mixed border, accents, or foundation plants.

WHEN TO PLANT

Plant summersweet in early spring for best success, although shrubs raised in containers can be planted anytime during the growing season. It is very vulnerable to stress and drying out when flowering.

WHERE TO PLANT

Summersweet is flexible about light. An understory situation that is mostly sunny, with some shade in the heat of the day, is ideal. Deeper shade forces it to stretch for light. Moist, woodsy soil on the acidic side assures yellow fall foliage. Because it likes wet soil, summersweet is also happy near streams or ponds. Plant it near a doorway or open windows or along walkways so passersby can stop and smell the flowers.

HOW TO PLANT

Choose containerized summersweet shrubs. If the soil in the planting area is thin or clayey, dig in organic matter to improve its texture. Then dig a saucer-shaped planting hole in the center of the prepared area as deep as the rootball is high and somewhat wider. Remove the summersweet from its container, and untangle or clip any circling roots. Set the plant in the empty hole with the top of its rootball exactly level with the surrounding soil. Then fill in the hole with soil, firm it gently, and water well. Space shrubs at least 6 feet from each other or from buildings.

CARE AND MAINTENANCE

Water regularly if rainfall is sparse over the summer while summersweet becomes established. Maintain a year-round, 2- or 3-inch layer of organic mulch over its root zone to retain soil moisture. Fertilize with slow-acting granular fertilizer in the spring. Prune then, too, because the flowers will form on the new growth to come. Clip off spent flowers or seedheads if desired. Periodically cut back any old or dead stems to the ground.

ADDITIONAL INFORMATION

Aside from occasional mites during periods of stress from dry soil, summersweet has no insect or disease problems. Rabbits, mice, and other rodents sometimes nest in weeds or thick winter mulch near its young stems and gnaw on their tender bark. Wrap stems temporarily with hardware cloth, chicken wire, or commercial tree guards.

ADDITIONAL SPECIES, CULTIVARS, OR VARIETIES

'Pink Spires' has light-pink flowers. 'Rosea' has dark-pink buds and paler-pink flowers, and it grows to 4 feet tall. 'Ruby Spice', with deep-pink flowers, is a winner of the Pennsylvania Horticultural Society's Gold Medal Award. *Clethra barbinervis* grows taller—to 18 feet or more—and bears tiny white flowers on drooping stems resembling lily-of-the-valley flowers. It has beautifully mottled bark.

 Did You Know?

Pennsylvania has its share of prominent plantsmen who know a good plant when they see it. Jim Plyler of Natural Landscapes Nursery popularized Clethra *'Hummingbird'. A charming dwarf (to 4 feet), compact shrub with dark-green leaves and white flowers, it won the Pennsylvania Horticultural Society's Gold Medal Award in 1994.*

Viburnum, Doublefile

Viburnum plicatum tomentosum

Type: Deciduous, flowering
Mature Size: 8 to 10 feet tall;
   10 to 12 feet wide
Bloom Time: May
Flower Color/Type: White; flat clusters
Features: Fruit; fall color; attracts birds

Color photograph on page 210.

Light Requirements:

Viburnums are beloved by home owners for their multiseason beauty and by birds for their fall berries. Perhaps the most easily identifiable during bloom time is the elegant doublefile type. From a distance it resembles a kousa dogwood, but its double rows of flat, white "lacecap" flowers that march along the tops of its tiered, horizontal branches are distinctive. Their central clusters of tight fertile florets ringed by open-petaled sterile florets, the flowers float in a row atop the paired green leaves, which droop on each side of the branches as if deferring to the blossoms. When they cover these stately, wide-spreading shrubs, the result is a stunning show. By fall when the foliage turns purplish red, the fertile flowers have become berries, first red, then maturing to black. Reportedly, deer in many areas tend to ignore this shrub.

When to Plant

Plant larger viburnums with burlap-wrapped roots and soil in either early spring or early fall. Smaller, container-grown ones can be planted anytime during the growing season. Their fibrous roots enable them to take transplanting in stride.

Where to Plant

Viburnums like full sun. They are happiest in any good garden soil that is moist but not soggy. It should be rich in organic matter, slightly acidic, and well-drained. This viburnum has a real problem with clay. Site it at the bottom of a hill or wall or deck so that people can view the flowers from above. Use one as a specimen or focal point. Group several for informal hedging or screens, or include them in a shrub border or edge of a woodland.

How to Plant

Incorporate lots of organic matter such as chopped leaves, compost, or peat moss into heavy clay soil to improve its drainage. Then in the center of the prepared area dig a planting hole with sloping sides as deep as the rootball is high and about twice as wide. Remove the viburnum from its container, and untangle any matted, circling roots. Set it in the hole so that the top of its rootball is exactly level with the surrounding soil. Cut as much burlap away from a wrapped rootball as possible. Then fill in the hole with soil, firm it gently, and water well.

CARE AND MAINTENANCE
Maintain a year-round, 2- or 3-inch layer of mulch over the viburnum root zone to retain soil moisture. Water it regularly if rainfall is unreliable until it is well established. After it has been in place for 6 months or so, sprinkle slow-acting granular fertilizer formulated for trees and shrubs on the mulch for the rain to soak in. After 1 or 2 years when the shrub is well established, there is no need for annual fertilizing. The constantly decomposing mulch layer nourishes the soil over its roots. Because they have a very symmetrical habit, these viburnums do not need pruning except to remove the occasional broken branch.

ADDITIONAL INFORMATION
To discourage rodents that sometimes gnaw on the tender bark of young shrubs during the winter, wrap their stems with hardware cloth or commercial tree guards.

ADDITIONAL SPECIES, CULTIVARS, OR VARIETIES

'Lanarth' has especially large outer sterile flowers. 'Mariesii' is also strongly horizontal. 'Summer Snowflake' blooms the entire summer. Japanese snowball viburnum (*Viburnum plicatum*) is similar except the flowers are composed of all sterile florets clustered into 2- to 3-inch-wide white balls. Immature lime-green ones are useful in floral displays. 'Grandiflorum' is highly rated.

 Did You Know?

Viburnum winners of the Pennsylvania Horticultural Society's Gold Medal Award:
- Viburnum × burkwoodii *'Mowhawk'*
- Viburnum *'Conoy'*
- Viburnum dilatatum *'Erie'*
- Viburnum × *'Eskimo'*
- Viburnum nudum *'Winterthur'*
- Viburnum plicatum tomentosum *'Shasta'*

Virginia Sweetspire

Itea virginica

Other Name: Virginia Willow
Type: Deciduous, flowering
Mature Size: 4 to 8 feet tall;
  3 to 6 feet wide
Bloom Time: June into July
Flower Color/Type: White; spikes
Features: Fall color

Light Requirements:

Color photograph on page 210.

Among the many wonderful flowering native shrubs that thrive in the Philadelphia area, Virginia sweetspire is widely grown and appreciated. It is so popular because it is so eminently satisfactory. The epitome of easy care, it has upright, slightly arching stems that tend to get twiggy at their tops. Virginia sweetspire initiates the season with wonderful bright, shiny, light-green spring foliage on its slender reddish twigs, which turns medium green in time for the flower display. Suddenly, the sweetspire is dripping with 2- to 6-inch-long, narrow tubes of tiny white florets. Later, the first tinges of burgundy that appear on the foliage in late August are an alert that the spectacular show of purple and/or bright-red leaves that lasts through most of the fall is beginning. Take advantage of this beauty as a specimen, foundation, or woodland plant. In rows they make great hedges, and massed on a bank, they hold the soil well.

WHEN TO PLANT

Plant rooted suckers from an existing plant in early spring. Small shrubs raised in pots at the nursery accept planting anytime during the growing season as long as they are well watered.

WHERE TO PLANT

Virginia sweetspires do fine as understory plants in woodland settings, but show to best effect in full sun. They are not fussy about soil type and positively enjoy wet soil. Site them at pond side or near other water, such as downspout outlets. Allow space for their suckering roots to spread and gradually widen the shrub.

HOW TO PLANT

If soil is sandy, prepare the planting area by mixing in organic matter such as peat moss, compost, or chopped leaves to help it hold moisture. In the middle of the prepared soil area dig a planting hole with sloping sides as deep as the rootball is high and about twice as wide. Remove the sweetspire shrub from its container, and untangle or clip any circling roots. Set it in the hole so that the top of its rootball is exactly level with the surrounding soil. Then fill in the hole, firm the soil, and water well. Set plants about 5 or 6 feet from each other or from buildings.

CARE AND MAINTENANCE

Mulch the root zone of the sweetspire bush with a 2- or 3-inch layer of organic matter such as chopped leaves or wood chips. Water the shrub regularly if rainfall is unreliable until it is well established. In the spring sprinkle slow-acting granular fertilizer formulated for trees and shrubs on the mulch for the rain to soak in. Also pull up any suckering stems that are spreading beyond their authorized limits, and plant them elsewhere or give them away. Prune only to control height and only if necessary.

ADDITIONAL INFORMATION

Virginia sweetspire tolerates drought well and is virtually pest and disease free. It also will grow in a container.

ADDITIONAL SPECIES, CULTIVARS, OR VARIETIES

'Henry's Garnet' has wonderful red fall color. It was one of the earliest winners of the Pennsylvania Horticultural Society's Gold Medal Award (Styer Award). 'Saturnalia' is reputed to be a bit smaller with a more orangish-red fall color.

 Did You Know?

'Henry's Garnet' put Virginia sweetspire on the horticultural map, and it all happened in the Philadelphia area. Professor Michael Dirr of the University of Georgia noticed a particularly deep-red-foliaged one on the Swarthmore College campus. Scott Arboretum spearheaded the process of correctly naming and introducing the plant. Since Josephine Henry provided some seeds and seedlings that she had brought to her garden in Gladwyn from Georgia, the name Henry was added to "garnet," representing one of Swarthmore College's colors and the rich color of this sweetspire's fall foliage.

Weigela

Weigela florida

Other Name: Old-Fashioned Weigela
Type: Deciduous, flowering
Mature Size: 6 to 10 feet tall;
  8 to 12 feet wide
Bloom Time: Late May and June
Flower Color/Type: White, pink, rose; tubular
Features: Old-fashioned; attracts hummingbirds

Color photograph on page 210.

Light Requirements:

Weigela has long been a tough, reliable bloomer in Philadelphia area yards and gardens. Paired with mockorange, it provides a flowerful transition into full summer. Its inch-long, funnel-shaped flowers arrayed in clusters along arching stems are in full show as the hummingbirds arrive on the scene. Branches may be so weighed down with flowers that their tips touch and root in the soil. Weigelas tend to have rangy, informal habits. Their foliage is a serviceable, plain green; although it might show a purple tinge in the fall, it is not significant. Traditionally low-key, older forms of weigela are content to serve unobtrusively in shrub borders or as hedges providing foliage backgrounds for other plants during the balance of the season. The newer, more flamboyant compact versions are more versatile, fitting happily into mixed borders or serving as foundation plants.

WHEN TO PLANT

Planting weigela in either spring or fall is preferred. If it has been raised in a container, anytime during the growing season is okay.

WHERE TO PLANT

Modern hybrids are easy to site and grow. They like sun or partial shade and almost any type of well-drained soil. They can handle pollution.

HOW TO PLANT

If soil is thin or sandy, improve it over the entire planting area by mixing in organic matter such as peat moss, compost, or chopped leaves to help it hold moisture. Then dig a planting hole as deep as the rootball is high and about twice as wide in the middle of the prepared soil area. Remove the weigela from its container, and untangle or clip any circling roots. Position the shrub in the hole so that the top of its rootball is exactly level with the surrounding soil. Then fill in the hole with soil, firm it, and water well.

Space standard shrubs at least 12 feet from each other or from buildings. Plant smaller hybrids 5 feet or so apart.

CARE AND MAINTENANCE

Mulch the root zone of the weigela with a 2- or 3-inch layer of organic matter such as chopped leaves or wood chips. Water the shrub regularly if rainfall is unreliable until it is well established. Each spring sprinkle slow-acting granular fertilizer formulated for trees and shrubs on the mulch for the rain to soak in. Since weigela blooms on the previous year's wood, prune immediately after it flowers. For maximum bloom, completely remove branches that have just bloomed as close to the base of the shrub as possible. Because shrubs tend to look unkempt, prune out dead wood on an ongoing basis. To renew a weigela shrub, either cut it entirely to the ground, or select the oldest, woodiest stems and cut them out every couple of years.

ADDITIONAL INFORMATION

Sometimes weigelas bloom sporadically later in the summer. They have no serious pest or disease problems.

ADDITIONAL SPECIES, CULTIVARS, OR VARIETIES

'Briant Rubidor' has pink flowers and chartreuse foliage, a striking combination! 'Bristol Ruby' has crimson flowers and a more upright posture. 'Candida', which is commonly cultivated, has white flowers. 'Polka' is noted for its long bloom period and pink flowers. 'White Knight' produces white flowers over most of the summer and is small at 5 to 6 feet tall. 'Wine 'n' Roses' is new, with maroon-purple-tinged foliate and medium-pink flowers. 'Variegata' foliage has cream-colored edges and pale-pink flowers.

 Did You Know?

Hummingbirds visit flowers to obtain nectar, and they incidentally pollinate their hosts. Flowers most attractive to hummers have red color, deep tubular shape, downward or sideways orientation, small petals and/or openings, and tough bases where they attach to their stems. Flowers such as weigela have these traits, which discourage bees and other pollinators, leaving them available to hummers.

Winged Euonymus

Euonymus alatus

Other Name: Burning Bush
Type: Deciduous
Mature Size: 8 to 15 feet tall;
   10 to 18 feet wide
Features: Ridged twigs; fall foliage color; winter architecture

Color photograph on page 210.

Light Requirements:

Most of the year it is simply a neat, somewhat horizontally branching, basic green shrub, content to bide its time unobtrusively among other shrubs in a border, as a hedge, or as a foundation plant near the house. The most remarkable thing about winged euonymus during this time is the peculiar ridges on its twigs that resemble flat wings. Most prominent on younger, vigorous stems, they are visible only in the winter. Eventually, they are obscured by the plain, dull-green foliage that densely covers the mounded shrub. By fall, however, this shrub takes on a whole new personality and a name to fit its alter ego. It truly becomes a burning bush, its foliage afire with brilliant scarlet reds verging on the fluorescent, visible from great distances. Adaptable, self-reliant, low-maintenance, winged euonymus is so popular that it verges on the overused. This may not be the case much longer, though, because it holds a prominent place on most short lists of plants that deer love to eat.

WHEN TO PLANT

Plant larger winged euonymus with roots wrapped in burlap in either spring or fall. Smaller shrubs raised in containers can be planted anytime during the growing season.

WHERE TO PLANT

The more sun, the better the scarlet fall foliage on winged euonymus. Shade, even periods of cloudy days in the early fall, may reduce its brilliance. It accepts just about any type of well-drained soil, but not alkaline or salty. Fall color is spectacular when backed by dark evergreens.

HOW TO PLANT

Add organic matter to sandy or thin soil to improve its ability to drain and hold moisture when preparing the planting area. Then dig a saucer-shaped planting hole as deep as the rootball is high and about twice as wide. Remove the euonymus from its container, and untangle or clip any circling roots. Set the shrub in the hole so that the top of its rootball is exactly level with the surrounding soil. Cut as much burlap as possible from wrapped rootballs. Then fill in the hole with soil, firm it gently, and water thoroughly.

CARE AND MAINTENANCE

Its masses of fibrous roots tend to migrate to near the surface of the soil, so mulch winged euonymus root zones year-round to prevent their drying out. Renew the 2- or 3-inch layer of organic matter periodically as it decomposes. Water if rainfall is unreliable until the shrub is well established. In the spring sprinkle slow-acting granular fertilizer formulated for shrubs on the mulch for the rain to soak in. After 1 or 2 years, the continuously decomposing mulch will enrich the soil instead. Winged euonymus grows very large without pruning. It takes shearing for a hedge very well. Of course, cut out broken or dead stems promptly.

ADDITIONAL INFORMATION

Unlike so many of its cousins, winged euonymus does not get scale or any other pests and diseases. Its bark is poisonous. Use bare, winged branches for fresh and dried floral arrangement and floral crafts. There is some concern that this shrub is "escaping" from home landscapes by promiscuous self-seeding and threatens to invade and pressure native plants in the wild because it tolerates shade and shades them out.

ADDITIONAL SPECIES, CULTIVARS, OR VARIETIES

'Compactus' is smaller, with a potential height and width of 6 to 10 feet, and is best suited to the typical residential landscape.

 Did You Know?

The beautiful foliage colors that many trees and shrubs develop in the fall are really there all along. They are not evident because the green chlorophyll pigment obscures them. But as winter approaches, reduced daylight ends its role of manufacturing energy from the sun, and chlorophyll is no longer produced. Then the reds, yellows, and oranges glow.

Winterberry Holly

Ilex verticillata

Other Names: Coralberry, Deciduous
Holly, Black Alder
Type: Deciduous
Mature Size: 6 to 10 feet tall; 6 to 8 feet wide
Bloom Time: June
Flower Color/Type: White; inconspicuous
Features: Berries; attracts songbirds, honeybees; winter interest

Light Requirements:

Color photograph on page 210.

Winterberry is another sturdy, locally native shrub that is at home in Philadelphia area residential landscapes. It is a holly and has berries, but instead of the classic spined, dark evergreen foliage, it has simple, oval, medium- to dark-green, finer-textured leaves that often turn yellowish or black after frost before they drop in the fall. Winterberry's glory is berry-encrusted bare branches that are exposed on female shrubs when the leaves drop. Usually red, but sometimes orange or yellow, they light up the drab winter landscape. The songbirds that flock to eat them add more excitement. These multistemmed, upright shrubs gradually spread into a thicket by means of suckering roots, but are easily controlled by pruning. Use them as focal points or accents in the winter landscape or in a shrub border or near streams or ponds.

WHEN TO PLANT

Plant in either early spring or early fall. To be sure of getting a female, buy named selections or mature shrubs whose sex can be confirmed. Container-grown winterberries can be planted anytime during the growing season.

WHERE TO PLANT

Site winterberry in full sun for best berry production. It prefers moist, acid, woodsy soils that are rich in organic matter and well-drained, although it does not mind wet or clayey soils. Plant winterberries as understory shrubs, backdropped by larger evergreens, and in view of a window to enjoy from indoors and with a male holly nearby.

HOW TO PLANT

Dig a saucer-shaped planting hole as deep as the rootball is high and about twice as wide. Remove the winterberry from its container, and untangle or clip any circling roots. Set it in its hole so that the top of its rootball is exactly level with the surrounding soil. If the roots are wrapped in burlap, cut as much of it away as possible. Then fill in the hole with soil, firm it gently, and water well. Set plants at least 8 feet apart from each other or from buildings.

CARE AND MAINTENANCE

Water newly planted winterberries during dry periods until they are established. Try not to let them dry out totally. Mulch their root zones year-round with a 2- or 3-inch layer of organic matter to retain soil moisture. As it decomposes it will add valuable organic matter to the soil. In the spring fertilize with slow-acting granular fertilizer formulated for acid-loving trees and shrubs. Also in the spring cut back old branches to ground level to stimulate new and denser growth that will produce lots of berries.

ADDITIONAL INFORMATION

Berry-laden winterberry branches are very useful for fall and holiday dried arrangements. They last about a week indoors. Because the berries are on bare branches, they have a different look from regular holly boughs. Beware, the berries are poisonous. Winterberry will grow in containers.

ADDITIONAL SPECIES, CULTIVARS, OR VARIETIES

'Scarlett O'Hara' and 'Winter Red' are winners of the Pennsylvania Horticultural Society's Gold Medal Award. ('Rhett Butler' is the male pollinator for 'Scarlett', of course!) Some excellent hybrid winterberries are 'Autumn Glow', which has more orangish yellow fall leaf color plus red berries; 'Sparkleberry', which produces lots of berries; and 'Harvest Red', which has purple fall foliage and red berries. 'Sparkleberry' and 'Harvest Red' are winners of the PHS Gold Medal Award. 'Raritan Chief', a male, has a long bloom period in spring, making it a good pollinator for many varieties of female winterberry.

Did You Know?

Birds that eat holly berries:
- *Bluebirds*
- *Catbirds*
- *Cedar waxwings*
- *Mockingbirds*
- *Robins*
- *Thrushes*

Witchhazel

Hamamelis mollis

Other Name: Chinese Witchhazel
Type: Deciduous, flowering
Mature Size: 10 to 15 feet tall;
  to 12 feet wide
Bloom Time: Late January through March
Flower Color/Type: Yellow; spidery petals
Features: Winter bloom; fragrance; fall color

Color photograph on page 210.

Light Requirements:

From a distance its vaselike shape, many stems, and tufts of yellow flowers along bare branches resemble forsythia, but up close there is no mistaking witchhazel. First the fragrance, and then the unique spiderlike flowers with twisting, inch-long, narrow petals confirm its identity. Over several weeks these flowers gleam in the winter sun, curling up when it is cold and expanding with milder temperatures. Chinese witchhazel is a handsome large shrub, with the largest, most colorful flowers and longest bloom period of all the witchhazels. When its dull green leaves appear in the spring, it blends into the landscape until they turn yellow in the fall and drop, exposing their dried seed capsules, which shoot their 2 black seeds as far as 20 feet away with a loud snap. Use witchhazels as focal points in the winter landscape or in shrub borders and woodland settings.

WHEN TO PLANT

For larger balled and burlapped witchhazels the best planting time is spring. Plant smaller ones in containers from the nursery anytime during the growing season.

WHERE TO PLANT

For best bloom and display, site witchhazels in full sun or under deciduous trees that are bare when they bloom. They can take some shade and do well in almost any soil that is acidic, rich in organic matter, and well-drained. They do not mind urban conditions. Allow them about 3 years to fully establish and bloom well.

HOW TO PLANT

Dig a saucer-shaped planting hole as deep as the rootball is high and some-what wider. Remove the witchhazel from its container, and untangle or clip any circling roots. Position it in the hole so that the top of its rootball is exactly level with the surrounding soil. Cut away as much burlap as possible from wrapped rootballs. Then fill in the hole with soil, firm it gently, and water well. Typically wider than they are tall, witchhazels tend to spread with age. Set shrubs at least 15 feet apart from each other and buildings.

CARE AND MAINTENANCE

Mulch witchhazel root zones year-round with a 2- or 3-inch layer of organic matter such as chopped leaves or wood chips. Water regularly if rainfall is unreliable until shrubs are well established, then only during droughts. Fertilize in the spring with slow-acting granular fertilizer formulated for trees and shrubs. Over time the decomposing mulch will enrich the soil, so regular fertilizing will not be necessary. Prune out the occasional broken branch promptly. Most named witchhazels are grafted; watch for suckers that branch out below the graft, and clip them off.

ADDITIONAL INFORMATION

Cut budded branches of witchhazel in late January for forced bloom indoors in just a few days. Their slender zigzag twigs are useful in dried arrangements and floral crafts. They have no significant pest or disease problems.

ADDITIONAL SPECIES, CULTIVARS, OR VARIETIES

Chinese witchhazel (*Hamamelis mollis*) includes 'Pallida', which is a 1989 Pennsylvania Horticultural Society Gold Medal Award winner with pale-yellow flowers, and 'Early Bright', which is espaliered against a stone wall at Clothier Hall at Swarthmore College. Hybrid witchhazels (*Hamamelis × intermedia*) are well suited to residential landscapes; examples include 'Arnold's Promise', which reaches 20 feet tall and blooms latest; 'Diana', which has reddish flowers, was a PHS Gold Medal Award winner, and blooms earliest in the Philadelphia area.

 Did You Know?

*Native Americans and early settlers used the bark of fall-blooming native witchhazel (*Hamamelis virginiana*) for medicine. An astringent, witchhazel is still available in pharmacies for first aid to halt minor bleeding and reduce inflammation. It is used in commercial eye drops, skin creams, ointments, and tonics. The "witch" in its name suggests the wood's occult powers. It has long been used to make divining rods to find water.*

Yew

Taxus × media

Other Name: Intermediate Yew
Type: Evergreen
Mature Size: 10 to 15 feet tall;
  to 15 feet wide
Foliage: Flat, green needles
Features: Red fruit

Color photograph on page 211.

Light Requirements:

Yews boast an ancient history according to the fossil record. They continue to offer long life, rich color, interesting needled foliage, and varied sizes for use in residential yards and gardens. The best ones are hybrids which combine the cold hardiness of Japanese yews and the dark-green foliage of the English yew. They have lustrous, soft, short, flat needles that are initially a bright spring green, turning dark green and paler beneath with age. Female yews bear red, fleshy fruit with a seed within that is poisonous to people but does not seem to deter deer from eating yew foliage with gusto. Part of their charm is their ability to take shearing to create hedges and even topiary. They are also useful for foundation planting and as background for colorful flowering plants.

WHEN TO PLANT

Plant yews that are balled and burlapped in spring or fall. Plant ones raised in containers anytime during the growing season.

WHERE TO PLANT

Easygoing yews are adaptable to full sun or shade, but they prefer some shade. They accept any type of reasonably fertile, well-drained soil. Overly wet soil turns their needles brown. They do not like very acid soil, so do not plant them near azaleas or hollies. Yews handle city conditions well.

HOW TO PLANT

If the soil in the planting area is clay, dig organic matter into it to improve its drainage. Then dig a planting hole with sloping sides in the center of the prepared area as deep as the rootball is high and about twice as wide. Remove the yew from its container, and untangle or clip any circling roots. Set it in the hole so that the top of its rootball is exactly level with the surrounding soil. If the roots are wrapped in burlap, cut as much of it away as possible. Then fill in the hole with soil, firm it gently, and water well. Set plants at least 5 feet apart from each other or away from buildings.

CARE AND MAINTENANCE

Mulch the root zone of the yew year-round with a 2- or 3-inch layer of organic matter such as chopped leaves or wood chips. Water it regularly if rainfall is unreliable until it is well established. In the spring sprinkle slow-acting granular fertilizer formulated for trees and shrubs on the mulch for the rain to soak in. To renew old shrubs, cut their stems back to within 6 inches of the ground. This stimulates new and dense growth over the next year or two. Prune to shape or control size in the spring before growth starts by clipping individual branches for a natural effect. Do not shear them into rigid shapes except for topiary. Hard shearing promotes the formation of dense, bare twigs within the plant. Clip hedges hard before May to maintain a maximum width of 2 feet and height of 6 or 8 feet.

ADDITIONAL INFORMATION

All parts of yews contain the toxic substance taxine, so lethal that approximately 50 small leaves may kill an adult. It is said that the ancient Celts used yew wood to make their longbows and then tipped their arrows with poisonous yew sap.

ADDITIONAL SPECIES, CULTIVARS, OR VARIETIES

'Brownii' and 'Brownii Globe' are rounded. 'Hicks' is narrow and upright. 'Densiformis' grows to 4 feet as a low spreader. Spreading English yew (*Taxus baccata* 'Repandens') has arching branches.

 Did You Know?

Yews have been in the medical news since 1991 when it was discovered that taxol, a drug derived from the bark of the Pacific yew, was a potent weapon in treating cancer. It was estimated that 600,000 of these yews would be needed to make enough taxol to treat a wider population of patients beyond ones who were critically ill. Because harvesting the bark would kill so many trees, every effort is being made to synthesize taxol.

Trees

Handsome Shade Trees and decorative flowering trees are significant elements in a residential landscape. Not only do they contribute aesthetically by defining its space—establishing scale, delineating borders, and roofing it with their canopies—but they also enhance its livability in numerous ways. They moderate the climate in the yard by transposing and filtering light and air, and creating shade and privacy. They provide habitat for wildlife—shelter and food—and add to the diversity of plants that interrelate to create a healthy ecosystem on the property. Deciduous trees reduce energy use indoors when carefully sited in the yard to block sun from windows and the roof in summer, and then permit it to shine on them after they drop their leaves in the fall. Trees are also economic assets. A healthy, mature shade tree can contribute up to $1500 to the value of the property.

TREES DEFINED

Trees are typically defined as single-stemmed plants that are 25 feet or taller. They are usually categorized as small (less than 30 feet), medium (30 to 60 feet), and tall (more than 60 feet) to facilitate their selection and use. Small trees are usually most appropriate near the house to frame it attractively. They are suitable for use under most utility wires and as understory plantings beneath taller trees. Medium trees do well in open areas a short distance from the house in typically suburban-sized properties. Tall trees are appropriate for very spacious lawns or along property boundaries where they are at least 35 feet from the house to allow for root growth. Before purchasing a tree, decide whether its purpose is to shade, to decorate, to screen a view, or to control erosion on a bank.

Buy locally, if possible, to assure that the tree is grown from local stock. Nurseries and garden centers will often provide a warranty for trees; some will plant them, too, for an extra fee. When trees are young, you can do the work, but it is safer for you and the tree to hire a professional to move or plant large trees. Also consider hiring a professional, a certified arborist, for any pruning job that requires a chain saw and a ladder and for spraying insecticides or fungicides on large trees.

In the last decade new insights into the growth of trees have affected how we plant and care for them. New planting practices reflect the understanding that a tree's feeder roots exist within the top 12 inches of soil and spread much farther than the leaf canopy is wide. Every effort is made to urge roots outward into the soil at the site. That is why the planting hole should have sloping sides, the fill soil should be the real thing (no pampering with special amendments), and fertilizer—a slow-acting type to provide nutrients gradually and uniformly—waits until after the roots get established. The roots' need for air and moisture explains why watering the first year is critical. Mulching eliminates turfgrass competition for water and nutrients and provides a steady infusion of moisture-retaining organic matter to condition the soil so that it holds air, too. Contemporary pruning techniques recognize that trees have special tissues that seal wounds; cutting a branch to preserve this "collar" of bark speeds healing. Painting wounds is no longer recommended, since the tree can take care of this job. The timing of pruning affects whether the size is controlled (spring or summer) or growth is stimulated (winter, during dormancy).

Finally, staking newly planted trees is no longer routine. Experts have come to appreciate the importance of movement to developing strength in stems of all kinds of plants. Young tree trunks need to flex a bit near their tops. Staking is recommended for special situations only, and for only 6 months to 1 year. Attach supporting lines down low on the trunk—about 18 inches from the ground—to stabilize it, but allow upper flexibility.

Did You Know?

Deer Greatest Hits—Trees and Shrubs[+]

American arborvitae   European mountain ash
Atlantic white cedar   Fraser fir
Azalea   *Hybrid tea roses*
Balsam fir   *Korean Lilac*
Buckeye   *Norway maple*
Cornelian dogwood   *Rhododendron*
Crabapple   *Winged euonymus*
Eastern redbud   *Yew*

[+]Subject to change daily   *Included in this book

Atlas Cedar, Blue

Cedrus atlantica 'Glauca'

Type: Needled evergreen
Mature Size: 40 to 60 feet tall;
40 to 60 feet wide
Foliage: Tufts of blue-green needles
Features: Sculptural habit; cones for wildlife; winter interest

Color photograph on page 211.

Light Requirements:

The only conifers that bloom in the fall, Atlas cedars are always elegant, dominant landscape features. They have distinctive angular, spurred branches adorned with tufted clusters of stiff, bluish, 1- to 2-inch-long needles and decorative, 3-inch cones. In youth they have an open, irregular, erectly pyramidal shape, then they develop even more character in maturity. They become more flat topped with distinctly tiered horizontal branches that suggest years of resistance to wind and other challenges. Fast-growing in youth, Atlas cedars slow as they age and may live for 300 years or more. Plant them as individual specimens in the lawn to show off their virtues, or use them nearer to the house to accent an architectural feature.

WHEN TO PLANT

Choose young trees in containers. Although they may seem thin and spindly, they accept transplanting best and will fill out soon. Fall is the best time to plant; spring is the next most desirable time.

WHERE TO PLANT

Atlas cedars do best in full sun, but tolerate very light shade. They prefer well-drained soil rich in organic matter, but readily adapt to sandy or more neutral soil. Site them where they will be protected from strong winds and storms.

HOW TO PLANT

Remove the young cedar from its container, and spread any circling roots to encourage them to grow outward in the hole. Dig a saucer-shaped planting hole just as deep as and 2 or 3 times wider than the rootball. Set the tree in the hole so that the top of its soilball is exactly level with, or even slightly above, the level of the surrounding ground. Fill in the hole with plain soil, firming it gently around the rootball. Form a small circular ridge of soil just beyond the edge of the root zone to create a moat to hold water, then water well.

CARE AND MAINTENANCE

Water the cedar regularly when rainfall is unreliable. Once established after 1 or 2 years, it is fairly drought resistant. Spread 2 or 3 inches of organic material over the root zone of the Atlas cedar and the water moat, but never against the tree trunk. The mulch will help the soil stay moist, discourage weeds, and improve the soil as it gradually decomposes. After at least 6 months, sprinkle granular slow-acting fertilizer formulated for trees on the mulch for the rain to soak in. Repeat this every year for 4 or 5 years. Eventually, continuous mulching will improve the soil, and the tree will not need regular fertilizing. Prune Atlas cedars only to remove broken, rubbing, or awkward branches.

ADDITIONAL INFORMATION

Occasionally, rodents nest in winter mulch under young trees and gnaw at their tender bark. To deny them a nesting spot, wait until the ground freezes hard before spreading the thicker winter mulch. Wrap cedar stems with hardware cloth or commercial tree guards. Atlas cedars do well in containers for a while. Be sure the pot has a drainage hole and is at least 2 feet deep.

ADDITIONAL SPECIES, CULTIVARS, OR VARIETIES

'Argentea' has silvery-blue needles. 'Aurea' has yellowish needles and a narrower, stiffer form than blue types. 'Fastigiata' is upright and has bluish green needles. 'Glauca Pendula' has weeping branches, which need supporting stakes. It can be espaliered on a wall to great effect. Deodar cedar (*Cedrus deodara*) is prized for its layers of drooping branches of feathery foliage. 'Shalimar' is the most cold hardy and has the best chance for survival in our area.

 Did You Know?

Many other conifers are commonly called cedar, but they are not true cedar because the first part of their Latin names is not Cedrus:

- *Alaskan cedar is* Chamaecyparis nootkatensis.
- *Western red cedar is* Thuja plicata.
- *Incense cedar is* Calocedrus decurrens.
- *Eastern red cedar is* Juniperus virginiana.

Bald Cypress

Taxodium distichum

Other Name: Swamp Cypress

Type: Deciduous conifer

Mature Size: 50 to 70 feet tall;
   30 to 40 feet wide

Foliage: Soft needles; green, then russet in fall

Features: 4-season appeal; knees (novelty)

Color photograph on page 211.

Light Requirements:

This stately East Coast native has traditionally been regarded as a Southern tree, its adaptability to swamps being the stuff of lore and legend. Fortunately, it likes conditions in the North equally well, and it is being planted as a landscape tree as well as a street tree. A conifer that is not evergreen (thus the sobriquet "bald"), it offers early appeal as soft, pale-green needles flush out on branches late in the spring. Among them on delicate twigs are the small, 1-inch cones that gradually turn brown. In fall bald cypress foliage turns red-bronze and drops, branchlets and all, revealing similarly colored, fibrous bark and a uniformly dense, narrow, pyramidal architecture. Excellent examples are planted in a marshy grove at the Taylor Arboretum in Nether Providence. On the way notice the bald cypress street trees on Chester Road in Swarthmore. There is a gorgeous specimen at the Morris Arboretum on Swan Road.

WHEN TO PLANT
Plant balled and burlapped nursery stock in the spring. Make sure the tree was grown from Northern seed so that it is hardy in our area. ontainerized trees can go in the ground anytime during the growing season. They transplant and establish easily, growing up to 2 feet or more a year.

WHERE TO PLANT
Bald cypresses like full sun best, but they can take some shade. They are flexible about soil—from dry to downright boggy. Site them so that their color and shape are shown to best effect in a spacious area. They can handle some wind in exposed sites and are ideal for floodplain areas. They are most effective in groves on large properties.

HOW TO PLANT
Dig a saucer-shaped planting hole just as deep as and somewhat wider than the rootball. Remove the young tree from its container, and spread any circling roots. Set the tree in the hole so that its root flare, where the roots meet

the trunk, shows and is exactly at soil level or even slightly above. Cut away as much burlap as possible from a wrapped rootball. Fill in the hole with plain soil, firming it gently around the rootball to remove air pockets. Form any excess fill into a small circular ridge just beyond the edge of the root zone for a water-holding moat, then water well. Allow plenty of space around the tree to accommodate its potential size.

CARE AND MAINTENANCE

Spread 2 or 3 inches of organic material over the root zone of the bald cypress and the water moat. This year-round mulch will help the soil stay moist, discourage weeds, and improve the soil as it gradually decomposes. Never pile it against the tree trunk. When the tree has been in place at least 6 months, sprinkle granular slow-acting fertilizer formulated for trees on the mulch for the rain to soak in. Do this for 1 or 2 years until it is established, and then the constantly decomposing mulch will maintain the soil.

ADDITIONAL INFORMATION

Prune bald cypress only to remove injured or overcrowded branches. The beautifully natural symmetry and form of this tree would be ruined by any attempt to control its size or shape by pruning. Bald cypress may lose its needles prematurely during drought, but it is not dead.

ADDITIONAL SPECIES, CULTIVARS, OR VARIETIES

'Shawnee Brave', a smaller, narrow form, is suited for ¾-acre yards and streetside. 'Monarch of Illinois' is more rounded and squatter, suited for very large properties.

 Did You Know?

Why do bald cypresses in swamps have knees? Knees grow only on trees in water or soggy soils. Since they protrude as far as 2 or 3 feet above the water vertically from the submerged roots, traditional wisdom was that they accessed oxygen from the air. Recent tests indicate that they are not necessary for oxygen-carbon dioxide exchange, however. The mystery remains.

Beech, European

Fagus sylvatica

Other Name: Common Beech
Type: Deciduous, shade
Mature Size: 60 feet tall; 45 to 60 feet wide
Foliage: Green
Features: Fall color; majestic presence; supports songbirds and other wildlife

Light Requirements:

Color photograph on page 211.

*E*uropean beeches are not for the average residential yard. These stately, slow-growing, long-lived shade trees dominate any landscape, their towering canopies eventually casting a huge sheltering shadow over what might once have been a sizable lawn. Beech leaves are typically 2 to 3 inches long, shiny gray-green in spring, turning dark green in summer, then bronze or yellow in fall. The smooth, gray bark that is revealed when they fall is reminiscent of an elephant's hide. The Philadelphia area has its share of wonderful specimens. Gorgeous examples quietly preside over daily life at Scott Arboretum on the Swarthmore College campus, at Longwood Gardens, and on many campuses and estates along the Main Line.

WHEN TO PLANT

Plant balled and burlapped nursery stock in the spring. Containerized trees can go in the ground then or anytime during the growing season.

WHERE TO PLANT

Beeches do best in full sun. They prefer moist, slightly acidic soil that is rich in organic matter, but they are quite adaptable to any soil type, even somewhat alkaline, as long as it drains well. Notorious for their shallow roots, which invariably become surface roots, they need a roomy site.

HOW TO PLANT

Beeches transplant best if as much soil as possible remains on their roots. Remove the young tree from its container, and spread any circling roots. Dig a saucer-shaped planting hole just as deep as and 2 or 3 times as wide as the rootball. Set the tree in the hole so that its root flare, where the roots join the trunk, is visible and is exactly at soil level or even slightly above. Cut away as much burlap as possible from a wrapped rootball. Fill in the hole with plain soil, firming it gently around the rootball. Form a water-holding moat over the root zone with any excess fill, then water well.

CARE AND MAINTENANCE

Maintain a 2- or 3-inch layer of organic material over the root zone of the tree (but not up against its trunk). A year-round mulch will help the soil stay moist, discourage weeds, and improve the soil as it constantly decomposes. Renew it periodically. After 6 months to 1 year, sprinkle granular slow-acting fertilizer formulated for trees on the mulch for the rain to soak in. Do this for 1 or 2 years until it is clear that the tree is well established.

ADDITIONAL INFORMATION

Beeches tolerate pruning well. Do it in the winter when they are dormant. Watch for the possibility of a second leader, or trunk, and cut it away. Lower branches on older trees will sweep the ground, and they can be removed to show off the trunk bark. Prune injured branches promptly. Young beeches can also be sheared for a hedge. Cut them back by ½ initially, then trim a full season later. Then trim as needed until the hedge forms and reaches the desired height. Always allow ¼ of the newest growth to remain when shearing beech hedges for maintenance.

ADDITIONAL SPECIES, CULTIVARS, OR VARIETIES

'Asplenifolia' has green, cutleaf foliage. 'Atropunicea' is the true deep-purple form, sometimes called copper beech in cases where the leaves are a paler purple. 'Tricolor' foliage is purple edged in cream and pink. Weeping beech (*Fagus sylvatica* 'Pendula') has drooping branches. 'Fastigata' is narrow.

 Did You Know?

*European beech is often confused with our native American beech (*Fagus grandiflora*), which also has smooth, gray bark and dark-green, somewhat coarse foliage. The easiest way to tell the difference is to count the pairs of veins in the leaves. If it has 5 to 9 pairs of veins, it is European. If it has 11 to 15 pairs of veins, it is American. There are no cultivars of American beech.*

Birch, River

Betula nigra 'Heritage'

Other Name: Heritage River Birch
Type: Deciduous, shade
Mature Size: 40 to 60 feet tall; equally wide
Foliage: Medium green, yellow in fall
Features: Fall color; peeling bark; attracts songbirds; hosts butterfly larvae

Light Requirements:

Color photograph on page 211.

*F*ine-textured birches are wonderful additions to home landscapes. In the Philadelphia area the perfect choice is the native river birch because it is not susceptible to the bronze birch borer that plagues the classic white-barked birches here. River birches are fast growing under preferred conditions—up to 5 feet in 1 year, 30 to 40 feet in 20 years. Columnar when young, their shape becomes more rounded as they age. Their toothed leaves are dark green with tiny hairs on the midrib beneath. Young trees have thin bark that peels to reveal variously reddish or tan and brown underneath. 'Heritage' is a special type of river birch because its bark color is paler, more closely resembling the classic white-barked birches of New England or Europe. Winner of the Gold Medal Award from the Pennsylvania Horticultural Society in 1990, it has slightly pendulous branches and larger leaves. It is listed among the top 10 trees for American landscapes and gardens and is amazingly adaptable to clay soils and intense summer heat. Use 'Heritage' as a specimen, naturalized along streambanks, or in groves.

WHEN TO PLANT

Plant larger balled and burlapped trees in the spring; those in containers can go in the ground anytime during the growing season until mid-August to assure that the roots have time to establish before winter weather gets harsh.

WHERE TO PLANT

River birch loves full sun and moist, acidic soil with lots of organic matter in it. It can handle drier soil and even truly wet soils as long as they are acidic.

HOW TO PLANT

River birch transplants well when young. Remove it from its container, and spread any circling roots. Dig a saucer-shaped planting hole just as deep as and considerably wider than the rootball. Set the tree in the hole so that the top of its soilball is exactly even with, or slightly above, the level of the surrounding ground. If its roots are wrapped in burlap, remove or cut away as much as possible. Fill in the hole with plain soil, firming it gently around the rootball to remove air pockets. Form any excess fill into a small circular ridge just beyond the edge of the root zone to make a moat to hold water, then water well.

CARE AND MAINTENANCE

Water regularly if rainfall is scarce for 1 or 2 years until the young birch is well established. Spread 2 or 3 inches of organic material such as chopped leaves, wood chips, or commercial bark product over its root zone, but not against its trunk. This mulch will help the soil stay moist, discourage weeds, and improve the soil as it gradually decomposes. Renew the mulch for winter. When the tree has been in place at least 6 months, sprinkle granular slow-acting fertilizer formulated for trees and shrubs on the mulch for the rain to soak in. When the tree gets older, keep an eye out for branches that have died deep in the dense canopy. Prune them promptly.

ADDITIONAL INFORMATION

To create a multiple-stemmed tree, cut back the original leader to nearly soil level when it is only 1 or 2 years old to stimulate new stem growth. The clump tree will be a bit shorter than a typical single-stemmed one.

ADDITIONAL SPECIES, CULTIVARS, OR VARIETIES

'Heritage' is the best and most available of numerous varieties of river birch.

 Did You Know?

Birches get their name from the ancient Sanskrit language. "Birch" evolved from Bhurga, *which signifies "a tree whose bark is used for writing upon." A distinguishing feature of most birches is their peeling, curling bark, which it is easy to believe, especially with the white-barked ones, could substitute for paper.*

Catalpa, Northern

Catalpa speciosa

Other Names: Cigar Tree, Hardy Catalpa, Western Catalpa

Type: Deciduous, shade

Mature Size: 60 feet tall; 20 to 40 feet wide

Foliage: Green; greenish yellow in fall

Features: Showy flowers; beanlike pods; supports honeybees

Light Requirements:

Color photograph on page 211.

Because of their coarse, rangy look, northern catalpas are an acquired taste. Though native to the Midwest, they are easily spotted in vacant lots in the city, along the Blue Route and other highways, and in the exurbs where they were common on former farm properties. Their fast-growing frames, festooned with huge, heart-shaped leaves that form a broad, oval leaf canopy, have a special appeal. They have late-spring flowers, composed of clusters of 2-inch-long, tubular white blooms featuring frilled edges and yellow or purple tinges and spots. The upright clusters on 4- to 8-inch stalks are visible from a distance. They produce an excellent honey, too. The 8- to 20-inch-long seedpods that develop later in the season and ridged, furrowed gray surface bark provide another season of interest. For the pioneer farmers catalpas were a source of durable wood suitable for fence posts because it resists rot when in contact with soil.

WHEN TO PLANT

Plant balled and burlapped trees in the spring. Catalpas have taproots, so choose young ones for successful transplanting.

WHERE TO PLANT

Catalpas prefer deep, moist, fertile soil, but they can handle either wet or dry, even alkaline, soil if they must. Site them in full sun in spacious yards and give them plenty of space. Because they drop their pods, it is best not to grow them near streets, walks, and gutters.

HOW TO PLANT

Remove the young tree from its container, and spread any circling roots. Dig a saucer-shaped planting hole just as deep as and twice as wide as the rootball. Set the catalpa in the hole so that the top of its rootball is exactly at soil level or even slightly above. If the rootball is wrapped in burlap, cut away as much of the wrapping as possible once the tree is positioned. Fill in the hole with plain soil, firming it gently around the rootball to remove air pockets. Form any excess fill into a small circular ridge just beyond the edge of the root zone to make a moat to hold water, then water well.

CARE AND MAINTENANCE

Maintain a year-round 2- or 3-inch layer of mulch over the root zone of the tree to protect it from mower or trimmer injury. Pods will fall on it and not onto the lawn. Increase the mulched area as the tree canopy spreads. It will also help the soil to stay moist, discourage weeds, and improve the soil as it gradually decomposes. Do not pile mulch up against the tree trunk.

ADDITIONAL INFORMATION

Catalpa has somewhat brittle wood that may break in wind or storms. Prune injured branches promptly, cutting them off cleanly at the branch collar, to facilitate healing. They can handle considerable heat and drought once they are established.

ADDITIONAL SPECIES, CULTIVARS, OR VARIETIES

There are several other types of catalpa, including one native to the South. Various hybrids have been developed in an effort to provide a smaller version that would suit residential landscapes. None are widely available yet.

 Did You Know?

If you like catalpa, you will love paulownia (Paulownia tomentosa), or empress tree. Paulownias are found in similar situations and also have big, coarse leaves, rangy habits, and drop-dead gorgeous flowers. Pale purple, the flowers appear in May and have a light scent. The trees can be cut back to the ground every year and maintained as a large, shrubby foliage-only accent in smaller residential yards. There are newly planted paulownias at the front entrance to the Philadelphia Museum of Art where aged ones long enjoyed the admiration of museum visitors.

Cherry, Ornamental

Prunus species and hybrids

Other Name: Japanese Flowering Cherry
Type: Deciduous, ornamental
Mature Size: 15 to 25 feet tall; equally wide
Bloom Time: April through June, depending
on the type
Features: Flowers; bark; attracts birds and butterfly larvae

Color photograph on page 211.

Light Requirements:

Ornamental cherry is a catchall label for a number of species of decorative cherry trees from Japan that flower in the spring. They are the wonderful trees that flower in Washington, D.C., at the Tidal Basin. Common in home landscapes all over the Delaware Valley, they are a major part of our region's incredibly gorgeous spring. They all offer a blizzard of pink or white, single or double, flowers and sometimes fragrance, too. Even though they have a relatively short life span, on average about 20 years, they are highly desirable as individual specimens, in rows to line walkways and boundaries, or grouped in threes on spacious properties.

WHEN TO PLANT
Plant 5- to 10-foot-tall nursery stock in containers in early spring (March or April). Fall is a good time, too.

WHERE TO PLANT
Ornamental cherries need full sun for best flowering. They can handle almost any kind of well-drained soil. Add organic matter to serious clay soil at the planting site before planting to improve its drainage.

HOW TO PLANT
Remove the tree from its container, and spread any circling roots. Dig a saucer-shaped planting hole just as deep as and twice or more as wide as the soilball. Set the tree in the hole so that its soil is exactly even with, or a bit above, the surrounding ground. Fill the hole with plain soil, firming it gently around the rootball to remove air pockets. Form any excess fill into a small circular ridge just beyond the edge of the root zone to make a moat to hold water, then water well.

CARE AND MAINTENANCE
Spread 2 or 3 inches of organic material over the root zone of the tree but not against its trunk. It will help the soil stay moist, discourage weeds, and

protect young tree trunks from injury by lawn mower or string trimmer. Maintained year-round, the mulch will improve the soil as it gradually decomposes. When the cherry tree has been in place at least 6 months, sprinkle granular slow-acting fertilizer formulated for trees and shrubs on the mulch for the rain to soak in. After 3 or 4 years, annual fertilizing will not be necessary. Years of decomposing organic mulch will improve the soil, which will then nourish the tree.

ADDITIONAL INFORMATION

Cut budded ornamental cherry branches and bring them indoors for preseason bloom. Prune suckers that emerge below the graft on grafted trees. Prune off incipient caterpillar tents at tips of branches as soon as possible. Guard against tree borers in young saplings. Cherry foliage is susceptible to Japanese beetles, so control grubs in the lawn.

ADDITIONAL SPECIES, CULTIVARS, OR VARIETIES

Prunus × 'Okame' is a 1988 Pennsylvania Horticultural Society's Gold Medal Award winner. It features long-lasting, early-season pink flowers and orange and yellow fall foliage. A lovely specimen shades the Hillman Family Garden at the library of Delaware Valley College. Weeping higan cherry (*Prunus subhirtella* 'Pendula') has weeping branches and pink flowers. Kwanzan cherry (*Prunus serrulata* 'Kwanzan') is vase shaped and produces loads of large, double, pink cotton candy flowers dangling among new green-bronze foliage. 'Mt. Fuji' has scented, double, white flowers. Yoshino cherry (*Prunus yeodensis*) bears white flowers in early April.

 Did You Know?

For more than 10 years the Philadelphia Horticultural Society (PHS) has sponsored a Gold Medal plant award program to select and promote woody plants that perform exceptionally well in Philadelphia-area gardens. A distinguished committee evaluates nominated plants for several years for their hardiness, pest and disease resistance, and durability. Initiated by the late J. Franklin Styer and originally named for him, the award has the goal of getting superior plants into Delaware Valley gardens.

Crabapple, Flowering

Malus species and hybrids

Other Name: Flowering Crab
Type: Deciduous, ornamental
Mature Size: 15 to 25 feet tall;
 18 to 30 feet wide
Bloom Time: Late April to June
Features: Flowers; fragrance; fruit; attracts hummingbirds and songbirds

Light Requirements:

Color photograph on page 211.

Because crabapples deliver such gorgeous spring flowers, we forgive them a host of problems including nudity by midsummer. Technically apple trees, they have more and better flowers, smaller fruit, and narrower leaves that may color in fall if the weather is right. Crabapple flower buds are typically deep pink, opening to white, and sometimes fragrant. Depending on the variety, they may be single, semidouble, or double, and the ½-inch fruits that follow in August or September may be red or yellow. Some trees bear lots of flowers one year, fewer the next. Select carefully for disease resistance. Their small but wide-spreading size is in scale with most residential landscapes.

WHEN TO PLANT

Crabapples establish with little fuss. Plant them in early fall; early spring is also fine. Those raised in containers can be planted anytime during the growing season.

WHERE TO PLANT

Crabs need full sun for maximum flowering. They accept most types of soil, even poor ones, if they are slightly acid and well-drained. Choose a site sheltered from strong winds.

HOW TO PLANT

Remove the young tree from its container, and spread any circling roots. Dig a saucer-shaped planting hole just as deep as and about twice as wide as the rootball. Set the tree in the empty hole, and cut away all twine and as much burlap as possible from a wrapped rootball. Assure that the top of the rootball is exactly level with the surrounding ground, then fill in the hole with plain soil, firming it gently. Then water well.

CARE AND MAINTENANCE

Water newly planted trees every 10 days to 2 weeks if rainfall is irregular. Spread 2 or 3 inches of organic material over the root zone of the tree, but not against its trunk, to help the soil stay moist and to catch falling fruit. When the tree has been in place at least 6 months, sprinkle granular slow-acting fertilizer formulated for trees and shrubs on the mulch for the rain to soak in. Do this for 1 or 2 years until the tree is established and growing. Thereafter, continuously decomposing mulch will nourish and condition the soil to maintain the tree's health.

ADDITIONAL INFORMATION

Branches pruned in the late winter can be forced to bloom indoors. Prune crabs when they are dormant to avoid stimulating excess leafy growth, which encourages fungal disease. Cut off damaged or diseased limbs whenever you spot them. Prune lightly to guide shape, and cut out any branches that rub against others. As they age crabapples often produce numerous thin branches, called water sprouts or suckers, along their main branches. Prune these off regularly to improve the appearance of the tree. If rodents gnaw at the bark of young trees in the yard in the winter, wrap the crabapple trunk with hardware cloth or commercial tree guards.

ADDITIONAL SPECIES, CULTIVARS, OR VARIETIES

Unfortunately, many old-fashioned crabapples are chronically afflicted with disease and lose their leaves for most of the summer. Among the more disease-resistant new selections are 2 winners of the 1989 Pennsylvania Horticultural Society's Gold Medal Award. 'Donald Wyman' has single, white flowers and red fruit. 'Jewelberry', which is a bit smaller, has flowers with pink edges and slightly larger red fruit.

 Did You Know?

Much smaller than regular apples, crabapples are generally sour and juiceless. Because they are mostly pectin and flavor, they make great jelly. Simmer them in water to create a mush, then press it through a food mill to remove the skins. Strain the resulting slurry through cheesecloth or a jelly bag to get a clear liquid. Use it for pectin for other jellies, or add a couple of pounds of sugar to it to produce a jelly with much more personality than the typical apple jelly.

Dogwood, Flowering

Cornus florida

Other Name: Native Dogwood
Type: Deciduous, ornamental
Mature Size: 20 plus feet tall; equally wide
Bloom Time: Late April, early May
Features: Flowers; fruit; fall color; attracts songbirds and butterfly larvae

Light Requirements:

Color photograph on page 211.

No list of Philadelphia-area trees can omit our native flowering dogwood. Until it began to disappear from our woods and yards due to a dieback disease, we tended to take for granted its 4 seasons of beauty. Its flowers, with their trademark notched petals (actually bracts), are white, sometimes tinged with pink, and bloom prior to its rich-green leaves. Crunchy red berries beloved by wildlife appear as the leaves turn merlot red in September prior to falling. Then the dark, deeply chiseled bark and horizontal branching winter silhouette remain for winter enjoyment. Visit Valley Forge National Park to see them in their natural setting.

WHEN TO PLANT

Plant nursery stock raised in a container in early spring while it is still basically dormant. Never transplant dogwood from the wild since that is the suspected source of dieback disease.

WHERE TO PLANT

Give dogwoods moist, well-drained, acidic soil rich in organic material as they would enjoy in their native woods. They are woodland edge plants, preferring their roots to be in the shade and their canopy in the sun much of the time—6 hours at least. (Many experts believe that full summer sun in the middle of a residential property is too stressful.) They need good air circulation. Most nursery-grown trees bloom by the third spring.

HOW TO PLANT

Remove the young dogwood from its container, and spread any circling roots. Dig a saucer-shaped planting hole just as deep as and considerably wider than the rootball. Set the tree in the hole so that the top of its rootball is level with, or even slightly above, the surrounding ground. Fill in the hole with plain soil, firming it gently around the rootball. Form any excess fill into a circular water-holding moat over the root zone, then water well. Dogwoods are very susceptible to drought, so water them anytime rainfall is scarce.

CARE AND MAINTENANCE

Mulch dogwood root zones year-round with 2 or 3 inches of organic material to keep the soil moist, discourage weeds, and prevent damage to trunks from weed trimmers and mowers. Never let it pile up against the tree trunk. The first spring after planting sprinkle granular slow-acting fertilizer formulated for trees on the mulch for the rain to soak in. Thereafter, the decomposing mulch will improve the soil, and the tree will not need regular fertilizing.

ADDITIONAL INFORMATION

Prune to shape dogwoods or remove rubbing branches right after flowering, before the next year's flower buds form in late summer. Inspect their trunks for borer holes as they age.

ADDITIONAL SPECIES, CULTIVARS, OR VARIETIES

'Cherokee Chief' has deep-reddish pink flowers. 'Rainbow' has yellow-and-green variegated leaves. 'Welchii' has narrow, pink, cream, and green leaves. Rutger's Hybrids of Japanese flowering dogwood feature good disease resistance. Two, Aurora® and Ruth Ellen®, are winners of the Pennsylvania Horticultural Society's Gold Medal Award. Japanese dogwood (*Cornus kousa*) blooms 3 weeks later than flowering dogwood with white, pointed flower bracts. Then fleshy, round, red fruits dangle from branches like ornaments in September. Its foliage turns reddish in mid-October.

 Did You Know?

For a while the cause of the decline or dieback disease plaguing native dogwoods both here and on the West Coast was elusive. Virtually unheard of 20 years ago, it creates purple-edged brown spots on leaves, starting on the lower branches. Eventually, the whole twig dies back. Infected trees struggle on, looking more sickly and losing more branches yearly. They produce water sprouts along the branches in a vain effort to overcome the disease. Energy reserves are soon exhausted by the output of twigs and foliage on these sprouts, and infected trees soon die. A fungus called Discula has finally been identified as the culprit.

Falsecypress, Hinoki

Chamaecyparis obtusa

Type: Evergreen, conifer
Mature Size: 50 to 75 feet tall;
  10 to 20 feet wide
Foliage: Dark green; flat-needled sprays
Features: Foliage; bark; cones

Color photograph on page 211.

Light Requirements:

Hinoki falsecypresses are stately, slow-growing trees from Japan. Their foliage grows in slightly drooping branchlets of flat sprays of needles that resemble those of arborvitae. Their blunt needles have pale lines or X patches beneath, and they come in many shades of green, some even yellow or bluish, depending on the variety. Hinokis produce male flowers (cones) that shed pollen in April on their bluish, 8-pointed, scaled female cones. As our native hemlocks succumb to an unrelenting infestation of woolly adelgid aphids in our area, these falsecypresses may be a good substitute for them. Fortunately, they like humid climates and are shade tolerant. Full-sized ones require large properties to show to advantage. Use dwarf shrubby types for small spaces and rock gardens.

WHEN TO PLANT

Dwarf Hinoki transplants well. Plant containerized nursery stock anytime during the growing season.

WHERE TO PLANT

Hinoki falsecypresses need sun to best show off their foliage color. A site where they get some shade during hot summer afternoons is ideal. They are flexible about soil as long as it is reasonably fertile and well-drained. Choose a site that is protected from strong wind.

HOW TO PLANT

Remove the young tree from its container, and spread any circling roots. Dig a saucer-shaped planting hole just as deep as and about twice as wide as the rootball. Position the rootball in the empty hole so that its soil is level with that of the surrounding area or even a bit higher. Fill in the hole with plain soil, firming it gently around the rootball to remove air pockets. Form a water-holding moat over the root zone with a ridge of excess soil, then water well. Continue to water over the next year when rainfall is unreliable.

CARE AND MAINTENANCE

Spread a 2- or 3-inch layer of organic material such as chopped leaves, wood chips, or commercial bark product over the root zone of the tree. This year-round mulch will help the soil stay moist, discourage weeds, and improve the soil as it gradually decomposes. Never let it pile up against the tree trunk. When the tree has been in place at least 6 months, sprinkle granular slow-acting fertilizer formulated for evergreen trees and shrubs on the mulch for the rain to soak in. Do this annually for the first few years. Thereafter, continuously decomposing mulch will improve the soil so that it can sustain the tree.

ADDITIONAL INFORMATION

Hinokis have lovely natural shapes, so they do not need routine pruning. To control the size of large varieties, clip their branches individually before new growth starts in the spring. Do not shear them. Cut out damaged ones promptly. Wash off any mite infestations with a forceful water spray. Deny gnawing rodents a nesting place by delaying winter mulching until after the ground freezes hard and wrapping vulnerable trunks with hardware cloth or commercial tree guards.

ADDITIONAL SPECIES, CULTIVARS, OR VARIETIES

The superiority of Hinoki falsecypress is evidenced by the numerous colorful varieties available in a wide range of sizes. 'Crippsii' at 10 to 20 feet is a top-rated, slower-growing, full-sized version with golden foliage. Sawara falsecypress (*Chamaecyparis pisifera*) is a bit narrower and potentially taller than Hinoki with fine-pointed needles. It has a tendency to lose its lower branches early in life. Golden thread ('Filifera Aurea') has handsome gold-tipped, cordlike foliage; 'Boulevard' grows to only 18 feet and has blue foliage.

 Did You Know?

To the average home owner, needled evergreen shrubs look pretty much alike. Sometimes only a practiced eye can easily distinguish some types of falsecypress from juniper, which they seem to resemble closely. Try the touch test. Juniper foliage tends to be prickly; falsecypress foliage is softer and smoother.

Fringe Tree

Chionanthus virginicus

Other Name: Old Man's Beard
Type: Deciduous, ornamental
Mature Size: 12 to 20 feet tall;
  12 to 20 feet wide
Bloom Time: Late May into June
Flower Color/Type: White florets in open clusters
Features: Flowers; scent; fall color; attracts birds

Light Requirements:

Color photograph on page 211.

---

*F*ringe trees are an ideal size for the typical residential yard, so shrublike that they easily fit under utility wires. Although fringe trees are native to the Southeast, their northern form has acclimated to our region since they were introduced in 1736. Consequently, they are rarely bothered by serious pests and diseases. They seem to be able to handle contemporary urban conditions, too. Fringe trees come as separate male and female trees. Both have interesting thready-petaled white flowers, the male ones being slightly longer and more showy. It is necessary to have both to produce their inconspicuous black fruit, which attract birds. To be sure of their sex, purchase young plants in flower. Their medium-green leaves that appear late in the spring develop yellowish tones in fall. Fringe trees are variable in shape, some shrubby, others lanky.

WHEN TO PLANT

Plant balled and burlapped fringe trees or smaller container-grown ones in early spring.

WHERE TO PLANT

Site fringe trees in full sun or partial shade. They accept just about any soil type as long as it is rich in organic matter to hold moisture. They like damp soil and are ideal for streambanks, but they do fine in drier spots if watered during droughts.

HOW TO PLANT

Fringe trees are not crazy about being transplanted, so plant a young tree. Remove it from its container, and spread any circling roots so that they aim outward. Dig a saucer-shaped planting hole just as deep as and somewhat wider than the rootball. Set the tree in the hole so that the top of the soilball is exactly even with, or slightly above, the level of the surrounding ground. Cut away as much burlap as possible if its roots are wrapped. Fill in the hole with plain soil, firming it gently around the rootball to remove air pockets. Form any excess fill into a small circular ridge just beyond the edge of the root zone to create a moat to hold water, then water well.

CARE AND MAINTENANCE

Water regularly if rainfall is scarce for 1 or 2 years until the fringe tree is well established. Maintain a year-round, 2- or 3-inch layer of organic mulch over its root zone, but not against its trunk. This mulch will help the soil stay moist, discourage weeds, and introduce valuable organic matter into the soil as it constantly decomposes. When the tree has been in place at least 6 months, sprinkle granular slow-acting fertilizer formulated for trees and shrubs on the mulch for the rain to soak in.

ADDITIONAL INFORMATION

Prune after the fringe tree blooms in the spring. Buds for next year's flowers will be set later in the season and will be lost to fall pruning. To establish a single trunk, clip off suckering stems that seem to want to make it into a bush.

ADDITIONAL SPECIES, CULTIVARS, OR VARIETIES

Chinese fringe tree (*Chionanthus retusus*) is smaller. Its flowers and fruit are similar, but they bloom on new wood. Its fruit are more obvious and ornamental, and its gray, diamond-patterned bark peels.

 Did You Know?

Fringe tree's scientific name, derived from Greek, is very descriptive. Chio means "snow," and anthos means "flower." Fringe trees grow in the wild from our region all the way to Florida. John Bartram offered them in his early plant catalog, and Thomas Jefferson grew them among the many trees at Monticello.

Ginkgo

Ginkgo biloba

Other Name: Maidenhair Tree

Type: Deciduous, shade

Mature Size: To 80 feet tall; 30 or 40 feet wide

Foliage: Scalloped fans; green

Features: Fall color; malodorous fruit on female

Color photograph on page 211.

Light Requirements:

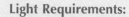

Ginkgos existed throughout the world millions of years ago. Today's trees are living survivors of the dinosaur period and have changed very little since then. Although almost all ginkgos eventually disappeared from the wild, some were grown and preserved in the temples of China, Japan, and Korea. They are the source of all ginkgos that we have today. Related to conifers, ginkgos have distinctive fan-shaped leaves that turn golden in the fall. They resemble those of the maidenhair fern, which explains their common name. Tyler Arboretum in Media boasts a huge specimen. Mature ones are slow growing, tough, and tolerant of most urban stresses except smog. They make great street trees and are well represented in Philadelphia, especially around the art museum and Fairmount Park. Male trees serve streetside best because they do not produce the malodorous fruit that females bear.

WHEN TO PLANT

Spring is the optimum planting time for ginkgos, although young trees in containers transplant well anytime during the growing season.

WHERE TO PLANT

Plant ginkgos in full sun. They prefer moist, well-drained soil rich in organic material, but are amazingly tolerant of a wide range of conditions. They can handle clay or sand and a range of pH.

HOW TO PLANT

Ginkgos are easy to plant when young and also to transplant when older. They take several years to recover, though. Remove the tree from its container, and spread any circling roots. Dig a saucer-shaped planting hole just as deep as and considerably wider than the rootball. Position the ginkgo in the empty hole so that its rootball is at exactly the same level in the soil as it was in its container. Cut away as much burlap as possible from a wrapped rootball. Double-check its depth, then fill the hole with plain soil, firming it gently around the rootball. Create a water-holding moat over the root zone with excess soil, then water well.

CARE AND MAINTENANCE

Water newly planted trees regularly for 1 or 2 years when rainfall is unreliable. Maintain a year-round, 2- or 3-inch layer of organic mulch such as chopped leaves, wood chips, or commercial bark product over the root zones. It will help the soil stay moist, discourage weeds, and improve the soil as it decomposes. Never pile it up against the tree trunk. After the first 6 months, sprinkle granular slow-acting fertilizer formulated for trees and shrubs on the mulch for the rain to soak in. Do this for 1 or 2 years while the roots are becoming established.

ADDITIONAL INFORMATION

Prune ginkgos in the spring when they are young to improve their branching. They are extremely resistant to pests—even Japanese beetles. Their branches are brittle and may suffer storm damage. A male ginkgo is preferable, but choosing from among young trees is a gamble. They do not flower for at least 20 years!

ADDITIONAL SPECIES, CULTIVARS, OR VARIETIES

Some good male ginkgos are 'Autumn Gold', which starts upright, then spreads; 'Fairmount', which was selected from a tree in Fairmount Park; 'Princeton Sentry', which is narrow and dense; and 'Saratoga'.

 Did You Know?

Taken internally, ginkgo is reputed to inhibit allergic responses and improve blood circulation, thus improving memory. The leaves contain chemical compounds that dilate bronchial tubes and blood vessels, and have antifungal and antibacterial properties. Ginkgo is reputed to be effective in treating asthma, circulation in the elderly, and varicose veins. Therapeutic preparations are made from foliage picked when it changes color in autumn. It is dried and processed for use in distilled extracts, infusions, powders, and tinctures.

Goldenrain Tree

Koelreuteria paniculata

Other Name: Varnish Tree
Type: Deciduous, ornamental
Mature Size: 30 feet tall; equally wide
Bloom Time: July
Features: Flowers; dried capsules

Color photograph on page 212.

Light Requirements:

A tree that flowers in the summer is always welcome. The 12- to 15-inch clusters of thin, small yellow flowers that halo the domed canopy of goldenrain trees are eye-catchers. They develop into green, lantern-shaped pods that turn yellow, then brown, and eventually release black seeds the size of peas. Goldenrain trees have a coarse, open structure, abetted by exotic-looking leaves composed of up to 15 coarsely toothed leaflets, which are reduced in size as the tree grows older. The leaves turn orange-yellow in fall. Fast growers (10 to 12 feet the first 7 years), these trees stay relatively small and are suitable for out in the lawn under utility wires or nearer the house to provide some shade. They do well in cities as street trees. They also work in smallish yards and they do not overpower one-story homes.

WHEN TO PLANT

Choose trees grown in the North from northern seed. They plant and transplant amazingly easily in the spring. Young trees look a bit gaunt at first, but fill out quickly.

WHERE TO PLANT

Goldenrain trees like full sun. They grow toward it if they are in shade. They appreciate decent soil, but are amazingly tolerant of poor soil as well as drought, air pollution, and wind.

HOW TO PLANT

Remove the young goldenrain tree from its container, and spread any circling roots. Dig a saucer-shaped planting hole just as deep as and somewhat wider than the rootball. Set the tree in the hole so that its soil is level with or just slightly higher than the surrounding ground. Fill in the hole with plain soil, using any excess fill to form a small circular ridge just beyond the edge of the root zone to create a temporary moat to hold water, then water well. Plant goldenrain trees at least 15 or 20 feet from buildings or other trees.

CARE AND MAINTENANCE

Water regularly if rain is sparse until the tree is established. Maintain a year-round, 2- or 3-inch layer of organic mulch, such as chopped leaves or wood chips, in a circle over the root zone of the goldenrain tree to help the soil stay moist and protect its trunk from weed trimmer and mower damage. Never let mulch pile up against the tree trunk.

ADDITIONAL INFORMATION

Prune damaged branches promptly. Prune for shape, or cut crowded or rubbing branches during dormancy in late winter. Always cut back to the crotch where the branch or twig is attached. Goldenrain tree self-sows its seeds, so lots of seedlings pop up in the area. They pull up easily before they get too woody.

ADDITIONAL SPECIES, CULTIVARS, OR VARIETIES

'September' is a 1997 Gold Medal (Styer) Award winner from the Pennsylvania Horticultural Society. It flowers into September. Chinese flame tree (*Koelreuteria bipinnata*) is a bit less cold hardy and flowers into September. It has rosy-pink fruit capsules.

Did You Know?

The other small "golden" tree with which goldenrain tree is sometimes confused is golden chaintree (Laburnum × watereri). It grows to only 12 or 15 feet tall with a narrower profile. Its glory is the scented yellow flowers that literally drip from its branches in long chains of up to 20 inches in late spring. It struggles a bit in our hot, humid climate.

Hawthorn, Green

Crataegus viridis 'Winter King'

Other Name: Winter King Thorn,
Winter King Hawthorn
Type: Deciduous
Mature Size: 20 to 30 feet tall; equally wide
Bloom Time: Mid-May
Features: Flowers; fruit; fall color; supports honeybees and
migrating birds

Light Requirements:

Color photograph on page 212.

Their beauty notwithstanding, most hawthorns are, as their name suggests, thorny. The thorns can be easily overlooked among the lustrous green leaves, especially when they turn to purplish scarlet in fall and the stems sport bright-red fruit the size of marbles. For all their beauty and toughness hawthorns also have their problems with fungal diseases. Often their foliage drops partway through the summer, leaving skeletons of dark, twiggy branches. 'Winter King' overcomes the typical liabilities of hawthorns, however. Winner of the 1992 Gold Medal Award of the Pennsylvania Horticultural Society, it has a broad vase shape and bears clusters of delicate white flowers each spring. Their musty scent attracts hoards of pollinating insects. After a show of bronze, red, and gold fall foliage, it reveals silvery bark patched with orange-brown and develops orange-red fruits that resemble rose hips. They persist through winter and are available for migrating birds such as cedar waxwings. Best of all 'Winter King' is disease resistant, and its sparse thorns are smaller than those on most types of hawthorn. It is on show at the Morris Arboretum English Park.

WHEN TO PLANT
Spring is the best time to plant hawthorns, although young trees raised in containers can be planted almost anytime during the season.

WHERE TO PLANT
Hawthorns do best in full sun, but some shade is fine. They agreeably tolerate almost any soil—either acid or alkaline, dry or wet sites, light or heavy. They also can handle air pollution. Use 'Winter King' as a specimen, and site it for viewing from indoors, too. Give it plenty of room for its spread.

HOW TO PLANT
Dig a saucer-shaped planting hole just as deep as and about twice as wide as the rootball. Remove the young tree from its container, and spread any circling roots so that they will grow outward. Set the tree in the hole so that

its soil surface is at the same level as the surrounding ground. Fill in the hole with plain soil, firming it gently around the root-ball to remove air pockets. Form any excess soil into a small circular ridge just beyond the edge of the root zone to form a moat to hold water, then water well.

CARE AND MAINTENANCE

Water newly planted trees when rainfall is sparse for a year or more until they are established. Mulching the soil over the root zone year-round with 2 or 3 inches of organic material such as chopped leaves or wood chips helps keep soil moist. Over the years the decomposing mulch will enrich the soil. Small trees may need temporary staking in sites exposed to wind.

ADDITIONAL INFORMATION

'Winter King' is grafted onto rootstock of the Washington hawthorn, and occasionally, suckers will develop from below the graft. Prune them away promptly. Prune off water sprouts if they appear along the branches.

ADDITIONAL SPECIES, CULTIVARS, OR VARIETIES

Washington hawthorn (*Crataegus phaenopyrum*) is another outstanding hawthorn. Native to the United States, it grows to about 20 feet tall and wide. It flowers a bit later than most hawthorns and bears the classic red fruit into winter. Its impressive thorns are 1 to 3 inches long!

Did You Know?

*Cedar-hawthorn rust plagues hawthorns, which are generally highly susceptible to it. It is one of several fungal diseases in plants that require alternate hosts. Fire blight is another notorious one. Rust needs two kinds of plants to survive, so chances of its being around are increased if there are Eastern red cedars (*Juniperus virginiana*) in the area. The disease starts on the hawthorn leaves—red or brown spots ringed with yellow. They develop horns protruding from the underside of the leaf which pop and release spores. They infect nearby junipers, which are not harmed, but host the spores over the winter. The following spring they pop over to the hawthorn again to cause further harm.*

Holly, American

Ilex opaca

Other Name: Christmas Holly
Type: Broadleaf evergreen
Mature Size: 30 to 40 feet tall;
  10 to 20 feet wide
Foliage: Green, spined
Features: Red or yellow berries; attracts birds

Color photograph on page 212.

Light Requirements:

Our native American holly is a stunning, extremely hardy landscape star. Its leathery, spined foliage is a lustrous medium green and paler beneath. Its handsome pyramidal shape with branching to the ground is undeniably elegant. If there is a male holly nearby, female trees bear bright-red, orange, or yellow fall berries, beloved of birds. Hollies are striking as individual specimens, in groups to screen a view or noise, or as background for other, lower shrubs and plants. They tolerate the sand and salt of the Shore. In some areas around Philadelphia deer have developed a taste for holly foliage. There are wonderful hollies in Longwood Gardens, the Morris Arboretum, the Tyler Arboretum, and in the Frorer Holly Collection at the Scott Arboretum.

WHEN TO PLANT

Hollies with rootballs wrapped in burlap plant best in spring. Those raised in containers can be planted anytime during the growing season, but spring is also best for them.

WHERE TO PLANT

Although naturalized American holly seedlings seem to do fine in woodland shade, cultivated trees do best in full sun. In shade they have fewer berries and are less compact. Holly prefers well-drained soil that is light and sandy and on the acidic side. Mix organic material into clay soil to improve its drainage. Plant a male in the yard to assure good pollination and berries on female trees. Site them with protection from harsh winter wind and sun.

HOW TO PLANT

Dig a saucer-shaped planting hole just as deep as and somewhat wider than the rootball. Remove the young tree from its container, and spread any circling roots outward. Set the tree in the hole so that the top of its rootball is level with the surrounding ground. Cut away as much burlap as possible from a wrapped rootball. Fill in the hole with plain soil, firming it gently around the rootball, and water well. Young hollies up to 5 years old need plenty of moisture. Water regularly if rainfall is sparse, but do not soak the soil excessively.

CARE AND MAINTENANCE

Be sure to water well in the fall before the ground freezes hard. Maintain a 2- or 3-inch layer of organic material over the root zone of the tree to help the soil stay moist. In the fall or when the tree has been in place at least 6 months, sprinkle granular slow-acting fertilizer formulated for acid-loving trees on the mulch for the rain to soak in. Do not overdo because hollies are sensitive to overfertilization. After a few years well-mulched hollies do not need regular fertilizing.

ADDITIONAL INFORMATION

Aging American holly branches become more open and irregular and benefit from tip trimming to maintain a uniform shape. Prune in winter, and select some branches to cut for holiday decorations. Never top specimen trees to reduce their height. Hollies can be sheared into hedges, but be sure the lower branches are wider than the upper ones so that they receive sunlight.

ADDITIONAL SPECIES, CULTIVARS, OR VARIETIES

'Jersey Knight' and 'Jersey Princess' have good form, dark-green foliage, and generous fruit. Local nurseries carry other varieties that are especially suitable for the Philadelphia area. English holly (*Ilex aquifolium*) is similar to American and even more beloved by deer. Its twigs are green or purple instead of yellow-brown. Less hardy, it flowers about a month earlier, in April.

 Did You Know?

To medieval monks, English holly, or "Holy Tree," was symbolic of Christianity. The sharp leaf spines recalled the crown of thorns, the white flowers symbolized purity and the virgin birth, and the red berries represented drops of blood. English holly became so closely associated with the celebration of Christmas that by 1598 surveys in England revealed that every house, church, and marketplace was decorated with English holly boughs.

Honeylocust, Thornless

Gleditsia tricanthos 'Inermis'

Type: Deciduous, ornamental
Mature Size: 30 to 50 feet tall; 30 feet wide
Bloom Time: June
Features: Fall color; pods; attracts butterflies
  and moths

Light Requirements:

Color photograph on page 212.

Wild honeylocusts abound in the woods of Pennsylvania, but they are not suitable for home landscapes because of the vicious thorns on their trunks and branches. Breeders have developed thornless versions of honeylocust that also have their nice proportions and typical light, airy foliage. Featuring 20 to 30 small leaflets, the green leaves turn pale yellow in autumn. While the honeylocust flowers that bloom among them in early summer are generally an inconspicuous green, they are scented. They give way to brown, twisted, strappy pods up to 8 inches long later in the summer. Their fine texture, salt tolerance, drought resistance, and adaptability to a range of city and suburban conditions account for honeylocusts' huge popularity all over the Delaware Valley and elsewhere as street trees and yard specimens.

WHEN TO PLANT

Plant trees raised in containers at the nursery anytime during the growing season. Plant larger ones with rootballs wrapped in burlap in the spring.

WHERE TO PLANT

Honeylocusts like full sun. They are not fussy about soil type as long as it is well-drained.

HOW TO PLANT

Remove the young tree from its container, and spread any circling roots. Dig a saucer-shaped planting hole just as deep as and somewhat wider than the rootball, and set the tree in the hole so that the rootball is level with the surrounding ground. Fill in the hole with plain soil, firming it gently around the rootball to remove air pockets. Form a temporary water-holding moat over the root zone with any excess soil, then water well. Honeylocusts take about 1 year per inch of trunk diameter to establish. During that time they need regular water over their root zone and adjacent soil.

CARE AND MAINTENANCE

Maintain a year-round, 2- or 3-inch layer of organic mulch over the honeylocust root zone. It will help the soil stay moist, discourage weeds, and improve the soil as it decomposes. It also protects its trunk from lawn mower and weed trimmer damage, which may promote disease and pest problems. Prune young trees to control their potential for erratic shape and to establish a single leader for a trunk. Prune broken or damaged branches promptly. Cut off any suckers growing from below the graft.

ADDITIONAL INFORMATION

Planting honeylocust too deeply fosters disease. Watch for webworms, which may produce brown patches of foliage or defoliate the tree. Prune out their nests.

ADDITIONAL SPECIES, CULTIVARS, OR VARIETIES

These choices have virtually no pods or thorns: 'Halka' is compact and rounded; 'Moraine' has deep-green foliage to yellow in fall; 'Shademaster' has good form with ascending branches, and it is the standard by which all other honeylocusts are judged; 'Skyline' is upright and pyramidal; and 'Sunburst' has golden spring foliage, then yellowish green.

 Did You Know?

Honeylocusts may be victims of their own success. Originally prized for their dearth of serious pest and disease problems, they were enthusiastically planted in huge numbers in the East and Midwest. They seemed the perfect plant to fill the gap left by the loss of the American elm to rampant disease. Experts now believe that they have been overplanted because they see a significant increase in the incidence of the many relatively minor problems that affect honeylocusts. Their ubiquity seems to be making them more vulnerable to webworm, borer, plant bugs, spider mite, and leaf canker. They risk becoming more of a liability than an asset.

Linden, Littleleaf

Tilia cordata

Other Name: Small-Leafed Lime
Type: Deciduous, shade
Mature Size: To 60 feet tall; 30 feet wide
Bloom Time: Late June into July
Features: Fragrant flowers; attracts honeybees and other wildlife

Light Requirements:

Color photograph on page 212.

*L*ittleleaf lindens abound in yards and along streets all over the Philadelphia area—and for good reason. Their dense foliage canopy of medium-sized, toothed, heart-shaped, dark-green leaves is neat and attractive. It shelters copious clusters of fragrant, small pale-yellow flowers that dangle on thin stalks beneath a single leafy bract. By late summer the flowers become tiny dried fruits that persist well after the foliage turns yellow and drops. Among their other virtues, lindens count a sturdy tolerance for pollution and shallow, disciplined root systems that make them good neighbors to buildings and other plants.

WHEN TO PLANT

Lindens transplant easily. Plant larger balled and burlapped trees in either spring or fall. Those raised in containers can be planted anytime during the growing season.

WHERE TO PLANT

Lindens do best in full sun, although they accept some shade. They prefer a good soil rich in organic matter, but will compromise as long as it is well-drained.

HOW TO PLANT

Dig a saucer-shaped planting hole just as deep as and twice as wide as the rootball. Remove the linden from its container, and spread any circling roots outward. Set the tree in the hole so that the top of its rootball where the roots visibly flare out from the trunk is exactly at soil level or even slightly above. Cut away as much burlap as possible from a wrapped rootball. Fill in the hole with plain soil, firming it gently around the rootball. Form a water-holding moat over the root zone with any excess soil, then water well. Space lindens as street trees 40 feet apart.

CARE AND MAINTENANCE

Water lindens if rainfall is unreliable over the 1 or 2 years it takes for them to become established and then during periods of drought in hot summers.

Maintain a year-round, 2- or 3-inch layer of organic mulch over the root zone (not against the trunk) to help the soil retain moisture. It also protects the tender bark on the trunk from damage by lawn mower or string trimmer. After a minimum of 6 months, sprinkle granular slow-acting fertilizer formulated for trees on the mulch for the rain to soak in. After 2 or 3 years annual fertilization will not be necessary because the constantly decomposing mulch will feed the soil.

ADDITIONAL INFORMATION

Lindens accept pruning well and can be trained as a hedge. Prune any suckers that appear on the trunk from below the graft. Often lindens have serious problems with Japanese beetles. Handpick or brush off the beetles on small trees into a jar of soapy water. Treat the lawn for white grubs to control the local beetle population. Do not hang bag traps in the tree or anywhere in the vicinity. Older, established trees seem to be able to withstand virtual defoliation by these pests every year.

ADDITIONAL SPECIES, CULTIVARS, OR VARIETIES

'Greenspire' is a fast grower, and its dense canopy and upright, straight trunk are the standard of comparison among lindens. 'Glenleven' is vigorous, with a more open-leaf canopy and more informal branching. American linden or basswood (*Tilia americana*) is larger and a bit more coarse-textured than littleleaf linden. Good varieties are 'Redmond' and 'Rosehill.' Silver linden (*Tilia tomentosum*) has silvery leaf undersides and is appropriate for city sites.

 Did You Know?

The bounty of the native American linden is generous. Its common names suggest its gifts. It is called bee tree because of the copious nectar its flowers produce, making it one of the best honey trees in the world. Its foliage is also used in tea for nerve, throat, and voice problems, and as an appetite stimulant. It is called basswood, or white wood, because its light, straight-grained wood is ideal for carving and joinery and piano sounding boards, keys, and cabinetry.

Magnolia, Saucer
Magnolia × soulangiana

Type: Deciduous, ornamental

Mature Size: Up to 30 feet tall; equally wide

Bloom Time: April

Features: Fuzzy buds; bark; fragrant flowers; seedpods

Color photograph on page 212.

Light Requirements:

Saucer magnolias, the products of a cross between Japanese and Chinese magnolias, provide a reliably cold-hardy version of magnolia for Northern yards. They cover themselves with glory every spring before their leaves emerge with 5- to 8-inch-wide, fragrant, saucer-shaped blossoms. Usually white with a pink or purplish blush on the undersides of their outer petals, they hold an annual contest with the last frost. More often than not they lose, their petals turning to brown mush, sometimes within hours of opening. Oh, but the years when they win!

WHEN TO PLANT
Magnolias' fleshy roots are tender and sparse. Damage delays recovery from transplant shock. Plant young trees with burlapped rootballs in either March or April. Smaller, potted ones transplant best, especially planted early in the season. They start flowering when they are 4 feet or so tall.

WHERE TO PLANT
Saucer magnolias do best in full sun in the open where air circulation is good. Sheltered sites heat up too soon, causing flower buds to open early and risk frost. Provide soil that is a bit on the acid side, rich in organic material, and well-drained.

HOW TO PLANT
Dig a saucer-shaped planting hole just as deep as and about twice as wide as the rootball. Remove the young tree from its container, and snip off any circling roots caused by confinement in the pot too long. They will never straighten out. Set the tree in the hole so that the top of its rootball is exactly at the level of the surrounding ground, no lower. Cut away as much burlap as possible from a wrapped rootball. Then fill in the hole with plain soil, firming it gently around the rootball. Create a water-holding moat over the root zone, and water well.

CARE AND MAINTENANCE

Water when rainfall is sparse during the first year or two.
Maintain a 2- or 3-inch layer of organic material over the magnolia's root zone year-round to help the soil stay moist and add
organic matter to it as it constantly decomposes. After the trees
have been in place 6 months, sprinkle granular slow-acting fertilizer formulated for trees on the mulch for the rain to soak in.
Prune the occasional damaged branch promptly. Cut off any
branch that crosses and rubs another and vertical water sprouts
or suckers along magnolia branches. Prune for size and shape
immediately after flowering because new buds form over the
summer for next year's show.

ADDITIONAL INFORMATION

Plant only permanent, shallow, small, hardy bulbs such as squill
or grape hyacinth under magnolias. Cultivating the soil damages
their shallow roots.

ADDITIONAL SPECIES, CULTIVARS, OR VARIETIES

Magnolia × 'Galaxy' is a 1992 winner of the Pennsylvania Horticultural Society's Gold Medal Award. Its April bloom time helps
its dark-pink flowers escape early frosts. Star magnolia (*Magnolia
stellata*) has smaller, white, double, fragrant flowers and grows
slowly to 20 feet. 'Centennial' is a 1997 Gold Medal Award winner. Southern magnolia (*Magnolia grandiflora*) 'Edith Bogue'
(Gold Medal, 1992) is hardy here; its creamy-white flowers
bloom in June and July. The USDA "girls" are 8 later-flowering
magnolia cultivars developed by the U.S. National Arboretum in
Washington, D.C., in the 1950s specifically for small yards and
gardens. 'Elizabeth' (Gold Medal) has yellow flowers in late
April and is fast growing. Sweetbay magnolia (*Magnolia virginiana*) is native with white flowers in June and takes wet soils.

 Did You Know?

*Saucer magnolias are named for Chevalier Etienne Soulange-
Bodin, a French soldier. A veteran of the Napoleonic Wars, he
devoted his retirement to gardening, becoming the director of
the Royal Institute of Horticulture in France. Around 1820
he crossed a white yulan magnolia with a purple lily one, and
the saucer magnolia was the result.*

Maple, Japanese

Acer palmatum

Type: Deciduous, ornamental

Mature Size: 3 to 20 feet tall; equally wide

Foliage: Red or green or variegated;
 palm shaped

Features: Fine texture; fall color; contorted shape; bark and twig color

Light Requirements:

Color photograph on page 212.

In their myriad forms and colors Japanese maples commonly grace suburban yards in the Philadelphia area as specimens or focal points anchoring an island bed. Weeping types integrate easily into small yards in containers or rock gardens. They make good understory plants because they tolerate some shade. Japanese maple flowers hang as small, purplish red clusters that develop into the classic maple winged seeds. Their leaves are 1 to 3 inches across, and depending on the variety, they have 5 to 11 lobes. Some are cut so deeply that they seem lacy. The most highly prized Japanese maples are the named cultivars, and their price reflects their value.

WHEN TO PLANT

Plant maples with roots wrapped in burlap in early spring immediately after winter dormancy ends. Transplant those raised in containers anytime during the growing season except during heat and drought spells.

WHERE TO PLANT

Most Japanese maples do best in full sun, but the color on the deep-red ones is enhanced in some shade. Maroon-leafed ones are greener in the shade. Find a somewhat protected site to avoid sunscorch in summer and frost in late winter. Almost any well-drained soil except unimproved clay or total sand is fine. Green-leaved Japanese maples are reportedly less fussy about sites than maroon or variegated types.

HOW TO PLANT

Dig a saucer-shaped planting hole just as deep as and somewhat wider than the rootball. Remove the maple from its container, and straighten any circling roots. Japanese maples tend to develop girdling roots as they age. Set the tree in the hole so that the top of its rootball is exactly at soil level or even slightly higher. Cut away the burlap from a wrapped rootball. Fill in the hole with plain soil, firming it gently around the rootball. With extra soil, create a water-holding moat over the root zone, then water well.

CARE AND MAINTENANCE

Provide a year-round, 2- or 3-inch layer of organic mulch over the root zone of the Japanese maple to help the soil stay moist, discourage weeds, and fend off lawn mowers. After at least 6 months, fertilize with granular slow-acting fertilizer formulated for trees. Do this annually for a few years, then the constantly decomposing mulch will enrich the soil. Prune mid- to late summer to shape and to remove suckers, rubbing branches, and excess twigs. Clip away damaged branches anytime.

ADDITIONAL INFORMATION

Rodents sometimes nest in mulch at the base of young trees and gnaw at their tender bark in winter. Delay spreading winter mulch until the ground freezes hard, and/or wrap trunks with hardware cloth or commercial bark guards. Japanese maples are susceptible to verticillium wilt in our area. Foliage on one or more branches may suddenly wilt, shrivel, and die. The rest of the tree may die suddenly or gradually. Prune off infected branches. Feed with high nitrogen (lawn) fertilizer to encourage new sapwood growth. Do not plant a Japanese maple where another has died.

ADDITIONAL SPECIES, CULTIVARS, OR VARIETIES

There are hundreds of named Japanese maples: 'Super Blood-good' is red all season; 'Versicolor' has green leaves variegated with pink and white. Threadleaf Japanese maple (*Acer palmatum* var. *dissectum*) has finely dissected foliage; 'Tamukeyama' (the 1997 Pennsylvania Horticultural Society Gold Medal winner) is the best of the purple-leafed cutleafs; and 'Waterfall' (1999 Gold Medal) has green foliage that turns yellow.

 Did You Know?

Bonsai is the ancient art of dwarfing regular trees and shrubs so that they age as containerized miniatures of their potential selves over decades—even centuries. It is possible to achieve something similar with less skill and patience using dwarf Japanese maples. Choose a regular outdoor container that is wider than tall, has a drainage hole, and can take winter outdoors. From a book on bonsai borrow the critical techniques for pruning roots and branches every few years.

Maple, Red

Acer rubrum

Other Names: Swamp Red Maple, Scarlet Maple

Type: Deciduous, shade

Mature Size: 40 to 60 feet tall; 30 to 50 feet wide

Foliage: Green, palm shaped

Features: Fall color; winged seeds; feeds and shelters wildlife

Color photograph on page 212.

Light Requirements:

Red describes them best. Swamp red maples have red buds in winter, red flowers and winged seeds in spring, red leaf stalks in summer, and red foliage in fall. This excellent native tree is fast growing, yet has strong wood (unlike its silver maple cousin and many other fast-growing trees). Furthermore, it prefers wet soil. Females have more conspicuous flowers, and the day when their seeds are released with the wind and cover the lawn is a delight for people and squirrels. Red maple sap is sweet, but it is not like that of its sugar maple cousin. Use red maples to be specimens in a large yard or to line drives or border the property.

WHEN TO PLANT

Plant in the spring. Transplant container-grown red maples anytime during the growing season. Avoid grafted trees.

WHERE TO PLANT

Red maples do best in full sun. They tolerate all kinds of soils, including wet ones. Their relatively shallow, wide-ranging roots tend to surface when crowded, so site them well away from buildings and curbs.

HOW TO PLANT

Dig a saucer-shaped planting hole just as deep as and about twice as wide as the rootball. Remove the red maple from its container. Position the rootball in the hole so that its top is even with, or slightly above, the surrounding ground. Cut away as much of the burlap and twine as possible from a wrapped rootball. Fill in the hole with plain soil, firming it gently around the trunk to remove air pockets. Form a water-holding moat over the root zone with any excess soil, then water well.

CARE AND MAINTENANCE

Continue to water newly planted trees regularly for 1 or 2 years whenever rainfall is sparse. Mulch their root zones year-round with 2 or 3 inches of organic material to help the soil stay moist and protect trunks from injury by mower or weed trimmer. When the maple has been in place at least 6 months, sprinkle granular slow-acting fertilizer formulated for trees on the mulch for the rain to soak in. Do this every year for 3 or 4 years. Thereafter, the constantly decomposing mulch will improve the soil, and the tree will not need regular fertilizing.

ADDITIONAL INFORMATION

Sometimes two leaders develop in young red maples. Prune one off early on to establish a single trunk. Trees pruned in late winter will leak sap but suffer no harm. Pruning in June avoids this. Prune diseased or injured branches immediately.

ADDITIONAL SPECIES, CULTIVARS, OR VARIETIES

'Autumn Flame' colors earliest in the fall. It has smaller leaves and is slower growing than most red maples. 'October Glory' turns color the latest—a display of crimson red to orange. An early hard frost sometimes preempts the color. Originally selected in nearby New Jersey, it is well adapted to our area. 'Red Sunset' is highly rated. It holds its red fall foliage longest and has a narrower canopy than many.

 Did You Know?

Norway maples (Acer platanoides) are among several brightly fall-colored foliage cousins of red maples. The beautiful maroon foliage of 'Crimson King' notwithstanding, it and other Norways have earned themselves the opprobrium of most local arborists, horticulturists, and environmentalists. More and more gardeners and home owners are also realizing the nuisance that they represent in our region. They seed everywhere, driving out native plants and hogging soil moisture. In his classic Manual of Woody Landscape Plants *(5th edition), Michael Dirr says, "I remember an early November drive from Swarthmore College to Longwood Gardens, PA and Norway Maple was everywhere in evidence in the local woodlands with the bright yellow leaves still persisting."*

Oak, Red and White

Quercus rubra; Quercus alba

Type: Deciduous, shade

Mature Size: 40 to 80 plus feet tall;
  60 feet or wider

Foliage: Dark green; deeply lobed

Features: Acorns; fall color; attracts birds, squirrels, and other wildlife;
  butterfly larvae

Light Requirements:

Color photograph on page 212.

Their presence echoing the hardwood forests that once covered this region, red oaks and white oaks are familiar, native shade trees that grace old properties and winding streets in and around Philadelphia. Their name often prefaced with the word *mighty*, these oaks have been used as street trees, but cruel restriction between curb and sidewalk forces bulging roots. They do best as specimens in spacious lawns. Red oaks are best for city sites; they tolerate air pollution and grow faster than white oaks. Their foliage has pointed lobes, while that of white oaks has rounded lobes. Neither produces acorns until trees are about 25 years old. Because they are extremely long-lived trees, attentive care bestowed on them as young trees (including protection from deer) is critical to their future. Old trees are extremely sensitive to damage to their widely spread roots by nearby construction projects and heavy machinery. The biggest red oak in the region is at Ridley Creek State Park near Media, Delaware County.

WHEN TO PLANT

For best results, plant oaks when they are young. The best planting time is in early spring, although trees raised in containers can be planted anytime during the growing season.

WHERE TO PLANT

Site oaks in full sun. They like soil that is loose, well-drained, and rich in organic matter. Their relatively shallow roots establish fairly easily.

HOW TO PLANT

Dig a saucer-shaped planting hole just as deep as and about twice as wide as the rootball. Remove the young oak tree from its container, and spread any circling roots outward. Set the tree in the hole so that the top of its rootball is exactly at soil level or even slightly above. Cut away as much burlap as possible from a wrapped rootball. Fill in the hole with plain soil, firming it gently around the rootball. Create a water-holding moat over the root zone with excess soil, then water well.

Care and Maintenance

Maintain a year-round, 2- or 3-inch layer of organic mulch over the oak's root zone to keep the soil moist, discourage weeds, and protect its trunk from mowers and weed trimmers. It will also catch the mess of acorn bits left by squirrel visitors and spare the lawn. When the tree has been in place at least 6 months, sprinkle granular slow-acting fertilizer formulated for trees on the mulch for the rain to soak in. After a few years the constantly decomposing mulch will improve the soil, and the tree will not need regular fertilizing. Prune damaged branches at any time. Prune to improve shape, to assure a single trunk, or to remove rubbing branches in the winter while the tree is dormant. Make proper cuts at the branch collar to assure that the wound seals naturally. Do not stake crooked or leaning red oaks to straighten them.

Additional Information

If oaks are relatively free of stress and injury, they usually escape serious pest and disease problems. Gypsy moths, their nemesis, defoliate full-grown trees in no time, but they seem to be under control lately.

Additional Species, Cultivars, or Varieties

Pin oak (*Quercus palustris*) is fast growing, with a uniform shape. Pin oak and swamp white oak (*Quercus bicolor*) both tolerate wetter soil.

 Did You Know?

Many colonial-era "Penn Oaks" still survive in the region and grace area Quaker meetinghouse yards and churchyards. William Penn often used oaks to mark boundaries such as Route 926 at the border of Chester and Delaware Counties. A Penn-era oak at the entrance to Longwood Gardens was greatly valued by Pierre S. duPont.

Pear, Ornamental

Pyrus calleryana

Other Name: Callery Pear
Type: Deciduous, ornamental
Mature Size: 30 to 45 feet tall;
   20 to 25 feet wide
Bloom Time: April
Features: Flowers; fall color

Color photograph on page 212.

Light Requirements:

Ornamental pear trees have become fixtures in home landscapes because of their uniform shape, rapid growth, and lovely white spring flowers. Relatively carefree, too, they do not develop real fruit, just inconspicuous little dried knobs. Their leaves turn wine red before dropping in October. A few have thorns, but many types are completely thornless. Once established, they are relatively drought tolerant. The most popular one has been 'Bradford', available since 1963, which offers the best flowers, disease resistance, and fall color. Its brittle dense branches, narrowly crotched where they join the trunk, tend to split from it in wind or weight of snow, however. Thus, their effective life span is generally less than 20 years. Recently introduced ornamental pear varieties have improved branching.

WHEN TO PLANT

Plant balled and burlapped trees when dormant in the spring. Containerized nursery stock can be planted anytime during the growing season, but spring or fall is preferred.

WHERE TO PLANT

Ornamental pears need full sun because shade makes them lose their shape. They accept almost any kind of soil, even clay, as long as it is reasonably fertile and well-drained. Site them where they have sufficient room to grow to their natural size.

HOW TO PLANT

Remove the young tree from its container, and spread or cut any circling roots. Dig a saucer-shaped planting hole just as deep as and somewhat wider than the rootball. Set the tree in the hole so that the top of its rootball is exactly at soil level or even slightly above. Cut away as much burlap as possible if its rootball is wrapped. Fill in the hole with plain soil, firming it gently around the rootball. Form a water-holding moat over the root zone from excess soil, then water well. Reserve an open space of 30 feet around the tree to accommodate its mature size.

CARE AND MAINTENANCE

Spread 2 or 3 inches of organic material over the pear root zone to keep the soil moist, discourage weeds, and protect the trunk from injury by mower or weed trimmer. Renew the mulch for winter. Never let it pile up against the tree trunk. When the tree has been in place at least 6 months, sprinkle granular slow-acting fertilizer formulated for trees and shrubs on the mulch for the rain to soak in. Do not overdo because excessive fertilizer promotes foliage disease. Eventually, the constantly decomposing mulch will improve the soil, and the tree will not need regular fertilizing.

ADDITIONAL INFORMATION

Ornamental pears do not need shaping because their habit is so uniform. Prune only to remove damaged or rubbing branches. The tender bark of young trees is sometimes a target for rodents, which nest in mulch. Delay winter mulch until the ground has frozen, and consider wrapping vulnerable trunks in hardware cloth or using commercial tree guards.

ADDITIONAL SPECIES, CULTIVARS, OR VARIETIES

Compared to 'Bradford', 'Aristocrat', with glossy leaves, no thorns, and upcurving branches, has stronger wood, so it is less likely to split; 'Autumn Blaze' sports gorgeous fall color, a stronger branching habit, and some thorns; 'Capital' has coppery fall foliage and a very narrow, upright habit; 'Chanticleer' ('Select') is upright and sturdier, less prone to damage, and narrower for an ideal street tree; and 'Whitehouse' is columnar and pyramidal with narrower leaves.

 Did You Know?

Ornamental pears make attractive espalier specimens. Plant them so that their straight trunks grow close to a wall trellis or a sturdy wire and post support. Prune them to establish strong lateral branches. Train the branches to grow horizontally, flat against the support. When they are pruned and displayed this way, their tendency to split with age is no longer a problem.

Pine, Eastern White

Pinus strobus

Other Name: White Pine
Type: Evergreen conifer
Mature Size: 80 to 100 feet tall;
  20 to 40 feet wide
Foliage: Bluish green, aromatic needles
Features: Winter color; cones; food and shelter for birds and
  other wildlife

Light Requirements:

Color photograph on page 212.

*E*ven though it grows quite large, our native white pine is so beloved that it is included in even modest residential yards. Its soft, 5-inch-long needles, bundled in fives, add colorful grace to any landscape, especially in the winter. White pines are long-lived, adaptable, and tolerant of pruning to control their size or create a hedge. As a bonus, in June and early July they produce male and female flowers, actually soft cones, which turn brown by fall and produce seeds for wildlife. When they are young, they are Christmas tree shaped, but they become lanky and flat topped with distinctive horizontal branching in adolescence. They are often planted as windbreaks or along berms as screens, but this is not a good idea. Their brittle wood is easily damaged in winds and storms. They are best in woodland settings or pruned as a screen. In many areas the deer seem to leave them alone.

WHEN TO PLANT

Plant pines with roots wrapped in burlap in early spring or fall. However, move a living Christmas tree back outdoors gradually, then plant it promptly if the ground is not frozen. Otherwise cover the rootball with chopped leaves to keep it moist. Store it in a sheltered, outdoor area until early spring. Small trees raised in containers can be planted anytime during the growing season.

WHERE TO PLANT

White pines like full sun and most soils that are reasonably fertile and drain well. They transplant fairly easily because they have shallow, spreading roots. Avoid sites exposed to winds to prevent breakage of their brittle branches. White pines cannot handle salt and car exhaust, so keep them away from roadsides.

HOW TO PLANT

Choose young trees raised in the North from northern stock. Keep the soil around the roots moist. Remove the young pine from its container, and cut or spread any circling roots. Dig a saucer-shaped planting hole just as deep as and somewhat wider than the rootball. Set the tree in the hole so that the top of its rootball is exactly level with or even a bit higher than the surrounding ground. Cut away as much burlap as possible from a wrapped rootball. Fill in the hole with plain soil, firming it gently around the rootball. Form a water-holding moat over the root zone with excess soil, then water well.

CARE AND MAINTENANCE

Water white pines well in the absence of rain for 1 or 2 years. Maintain a 2- or 3-inch year-round layer of organic mulch over their root zones to retain soil moisture and eliminate turfgrass whose roots release a growth-inhibiting substance to which pines are sensitive. If the soil is poor, sprinkle granular slow-acting fertilizer formulated for conifers on the mulch for the rain to soak in about 6 months after planting, then annually for 1 or 2 years. Temporarily stake young, fall-planted trees only if they are exposed to winter winds.

ADDITIONAL INFORMATION

Prune white pines to remove broken branches anytime. To encourage compactness or train to a hedge, prune them in the spring before their new growth, "candles," appears at their branch tips. Boughs and cones pruned from white pine are traditional greens used in wreaths and other Christmas decorations.

ADDITIONAL SPECIES, CULTIVARS, OR VARIETIES

'Pendula' is a weeping variety with arching branches. 'Fastigiata' is narrow, columnar, and best for hedges and screens. 'Nana' is dwarf and mounded.

 Did You Know?

The Pinetum at Haverford College has a fine collection for conifer study. Located on the campus between Haverford Road, College Avenue, and Featherbed Lane, the Pinetum displays 332 individually labeled conifers arranged in 5 family groups for easy access and identification. The arboretum is open dawn to dusk every day of the year.

Redbud, Eastern

Cercis canadensis

Other Names: American Redbud, Judas Tree
Type: Deciduous, ornamental
Mature Size: To 30 feet tall; 25 to 30 feet wide
Bloom Time: Late April, early May
Features: Flowers; seedpods; fall color; edible flowers

Light Requirements:

Color photograph on page 212.

An ideal size for small yards, redbuds, native to Pennsylvania, introduce the beauty of the flowering forest into the landscape. At 4 or 5 years old young trees start to flower along still-leafless branches and sometimes even their trunks. The spring blooms resemble sweet peas and are lilac-pink or white. Flat tiers of heart-shaped leaves up to 5 inches long eventually develop on the long, dipping branches; flat brown seedpods appear as summer progresses. Their season finale is yellow fall foliage. Older trees become architecturally interesting with open branches and sometimes knobs or burls on their trunks, making them visually interesting even in winter. Redbuds generally live only about 20 years, often falling victim to a fungal canker disease which enters through wounds in the bark. They also are victims of browsing deer.

WHEN TO PLANT

Plant young containerized nursery trees, raised in the North from northern seed, anytime during the growing season. The smaller and younger they are, the easier they transplant.

WHERE TO PLANT

Give redbuds full sun or light shade such as an understory site in the protective lee of larger pines, maples, or oaks or at the edge of woodland settings. They accept any soil from sand to clay that is reasonably fertile and well-drained. Once established, they tolerate some drought.

HOW TO PLANT

Remove the young tree from its container, and spread any circling roots. Dig a saucer-shaped planting hole just as deep as and somewhat wider than the rootball, and set the tree in the hole so that the top of the rootball is level with or slightly above the surrounding ground. Fill in the hole with plain soil, firming it gently around the rootball. Create a water-holding moat over the root zone, and water well and regularly over the first year in the absence of rain.

CARE AND MAINTENANCE

Spread a 2- or 3-inch layer of organic material as a year-round mulch over the redbud's root zone, but not against its trunk. It will help the soil stay moist, discourage weeds, and protect against mower damage. When the redbud has been in place at least 6 months, sprinkle granular slow-acting fertilizer formulated for trees and shrubs on the mulch for the rain to soak in. After 2 or 3 years, the constantly decomposing mulch will enrich the soil, and the tree will not need regular fertilizing.

ADDITIONAL INFORMATION

Cut budded branches in late winter to force preseason indoor bloom. Prune a redbud in the spring after flowering to remove low or excess branches if necessary. Train it to a single trunk, or cut it back to the ground after it flowers to make it multi-stemmed. Cut off all but the sturdiest stems that sprout from the stump. Prune canker infection by cutting off the entire affected branch below where healthy wood starts, so it can generate new, healthy growth. Afterward, sterilize tools in a solution of hot water and household bleach.

ADDITIONAL SPECIES, CULTIVARS, OR VARIETIES

'Flame' ('Plena') is double flowered and faster growing, and it has few pods. 'Forest Pansy' has black-purple new leaves, which fade to greenish in summer humidity and heat. Chinese redbud (*Cercis chinensis*) is smaller (12 feet tall) and shrubby with several upright stems. 'Avondale' flowers exuberantly.

 Did You Know?

Redbud flowers are edible—either as buds or fully opened. They make a colorful, crunchy addition to salads. Buds can be pickled or sautéed in butter and served as a single vegetable or included in mixed vegetables such as peas and mushrooms. Their flavor is slightly tart and beanlike. (Information courtesy of Cathy Wilkinson Barash, Edible Flowers from Garden to Palate, *Fulcrum Publishing, 1993.)*

Sourwood

Oxydendron arboreum

Other Names: Sorrel Tree,
Lily-of-the-Valley Tree

Type: Deciduous, ornamental

Mature Size: 25 to 30 feet tall;
15 to 20 feet wide

Bloom Time: July

Features: Flowers; fall color; supports honeybees; hard,
close-grained wood

Light Requirements:

Color photograph on page 213.

Native to Southwestern Pennsylvania and the South, sourwoods are our best-kept tree secret. They are ornamental in every respect, their unflattering name deriving from the sour taste of their leaves. Sourwood leaves resemble peach foliage in shape and are a bit leathery. Shiny green in spring, they are destined to become a gorgeous glossy red or burgundy starting in September. Meanwhile, sourwood branches also literally drip with clusters of 6-inch strands of tiny, white, drooping urn-shaped florets most of the summer. Not only are they beautiful, but their nectar makes great honey. Later, they give way to tan fruits that contrast with the green foliage and feed the birds. Typically upright and narrow when young, sourwoods' irregular, upright branches sometimes get distracted, and they form a rounded or flattened top as the tree ages. Sourwoods are slow growing, so they are shrubby for the first decade or so. They are best used as specimens to show off their multiseason virtues.

WHEN TO PLANT

Plant balled and burlapped trees in the spring. Transplant sourwoods raised in containers anytime during the growing season. Young trees up to 3 feet tall transplant easily. Their coarse, deep, lateral roots make them trickier to transplant when older.

WHERE TO PLANT

Sun shows off their fall color best, but they are comfortable in their familiar shady understory native habitat at the edge of woods. They appreciate rich, acidic, moist, well-drained soil. Once established, they can handle dry soil. They are a good substitute for dogwood.

HOW TO PLANT

Dig a saucer-shaped hole just as deep as and 2 or 3 times wider than the rootball. Remove the young sourwood from its container, and spread any circling roots. Set the tree in the hole so that the top of its rootball is exactly at soil level or even slightly above. Cut away as much burlap as possible from a wrapped rootball after it is positioned in the hole. Fill in the hole with plain soil, firming it gently around the rootball. Fashion a water-holding moat over the root zone, and water.

CARE AND MAINTENANCE

Water newly planted sourwoods regularly for a year when rainfall is sparse. Maintain a year-round, 2- or 3-inch layer of organic mulch over the tree root zone to retain soil moisture, discourage weeds, and protect the trunk from mower injury. Never pile it against the tree trunk. When the tree has been in place at least 6 months, sprinkle granular slow-acting fertilizer formulated for trees on the mulch for the rain to soak in. After 3 or 4 years the continuously decomposing mulch will enrich the soil, and the tree will not need annual fertilizing.

ADDITIONAL INFORMATION

Prune off competing leaders, if necessary, to assure a single trunk. Cut off injured or rubbing branches, making a smooth cut at the branch collar to promote healing. Newly planted trees are no longer routinely staked, but if the site is exposed to winter wind, temporary staking may be necessary the first winter. Keep an eye out for nests of fall webworm, and prune them out before the caterpillars venture forth to eat the sourwood leaves.

ADDITIONAL SPECIES, CULTIVARS, OR VARIETIES

Selected forms of sourwood are not widely available yet.

 Did You Know?

Multiseason Hall of Fame
Sourwood tops any list of landscape trees offering ornamental features virtually year-round. Here are some others, not covered in this book:
- *Katsura tree* (Cercidiphyllum japonicum)
- *Japanese tree Clethra* (Clethra barbinervis)
- *Franklin tree* (Franklinia alatamaha)
- *Pagoda tree* (Sophora japonica)
- *Japanese Stewartia* (Stewartia pseudocamellia)

Spruce, Colorado Blue

Picea pungens 'Glauca'

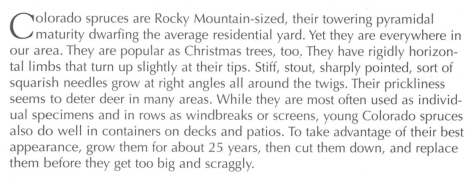

Other Name: Colorado Spruce
Type: Evergreen conifer
Mature Size: 30 to 60 feet tall;
    10 to 20 feet wide
Foliage: Bluish needles
Features: Foliage color; cones; aromatic; shelters wildlife

Light Requirements:

Color photograph on page 213.

Colorado spruces are Rocky Mountain-sized, their towering pyramidal maturity dwarfing the average residential yard. Yet they are everywhere in our area. They are popular as Christmas trees, too. They have rigidly horizontal limbs that turn up slightly at their tips. Stiff, stout, sharply pointed, sort of squarish needles grow at right angles all around the twigs. Their prickliness seems to deter deer in many areas. While they are most often used as individual specimens and in rows as windbreaks or screens, young Colorado spruces also do well in containers on decks and patios. To take advantage of their best appearance, grow them for about 25 years, then cut them down, and replace them before they get too big and scraggly.

WHEN TO PLANT

Plant trees with roots wrapped in burlap in early spring. Plant a living Christmas tree after a period of acclimatization to the outdoors, immediately after the holidays if the ground is not frozen. Otherwise cover the rootball with chopped leaves to keep it moist, and store it in a sheltered, outdoor area until early spring.

WHERE TO PLANT

Colorado blue spruces like full sun and moist, slightly acidic, well-drained, soil of almost any type. They do not like soggy or very dry soil, however. Plant them away from buildings for good air circulation and space to grow. Too much wind may cause them to lose some of their blue color, which is a powdery coating on the outer needles.

HOW TO PLANT

Keep soil around the roots moist until planting time. Remove the young spruce from its container, and cut or spread any circling roots. Dig a saucer-shaped planting hole just as deep as and somewhat wider than the rootball. Set the tree in the hole so that top of the rootball is exactly level with or even a bit higher than the surrounding ground. Cut away as much burlap as possible from a wrapped rootball. Fill in the hole with plain soil, firming it gently around the rootball. Fashion a water-holding moat over the root zone, and water well.

CARE AND MAINTENANCE

Mulch the spruce's root zone year-round with 2 or 3 inches of organic material to retain soil moisture and discourage weeds. After at least 6 months, sprinkle granular slow-acting fertilizer formulated for conifers on the mulch for the rain to soak in. Do this for 3 or 4 years if the spruce is in poor soil. Adequate nutrition is essential to assure good blue color. Eventually, the constantly decomposing mulch will enrich the soil and sustain the tree.

ADDITIONAL INFORMATION

If you anticipate that the Colorado blue spruce will grow too large (a fair assumption with these spruces), start annual shearing when the tree is still young during its active growth over 3 or 4 weeks in late spring. When it eventually achieves its allowed height, shear more closely each year. Do it after a rain when the needles are damp. Cut off the ratty lower branches that develop on older trees to improve their appearance. Snip off any galls caused by spruce gall aphid infestation (they look like distorted cones on the branch tips).

ADDITIONAL SPECIES, CULTIVARS, OR VARIETIES

'Fat Albert' is semidwarf, rounded, and bushy. 'Glauca Pendula' has sprawling, drooping branches for a weeping effect. 'Hoopsii' has good silver-blue color. 'Montgomery' is silver-blue, cone shaped, and dwarf.

 Did You Know?

*Spider mites are occasionally a nuisance on Colorado spruces and other conifers. Their feeding causes needles to turn a sickly yellow and drop off. Sometimes fine webbing is visible around affected foliage. A spray of horticultural oil would kill overwintering eggs in the spring and prevent any problems; however, it is **not** recommended for use on blue spruces. Instead, spray visible mites with a commercial insecticidal soap product as directed on its label.*

Sweetgum

Liquidambar styraciflua

Other Name: Gumball Tree
Type: Deciduous, shade
Mature Size: 60 to 75 feet tall;
  30 to 50 feet wide
Foliage: Green, starlike
Features: Prickly balls; fall color

Color photograph on page 213.

Light Requirements:

The tall trunks and shapely foliage canopies of sweetgum trees are easily overlooked in their native Pennsylvania woodland settings, but they are standouts in spacious home landscapes. Their leaves resemble those of maples, but a closer look reveals a more lustrous, smoother surface and lobes resembling a 5-pointed star. They emerge later than most in the spring on branches that sometimes have ridges of corky bark along them. In fall the leaves turn degrees of yellow, orange, and red to purple. Fast-growing in moist soils, sweetgums grow more elongated as they age. One of the biggest sweetgums in the region is at Curtis Arboretum in Montgomery County.

WHEN TO PLANT

Plant young sweetgum trees with roots wrapped in burlap in early spring. Those raised in containers have the best chance because their coarse, fleshy roots are more compact. They may take 1 or 2 years to establish. Be sure your tree is grown from seed that comes from the North, which is genetically programmed to handle our winters.

WHERE TO PLANT

Plant sweetgums in full sun and in any type of soil that is slightly acidic, rich in organic matter, and well-drained. They often settle for less and do well in wet soil on floodplains. Site them away from foot traffic because their prickly balls may be a hazard. They develop sturdy, broad root systems, so they must keep their distance from buildings and sewer lines. Their sensitivity to pollution makes them a dubious choice for many city sites, but they can handle the compacted soil in the average suburban yard, especially where builders have stripped away topsoil.

HOW TO PLANT

Dig a saucer-shaped planting hole just as deep as and about twice as wide as the rootball. Remove the sweetgum from its container. Position the rootball in the hole so that its top is even with, or slightly above, the surrounding ground. Cut away as much of the burlap and twine as possible from a wrapped one. Fill in the hole with plain soil, firming it gently around the rootball, and form any excess soil into a water-holding moat over the root zone. Water well and regularly in the absence of rain for 1 or 2 years while the roots become established.

CARE AND MAINTENANCE

Maintain a year-round, 2- or 3-inch layer of organic mulch on the root zone of the sweetgum out as far as the leaf canopy extends. It will help the soil stay moist, protect the trunk from mowers and trimmers, and catch the prickly balls when they fall from the branches. Expand the mulched area as the tree canopy grows wider. After the tree has been in place at least 6 months, sprinkle granular slow-acting fertilizer formulated for trees on the mulch for the rain to soak in. Do this annually for 3 or 4 years if the tree is in mediocre soil. Thereafter, the constantly decomposing mulch will improve the soil, and the tree will not need regular fertilizing.

ADDITIONAL INFORMATION

Sweetgums' hard wood makes them resistant to wind damage and commercially useful for furniture. These trees also contribute a resin for making chewing gum. Their prickly balls are useful in dried floral crafts.

ADDITIONAL SPECIES, CULTIVARS, OR VARIETIES

'Gumball' is a rounded, fruitless, large shrub. 'Variegata' has green foliage marked with yellow streaks and blotches. 'Rotundi-loba' ('Obtusiloba') is fruitless; the tips of the lobes on its foliage are rounded.

 Did You Know?

More than one creative gardener and sweetgum fan has struggled to find a use for its interesting, but prickly, gum-balls. One of the best uses is as slug barriers. Collect the gumballs, and then lay them down as a mulch around plants vulnerable to slugs, such as hostas or lettuce. There are no guarantees, but give it a try.

Sycamore, American

Platanus occidentalis

Other Name: Buttonwood
Type: Deciduous, shade
Mature Size: Up to 100 feet tall;
  40 to 80 feet wide
Bloom Time: Late May, early June
Features: Colorful bark

Color photograph on page 213.

Light Requirements:

Although sycamores have limited uses in residential landscapes, no list of Philadelphia-area trees would be complete without mention of these stately shade trees with massive trunks and huge gnarled branches that are so ubiquitous in our parks, on campuses, and, yes, in our yards. These rapid-growing natives offer something messy every season. They grow rapidly, shedding their bark in large patches, creating mottled cream, red, and gray-brown-green trunks. New bark gleams almost white in the winter. Large, coarse, gray-green leaves resembling maple leaves with sharply pointed lobes (some the size of dinner plates) are their trademark. They present a challenge to power vacuum shredders in the fall. Inconspicuous sycamore flowers yield fuzzy balls that dangle from twigs, one to a stalk through fall and winter. When they drop, they release wind-borne hairs that may cause minor respiratory problems. Naturally hollowed out sycamore trunks sheltered pioneer families along the streams. Some sycamores in our region date from the arrival of William Penn.

WHEN TO PLANT

Sycamores transplant easily because they have fibrous, shallow roots. Plant young trees with roots wrapped in burlap in either spring or fall. Plant more commonly found London planetrees raised in containers anytime during the growing season.

WHERE TO PLANT

Sycamores like full sun and the moist soil along streams, typical of their native habitat. In moist soil, they can handle dry air, pollution, and soil compaction. They tolerate neutral or even somewhat alkaline soil if it is well-drained. Give them lots of room.

HOW TO PLANT

Dig a saucer-shaped planting hole just as deep as and 2 or 3 times wider than the rootball. Remove the young sycamore from its container, and spread any circling roots. Set the tree in the hole so that the top of its rootball where the roots visibly flare out from the trunk is exactly at soil level. Cut away as much burlap as possible from the wrapped rootball. Then fill in the hole with plain soil, firming it gently around the rootball. Fashion a moat over the root zone to hold water, then water well.

CARE AND MAINTENANCE

Maintain a year-round, 2 -or 3-inch layer of organic mulch over the sycamore's root zone, but not against its trunk. It will retain soil moisture, discourage weeds, and protect the tender trunk from mower injury. When the tree has been in place at least 6 months, sprinkle granular slow-acting fertilizer formulated for trees and shrubs on the mulch for the rain to soak in. After 2 or 3 years, the decomposing mulch will enrich the soil and no fertilizer will be needed.

ADDITIONAL INFORMATION

Sycamores self-prune, periodically dropping their dead branches. They also seed in, so watch for uninvited seedlings. Because their bark may be toxic to certain plants, rake it up from lawns and planted beds. American sycamore is notoriously susceptible to anthracnose, a fungal disease also known as blight or scorch. Large trees take this in stride, but young, barely established ones need treatment. Consult a certified arborist.

ADDITIONAL SPECIES, CULTIVARS, OR VARIETIES

London planetree (*Platanus* × *acerfolia*) is a hybrid of sycamore. 'Bloodgood' is reputed to be more resistant to anthracnose. Eminently suitable for city streets, London planes line Kelly Drive and Benjamin Franklin Parkway.

 Did You Know?

Sometimes it is difficult to tell the difference between London planetrees and sycamores. London planetrees are obviously planted on purpose, whereas sycamores are typically self-sown and randomly occurring. London planetree is usually smaller and less wide-spreading (though still impressive) than sycamore. Its bark is more olive green, and it typically bears 2 fruit per stalk. Its leaves are more maplelike and deeply cut but straight across the bottom.

Tuliptree

Liriodendron tulipifera

Other Names: Yellow Poplar, Tulip Poplar   **Light Requirements:**

Type: Deciduous, shade

Mature Size: 70 to 90 feet tall;
   40 to 50 feet wide

Bloom Time: Late May

Features: Flowers; fall color; attracts hummingbirds; honeybees, and
   butterfly larvae

Color photograph on page 213.

Tuliptrees are often described as majestic, and it is no wonder. They are the tallest Eastern deciduous tree growing in the wild—as tall as 200 feet. Although they are shorter when grown in a landscape setting, they retain their trademark, ramrod-straight trunks, typically branchless until ⅔ of the way up. Related to magnolia, they are one of the earliest trees to leaf out in spring. Tuliptrees are easily recognized by their distinctive leaves, as broad as long, the squarish shape suggesting a cat's face (the top 2 lobes resembling the cat's ears) or a keystone. Their flowers are greenish yellow tulips with an orange blotch in the center. Although they are 2 to 3 inches wide, they are obscured by the leaves, especially high in the canopy of mature trees. Often the only evidence they have bloomed is dropped petals on the ground. The honeybees know when they flower, however, and they produce wonderful honey from tuliptrees. Tuliptrees are considered to be drought indicator plants. They are among the first to show stress—yellowed leaves in August and September—from lack of rain.

WHEN TO PLANT

Plant or transplant tuliptrees carefully in the spring. They are a bit difficult to transplant because their fleshy roots break easily. Choose young containerized nursery stock.

WHERE TO PLANT

Site tuliptrees in full sun and in deep, rich, moist, well-drained soil. They prefer acidic soil but can handle higher pH. They are ideal for floodplains, growing up to 3 feet per year when young and happily situated. Keep them away from the house because they are brittle and lightning prone.

HOW TO PLANT

Dig a saucer-shaped planting hole just as deep as and 2 or 3 times as wide as the rootball. Remove the young tuliptree from its container, and spread any circling roots. Set the tree in the hole so that the top of its rootball where the roots visibly flare out from the trunk is exactly at soil level or even slightly above. Cut away as much burlap as possible from a wrapped rootball. Fill in the hole with plain soil, firming it gently around the rootball. Fashion a water-holding moat with extra soil extending just beyond the edge of the root zone. Water well and as often as necessary to keep the soil moist while the tuliptree gets established over the next 1 or 2 years.

CARE AND MAINTENANCE

Maintain a 2- or 3-inch layer of organic mulch over the root zone of the tuliptree year-round. It will keep the site moist, discourage weeds, and protect the tender bark from injury by mower or trimmer. Because mulch improves the soil as it gradually decomposes, a tuliptree in moist, decent soil will not require annual fertilization after 1 or 2 years.

ADDITIONAL INFORMATION

Tuliptrees are not without their drawbacks. Their nectar-filled flowers attract aphids and promote unsightly sooty mold. Their ability for self-cleaning means that they drop twigs and branches readily. Other nuisance debris consists of leaves, flower petals, and abundant hard seeds, which germinate with abandon.

ADDITIONAL SPECIES, CULTIVARS, OR VARIETIES

'Aureo-Marginata' ('Majestic Beauty') has yellow-and-green variegated foliage. 'Fastigiatum' is narrow.

 Did You Know?

- *Daniel Boone used tuliptree for his 60-foot canoe.*
- *Tuliptrees indicated to pioneers the location of the best farming soils.*
- *Thomas Jefferson, a great admirer of trees, planted thousands at Monticello. Today only about a half-dozen remain. Of those, two are magnificent tuliptrees. One has a 7-foot-diameter trunk. Jefferson called tuliptrees the "Juno of the woods."*
- *Tuliptrees have fine-textured, light-grained wood that is easy to work, but difficult to split. Within is a compound called hydrochlorate of tulipiferine, which is a heart stimulant.*

Willow, Weeping

Salix species

Other Names: White Willow, Babylon Weeping Willow

Type: Deciduous, shade

Mature Size: 30 to 40 feet tall; 15 to 20 feet wide

Bloom Time: Late February, early March

Features: Fuzzy flowers; fall color; supports wildlife and butterfly larvae

Light Requirements:

Color photograph on page 213.

There are many kinds of willows, each with ornamental features. Pussy willows feature fuzzy catkins; curly or corkscrew willows have decoratively contorted branches. To many gardeners, however, willow means the good old weeping willow whose graceful, drooping branches seem, on looking back, to have sheltered our childhoods. It is easy to forgive them their brittle wood, their tendency to drip twigs and leaves onto the ground, their susceptibility to pest and diseases, and their need for extra watering during periods of drought. After all, their yellow-green halo of new twigs signals spring for us. Then narrow, pointed, fine-textured leaves emerge to clothe curtains of long, thin, flexible branches that have a charm offered by no other tree. It remains in its wonderful winter silhouette long after the leaves yellow and fall late in the season.

WHEN TO PLANT

Mail-order willows will be bare root and dormant. Plant them in early spring. They are among the first trees to leaf out in spring, so get them into the ground promptly. Plant container-grown nursery stock anytime during the growing season.

WHERE TO PLANT

Weeping willows need full sun. The soil type is less critical than its moisture. The richer it is in organic matter, the more moisture it will hold. Site willows at the edge of a stream or pond, or in boggy areas and floodplains, but away from wells and septic systems. Their notorious extensive, suckering root systems will search widely for water if necessary. Plant them away from buildings or parked cars because they sometimes fall over.

HOW TO PLANT

Willow branches stuck haphazardly into the ground will root, but take care in planting nursery stock. Remove the young tree from its container, and clip off any roots tightly circled from confinement there. Dig a saucer-shaped planting hole just as deep as and somewhat wider than the rootball. Set the tree in the hole so that its rootball is exactly at soil level. Support bare-root trees at the correct height in the hole with a cone of packed soil. Fill in the hole with plain soil, firming it gently around the rootball. Fashion a water-holding moat from extra soil over the root zone. Then water well, and follow up with regular watering whenever rainfall is scarce.

CARE AND MAINTENANCE

Maintain a 2- or 3-inch layer of organic mulch over the root zone of the willow year-round. It will retain soil moisture, discourage weeds, and add organic matter to the soil as it continuously breaks down. After 6 months, sprinkle granular slow-acting fertilizer formulated for trees on the mulch for the rain to soak in. Do this for 1 or 2 years to give the willow a good start.

ADDITIONAL INFORMATION

There is no need to routinely prune weeping willows. Their brittle wood is prone to storm damage, however. Promptly prune broken branches with smooth cuts to promote healing.

ADDITIONAL SPECIES, CULTIVARS, OR VARIETIES

Babylon weeping willow (*Salix babylonica*) is the most "weeping" of all willows, with a rounded leaf crown and stocky trunk. Golden weeping willow (*Salix alba* 'Tristis') has an upright habit and distinctive yellow bark on young branches. Many shrub versions of willow are decorative and appropriate for small yards. They may be available at mail-order specialty nurseries: black pussy willow (*Salix melanostachys*) has black fussy catkins; dragon's claw (corkscrew) willow (*Salix matsudana* 'Tortuosa') has curly branches for floral arrangements; and fantail willow (*Salix sachalinensis* 'Sekka') has distinctive flattened branch tips.

 Did You Know?

Willows have contributed their flexible branches to many cultures for weaving baskets, mats, and wattle fences. Arguably, their greatest gift has been the compound salicin, found in their bark and tender branches. Used by Native Americans for treating inflammations and fevers, it has been synthesized in modern times as salicylic acid, or aspirin.

Zelkova, Japanese

Zelkova serrata

Other Name: Zelkova
Type: Deciduous, shade
Mature Size: 60 to 70 feet tall;
 50 to 55 feet wide
Foliage: Bright green, toothed oval
Features: Fall color; mottled bark

Color photograph on page 213.

Light Requirements:

Zelkovas, first recognized as good substitutes for the dying American elms on Eastern streets and campuses, have earned a reputation of their own as versatile, attractive trees. Their moderate size suits them to residential yards, and their vaselike profile of upright branches fanning out above a short trunk qualifies them to be street trees as well. Furthermore, they grow rapidly, doubling their height in 4 to 6 years, to provide welcome shade. Since their flowers and fruit are inconspicuous, their dark-green foliage that turns reddish purple in the fall and their interesting patchy mature bark are the closest they get to ornamental. Zelkovas do fine in suburban and coastal environments where, properly sited and cared for, they thrive. There is a huge specimen at the Morris Arboretum.

WHEN TO PLANT
Zelkovas transplant well. Plant container-grown stock anytime during the growing season.

WHERE TO PLANT
Site zelkovas in full sun. They are agreeable to almost any type of well-drained soil except sand. They tolerate a range of pH, compacted soil, pollution, and even drought, once they are established. Do not plant near where a diseased elm may formerly have been located.

HOW TO PLANT
Dig a saucer-shaped planting hole just as deep as and about twice as wide as the rootball. Remove the zelkova from its container. Position the rootball in the hole so that its top is even with, or slightly above, the surrounding ground. Cut as much burlap as possible from a wrapped rootball at this point. Then fill in the hole with plain soil, firming it gently around the rootball. Form a water-holding moat over the root zone, then water well.

CARE AND MAINTENANCE

Spread a 2- or 3-inch layer of organic material such as chopped leaves, pine needles, wood chips, or commercial bark product over the zelkova's root zone (not against its trunk) to improve the soil as it continuously decomposes. Expand the circle of mulch as the tree canopy grows wider. When the tree has been in place at least 6 months, sprinkle granular slow-acting fertilizer formulated for trees on the mulch for the rain to soak in. Do this yearly for 3 or 4 years if the tree is in mediocre soil. Thereafter, the constantly decomposing mulch will improve the soil, and the tree will not need regular fertilizing. Newly planted zelkovas are susceptible to wind and may need temporary staking their first year.

ADDITIONAL INFORMATION

Prune young trees to establish a branching framework and remove rubbing branches. Sometimes the narrow angle of the crotches where upright branches attach to the trunk causes splitting. Zelkovas are highly resistant to Dutch elm disease, but they have occasional problems with Japanese beetles.

ADDITIONAL SPECIES, CULTIVARS, OR VARIETIES

'Green Vase' features rapid growth, good form, and fall color. It won the Pennsylvania Horticultural Society's Gold Medal (Styer) Award in 1988. 'Village Green' has rusty-red fall foliage color and a broader crown. It is resistant to Japanese beetles.

 Did You Know?

Dutch elm disease was introduced into the United States from Europe in the 1930s on elm logs intended for manufacture into veneer in Ohio. The logs were infested with bark-eating beetles carrying the fungal disease. They triggered an epidemic whose toll was an estimated 77 million dead elms. Among the many lessons learned were these:

- *Sterilize pruning equipment after use on diseased plants.*
- *Time pruning to avoid aggravating the situation (the fresh pruning wounds made on healthy elms just when the beetles started their flight attracted them).*
- *Limit the population of any tree species in an area to only 10 percent of total trees there to maintain diversity and avoid a monoculture.*

Vines

*I*N ADDITION TO BEAUTY, upwardly mobile plants offer a third spatial dimension to the landscape. By taking advantage of airspace, vines and other climbers increase its size while defining it in wonderful new ways.

Vines also solve landscape problems. Their foliage tapestry cools bare walls exposed to summer sun. It muffles street noise, insures privacy, and obscures eyesores such as utility meters and old stumps. Clambering over pergolas or arbors, vines provide a transition between hardscape and softscape and substitute for trees to create shade for other plants. Planted as specimens on trellises, they become focal points. Of course, they are ideal for small properties where planting ground is at a premium, requiring just a few square inches of soil. Many will grow happily in pots. In the winter the ropes of woody stems of some perennial vines add drama and structure to an otherwise bleak landscape.

ABOUT VINES

Vining and climbing plants may be annuals or perennials. The annual ones grow from seed or seedlings, starting slowly in the cool spring, then exploding with bloom when the heat arrives until frost kills them back. Many self-sow their seeds to assure a vine the next season. Perennial vines tend to proceed more decorously, taking time their first season to develop strong roots and sturdy stems that will hold them up over the long term. Most are deciduous, and many benefit from pruning back in the fall or late winter so that they can bloom on new wood next year.

A vine's distinction is its willingness to grow vertically. Vines and other climbers achieve this in one of several ways. Some, like ivy, are clingers. They attach themselves directly to a surface with sticky rootlets on their stems. Others, like wisteria, are twiners and wrap themselves around supports. Still others, such as clematis, are grabbers, latching onto the nearest support with special tendrils that they produce from their leaf stems. Finally, there are sprawlers, such as climbing roses. Their elongated branches lean on whatever is convenient and stretch up or across it.

SUPPORT

Proper support is a critical issue with vines and climbers. Choose a support that accommodates each vine's growing style and its future size. Mount trellises a bit away from walls that will need maintenance over the years.

Chapter Eight

Clingers adhere directly to a smooth surface, but they may damage walls where mortar or stucco is deteriorating or soft. Grabbers do best with thin supports such as wire, lattice, or netting that their tendrils can grasp easily. Tie the long canes of sprawlers to a sturdy trellis or arbor that can hold their mature weight. Twiners are the biggest challenge. Vines such as kiwi and wisteria last for many years, so the support should be very strong like a pergola.

Vines, like ground covers (which are sometimes—as with ivy and wintercreeper—the same plant), earn their keep by spreading. Some are so vigorous, however, that the words *rampant* and *invasive* come to mind. Only faithful pruning qualifies them as garden assets. Virginia creeper is a good example—it roams at will up phone poles and over utility lines if permitted. Because this rowdyism is balanced by the fact that it is relatively easy to pull up and it offers food and shelter to wildlife, it earns a place in a residential landscape. Alan Lacey points out that there is a bargain required with rampant vines—to have the beauty, you must be willing to do the pruning.

Sometimes it is a close call as to whether a particular vine can truly be controlled enough. Many lovely vines pose an environmental problem when they "escape" from backyard cultivation into the wild. Their uncontrolled spread suffocates natural vegetation and degrades the health of the forest. Although plants introduced into the area from elsewhere are often the worst culprits, sometimes native plants are a problem, too.

FLORA NON GRATA

These vines are generally regarded as having more vices than virtues and should not be planted in residential gardens in our area:

- Hall's honeysuckle (*Lonicera japonica* 'Halliana')
- Fiveleaf akebia (*Akebia quinata*)
- Porcelainberry (*Ampelopsis brevipedunculata*)
- Oriental bittersweet (*Celastrus orbiculatus*)

Boston Ivy

Parthenocissus tricuspidata

Other Name: Japanese Creeper
Type: Woody clinger
Mature size: To 60 feet
Bloom Time: Mid-June
Flower Color/Type: insignificant whitish green florets in clusters
Foliage: Deciduous; glossy green, then scarlet in fall
Features: Blue-black berries on red stems; attracts songbirds

Light Requirements:

Color photograph on page 213.

Boston ivy enjoys a certain distinction because it is the "ivy" of Ivy League colleges. It is well represented on the stone walls of highly respected local institutions such as Villanova University, Swarthmore, Haverford, and Bryn Mawr colleges, where it confers a similar aura of tradition. Its dense, glossy, trilobed leaves also reflect heat, cooling campus courtyards and walkways. They do the same in residential landscapes where they provide a stunning fall show of deeply red leaves and blue berries.

WHEN TO PLANT

Transplant containerized nursery stock anytime during the growing season. Plant when young vines will not be stressed by the sun.

WHERE TO PLANT

Boston ivy can handle full sun in most situations. It is sensitive to bright light and extreme heat, however, so an eastern or northern exposed wall is better in these conditions. On trees it is shaded in summer. It does well in almost any type of well-drained soil, but prefers it to be woodsy, moist, and slightly acidic.

HOW TO PLANT

Purchase containerized nursery stock to assure a good root system. Cultivate the soil down 8 to 10 inches, and mix in granular slow-acting fertilizer to assure plants a good first season. Add organic matter, too, if the soil is thin or clay. Dig the planting hole about as deep as and considerably wider than the container within a foot of the intended support for the Boston ivy. Gently tap the base of the pot to dislodge the young plant, and cut or loosen any matted, encircling roots. Set the plant in the empty hole so that its soil is level with the surrounding ground. Fill in the hole with soil, firm it around plant stems, and water well.

CARE AND MAINTENANCE

Water Boston ivy transplants well until they become established. Mulch around their stems to hold soil moisture and to protect against string trimmer encounters. Once established, it does not need fertilizing. Prune away broken or discolored stems. When the vine threatens to outgrow its allotted space, either lightly prune it frequently to control it, or cut it back hard at longer intervals.

ADDITIONAL INFORMATION

Boston ivy screens unpleasant views if trained on trellises or lattice panels. It vastly improves chain-link fencing and looks great climbing up trees (it will not harm them). It is not suitable on wood—the humid environment among dense leaves tends to rot it and interfere with regular painting. Because it is a clinger, it will leave rootlet marks on walls from which it is removed.

ADDITIONAL SPECIES, CULTIVARS, OR VARIETIES

'Beverly Brooks' has large leaves; 'Lowii' has smaller leaves, and sometimes immature leaves have extra lobes. 'Purpurea' has reddish-purple foliage all season; 'Veitchii' has smaller leaves that are finer textured. Small-leaved types are less hardy than regular Boston ivy. Our native Virginia creeper, sometimes called woodbine (*Parthenocissus quinquefolia*), is similar to Boston ivy. Its leaves have 5 lobes, however. Also shiny and rich green, they have long-lasting fall color to set off dark berries. Silver vein creeper (*Parthenocissus henryana*) has similar foliage with attractive silver veins.

Did You Know?

Boston ivy sometimes suffers from mistaken identity because its juvenile foliage closely resembles poison ivy. The leaves of Boston ivy seedlings also have 3 leaflets, and the admonition "leaves of three, let it be" seems appropriate. A closer look will confirm its true identity, however. The mature leaves of Boston ivy are single with 3 lobes at their tips. While its foliage is safe, Boston ivy's berries are poisonous to people.

Clematis

Clematis hybrids

Other Names: Hybrid Clematis, Jackman Clematis, Large-Flowered Clematis
Type: Woody grabber
Mature size: Up to 15 feet
Bloom Time: May; through summer intermittently
Flower Color/Type: Purple, pink, white, rose
Foliage: Deciduous; medium green
Features: Whorled, feathery seedheads

Color photograph on page 213.

Light Requirements:

Clematis vines look so exotic and elegant that the assumption is that only the gifted gardener can manage them. Nothing could be farther from the truth. In recent years their progress from estate gardens to neighborhood mailboxes and light posts testifies to their increased popularity and availability at garden centers as people realize they are not a big deal to grow. Hybrid types deliver the biggest color splash, their broad, flat flowers—often as large as 4 or 5 inches across—typically featuring 4 to 6 beautifully colored petals. Their fancy seedheads of curved filaments are a continuing decorative feature as the summer progresses.

WHEN TO PLANT
Plant containerized young clematis vines anytime during the growing season. Spring is best, of course, to get in a full first season. They often take two seasons to get up to speed. Plant in the evening or on an overcast day to minimize transplant shock.

WHERE TO PLANT
Clematis are of two minds about their favorite location. They like full, warm sun for their flowers and foliage, but cool soil for their roots. Choose an open site among low plants that shade the soil. They like rich, well-drained, good garden soil.

HOW TO PLANT
Loosen and aerate the soil down 12 to 16 inches and over a 2-foot-wide area. Mix in granular slow-acting fertilizer and organic matter to improve the soil. Dig the planting hole deeper and slightly wider than the plant's container or root system. Set the plant deeply in the hole so that its crown is 4 inches below soil level to encourage roots to grow from the stem, too. Form a cone of packed soil in the bottom of the hole for a bare-root plant,

and set the plant on it, arranging the loose roots down the sides of the cone. Fill in the hole with soil, firming it gently around plant stems, and water well. Spread organic mulch over the soil to keep it cool and moist, but not against plant stems.

CARE AND MAINTENANCE

Clematis vines need temporary support in their floppy, newly planted phase before they can reach the support they are intended to climb. As they reach it, guide the stems around it to encourage them to climb. Flowers bloom on old and new growth, so prune in the spring to remove any dead stems and stem ends, cutting back to where new leaf buds are appearing. Cutting back nearly to the ground revitalizes the plant and delays bloom a bit.

ADDITIONAL INFORMATION

It will readily climb traditional vine supports, yet clematis is willing to be creative. It does not mind growing horizontally on a chain-link or rail fence. It grabs on best to thin materials such as wire or poly mesh. It will scramble over drab, green shrubs, endowing them with gorgeous blooms.

ADDITIONAL SPECIES, CULTIVARS, OR VARIETIES

Among the large-flowered types, there are many from which to choose. Jackman clematis (*Clematis × Jackmanii*) has the showiest flowers. 'Betty Corning', a hybrid of *Clematis itacella* with fragrant, bell-shaped summer flowers, is a Pennsylvania Horticultural Society Gold Medal winner (1992). Sweet autumn clematis (*Clematis terniflora*) is the rampant cousin whose zillions of tiny white flowers fill humid August and September evenings with fragrance. To control its spread, cut back stems with spent flowers before they have a chance to set seed.

 Did You Know?

Pronunciation of plant names is always fraught with uncertainty. Clematis *is a perfect example of this problem. CLEM-a-tis is the way the British pronounce it, so many horticulturists and professional gardeners say it that way because classical horticultural training is steeped in British tradition. Clem-A-tis is the way everyone else says it because in the United States we tend to emphasize the second syllable in three-syllable words. Either pronunciation is correct.*

Climbing Hydrangea

Hydrangea anomala var. *petiolaris*

Type: Woody clinger
Mature Size: Over 60 feet if permitted
Bloom Time: Late May
Flower Color/Type: White florets in flat clusters
Foliage: Deciduous; textured, dark green
Features: Attracts beneficial insects

Color photograph on page 213.

Light Requirements:

Here is a vine that signals substance and permanence. Essentially an elongated, vertical shrub, a mature climbing hydrangea becomes a dominant landscape feature that commands attention through the seasons. It takes several years before these slow starters catch on, climb, and deliver on the promised layers of faintly scented, lacy flat spring flowers among rich green, textured leaves. Its vertical progress against a building eventually turns it into an architectural element, softening corners, delineating adjacent stairways, and defining patio spaces to create an entirely original profile. Clinging by means of holdfast rootlets, the woody stems of climbing hydrangea develop a rough, cinnamon-colored bark that becomes a landscape feature after the leaves drop late in fall or early winter. Plant one if you plan to stay on the property for several years or want to give a gift to future owners.

WHEN TO PLANT

Typically, climbing hydrangeas are sold in containers. A spring planting gives them a full growing season their first year in place, but they can be planted almost anytime that it is not very hot and dry. Overcast days or late afternoons are the best planting times to minimize transplant shock.

WHERE TO PLANT

For best flowering, locate climbing hydrangea in full sun. It can cope with shade, but it will grow more slowly there. A site sheltered from winter winds is ideal. It likes moist, well-drained garden soil.

HOW TO PLANT

Dig the soil down at least 12 inches, mixing in granular slow-acting fertilizer at the same time. Add organic matter to improve drainage in clay soil. Dig the planting hole about as deep as and slightly wider than the container. Gently tip the pot, and tap it on the bottom to dislodge the plant. Hydrangea roots are fragile; if they are circling the rootball because of confinement in the pot too long, untangle them very gently. Set the plant in the hole so that the top of the soilball is exactly level with the sur-rounding ground. Fill in the hole with soil, firming it gently around plant stems to remove air pockets, and water well. Place the plants at least 1 foot out from the supporting wall or structure.

CARE AND MAINTENANCE

While the young climbing hydrangea recovers from transplant-ing, keep it moist, but do not overwater. Compared to many other woody vines, it is slow to catch on and grow. There is no need to prune for the first few years. Prune it after it flowers to train it to grow as desired. Periodically, in its fullness of years, it will need thinning to improve air circulation and appearance.

ADDITIONAL INFORMATION

Climbing hydrangea looks especially good on stone or brick walls. It will grow up trees without hurting them. If the tree eventually dies, the topped trunk continues to provide sturdy support, creating essentially a free-standing vine-tree that is a real eye-catcher.

ADDITIONAL SPECIES, CULTIVARS, OR VARIETIES

Good substitutes for climbing hydrangea are Japanese hydrangea vine (*Schizophragma hydrangeoides* 'Moonlight') and wood vamp (*Decumaria barbara*), which has deciduous, dark-green leaves and white flowers.

 Did You Know?

There are wonderful climbing hydrangeas at some of the old, elegant homes on Philadelphia's Main Line where they have climbed substantial stone walls for several generations. There is a stunning one at Ker-feal, country home of the late Dr. Alfred C. Barnes and his wife, Laura, whose home in Merion is surrounded by an arboretum and houses a world renowned art collection. Many cultivars are on view at the Scott Arboretum on the Swarthmore College campus.

Hardy Kiwi

Actinidia kolomikta

Other Names: Kolomikta Vine,
Siberian Kiwi Vine
Type: Woody twiner
Mature Size: To 30 feet
Bloom Time: May
Flower Color/Type: Inconspicuous white
Foliage: Deciduous; green with white blotch, fading to pink, then green
Features: Multicolored foliage; edible fruit

Color photograph on page 213.

Light Requirements:

This kiwi is renowned for its unusual calico foliage rather than its fruit, although by the end of summer, mature female vines drip with sweet, yellow-green tasty berries that are much smaller than the subtropical kiwis usually available at the grocery store. The exotic variegated 4- or 5-inch-long leaves on both male and female vines are blotched with white and pink. They look like a painter has dripped white paint on them. The markings are reputedly a bit more striking in male plants and grow richer in color as the vine matures. Kolomikta kiwi turns an ordinary wall into a showpiece. It needs a sturdy trellis set solidly in the soil a few inches out from the wall surface or a wire grid fastened to hooks embedded in wood or masonry.

WHEN TO PLANT
Plant containerized nursery stock anytime during the growing season. Choose an overcast day or plant in the evening so that it is not stressed by the sun while it copes with transplant shock.

WHERE TO PLANT
For best foliage color, plant kiwi vines in full sun. They prefer average soils that are well-drained. Reportedly, soil that is a bit on the alkaline side promotes stronger foliage color.

HOW TO PLANT
Dig the soil to loosen and aerate it down 8 to 10 inches, and add coarse sand or organic matter to improve drainage if necessary. Mix in just a trace of slow-acting fertilizer to give the young plant a boost its first season. Dig the planting hole about as deep as and slightly wider than the rootball when it is removed from the container. Set the plant in the hole so that its crown, where the stems meet the roots, is exactly at soil level. Fill in the hole with soil, firming it gently around vine stems, and water well. Spread

organic mulch on the soil around, but not touching, the stems to help soil retain moisture and to discourage weeds. Set each plant about 1 foot from its support to allow room for roots to grow.

CARE AND MAINTENANCE

Once established, kiwi vines are fairly self-reliant. They will not need any encouragement from annual fertilizing. In fact, a rich diet tends to wash out the foliage color. Prune kiwi in late winter to establish a few main stems and then to control the number of subsidiary stems that spread across the trellis or pergola.

ADDITIONAL INFORMATION

Apparently, cats are admirers of kiwi foliage, too. They love its taste, which must resemble catnip. To protect newly planted young vines from their attention, spray them with pet repellent as directed on its label, or surround them with a chicken wire cage. Once vine stems turn woody, it is safe to remove the barrier.

ADDITIONAL SPECIES, CULTIVARS, OR VARIETIES

Silver vine (*Actinidia polygama*) also has white-tipped leaves, but it is less energetic. Bower actinidia (*Actinidia arguta*) has deep-green leaves and edible fruit.

 Did You Know?

Hardy kiwis will produce edible fruit in our region if certain conditions exist. Plant both a male and a female vine within about 15 feet of each other to assure good pollination. Site them where they get at least 5 hours of sun daily. Fruit will set on shoots that emerge from the first 3 to 6 buds of this year's growth, so later in the summer you can prune excess foliage back almost to the maturing fruit. Kiwis are ready to pick when they feel slightly soft between thumb and fore-finger, usually in September. Yields will be sparse until the vines are 7 or 8 years old.

Hyacinth Bean

Dolichos lablab (Lablab purpureus)

Other Names: Lablab, Bonavista Vine
Type: Annual twiner
Mature Size: 10 feet
Bloom Time: Midsummer to fall
Flower Color/Type: Lavender; pealike
Foliage: Dark green with purple stems
Features: Shiny, flat purple pods

Color photograph on page 213.

Light Requirements:

Hyacinth bean vine is decorative and fun. Even its nickname, lablab, is fun, making it memorable to kids as well as adults. Like most annual vines, it is a vigorous grower and prolific bloomer once it gets started and the season's heat arrives. It produces purplish-tinged leaves in threes on reddish stems that are willing to climb up anything handy. Lablab blossoms are actually upright clusters of small lilac-purple flowers that resemble sweet peas. In no time they give way to flat, shiny maroon bean pods, which dangle from the vine as new flowers, then more pods, form in lush succession over the summer. The seeds within the pods are black with a curious white line on them. They are so interesting that they are responsible for this vine being the ultimate pass-along plant. When visitors admire and inquire, hand them some seeds.

WHEN TO PLANT

Plant seeds indoors in early April for seedlings to plant in May when the soil has warmed and dried out. Or plant seeds outdoors in May. If the pods are left on the vine the previous season until they dry out and pop open, hyacinth bean is likely to self-sow.

WHERE TO PLANT

This vine loves sun. It can handle almost any type of soil, but it is most vigorous in good garden soil that is well-drained. Set it near a post, trellis, or other intended support.

HOW TO PLANT

Dig the soil in the planting area down a few inches to loosen and aerate it. Set seeds, the white "eye" facing upward, 1 or 2 inches down, 2 or 3 inches apart. Cover them with soil, then water. Expect germination in 2 weeks. When young seedlings are several inches tall, thin them to the desired number and spacing, then mulch them to keep down weeds and retain soil moisture. Transplant seedlings grown in pots into soil dug down 6 to 8 inches. Set them in holes so that the soil of their rootball is level with the surrounding ground. Space them about 1 foot apart. Water well, and mulch with organic material to discourage weeds.

CARE AND MAINTENANCE

Hyacinth bean vine needs little attention. Water plants when rainfall is particularly scarce. Provide them a place to climb or they will find one themselves. No special pruning is needed; the lusher the foliage and flowers, the better. Pick off bean pods when they start to dry up.

ADDITIONAL INFORMATION

Gardening sources conflict over whether hyacinth beans are edible. Some indicate that they are used for food in the tropical regions where they are perennial. They are used for animal forage in the Northern Hemisphere, but are not included on general lists of flowers or plants edible by humans. It is likely that they are unpalatable, but not necessarily poisonous. Because children are particularly attracted to this plant, to be on the safe side, warn them against tasting it.

ADDITIONAL SPECIES, CULTIVARS, OR VARIETIES

There are none.

 Did You Know?

It is entirely possible that the hyacinth bean is the "purple bean" that Thomas Jefferson mentioned in the garden journals he kept on his wonderful garden at Monticello. He planted more than 44 varieties of garden beans during the years he kept his journals. An entry for April 17, 1812, which mentions "Arbor beans white, scarlet, crimson, purple at the trees of the level on both sides of terrasses, and on long walk of garden," suggests that he used colorful beans as decorative features. Perhaps the tropical lablabs were among them.

Moonflower

Ipomea alba

Other Name: Moon Vine
Type: Annual twiner
Mature Size: Up to 15 feet
Bloom Time: Midsummer to fall
Flower Color/Type: Luminous white funnel
Foliage: Light green
Features: Night blooming and scented; attracts moths

Color photograph on page 214.

Light Requirements:

Moonflower is not just another morning glory, although it is a member of that family. This is the exotic, sophisticated cousin that stays up all night and closes the next day. Its white flowers are a spectacular 6 inches across where their fluted petals come to points, forming a starlike face. The show actually begins with their coiled, pointed buds that unfurl before your eyes among oversized heart-shaped rich green leaves on hot evenings. It is the centerpiece of an evening garden. Moonflower seeds are notoriously reluctant to germinate, so it gets a late start. By August, however, it twines with abandon on fences, arbors, and trellises. It may be the only plant needed on an apartment balcony or patio.

WHEN TO PLANT

Because seedlings are tricky to transplant, moonflower is usually direct seeded into the garden. Wait until the weather has turned warm—the middle of May—to sow the seeds.

WHERE TO PLANT

Choose a sunny site that has well-drained, average garden soil. Soil that is too rich in nutrients will stimulate foliage at the expense of flowers. If it is near a doorway or an arbor so that passersby can enjoy the scent, all the better.

HOW TO PLANT

Dig down about 6 to 8 inches to loosen and aerate the soil. Mix in organic material to improve soil drainage if necessary. Cut or scrape the hard coating on the seeds prior to planting to encourage germination. It seems to take forever, but if the soil is warm and summer is under way, they will sprout in about 2 weeks. Plant seeds in groups of 2 or 3, poking them into the soil about 1 inch deep. Lightly tamp the soil over them, and water well.

CARE AND MAINTENANCE

Moonflower vine takes care of itself very well once it is established. Do not fertilize it. Water only during periods of extended drought. Prune only if the vine has exceeded its bounds and engulfed the lawn furniture. In the fall when the frost kills it, pull down the dead stems.

ADDITIONAL INFORMATION

Like most vines, moonflower is useful for covering eyesores such as chain-link fences, drainpipes, and utility boxes out by the front walk. Plant it with white morning glory to enjoy continuous bloom, day and night. It will grow in a container and climb the nearest vertical support.

ADDITIONAL SPECIES, CULTIVARS, OR VARIETIES

Common morning glory (*Ipomea purpurea*) has similar, but smaller leaves and flowers (blue, white, pink, and bicolor). Morning glory (*Ipomea tricolor*) 'Heavenly Blue' is an All-America Selection winner; 'Pearly Gates' is a white-flowered form. There is also a red-flowered version with white trim. Other, more delicate, members of the morning glory family are cypress vine (*Ipomea quamoclit*) and cardinal climber (*Ipomea × sloteri*), which have small, red tubular flowers, and finer, cutleaf or deeply lobed foliage. They attract butterflies and hummingbirds.

 Did You Know?

*Sweet potato vine (*Ipomea batatas *'Blackie') is a member of the same family as morning glory and moonflower. It is both ornamental and edible. Extremely vigorous, it bears large, 3 deeply lobed leaves of deep black-purple on tender, trailing stems. Its flowers are lavender and tubular, but are small and take a back seat to the foliage. The tuberous roots are the sweet potatoes. More interested in traveling horizontally than vertically, it makes a handsome addition to windowboxes and other containers. Versions with chartreuse ('Margarite') and multicolored foliage are equally decorative.*

Rose

Rosa × hybrida

Other Names: Climbing Rose, Rambler

Type: Woody sprawler

Mature Size: 10 to 15 feet tall

Bloom Time: Spring; some rebloom
over the season

Flower Color/Type: White, shades of red, yellow, and pink; single,
semidouble, double flowers

Foliage: Medium- to dark-green toothed leaflets

Features: Fragrance (some)

Light Requirements:

Color photograph on page 214.

A rose may always be a rose, but depending on the situation, it may act as a ground cover or vine. Climbers are distinguished from bush roses by their arching canes that, if permitted, will grow more than 10 feet long. They are the roses celebrated in the romantic notion of the rose-covered cottage. Among the types of roses that have aerial ambitions are old-fashioned roses, large-flowered climbers, and ramblers. Traditional ramblers bloom only once and have more flexible canes. Large-flowered climbers and their kin, pillar roses, have stiffer canes. All climbers are sprawlers, or leaners, and need to be fastened to a sturdy supporting structure of some kind. Use soft material for tying; wire may cut into the canes. Check periodically for tightness.

WHEN TO PLANT

Plant bare-root climbers while they are still dormant in spring when danger of frost is past and the soil has warmed a bit. Be sure to keep their roots moist if planting is delayed. Transplant containerized nursery stock anytime during the growing season.

WHERE TO PLANT

Roses need full sun to do their best. They also need good garden soil, rich in organic matter, that is slightly acid and well-drained. Site them where they have plenty of air circulation.

HOW TO PLANT

Dig the soil down 2 feet. Unless it is already wonderful, add organic material such as compost, mushroom soil, or chopped leaves to improve it. Also mix in granular slow-acting fertilizer or a rose fertilizer. Dig a saucer-shaped planting hole about as deep as and twice as wide as the bare-root system or the soilball when the container is removed. Set the plant in the hole so that it is at the same level that it was in its container. Set bare-root plants on a hump of packed soil so that their roots can extend downward as the crown is supported. Grafts, swollen knobs where two different roses are connected, should be just below the soil level. Fill in the hole with soil, firm it, and water well. Spread a 2- or 3-inch layer of organic mulch over the root zone to discourage weeds and retain soil moisture.

CARE AND MAINTENANCE

Roses need good, steady moisture and nutrition. When needed, water early in the day to avoid moist leaves overnight, which encourages fungal disease. Some climbers take 2 years to establish themselves and start blooming. Prune away dead canes anytime, but wait 2 or 3 years to begin maintenance pruning. Prune after flowering to control the size and direction of growth or to thin the foliage to permit better air circulation. At the end of the season cut back the oldest canes to their base. Train the young ones to take their place. Leave at least 4 healthy, younger canes securely tied to the support. Mulch plants well over the winter.

ADDITIONAL INFORMATION

If they are not tied to a vertical support, climbing roses will sprawl along the ground. They are particularly effective spilling over a wall or down a steep hill.

ADDITIONAL SPECIES, CULTIVARS, OR VARIETIES

'New Dawn' is a large-flowered climber featuring copious semi-double pale-pink flowers on very thorny stems in the spring, and then sporadically over the summer. The red 'Blaze Improved' blooms continuously. 'Golden Showers', All-American Rose Society (AARS) winner for 1957, bears large, fragrant double yellow flowers all summer. Almost thornless, it has good disease resistance and is very hardy.

 Did You Know?

Many of Philadelphia's notable gardens and arboretums display climbing roses to wonderful effect. Among them are the Scott Arboretum and the Morris Arboretum.

Scarlet Honeysuckle

Lonicera sempervirens

Other Names: Coral Honeysuckle, Trumpet Honeysuckle

Type: Woody twiner

Mature Size: To 15 feet tall

Bloom Time: Late spring to fall frost

Flower Color/Type: Bright red; tubular

Foliage: Semievergreen; grayish green becoming darker blue-green

Features: Attracts hummingbirds

Light Requirements:

Color photograph on page 214.

Scarlet honeysuckle is hardy and dependable. This Pennsylvania native is also drought resistant, taking our hot, humid summers in stride. The bright red 2-inch-long tubular blossoms cluster at the tips of stems from the previous year during its peak bloom period in late spring and early summer. Subsequently, flowers appear sporadically on new wood until fall when reddish orange berries develop. Left to its own devices, this vine will flop on the ground and twine around whatever is nearby. To best display its beauty, train it to a support such as a wood fence or trellis.

WHEN TO PLANT

Plant bare-root plants in the spring for maximum opportunity for root establishment before winter frost. Plant containerized nursery stock anytime during the growing season.

WHERE TO PLANT

Scarlet honeysuckle flowers best in full sun, but it can handle some shade. It likes moist, good garden soil but will accept soil of almost any type and pH, even limestone.

HOW TO PLANT

Because it has sparse roots, this honeysuckle is a bit tricky to transplant. Choose nursery stock that is 1 to 2 feet tall. Loosen the soil down 8 to 10 inches, and add granular slow-acting fertilizer and organic matter to enhance its drainage and moisture retention. Dig the planting hole to accommodate the rootball when it is removed from the nursery pot. Set the plant in the hole so that its soil surface is level with the surrounding ground. Fill in the hole with soil, firm it gently around plant stems, and water well. Set plants about 2 feet apart from each other and 1 foot from the base of their support.

CARE AND MAINTENANCE

Water vines when first planted and during periods of severe drought. Using organic mulch around the roots will help the soil retain moisture. Honeysuckle is used to fending for itself, so there is no need to fertilize it annually. A rich diet only stimulates excess foliage. Prune after flowering to train it. Winter is a good time because the stems are visible. Make fence or trellis supports at least 8 feet tall. Or use tautly strung galvanized wire fastened with screw eyes set in a grid pattern about 1 inch from a wall.

ADDITIONAL INFORMATION

Early in the season tender tips of new stems and their flower buds may attract aphids. A strong water spray every 1 or 2 days will dislodge them. Honeysuckle is phytotoxic to insecticidal soaps, so spot treat a major infestation with a product featuring pyrethrins. When the stems harden, aphids turn to newly emerging perennials. Foliage sometimes develops powdery mildew from lack of good air circulation. Thin vines by clipping out excess branches.

ADDITIONAL SPECIES, CULTIVARS, OR VARIETIES

Lonicera sempervirens 'Sulphurea' has deep yellow flowers. 'Magnifica' has deeper red flowers, and 'Superba' has larger red ones. 'Manifich' flowers are lighter tangerine. 'Cedar Lane' is resistant to aphids. Goldflame honeysuckle (*Lonicera × heckrottii* 'Goldflame') has red flowers that turn to pink highlighted by a yellow throat and blooms May through midsummer, then intermittently until fall. *Lonicera flava* is rare, but beautiful. Catch its golden-yellow blossoms tinted orange during their week of bloom in May at the Henry Foundation in Gladwyne.

 Did You Know?

*Hall's or Japanese honeysuckle (*Lonicera japonica *'Halliana') is the one whose white and yellow flowers smell so deliciously fragrant on hot summer nights along roadsides where it was originally planted to control erosion. Now a weedy nuisance, it has invaded woodland areas, opportunistically climbing over trees and shading native understory plants, killing them. Although it is reportedly much better behaved in New England, it is not recommended as a garden plant here.*

Wisteria

Wisteria species and hybrids

Type: Woody twiner
Mature Size: More than 40 feet tall
Bloom Time: May
Flower Color/Type: Lavender, pink, white
in pendant clusters
Foliage: Deciduous; green

Light Requirements:

Color photograph on page 214.

The incredible drooping cascades of wisteria's pea-type flowers are worth the wait for it to bloom and the effort to control it. Its numerous foliage leaflets along thin stems are also attractive and turn yellow in fall before frost. Furry, green seedpods that persist into winter complete the show. Wisteria can be trained as a shrub with a single stem, but is most effective as a vine. It is potentially invasive, so it appears on some lists of nuisance plants. Beware of allowing it to climb trees; it is capable of strangling them. Beautifully controlled wisteria vines are on display at Longwood Gardens.

WHEN TO PLANT

Transplant containerized nursery stock anytime during the growing season when it is not extremely hot and/or dry.

WHERE TO PLANT

Wisteria needs at least 6 hours of sun daily. Avoid planting it on the north side of a building or where a tree will shade it or under eaves or roof overhangs that may obstruct rainfall. It is not fussy about soil type as long as it is well-drained.

HOW TO PLANT

Purchase as large a plant as is affordable to hasten bloom. Already-blooming grafted stock in containers is most dependable. Loosen the soil down 12 inches, and mix in organic matter to improve its drainage if necessary. Add a little slow-acting granular fertilizer. Dig the hole out 1 foot from the wisteria's supporting structure. Make it as deep as the plant's container. When it is set in the hole, the graft, the swollen knob on the stem where the wisteria plant is joined to a different rootstock, should be below the soil level. Fill the hole with plain soil, and water well. Mulch to keep soil moist and protect against string trimmers.

CARE AND MAINTENANCE

Skip fertilizing if the soil is fairly decent; deprivation may promote flowering. Once it is established and new leaves appear, water wisteria only when rainfall is scarce. Train the vine to a **very sturdy** supporting structure at least 6 inches from a wall to assure air circulation. Use galvanized supporting wires or pipe. Identify the strongest shoot, and attach it to the vertical wire or post to twine on its own. Clip off all other tendrils. When the vertical leader sends out horizontal side branches, select some to train along horizontal supports. The shoots that form flower buds will grow from these branches. Prune off all others. When the vertical leader reaches the desired height, clip off its tip. Severely cut back all main branches by half in late winter to stimulate spring growth. Trim flower-producing spurs to only 2 or 3 buds at the base of the shoots where they are close together.

ADDITIONAL INFORMATION

Wisterias are notoriously reluctant to bloom; some take up to 12 years. Various violent measures may speed the event. Dig down around roots with a sharp spade to cut them, or tie constricting wire or string around stems for a season. Or buy grafted plants in pots that already have buds or blooms.

ADDITIONAL SPECIES, CULTIVARS, OR VARIETIES

Japanese wisteria (*Wisteria floribunda*) has 2- to 3-foot-long flowers. 'Issai Perfect' has white blossoms and is reputed to bloom on young plants. 'Rosea' has rose to pink flowers. 'Macrobotrys' has lavender-blue, very long blossoms. 'Violacea Plena' has double-flowered blossoms. Chinese wisteria (*Wisteria chinensis*) has smaller flower clusters and leaves, and blooms before its leaves emerge. It twines left to right around its support, whereas Japanese wisteria twines right to left. 'Alba' has fragrant white flowers. Two native wisterias (*W. frutescens* and *W. macrostachys*) are less spectacular but also less aggressive.

 Did You Know?

The similarity of the plant name wisteria to the old Philadelphia area family name of Wister (or Wistar) is not coincidental. The plant was named for Caspar Wistar, professor of anatomy at the University of Pennsylvania in the early nineteenth century.

CHAPTER NINE

Water Plants

GARDENING IN WATER represents another dimension in gardening. It is possible because some plants are hydrophytic, able to live in water. Their roots are specially adapted to wet environments, either soggy soil or outright water, so that they do not suffocate for lack of air as terrestrial plants would. In nature these aquatic plants inhabit oceans, lakes, streams, tidal marshes, and swamps, adjusting as well to man-made drainage ditches and retention basins. Tamed by hybridization and/or cultivation in pots, which curbs their natural tendency to run rampant and controls their overall size, many qualify as lovely ornamental plants. When they are planted in containers before they are set in the water, they are easy to arrange, maintain, and remove from a water garden.

Once cultivating aquatic plants in water gardens was limited to the very rich who could afford to build expensive concrete or tile ponds and pools. Now water gardening is accessible to almost everyone, thanks to the availability of relatively inexpensive flexible liners, preformed fiberglass pools, and interesting tubs and kettles. Dwarf and miniature versions of aquatic plants make it possible to garden in water almost anywhere—on a balcony, in a tiny yard, or even on the dining room table!

GROWING WATER PLANTS

Water plants are no more difficult to grow than terrestrial plants. Some are frost tender and are therefore treated as annuals in the Philadelphia area. Many others are cold hardy and are perennial, growing year after year in the water garden. According to their habit, size, and nature, some water plants function as specimens or focal points, others as ground(water) covers, and still others as screens at the edge of the water garden. Certain ones live below the water surface and specialize in maintaining a healthy water environment. Some feature foliage; others flowers, fragrance, decorative seeds, or pods. They are planted in soil in containers that are set at different levels in the water garden pond depending on whether they prefer to have just their roots wet (bog plants) or both their roots and their stems submerged (floaters).

Plants that grow in water require the same type of maintenance that terrestrial ones do. They need routine fertilization, deadheading of faded blossoms, and removal of yellowed leaves and stems over the growing

Chapter Nine

season. Some especially tall ones may need staking to keep them from flopping over. Perennial aquatic plants spread and crowd their pots after a season or two, and they need to be divided, usually in the spring, just as other perennials do. Water gardens do not need to be weeded exactly, but sometimes overenthusiastic submerged or surface-floating plants need to be thinned or hauled out to make water space for spreading water lily foliage.

A Healthy Water Environment

A healthy water environment is as important for aquatic plants as good soil is for terrestrial plants. Oxygenating plants, waterfalls, and fountains aerate the water, just as tilling and digging in organic matter aerate the soil. Microbial life assures balanced nutrients and pH in water, just as it does in soil. Water gardens do not have earthworms, but they have fish and snails to do housekeeping chores. The biggest chore, however, is left to the water gardener. Even though the water is filtered during the season and a net cover prevents falling leaves from fouling the water every autumn, organic debris builds up over time in the bottom of a water garden pond that has a liner. Every fall or two it needs to be cleaned out before too much accumulates, turns anaerobic, and begins to suck the oxygen from the water. Some years dredging the bottom of the pond with a sturdy net after the plants are removed will do the trick. Periodically, nothing less than draining the pond and scrubbing the liner bottom will assure healthy water and plants for the next season.

Traditionally, water garden supplies and aquatic plants have been sold by mail order, and they still are. It is possible to have the entire garden— liner, containers, plants, fish, food, snails, fertilizer, pump, filter, tubing, and assorted peripherals—delivered to the front door. These days, however, with the increased interest in aquatic plants, many garden centers and home centers carry these supplies, a selection of aquatic plants, and books on water gardening.

The place to see aquatic plants, especially water lilies, is Longwood Gardens. Visit during the warm summer months when their outdoor pools fairly glow with the luster of huge, exotic tropical lilies and an assortment of other aquatic plants. Plan to stay through the evening to see, and smell, the night bloomers.

Anacharis

Egeria densa

Other Name: Elodea
Type: Submerged, hardy
Mature Size: Indefinite
Bloom Time: Summer
Flower Color/Type: White; insignificant

Color photograph on page 214.

Light Requirements:

Although they are not considered ornamental assets to water gardens, submerged plants such as anacharis have a delicate beauty as they float just under the surface of the water. They are also certainly assets, integral to the healthy functioning of the aquatic ecosystem that a water garden represents. Anacharis stems resemble seaweed, laddered with small dark-green leaves that create an efficient water filter. Later in the season their stem tips at the water surface bear tiny white flowers that have 3 petals with yellow centers. Anacharis's main job as an oxygenator is to maintain water quality. It replenishes the oxygen in water that proliferating algae may be stealing, and it absorbs excess nutrients such as nitrates, ammonia, and phosphates that promote the development of stagnant water.

WHEN TO PLANT

Submerged plants such as anacharis are the first plants introduced into a new water garden. Set potted stems under water in existing ponds in the spring or in a new pond whenever it is built.

WHERE TO PLANT

Anacharis likes full sun but can manage in incidental shade. Set pots of stems at the bottom of the pond so that 1 or 2 feet of water cover them. They should be visible under the water, not shaded by foliage of surface plants.

HOW TO PLANT

Anacharis and other submerged plants are usually packaged as bunches of 6-inch-long foliage-covered stems. Use 1 bunch, or about 6 stems, per 2 square feet of pond surface, more if there are many fish in the water garden. Plant 2 or 3 bunches together in an 8-quart pot filled with clean sand. Insert each stem end 1 inch or more down in the sand, then cover the sand with gravel to prevent fish from stirring it up and dislodging the anacharis. Soak the container with water to remove any air bubbles from the sand, then sink it in the pond.

CARE AND MAINTENANCE

Submerged plants do not need any routine care, except possibly to thin excessively crowded stems later in the season. Clip off and pull up as many stems as seems necessary to restore some clear water. Do not fertilize submerged plants.

ADDITIONAL INFORMATION

Sometimes anacharis foliage is coated with fine, brown silt from its water-filtering efforts. This will wash off if the stems are swished around a bit. Submerged plants are potentially invasive. Do not plant them directly in soil at the bottom of a natural pond. Take care when discarding stems that they do not "escape" into natural waterways.

ADDITIONAL SPECIES, CULTIVARS, OR VARIETIES

Milfoils (*Myriophyllum* species) have delicate hairy foliage for efficient filtration of water debris in ponds, water gardens, and indoor aquariums. Washington grass (*Cabomba caroliniana*) has fanned, lacy foliage and tiny white or purple flowers.

WATER PLANTS

 Did You Know?

Fish are both ornamental and practical additions to a water garden. Part of the natural housekeeping staff, they eat mosquito eggs and algae. Be aware, however, that their waste adds nutrients to the water and fosters excess algae production if there are no oxygenating plants to absorb them. Fish depend on these submerged plants to protect them from bird predators and to provide a thicket of undulating fronds in which to lay eggs.

Cattail

Typha angustifolia

Other Name: Narrowleaf Cattail
Type: Marginal, hardy
Mature Size: To 7 feet tall
Bloom Time: Late summer
Flower Color/Type: Beige; spikes of florets
Features: Attracts birds; 4-season interest

Color photograph on page 214.

Light Requirements:

Cattails are native to Pennsylvania, so they are familiar, abounding in roadside drainage ditches and water retention basins where they are home to red-winged blackbirds and other wildlife. They are easily recognized by their distinctive seedheads, resembling velvety brown cigars at the tops of slender stalks. Ideal for stabilizing soils along stream banks, they spread rapidly as long as boggy soil is available, but stop when they hit dry soil. Narrowleaf cattails are similar, having more slender leaves and therefore a finer texture. More ornamental, they provide vertical interest at the edge of a water garden that contrasts with its flat surface expanse. They catch the breeze and provide sound and movement through the entire year. Like other cattails, their flowers are densely packed spikes of tiny beige florets, male and female on the same stalk, clustered at the top of stems rising amid long, narrow-pointed green leaves. Use tall, narrow-leafed cattails to frame a large pond as background or as a screen. Use smaller cousins in the water at the edge of the water garden.

WHEN TO PLANT

Plant cattails anytime prior to a month before expected first frost in mid-October. Wait to set out young plants in the spring until the water is over 50 degrees Fahrenheit.

WHERE TO PLANT

Cattails like full sun but accept some light shade. Set their pots in the water at the edge of the water garden on a shelf or submerged support so that they have no more than 12 inches of water over their soil.

HOW TO PLANT

Plant thick cattail rhizomes in containers that hold a minimum of 3½ quarts of heavy soil. Slightly acid garden soil that has a bit of organic matter in it is ideal for anchoring the plant securely in the pot when it is lowered into the water. A mulch of washed gravel or decorative stones over the soil helps keep it settled. Set potted cattail seedlings in only 1 inch of water at first, lowering the pots as the plants grow taller to maintain several inches of water over the edge of the pots. Make holes in the bottom of each container so that the roots can stay wet if the pond water level drops below the edge of the pot from evaporation and lack of rain.

CARE AND MAINTENANCE

Cattails of all types are hardy here in the Philadelphia area; they can spend the winter at the pond side. Over the season cut back any ratty leaves and stalks, but do not cut them below the water line or it will kill them. The dried flower stems usually look good all winter. Cut them all back in spring to prepare for the emergence of new shoots. Divide crowded clumps also in the spring. Lift the pots from the water, and remove the plants. Cut chunks of rooted young shoots from the clump with a sharp knife or shovel edge. Replant the healthy portions in pots of fresh soil, and immerse them in shallow water at the edge of the pond or share them with friends.

ADDITIONAL INFORMATION

Take care when discarding cattail roots after dividing plants. They can be invasive nuisances if they find their way into natural wet areas.

ADDITIONAL SPECIES, CULTIVARS, OR VARIETIES

Graceful cattail (*Typha lamannii*) is about 4 feet tall and forms seedheads sooner than other cattails. It has good proportions for small ponds. Dwarf cattail (*Typha minima*) is only 30 inches tall, ideal for a container water garden.

 Did You Know?

Cattails are useful for floral crafts if picked at the correct time. Harvest them in July when the male flowers—gold tassels on the top part of the flower stalk—are still blooming. Cut them with long stems to set in empty containers for air drying.

Lotus

Nelumbo nucifera

Other Name: Sacred Lotus
Type: Ornamental, hardy
Mature Size: 1 to 7 feet tall; 2 to 6 feet wide
Bloom Time: Mid-July through August
Flower Color/Type: Shades of yellow, cream, pink, rose; single, double, goblet
Features: Fragrance; pods

Light Requirements:

Color photograph on page 214.

Lotus is the ultimate water garden plant. By virtue of its dominating size and exotic appearance, it is a commanding specimen, whether alone in a barrel or tub, or as part of a community of plants in a water garden. The rounded bluish green saucer leaves, 10 to 30 inches across, glisten with beads of water trapped on their waxy surface. Lower ones float water lily style on the surface of the water, and others float in the air on tall stems. Among them, the incredibly fragrant 6- to 12-inch-wide flowers open from pointed buds at the tips of their own stems. Resembling water lilies in shape, they open early and close at midday, their petals falling after 3 days. In their wake they leave their trademark flat pods. The good news is that lotus is winter hardy in the Philadelphia area; the bad news is that deer like it.

WHEN TO PLANT

Pot lotus in the spring during the few weeks the rootstock is actually a tuber. Soon it atrophies, and runners develop for the summer, forming tubers again in the fall. Set it in the water garden when all danger of frost is past and the water in the pond is above 50 degrees Fahrenheit. It will bloom after enjoying 3 or 4 weeks of sunny weather with air temperatures above 80 degrees Fahrenheit.

WHERE TO PLANT

Lotus needs a minimum of 5 to 6 hours of direct full sun and warmth. Locate it in still water. Miniature lotus is suitable for a 10-by-10-foot pond, or a tub or kettle.

HOW TO PLANT

Plant full-sized lotus in 30-quart containers that are 16 inches or more across and at least 10 inches deep. Miniatures need pots half that size. Orient the tuber horizontally, laying it on the soil about 2 to 4 inches below the pot rim so that its growing tip protrudes ½ inch when the tuber is covered with heavy soil. Insert fertilizer pellets deep into the soil but not touching the tuber, then water the container to eliminate air bubbles. Submerge the pot so that its soil level is 4 to 12 inches below the water surface. Shallower is better the first year. Gradually lower the pot as the lotus shoots grow taller. Lotus takes 1 or 2 years to establish, blossoming the second summer.

CARE AND MAINTENANCE

For continuous blooms, fertilize lotus twice a month until about mid-September. Routinely clip off limp, faded foliage and flowers. At season's end cut back all the stems, and sink the pot in at least 2 feet of water, safely below the frost line. An alternative is to wrap the bare tubers and store them moist indoors in a cool area. In the spring, divide overlarge potted or stored tubers so that they have 2 joints and a growing tip, and repot them.

ADDITIONAL INFORMATION

Cut first-day-bloom lotus buds for indoor display in a tall, narrow vase to support their stems or they will sag. Harvest seedpods after they have turned from green to brown and doubled in size. Left too long, they will fall toward the water to release their seeds.

ADDITIONAL SPECIES, CULTIVARS, OR VARIETIES

'Alba Grandiflora' is large with dramatic single, white flowers. 'Charles Thomas' has medium-sized deep-pink flowers. 'Momo Botan Minima' has miniature double, rose-colored flowers and stays small for tubs, growing a bit larger in pond gardens. 'Mrs. Perry D. Slocum' flowers are pink, becoming yellow, and they grow to 6 feet.

 Did You Know?

American lotus (Nelumbo lutea) grows to 5 feet tall and produces single, 5- to 7-inch light-yellow flowers and huge 2-foot-wide leaves. Native Americans called it Chinquapin or "pond nuts" because its starchy tubers were useful for food.

Papyrus

Cyperus isocladus

Other Name: Dwarf Papyrus
Type: Marginal, tender
Mature Size: To 30 inches tall
Flower Color/Type: Brown; insignificant
Features: Novelty; indoor

Light Requirements:

Color photograph on page 214.

Fortunately, papyrus comes in dwarf form, an appropriate scale for most backyard water gardens because it is such an interesting marginal plant. Its trademark 3-angled, leafless stems stand upright like reeds in crowded clumps, each one topped with a 2- to 3-inch-wide tuft of radiating spiky, grassy leaves that resembles a Fourth of July sparkler. They bear little green seedpods at their tips that eventually turn brown. As the season wanes, older stalks bend and flop, the brown seedpods dipping into the water. Use any papyrus as a vertical accent or screen at the edge of a water garden, similar to an ornamental grass. Dwarf papyrus can also be grown as a houseplant indoors during Philadelphia winters.

WHEN TO PLANT
Set out seedlings or potted rooted divisions from larger papyrus plants whenever air temperatures are reliably warm and the water temperature is around 70 degrees Fahrenheit. Anytime all summer is also fine for planting.

WHERE TO PLANT
Papyrus thrives in full sun or partial shade at pond's edge or in water about 6 inches deep.

HOW TO PLANT
Plant papyrus seedlings or rooted divisions from a larger plant in containers that hold a minimum of 3½ quarts of heavy soil. Slightly acid garden soil that has a bit of organic matter in it is ideal, as is clay. Avoid soilless potting mixes and other light, peat moss-based media because they will not anchor the plant securely in the pot when it is lowered into the water. Also particles will float to the surface and foul the water. A mulch of washed gravel or decorative stones over the soil in the pot helps keep it settled. Set potted dwarf papyrus in only 1 inch of water at first, lowering the pots as the plants grow taller to maintain several inches of water over their edges. If the pots have holes in their bottoms, the roots will be in water even though the pond water level drops below the edges of the pots.

CARE AND MAINTENANCE

Cut off any stalks that start to flop into the water near the crown of the plant to neaten its appearance. At the end of the season, most of its stems will brown and flop over. Because papyrus is frost tender, it will not survive outdoors during the winter. Either let it die, or before frost kills it, bring it indoors to overwinter as a houseplant in a container of water to keep its soil moist. It will eventually send up new shoots. Divide crowded clumps, and repot them in the spring. Otherwise, after a hard frost, throw papyrus away.

ADDITIONAL INFORMATION

By virtue of being indoors, plants suffer unavoidable stress and are vulnerable to pest insect infestations. Watch for aphids or spider mites on dwarf papyrus. Wash them off under the faucet, or spray them with insecticidal soap as directed on the product label.

Did You Know?

Egyptian paper reed or Cyperus papyrus *grew as marginal plants along the Nile, the resource upon which the entire ancient Egyptian culture was built. Among other uses, its huge 14-foot reeds were processed for paper and woven into baskets. It is highly likely that Moses was hidden among papyrus reeds, not bulrushes. English translators of the King James Bible could more readily imagine the English bulrushes than papyrus, which was unfamiliar to them.*

Parrot's Feather

Myriophyllum aquaticum

Other Name: Diamond Milfoil
Type: Surface, hardy
Mature Size: 6 feet long
Bloom Time: Summer
Flower Color/Type: Yellow-green; insignificant
Features: Trailing

Color photograph on page 214.

Light Requirements:

Parrot's feather is the aquatic equivalent of a ground cover. Although parts of the stems are submerged, trailing thin rootlets and sparse, yellowish hairlike foliage below the water, their top 2 or 3 inches protrude above the water surface. These stem tips are whorled with lovely fine-textured, feathery, pale-blue-green foliage, and they emerge farther out of the water as the summer progresses. They fill in the open water spaces between the other plants, their soft tufts weaving a tapestry of floating water foliage. Parrot's feather leaves open and close each day, their soft, fine texture contrasting with the round, flat foliage of neighboring water lily or lotus plants. Fast growers, overachieving parrot's feather stems grow crowded rapidly and will literally crawl out of a kettle or tub water garden, draping themselves down its side.

WHEN TO PLANT

Immerse pots of parrot's feather stems in existing ponds in the spring or in a new pond whenever it is built.

WHERE TO PLANT

Parrot's feather likes full sun, but does fine in light shade part of the day. Set the pots under open water at the bottom of the pond so that the sun reaches the plants and encourages them to grow.

HOW TO PLANT

Use 1 bunch, or about 6 stems, of parrot's feather per 2 square feet of pond surface. Use more if there are many fish. Their roots are primarily to anchor themselves in the soil at the bottom of a natural pond and to winter over. They need controlling for display in a water garden, natural bottom or lined, however. Insert the ends of parrot's feather stems at least 1 inch deep in heavy soil or washed sand in a quart container. Cover its surface with gravel to prevent fish from stirring up the soil. Water the container thoroughly to remove any air bubbles, then immerse it in the pond to sit on the bottom so that the soil level is from 2 to 6 inches under the water surface.

CARE AND MAINTENANCE

There is no need to fertilize parrot's feather. It may need trimming or thinning as the season progresses. If it gets crowded, its stems will rise practically upright several inches above the water. To acquire more parrot's feather, break off existing stems in 6- or 8-inch lengths, and put them in pots as described above.

ADDITIONAL INFORMATION

Parrot's feather is potentially invasive. Do not plant it directly in soil at the bottom of a natural pond. Take care when discarding stems that they do not "escape" into the wild where they may move into and take over natural ponds and waterways.

ADDITIONAL SPECIES, CULTIVARS, OR VARIETIES

Other small-leafed floating plants that act as "ground covers" in a water garden are four leaf water clover (*Marsilea mutica*), which has 4-part leaves with yellow or brown patterning and measures 3 inches across; yellow snowflake (*Nymphoides crenata*), which has green-veined, dark-brown leaves and yellow flowers; and white snowflake (*Nymphoides cristata*), which has maroon, mottled-green leaves and ¼-inch white, fragrant flowers.

 Did You Know?

Aquatic plants have their share of pest insect predators, among them aphids and the occasional caterpillar such as corn earworm. Aphids infest lily pads, speckling the leaves and turning them yellow. Caterpillars chew holes in foliage surfaces, leaving only a network of veins at the site. Either pinch off the infested leaves down low on their stems and throw them away, or dunk them in the water to wash off the pests. The fish, especially koi, will make short work of the insects or caterpillars.

Pickerel Rush

Pontederia cordata

Other Name: Pickerel Weed
Type: Marginal, hardy
Mature Size: 2 to 3 feet tall
Bloom Time: Spring through summer
Flower Color/Type: Blue or white; floret spikes
Features: Attracts butterflies, beneficials; cut flowers

Color photograph on page 214.

Light Requirements:

*I*n the South where it chokes lakes and streams, it is called pickerel weed. It is also native to Pennsylvania where it can be found growing in tidal marshes. In an ornamental role, confined to a pot and planted as a marginal plant to frame the edge of the water garden, it is called pickerel rush. Tamed medium-sized clumps send up clusters of bare stems with waxy, arrowhead-shaped leaves branching off just below their flowered tips. The flowers are spikes of clusters of tiny florets usually blue, but also available in white. Each floret has 2 petals per flower, the upper one having 2 yellow dots. They make nice cut flowers, too.

WHEN TO PLANT

Plant rooted sections of pickerel rush in pots, and immerse them in the water garden pond or tub anytime from spring until a month or so before frost is likely in mid-October. Water temperature should be above 50 degrees Fahrenheit.

WHERE TO PLANT

Pickerel weed, especially the white-flowered type, likes full sun. Blue ones can take some shade if necessary. Set pots of pickerel rush at the shallow part of the pond or on a shelf so that 2 to 10 inches of water cover their rims.

HOW TO PLANT

Plant pickerel rush seedlings or rooted divisions from a larger plant in containers that hold a minimum of 3½ quarts of heavy soil. Slightly acid garden soil that has a bit of organic matter in it is ideal. Avoid soilless potting mixes and other light, peat moss-based media because they do not anchor the plant securely in the pot when it is lowered into the water. Also particles float to the surface and foul the water. A mulch of washed gravel or decorative stones over the heavy soil in the pot helps keep it settled. Set potted pickerel rush in very shallow water at first, lowering the pots as the plants grow taller to maintain several inches of water over their edges.

Make holes in the bottom of the container so that the roots will be in water in case the pond water level drops because of evaporation or lack of rain.

CARE AND MAINTENANCE

Cut back dead stems after frost to within 1 or 2 inches of the pot surface, then lower the pot to the deepest part of the pond. If that is about 2 feet, it is safely below the frost line. Bring pickerel rush back up to divide and repot in the spring. Remove its pot, and slice through the mass of roots to separate chunks of rooted shoots. Replant them as described above.

ADDITIONAL INFORMATION

Discard perennial plants such as pickerel rush carefully so that they do not "escape" into local waterways. Put them on a compost pile or in a plastic bag in the trash.

ADDITIONAL SPECIES, CULTIVARS, OR VARIETIES

Hardy thalia (*Thalia dealbata*) is similar to pickerel rush, but bolder, with similar cultural requirements. Its stiff, slender stems are 4 to 6 feet tall with narrow-tipped, oval, 20-inch-long leaves jutting from them at right angles. Delicate, deep-purple florets tip flexible stems that protrude another 1 to 5 feet taller. Red-stemmed thalia (*Thalia geniculata* 'Ruminoides'), as tall as 10 feet, has red or purple stems and purplish flowers. Less cold-hardy than regular thalia, it is treated as an annual in the Philadelphia area.

 Did You Know?

Pickerel rush is growing at the John Heinz National Wildlife Refuge at Tinicum. This 900-acre wetlands preserve along Route 95 near the airport features a tidewater marsh and foot trails for observation of the 280 species of birds, mammals, and reptiles that find sanctuary there.

Taro

Colocasia esculenta

Other Names: Dasheen, Cocoyam
Type: Marginal, tender
Mature Size: 2 to 4 feet tall; 2 to 3 feet wide
Flower Color/Type: Pale yellow; insignificant
or absent
Features: Tropical look; edible

Color photograph on page 214.

Light Requirements:

Although it is typically used as a marginal plant, taro is handsome and dramatic enough to be a featured foliage specimen in a water garden. It is available in both regular and dwarf sizes, and its distinctive leaves may be green, purple, or variegated, many marked with indented, pale veins that accentuate their texture. Taro usually bears 2 leaves per stem at any one time, each up to 2 feet long. They are acutely angled downward so that their surfaces are practically vertical, resembling elephant ears. Taro provides a vertical element to the water garden, its large leaves adding foliage contrast, color, and texture simultaneously.

WHEN TO PLANT

Put out potted young plants or divisions of larger plants in the spring when the air temperature has warmed to around 70 degrees Fahrenheit.

WHERE TO PLANT

Taro likes full sun or some shade. Some of the darker-leafed ones show better in the shade. Set them on a shelf of bricks or rocks to elevate their pots in the water so that they have constantly moist soil. They can handle up to 12 inches of water over their roots, but 2 or 3 inches are better. They have less vigor if they are deeper in the water.

HOW TO PLANT

Plant taro seedlings or rooted divisions from a larger plant in containers that hold a minimum of 3½ quarts of heavy soil or are at least 5 inches in diameter. Slightly acid heavy garden soil that has a bit of organic matter in it is ideal. Avoid soilless potting mixes and other light, peat moss-based media because they will not anchor the plant securely in the pot when it is lowered into the water. Inevitably, particles float to the surface and foul the water. A mulch of washed gravel or decorative stones over the soil surface helps keep it settled. Set potted taro in only 1 inch of water at first, lowering the pots as the plants grow taller to maintain several inches of water over their edges. Make holes in the bottom of each container so that the roots will be in water even though the pond water level drops below the edge of the pot from evaporation or lack of rain.

CARE AND MAINTENANCE

During the season trim off yellowed, limp leaf stalks to groom the taro plant. They do not need regular fertilizing. Like other annuals in the yard, taro will yellow and die when frost hits. To divide an overgrown clump of taro in the spring, remove it from its pot, and slice through the mass of roots to separate chunks of rooted shoots. Repot them in fresh soil, and immerse the pots in shallow water at the edge of the pond when spring arrives.

ADDITIONAL INFORMATION

Taro can also double as a houseplant, set in a container of water, during the winter when the temperature is too cold for it outdoors. Because indoor conditions are less than ideal, houseplants are always a bit stressed. They are more prone to pest and disease problems. Watch for aphids, mites, or whiteflies, and wash them off or spray them with insecticidal soap as directed on the product label. Taro tissues have a sap that may irritate skin.

ADDITIONAL SPECIES, CULTIVARS, OR VARIETIES

'Hilo Beauty' has green leaves mottled with white. 'Fontanesii' has purple stems with dark-green leaves. 'Illustris', or imperial taro, has violet leaf stalks and green leaves with dark-purple coloration between the veins.

 Did You Know?

In Hawaii and other tropical cultures taro is an agricultural crop because it is a diet staple much like potatoes are for many other cultures. The starchy tuber is prepared numerous ways, including baked, fried, and boiled. Poi, a classic Hawaiian dish, is made of pounded taro root. Taro must always be cooked to be edible.

Water Hyacinth

Eichhornia crassipes

Other Name: Water Orchid
Type: Floater, tender
Mature Size: 10 to 12 inches tall;
  6 to 8 inches wide
Bloom Time: Late summer
Flower Color/Type: Lilac-blue; floret spikes
Features: Novelty; water cleaning

Color photograph on page 214.

Light Requirements:

Water hyacinths have a dual personality. In the Philadelphia area they are valued in water gardens where they maintain water quality and produce attractive flowers, then succumb to frost. In the warm South, however, they are regarded as major problems because they multiply with abandon in the wild, choking waterways and canals year-round. In fact, federal law prohibits interstate shipment of these plants to prevent their further naturalization. Actually, water hyacinths are amazing water cleaners in the wild or the water garden. Their bizarre feathered roots trailing below the surface in thick bunches absorb prodigious amounts of water pollutants as well as provide shelter for spawning fish. A single water hyacinth is as effective at controlling algae as 6 bunches of submerged plants. Water hyacinths are particularly useful in ponds lacking filters. Above the water they sport crisp, glossy-green, rounded foliage with bulbous stalks that enable them to float. They multiply very quickly by means of radiating surface stems. Water hyacinths bloom toward the end of summer, their flowering prompted by water rich in nutrients and crowding. Their flowers vaguely resemble Dutch hyacinths, 4- to 9-inch-tall stalks arrayed with violet-blue florets. The florets open and close daily, each floret lasting only 1 day, and the entire spike lasting 2 days.

WHEN TO PLANT
Put water hyacinths into the pond, tub, or kettle when the water is over 70 degrees Fahrenheit. They are not usually available in stores that sell aquatic plants until well into June.

WHERE TO PLANT
As floaters, water hyacinths have the run of the pond. They need still water, so they do not do well where water is disturbed by a fountain. Any pond over 6 inches deep is fine. They are suitable for tubs and kettles. If they have been accustomed to indoor or greenhouse conditions over the winter,

they will need some afternoon shade when first introduced to the outdoors in the spring.

HOW TO PLANT

Simply drop water hyacinths into the water. If they land upside down, they will right themselves.

CARE AND MAINTENANCE

Water hyacinths multiply by means of stem offshoots in several directions from the mother plants. Usually, it is easy to remove excess by just pulling them out of the water. Sometimes their long roots reach into the soil bottom of natural ponds or the accumulated gunk on the bottom of lined ponds overdue for cleaning, so pulling them may take a bit more effort. Water hyacinths are killed by frost instantly. Scoop them out of the water garden, and discard them. Or in mid-October, before frost, pull some from the water garden to winter over indoors in a tub of water in a sunny room with moist air.

ADDITIONAL INFORMATION

A good way to restrict water hyacinths in the pond is to corral them. Fashion a large ring from some tubing or other material that floats on the water, and trap the water hyacinths inside it.

ADDITIONAL SPECIES, CULTIVARS, OR VARIETIES

Water lettuce (*Pistia stratiotes*) is a tropical floater also, with small rosettes of yellow-green-ridged foliage and roots that clean water.

Did You Know?

Wherever there are warm water, sunshine, and nutrients, there will be algae. There are many kinds, some good, some bad, in a water garden. The brown type that coats surfaces of liners, pumps, pots, and submerged plants with a furry layer is not a problem. In fact, like organic matter in soil, it supports beneficial microorganisms to maintain a balanced system and water quality. The bright-green, stringy stuff is a problem. Water hyacinths and submerged plants such as anacharis help control it by taking up the nitrates that would otherwise nourish this algae.

Water Lily

Nymphaea species

Other Name: Nymphaea
Type: Specimen, tender or hardy
Mature Size: 6 to 8 inches above water
surface; spread from 1 to 10 feet
Bloom Time: June to September
Flower Color/Type: Red, pink, yellow, white, lilac, bicolor;
goblet shaped
Features: Cut flower; fragrance (some); evening garden (some)

Light Requirements:

Color photograph on page 215.

Tropical or hardy, water lilies are the stars of a water garden. As exotic as they look, they are easy to grow and generous with their blossoms. Their classic, round, lily pad foliage—green, bronze, maroon, mottled, or ripple edged—is decorative even as it shades the water, sheltering fish and discouraging algae growth. Their wonderful blossoms are from 2 to 12 inches wide, semidouble or double, and bloom at the tips of submerged stalks at, or just above, the water surface. Hardy lilies and daytime tropicals bloom between 9:00 a.m. and 4:00 p.m. Night-blooming tropicals open after sundown and close the following midday. Tropical water lily flowers bloom higher above water and are more likely to be fragrant than the hardy types. They also bloom longer into the fall, stopping finally when water temperatures dip to 50 degrees Fahrenheit. They die when frost arrives.

WHEN TO PLANT

Pot water lily rhizomes in the spring. Hardy types can go in the water anytime. Wait until the water temperature reaches a minimum of 70 degrees Fahrenheit to put in tropical (tender) ones.

WHERE TO PLANT

Water lilies need at least 5 or 6 hours of sun daily; less sun means fewer blooms. Set their containers 6 to 18 inches deep under still water on the bottom of the pond. Use dwarf varieties in tub or kettle water gardens.

HOW TO PLANT

Plant water lily rhizomes in shallow, dishpan-type containers that hold at least 15 quarts of heavy or clay soil. Soilless potting mixes and other light, bark- or peat moss-based media do not anchor the plant securely enough in the pot in the water. Lay the rhizome horizontally on several inches of soil, its growing tip tilted upward. Cover the rhizome, but not the tip, with soil.

Insert 2 fertilizer tablets into the soil near the rhizome, and mulch the soil with washed gravel or decorative stones to keep it settled. Water the plant to soak the soil and eliminate air pockets, then sink the container to the bottom of the water garden pond or tub.

CARE AND MAINTENANCE

Fertilize with pellets twice a month when the air temperature is more than 75 degrees Fahrenheit and the plants are flowering. Routinely pinch off dead flowers and yellowed leaves to groom the plant and to remove organic debris from the water. Winterize hardies by cutting back their stems and setting them at the deepest part of the pond if it is 2 feet deep, so they are safely below the Philadelphia area frost line. Otherwise, wrap the water lilies, containers and all, in damp newspaper, and put them in plastic bags. Store them in the basement, checking periodically to be sure they stay moist. Divide hardy water lilies every year or two. In the spring lift them from the pond when their new leaf shoots show, remove the rhizome from the container, and rinse off the soil. Locate a growing tip, and cut a 4- to 6-inch piece of tuber that includes it. Repot as described above.

ADDITIONAL SPECIES, CULTIVARS, OR VARIETIES

Innumerable water lily varieties are available. Consult with a local retailer or study a mail-order catalog. Native water lily (*Nymphaea odorata*) has yellow flowers.

Did You Know?

Water lilies make great cut flowers. Cut water lily blossoms on their opening day. Clip their stems about 1 foot under the water if possible. Float them stemless on the surface of bowls of water, or place stems in a tall vase so that the water is within 1 inch of the flower base. A drop of melted candle wax between their petals will keep blossoms open for evening viewing. They last 3 or 4 days.

Yellow Flag

Iris pseudacorus

Other Name: Yellow Water Iris
Type: Marginal, hardy
Mature Size: 3 to 5 feet tall
Bloom Time: June and July
Flower Color/Type: Yellow; iris
Features: Vertical interest; cutting flower

Color photograph on page 215.

Light Requirements:

Several types of irises like boggy soil and make wonderful marginal plants for a water garden. Although they are not native to Pennsylvania, they are naturalized here in lakes and farm ponds. Yellow flag combines ribbed, bright-green to gray-green straplike foliage 1 to 2 inches wide with cheery yellow flowers for a lovely effect. Yellow flag flowers are typical iris with 3 inner petals that stand up, called standards, and 3 outer ones that jut out horizontally or droop a bit, called falls. They do not have beards as some soil irises do. Flowers are typically 3 to 4 inches across, and there are several on each branched stem. Some have brown or violet veins, and various hybrids are paler or darker yellow, or even double. Early bloomers, they are the first of all water irises to bloom in spring when air is still quite chilly. They spread, but slowly.

WHEN TO PLANT
Pot new or divided iris rhizomes in spring, summer, or early fall. Fall-planted ones will bloom in the spring; spring-planted ones may not bloom until the following spring.

WHERE TO PLANT
Yellow flags do fine in full sun or partial sun on a shallow pond shelf or on bricks to support their pots near the water surface. They can take from 2 to 10 inches of water over their pots; however, double-flowered types prefer only 4 inches.

HOW TO PLANT
Plant up to 3 rhizomes in a container 9 inches across. Use heavy soil to be sure they are anchored well in the pot. Lay each rhizome on the soil on a slant so that its growing tip tilts upward. Allow it to protrude from the 2-inch layer of soil that covers the rest of each rhizome. A layer of washed gravel or small stones on the soil will help hold it. Wet the container and

soil first to eliminate air bubbles, then lower it onto a shallow shelf or support at the edge of the water garden.

CARE AND MAINTENANCE

Over the summer cut off the faded flowers and leaves to groom the plant. In October put fertilizer pellets in the soil as directed on the product label, then cut back the frosted foliage. Lower the pot to the bottom of the pond so that yellow flag winters over below the frost line. Divide crowded yellow flag rhizomes every 3 to 5 years after they bloom, midsummer through early fall. Remove them from their pot, and cut them in pieces 2 or more inches long, each with growing tip. Replant the healthy pieces, and throw old, woody ones in the trash.

ADDITIONAL INFORMATION

Discard perennial plants such as yellow flag carefully so that they do not "escape" from the garden into the wild. Put them on a compost pile or in a plastic bag in the trash.

ADDITIONAL SPECIES, CULTIVARS, OR VARIETIES

'Flora Plena' is a 2-foot-tall, double-flowered yellow flag hybrid. Siberian iris (*Iris sibirica*) has blue white, purple, and yellow flowers in late spring; it grows in regular soil, too. Japanese iris (*Iris ensata*) flowers are flattened. Blue flag (*Iris versicolor*) is native and has blue flowers.

 Did You Know?

Many aquatic plants appropriate for Philadelphia area water gardens grow in the wild in the region. Some are native; others are not, but have made themselves at home here. It is tempting to dig up plants such as pickerel rush or yellow flag found in a remote area and bring them home. Not only is digging them up likely to be against the law, but wild plants may carry disease pathogens or pest insects that would endanger the fish and plants in your water garden. Buy aquatic plants from reputable sources that raise them for ornamental use.

Philadelphia Area Gardening Quick Facts

Frost Dates

First expected frost . . . . On or about October 20
First hard frost . . . . On or about November 10
Last hard frost . . . . On or about March 31
Last expected frost . . . . On or about April 20

Precipitation

Average annual total precipitation . . . . About 42 inches

Cold Hardiness Zones (see map on page 215)

**Most of Philadelphia and its Northern and
   Western suburbs** 6B
Eastern half of Delaware Country . . . . Borderline 7A

Soil

pH . . . . Typically 6.3
Type . . . . Clay/loam

Test kits are available from the office of your County Extension Agent.

Pennsylvania State University
Cooperative Extension Program Offices

Bucks County 215-345-3283
Chester County 610-696-3500
Delaware County 610-690-2655
Montgomery County 610-489-4315
Philadelphia County 215-471-2200

The Pennsylvania Horticultural Society's Gold Medal Plant Awards

The Pennsylvania Horticultural Society's Gold Medal Plant Award program honors little-known and underused woody plants of exceptional merit in the Philadelphia area and promotes their use. Awards have been given to 64 plants since 1988. All are superb garden plants. For additional information, please feel free to contact the Pennsylvania Horticultural Society at 215-988-8800.

1988 Winners
Hedera helix 'Buttercup'
Ilex 'Sparkleberry'
Itea virginica 'Henry's Garnet'
Magnolia 'Elizabeth'
Prunus 'Okame'
Zelkova serrata 'Green Vase'

1989 Winners
Callicarpa dichotoma
Deutzia gracilis 'Nikko'
Hamamelis mollis 'Pallida'
Hydrangea quercifolia
 'Snow Queen'
Malus 'Donald Wyman'
Malus 'Jewelberry'

1990 Winners
Betula nigra 'Heritage'
Cornus sericea 'Silver and Gold'
Daphne caucasica
Fothergilla gardenii 'Blue Mist'
Hydrangea macrophylla
 'Blue Billow'
Stewartia pseudocammellia
 var. *koreana*

1991 Winners
Hamamelis × intermedia 'Diane'
Hibiscus syriacus 'Diana'
Ilex 'Harvest Red'
Sciadopitys verticillata
Viburnum nudum 'Winterthur'
Viburnum plicatum f. tomentosum
 'Shasta'

1992 Winners
Clematis 'Betty Corning'
Crataegus viridis 'Winter King'
Magnolia 'Galaxy'
Magnolia grandiflora 'Edith Bogue'
Picea orientalis
Viburnum 'Eskimo'

1993 Winners
Acer griseum
Cornus kousa (*C. florida* 'Rutban'
 Aurora™)
Cornus kousa (*C. florida* 'Rutlan'
 Ruth Ellen™)
Cryptomeria japonica 'Yoshino'
Viburnum burkwoodii 'Mohawk'
Viburnum dilatatum 'Erie'

1994 Winners

Abies nordmanniana, Prunus
   'Hally Jolivette'
Cephalotaxus harringtonia
   'Prostrata'
Cladrastis kentukea
Clethra alnifolia
   'Hummingbird'
Ilex glabra 'Densa'

1995 Winners

Aesculus pavia
Buxus 'Green Velvet'
Heptacodium miconioides
Ilex verticillata 'Winter Red'

1996 Winners

Acer triflorum
Ilex × meserveae 'Mesid' Blue
   Maid™
Ilex verticillata
   'Scarlett O'Hara'
Syringa reticulata 'Ivory Silk'

1997 Winners

Acer palmatum 'Tamukeyama'
Buxus 'Green Velvet'
Juniperus virginiana 'Corcorcor'
   Emerald Sentinel™
Koelreuteria paniculata
   'September'
Magnolia kobus var. *stellata*
   'Centennial'
Viburnum × burkwoodii 'Conoy'

1998 Winners

Aesculus parviflora
Clethra alnifolia 'Ruby Spice'
Mahonia bealei
Schizophragma hydrangeoides
   'Moonlight'
Thuja 'Green Giant'

1999 Winners

Acer palmatum 'Waterfall'
Enkianthus perulatus 'J. L. Pennock'
Metasequoia glyptostroboides

List courtesy of Pennsylvania Horticultural Society

Southeastern Pennsylvania Public Gardens

For detailed information on many of these gardens, write to The Gardens Collaborative, c/o Morris Arboretum of the University of Pennsylvania, 9414 Meadowbook Avenue, Philadelphia, PA 19118; *or call* 215-248-5777. *(See map on page 216.)*

The American College Arboretum
270 South Bryn Mawr Avenue
Bryn Mawr, PA 19010
610-526-1228
http://www.fieldtrip.com/pa/05261228.htm
This 35-acre campus was developed as an arboretum when the college purchased the property in 1959. It features fine old trees, plus planted annual, perennial, and vegetable gardens.

Appleford Manor
770 Mount Moro Road
Villanova, PA 19085
610-525-9430
http://www.mainlineevents.com/facilities/appleford.htm
This municipally owned 22-acre property features formal and informal planted areas, including a parterre garden.

Arboretum Villanova
Villanova University
800 Lancaster Avenue
Villanova, PA 19085
610-519-4426
The 222-acre campus has 100 tree species plus flowering annuals, perennials, and bulbs.

Awbury Arboretum
The Francis Cope House
One Awbury Road
Philadelphia, PA 19138-1505
215-849-2855
http://www.phila.gov/tourism/sightsbrowse.html#
This house with its planted grounds, 55 acres of green, was the summer retreat of Henry Cope, Quaker businessman and philanthropist. It features trails and open lawns reminiscent of an English park.

Resources

The Barnes Foundation Arboretum
300 North Latches Lane
Merion, PA 19066
610-667-0290
http://www.msue.msu.edu/son/mod70/70000209.html
This arboretum was established by Albert C. and Laura Barnes in 1922 on the grounds of their home, which housed an art gallery filled with Mr. Barnes's unique collection of Impressionist and post-Impressionist paintings. The gardens were designed to supplement the art appreciation classes held there.

Bowman's Hill Wildflower Preserve
Washington Crossing State Park
Route 32
New Hope, PA 18938-0685
215-862-2924
http://www.msue.msu.edu/son/mod70/70000203.html
A subdivision of Washington Crossing Historic Park, this first wildflower preserve in Pennsylvania is dedicated to educating the public about preserving native plants. Among the 800 species of native plants there are 80 that are endangered to some degree. Birders will enjoy the Sinkler Observation Area for nesting and migrating birds and indoor displays.

Brandywine Conservancy and Brandywine River Museum
Route 1 (near Route 100)
P.O. Box 141
Chadds Ford, PA 19317
610-388-2700
http://www.brandywinemuseum.org/conserve.html
On the grounds of the Brandywine River Museum, which features the art of the Wyeth family, naturalistic wildflower plantings in varied habitats, including parking areas, embody the mission of preserving, protecting, and sharing the natural resources of the Brandywine Valley area.

Resources

Chanticleer

786 Church Road
Wayne, PA 19087
610-687-4163
http://www.fieldtrip.com/pa/06874163.html

The former estate of Adolph Rosengarten is now a 30-acre pleasure garden featuring thousands of bulbs, roses, vegetables, fruit trees, containers, and courtyards.

Cliveden of the National Trust

6401 Germantown Avenue
Philadelphia, PA 19144
215-848-1777

This was the summer home of Chief Justice Benjamin Chew (1763-67), and scene of the Battle of Germantown, October 4, 1777. There are a museum and 60 acres of trees and gardens.

Colonial Pennsylvania Plantation

Ridley Creek State Park
Sycamore Mills Road
Media, PA 19063
215-566-4800

This farm museum re-creates daily 18th-century farm life. Authentically dressed staff provide educational demonstrations of traditional tasks on a farm. It features an enclosed vegetable garden and animal pens as well as the farmhouse and outbuildings.

Crozer Arboretum

1 Medical Center Boulevard
Upland, PA 19018
610-447-2281

The grounds of the former theological seminary, now part of a hospital campus, feature fine trees and other plantings.

Resources

Ebenezer Maxwell Mansion
200 West Tulpehocken Street
Philadelphia, PA 19444
215-438-1861

This accurately re-created Victorian garden is composed of more than 150 varieties of period plants—trees, shrubs, herbaceous plants, ferns, and vines.

Fairmount Park Horticulture Center
North Horticultural Drive and Montgomery Avenue
P.O. Box 21601
Philadelphia, PA 19131
215-685-0096

The center anchors the 8000 acres of Fairmount Park, the largest urban park in North America. The conservatory is the site of the Pennsylvania Horticultural Society's annual Harvest Show and contains a year-round display. It is surrounded by lovely grounds with gardens and display areas.

Friends Hospital
4641 Roosevelt Boulevard
Philadelphia, PA 19124
215-831-4781

The grounds of this hospital feature woodland trails through groves of azaleas and rhododendrons, plus interesting plantings among its various buildings.

The Grange
Myrtle Avenue and Warwick Road
Havertown, PA 19083
610-446-4958

This country estate of Henry Lewis, a Welsh Quaker, is listed on the National Register of Historic Places. It features sheltered gardens and woodlands overlooking Cobb's Creek.

Haverford College Arboretum

370 Lancaster Avenue (Route 3)
Haverford, PA 19041
610-896-1101

This arboretum is on 216 acres of a tract originally deeded to Welsh Quakers and purchased in 1831 for a college. It features 3 Pennsylvania State Champion trees, a duck pond, an herb garden, and a Japanese Zen garden.

The Henry Foundation for Botanical Research

801 Stony Lane (off Henry Lane)
Gladwyne, PA 19035
610-525-2037

It was founded by Mary Gibson Henry in 1948 for her collection of plants acquired over 40 years of extensive plant-collecting travels.

The Henry Schmeider Arboretum

Delaware Valley College of Science and Agriculture
Route 202 and New Britain Road
Doylestown, PA 18901
215-345-1500

Named to honor a revered professor, this campus arboretum serves as an outdoor laboratory for Delaware Valley College's horticulture programs. In addition to century-old trees, there are special collection gardens to aid study. The Lois Burpee Herb Garden and others are featured on the self-guided tour.

The Highlands Mansion and Gardens

7001 Sheaff Lane
Fort Washington, PA 19034
215-646-9355

Originally the estate of Anthony Morris, a Quaker lawyer, it represents a remarkable blend of the taste and technology of its day. Caroline Sinkler bought it in 1917 and installed formal gardens, which won a Gold Medal for Excellence from the Pennsylvania Horticultural Society in 1933.

Hill-Physick-Keith House
321 South Fourth Street
Philadelphia, PA 19106
215-925-7866

For 20 years, this was the home of Philip Syng Physick, a famous colonial doctor. It features a small 19th-century walled city garden.

Historic Bartram's Gardens
Fifty-fourth Street and Lindbergh Boulevard
Philadelphia, PA 19143
215-729-5281
http://www.fieldtrip.com/pa/57295281.html

Home of King George III's Royal Botanist for North America and a National Historic Landmark, this is America's oldest living botanical garden. It is a repository of the plants discovered by Quaker farmer John Bartram and his son in the attempt to document all the native plants in the New World. The interesting house reflects the complex character of its owner, and the grounds contain the oldest ginkgo tree in the country.

Independence National Historical Park
Visitors' Center
Third and Chestnut Streets
Philadelphia, PA 19106
215-597-8974

The historical district of Philadelphia contains plantings and individual gardens at Franklin Court, Independence Square, and other sites that reflect the fact that Philadelphia was the center of American horticulture. Directions and self-guided tour information are available at the visitors' center.

The Japanese House and Garden
The Horticulture Center
North Horticulture Drive at Montgomery Drive
Philadelphia, PA 19131
215-878-5097

Originally landscaped for the 1876 Centennial Exposition held in Philadelphia, the current garden was designed in 1958 when the tea house was moved from the Museum of Modern Art in New York to Fairmount Park. It was subsequently renovated for the 1976 bicentennial celebration.

Resources

Jenkins Arboretum
Elizabeth Phillippe Jenkins Foundation
631 Berwyn-Baptist Road
Devon, PA 19333
215-647-8870

A preserved remnant of the hardwood forest of Southeastern Pennsylvania, it features the native flora of Eastern North America and specializes in rhododendrons from all over the world.

John Heinz National Wildlife Refuge and Environmental Center
Lindbergh Boulevard and Eighty-sixth Street
Philadelphia, PA
215-365-3118
http://www.refugenet.com/r5tin.html

The refuge and center feature a tidal wetlands habitat and trails for biking.

Longwood Gardens
Routes 1 and 52
Kennett Square, PA 19348
610-388-1000
http://www.longwoodgardens.org

This former home of Pierre duPont is the premier display garden in the United States, featuring 11,000 types of plants on 1050 acres of meticulously maintained conservatory displays, formal gardens, and woodlands, augmented by fountain and firework displays.

Morris Arboretum of the University of Pennsylvania
100 Northwestern Avenue
Philadelphia, PA 19118
215-247-5777
http://www.upenn.edu/morris/drctns.html

Established in 1932 on the site of the home of siblings John and Lydia Morris, it is today 92 acres of rare woody plants set in a Victorian landscape. It is the official arboretum of the Commonwealth of Pennsylvania.

Resources

Pennsbury Manor

East of Bordentown Road and north of Exit 29 of
   Pennsylvania Turnpike
Morristown, PA
215-946-0400
http://www.libertynet.org/pensbury

The grounds of this former county home of William Penn have 23 buildings and gardens that represent colonial living of his era. Among them are a formal flower garden, a kitchen garden, a vineyard, and an orchard.

Philadelphia Zoological Garden

Thirty-fourth Street and Girard Avenue
Philadelphia, PA 19104
215-243-1100
http://www.phillyzoo.org

The oldest zoo in America is also a garden, featuring some fine old trees and naturalistic plantings to complement the animals on display and provide them habitat.

Physick Garden

Eighth and Pine Streets
Philadelphia, PA 19107
215-829-3971

This tiny garden of 18th-century medicinal plants was the dream of doctors at nearby Pennsylvania Hospital in 1774. It would provide them a source of botanical compounds for treatment of patients. Only in 1976, as a celebration of the bicentennial, were appropriate plants actually planted at the site.

Scott Arboretum

Swarthmore College
Route 320 (Chester Road)
Swarthmore, PA 19081
610-328-8025
http://www.sccs.swarthmore.edu/~maya/scott.html

Integrated into the 300-acre campus of Swarthmore College, this arboretum showcases trees, shrubs, and perennials recommended for Philadelphia-area gardens. Labeled collections of hollies, maples, lilacs, rhododendrons, and many others share the grounds with several special gardens and a remarkable outdoor amphitheater where graduation is held annually.

Taylor Memorial Arboretum
10 Ridley Drive
Wallingford, PA 19086
610-876-2649

These 30 acres nestled along Ridley Creek were dedicated to the public for their health, education, and pleasure in 1931 by Chester lawyer and banker Joshua C. Taylor. The arboretum features a fern grotto at a former quarry site and a waterfall and millrace dating from 1740. The bald cypress marsh supports cattails and other water plants, which are habitat for a variety of wildlife. Trails reveal meadows and collections of azaleas, viburnum, and three Pennsylvania Champion trees.

Temple University, Ambler Campus
School of Landscape Architecture/Horticulture
Butler Pike and Meeting House Road
Ambler, PA 19002-3994
215-283-1292
http://www.temple.edu/

Around this campus garden 800 species of plants are on view. Among the attractions are special dwarf shrubs, woodlands, and a herb garden, as well as an orchard and formal perennial garden.

Tyler Arboretum
515 Painter Road
Media, PA 19063
610-566-5431

Presently encompassing 650 acres, the arboretum is composed of several parcels of land dating to a land grant in 1681, including one owned by the Quaker Painter brothers who planted enormous numbers of shrubs and trees. There are trails through woods and planted collections, and a meadow maze for fun. Two especially unique features are the huge sequoia and a remnant of serpentine barrens.

Resources

Wyck House
6026 Germantown Avenue
Philadelphia, PA 19144
215-848-1690

This was home to generations of the horticulturally inclined Quaker families of Wistars and Hainses. The landscape includes a garden of old roses and has not been altered since the 1820s.

The Woodlands
4000 Woodland Avenue
Philadelphia, PA 19104
215-386-2181

The 55 acres of this Victorian garden cemetery and remarkable home are a National Historic Landmark.

Plant Societies in the Philadelphia Area

American Conifer Society
Central Region Chapter
Frank Goodhart
27 Oak Knoll Road
Mendham, NJ 07945
(908) 879-4788

American Rhododendron Society
Greater Philadelphia Chapter
Tom Conover
505 East Wynnewood Road
Wynnewood, PA 19096
610-896-7584

American Rhododendron Society
Valley Forge Chapter
Winfield Howe
7 Surrey Lane
Downingtown, PA 19335-1507
610-458-5291

Azalea Society of America
P.O. Box 34536
West Bethesda, MD 20087-0536

Delaware Valley Chrysanthemum Society
Ralph B. Parks
821 Meredith Drive
Media, PA 19063-1740
610-566-5644

Delaware Valley Daffodil Society
Ann M. Howe
7 Surrey Lane
Downingtown, PA 19335-1507
610-458-5291

Delaware Valley Daylily Society
Beth Creveling
980 Bypass Road
Perkasie, PA 18944
215-249-0682
Cathy Tomlinson
610-458-0177

Delaware Valley Fern and Wildflower Society
Ralph Wilen
143 Ridge Road
Southhampton, NJ 08088
(609) 859-8685

Delaware Valley Hosta Society
Warren Pollock
202 Hackney Circle
Surrey Park
Wilmington, DE 19803-1911
(302) 478-2610

Delaware Valley Iris Society
Charles and Betsy Conklin
91 Duncan Lane
Springfield, PA 19064
610-544-3984

Resources

Delaware Valley Water Garden Society
Fred Weiss
339 Valley Road
Merion Station, PA 19066
610-667-7545

Greater Philadelphia Dahlia Society
Steve Thomas
566 Sugartown Road
Malvern, PA 19355
610-644-4581

Hardy Plant Society/Mid-Atlantic Group
Sylvia Cooperman
20 Crown Oak Drive
Chester Springs, PA 19425
610-363-7840

Herb Society of America
Philadelphia Unit
Kathy Bepler
1515 Ridley Creek Road
Media, PA 19063
610-566-6261

Ivy Society
Hedera Etc.
Lionsville, PA 19353-0461
610-970-9175

Mid-Atlantic Lily Society
Ellen Ressler
510 East Conestoga Street
New Holland, PA 17557
(717) 354-9556

Native Plant Society
P.O. Box 281
State College, PA 16804
(814) 238-8879

North American Rock Garden Society
Delaware Valley Chapter
Dr. Jim McClements
50 South Prestwick Court
Dover, DE 19904
(302) 734-2836

Philadelphia Botanical Club
Elizabeth B. Farley
Academy of Natural Sciences
1900 Benjamin Franklin Parkway
Philadelphia, PA 19103-1195
610-667-0625

Philadelphia Rose Society
Pat Pitkin
923 Springfield Drive
West Chester, PA 19382
610-692-4076

List courtesy of Erin Fournier and Green Scene *magazine published by the Pennsylvania Horticultural Society.*

Some Greater Philadelphia Garden Centers

BUCKS COUNTY

Bucks Country Gardens
Route 611 North
Doylestown, PA 18901
215-766-7211

Lawn Depot
275 Edison Furlong Road
Doylestown, PA 18901-3029
215-348-5553

Russell Gardens Center
600 New Road
Southampton, PA 18966-1077
215-322-2339

Snipes Farm and Nursery
890 West Bridge Street
Morrisville, PA 19067
215-295-1138

Spring Valley Nurseries
4038 Route 202
Doylestown, PA 18901-1624
215-794-7159

CHESTER COUNTY

Main Line Gardens
376 Paoli Pike
Malvern, PA 19355-3312
610-644-2300

Stephens Garden Creations
North Middletown and
  Sycamore Mills Roads
P.O. Box 321
Gradyville, PA 19039
610-328-3008

Waterloo Gardens
136 Lancaster Avenue
Devon, PA 19333
or
200 North Whitford Road
Exton, PA 19341
610-363-0800

DELAWARE COUNTY

Rose Valley Garden Center
684 South New Middletown
  Road
Media, PA 19063-5020
610-876-7673

Bonnie's Wonder Gardens
233 Scottdale Road
Lansdowne, PA 19050-2328
610-259-1733

Bryn Mawr Feed and Seed Co
1225 Montrose Avenue
Bryn Mawr, PA 19010-2711
610-525-7011

J. Franklin Styer Nurseries
914 Baltimore Pike
Concordville, PA 19331
610-459-2400

**Mostardi's Nursery and
  Greenhouses**
4033 West Chester Pike
Newtown Square, PA 19073
610-356-8035

Resources

Orner's Garden Center
15 West Eagle Road
Havertown, PA 19083-2204
610-446-8971

Woodland Gardens
261 East Woodland Avenue
Springfield, PA 19064-3049
610-328-9697

MONTGOMERY COUNTY

Albrecht Nurseries Inc.
650 Montgomery Avenue
Narberth, PA 19072
610-664-4300

Meadowbrook Farm
1633 Washington Lane
Meadowbrook, PA 19046
215-887-5900

Primex Garden Center
435 West Glenside Avenue
Glenside, PA 19038-3315
215-887-7500

PHILADELPHIA COUNTY

Laurel Hill Gardens
8125 Germantown Avenue
Philadelphia, PA 19118-3422
215-247-9490

Information Resources

All-America Selections
Nona Wolfram-Koivula
1311 Butterfield Road
Suite 310
Downer's Grove, IL 60515
(630) 963-0770

American Rose Society
P. O. Box 30,000
Shreveport, LA 71130-0030
(318) 938-5402
http://www.ars.org

International Society of Arboriculture
Derek Vannice
P.O. Box 3129
Champaign, IL 61826
(217) 355-9411
E-mail: isa@isa-arbor.com

National Audubon Society
700 Broadway
New York, NY 10003
(212) 979-3000
http://www.audubon.org

National Wildlife Federation
Backyard Wildlife Habitat
   Program
8925 Leesburg Pike
Vienna, VA 22184-0001
(703) 790-4434
http://www.carskaddan@nwf.org

Netherlands Flower Bulb Information Center
Sally Ferguson
30 Midwood Street
Brooklyn, NY 11225
(718) 693-5400
http://www.bulb.com

Pennsylvania Horticultural Society
100 North Twentieth Street
5th Floor
Philadelphia, PA 19103-1495
215-988-8800
http://www.libertynet.org/phs

Turfgrass Producers International
Douglas H. Fender
1855-A Hicks Road
Rolling Meadows, IL 60008
(800) 405-TURF

Mail-Order Sources

Burpee Seed Company
300 Park Avenue
Warminster, PA 18974
http://www.burpee.com
215-674-9633
Seeds, flowering plants

Brent and Becky's Daffodils
7463 Heath Trail
Gloucester, VA 23601
(804) 693-3966
Bulbs

Duncraft
102 Fisherville Road
Concord, NH 03303-2086
(800) 593-5656
Bird supplies

Ferry-Morse Seeds
Linda D. Harris
P.O. Box 488
Fulton, KY 42041-0488
(800) 283-3400
Seeds, plants, bulbs

Forest Farm
990 Tetherow Road
Williams, OR 97544-9599
(541) 846-7269
http://www.forestfarm.com
Trees, shrubs, perennials

Gardener's Supply Company
128 Intervale Road
Burlington, VT 05401
(802) 863-1700
http://www.gardeners.com
Tools and supplies

Jackson and Perkins
1 Rose Lane
Medford, OR 97501-0702
(541) 776-2145
Roses

Lilypons Water Gardens
7000 Lilypons Road
P.O. Box 10
Buckeystown, MD 21717-0010
(301) 874-5504
Aquatic plants, fish, supplies

Musser Forests
P.O. Box S-91M
Indiana, PA 15701
(412) 465-5685

Park Seed Company
P.O. Box 31
Greenwood, SC 29647
(800) 845-3369
http://www.parkseed.com
Flower and vegetable seeds

Plow and Hearth
560 Main Street
Madison, VA 22727
(800) 627-1712
Tools and supplies

Seeds of Change
P.O. Box 15700
Santa Fe, NM 87506-5700
*Organically grown vegetable and
flower seeds*

Resources

Wayside Gardens
1 Garden Lane
Hodges, SC 29695-0001
(800) 845-1124
http://www.waysidegardens.com
Perennials, shrubs, roses, bulbs

We-Du Nurseries
Route 5, Box 724
Marion, NC 28752-9338
Perennials, wildflowers

Windrose
1093 Mill Road
Pen Argyl, PA 18072-9670
610-588-1037
http://www.windrosenursery.com
Trees, shrubs, perennials

Glossary

Alkaline soil: soil with a pH greater than 7.0. It lacks acidity, often because it has limestone in it.

All-purpose fertilizer: powdered, liquid, or granular fertilizer with a balanced proportion of the three key nutrients—nitrogen (N), potassium (P), and phosphorus (K). It is suitable for maintenance nutrition for most plants.

Annual: a plant that lives its entire life in one season. It is genetically determined to germinate, grow, flower, set seed, and die the same year.

Balled and burlapped: describes a tree or shrub grown in the field whose soil ball has been wrapped with protective burlap and twine when the plant is dug up to be sold or transplanted.

Bare root: describes plants that have been packaged without any soil around their roots. (Often young shrubs and trees purchased through the mail arrive with their exposed roots covered with moist peat or sphagnum moss, sawdust, or similar material, and wrapped in plastic.)

Barrier plant: a plant that has intimidating thorns or spines and is sited purposely to block foot traffic or other access to the home or yard.

Beneficial insects: insects or their larvae that prey on pest organisms and their eggs. They may be flying insects (such as ladybugs, parasitic wasps, praying mantids, and soldier bugs) or soil dwellers such as predatory nematodes, spiders, and ants.

Bract: a modified leaf structure on a plant stem near its flower that resembles a petal. Often it is more colorful and visible than the actual flower, such as in dogwood.

Canopy: the overhead branching area of a tree, usually referring to its extent including foliage.

Cold hardiness: the ability of a perennial plant to survive the winter cold in a particular area. Plants that are listed as cold hardy to -10 degrees Fahrenheit do well in the Philadelphia area.

Composite: a flower that is actually composed of many tiny flowers. Typically, they are flat clusters of tiny, tight florets, sometimes surrounded by wider-petaled florets. Composite flowers are highly attractive to bees and beneficial insects.

Compost: organic matter that has undergone progressive decomposition by microbial and macrobial activity until it is reduced to a spongy, fluffy texture. Added to soil of any type, it improves the soil's ability to hold air and water and to drain well.

Corm: the swollen energy-storing structure, analogous to a bulb, under the soil at the base of the stem of plants such as crocus and gladiolus.

Crown: the base of a plant at, or just beneath, the surface of the soil where the roots meet the stems.

Cultivar: a CULTIvated VARiety. It is a naturally occurring form of a plant that has been identified as special or superior and is purposely selected for propagation and production.

Deadhead: a pruning technique that removes faded flower heads from plants to improve their appearance, abort seed production, and stimulate further flowering.

Deciduous plants: unlike evergreens, these trees and shrubs lose their leaves in the fall.

Desiccation: drying out of foliage tissues, usually due to drought or wind.

Division: the practice of splitting apart perennial plants to create several smaller-rooted segments. The practice is useful for controlling the plant's size and for acquiring more plants; it is also essential to the health and continued flowering of certain ones.

Dormancy: the period, usually the winter, when perennial plants temporarily cease active growth and rest. Some plants such as spring-blooming bulbs go dormant in the summer to cope with the heat.

Established: the point at which a newly planted tree, shrub, or flower begins to produce new growth, either foliage or stems. This is an indication that the roots have recovered from transplant shock and have begun to grow and spread.

Evergreen: perennial plants that do not lose their foliage annually with the onset of winter. The term refers to needled or broadleaf foliage that persists and continues to function on a plant through one or more winters, aging and dropping unobtrusively in cycles of three or four years or more.

Foliar: of or about foliage. It usually refers to the practice of spraying foliage, as in fertilizing or treating with insecticide; leaf tissues absorb liquid directly for much faster results, and the soil is not affected.

Floret: a tiny flower, usually one of many forming a cluster that comprises a single blossom such as a lilac or spider flower.

Germinate: to sprout. Germination is a fertile seed's first stage of development.

Graft (union): the point on the stem of a woody plant with sturdier roots where a stem from a highly ornamental plant is inserted so that it will join with it. Roses are commonly grafted.

Hardscape: the permanent, structural, nonplant part of a landscape, such as walls, sheds, pools, patios, arbors, and walkways.

Herbaceous: plants having fleshy or soft stems that die back with frost; the opposite of woody.

Hybrid: a plant that is the result of intentional or natural cross-pollination between two or more plants of the same species or genus.

Low-water-demand: describes plants that tolerate dry soil for varying periods of time. Typically, they have succulent, hairy, or silvery-gray foliage and tuberous roots or taproots.

Mulch: a layer of material over bare soil to protect it from erosion and compaction by rain, and to discourage weeds. It may be inorganic (gravel, fabric) or organic (wood chips, bark, pine needles, chopped leaves).

Naturalize: (*a*) to plant seeds, bulbs, or plants in a random, informal pattern as they would appear in their natural habitat; (*b*) to adapt to and spread throughout adopted habitats (a tendency of some nonnative plants).

Nectar: the sweet fluid produced by glands on flowers that attract pollinators such as hummingbirds and honeybees for whom it is a source of energy.

Organic material, organic matter: any material or debris that is derived from plants. It is carbon-based material capable of undergoing decomposition and decay.

Peat moss: organic matter from peat sedges (United States) or sphagnum mosses (Canada) often used to improve soil texture. The acidity of sphagnum peat moss makes it ideal for boosting or maintaining soil acidity while also improving its drainage.

Perennial: a flowering plant that lives over two or more seasons. Many die back with frost, but their roots survive the winter and generate new shoots in the spring.

pH: a measurement of the relative acidity (low pH) or alkalinity (high pH) of soil or water based on a scale of 1 to 14, 7 being neutral. Individual plants require soil to be within a certain range so that nutrients can dissolve in moisture and be available to them. Philadelphia-area soil is typically slightly acidic, measuring about 6.3.

Pinch: to remove tender stems and/or leaves by pressing them between thumb and forefinger. This pruning technique encourages branching, compactness, and flowering in plants. It also removes aphids clustered at growing tips.

Pollen: the yellow, powdery grains in the center of a flower. A plant's male sex cells, they are transferred to the female plant parts by means of wind or animal pollinators to fertilize them and create seeds.

Pond liner: a molded fiberglass form or a flexible butyl or poly fabric that creates an artificial pond for the purpose of water gardening.

Rhizome: a swollen energy-storing stem structure, similar to a bulb, that lies horizontally in the soil, with roots emerging from its lower surface and growth shoots from a growing point at or near its tip, as in bearded iris.

Rootbound (or potbound): the condition of a plant that has been confined to a container too long, its roots having been forced to wrap around themselves and even swell out of the container. Successful transplanting or repotting requires untangling and trimming away of some of the matted roots.

Root flare: the transition at the base of a tree trunk where the bark tissue begins to differentiate and roots begin to form just prior to entering the soil. This area should not be covered with soil when planting a tree.

Self-seeding: the tendency of some plants to sow their seeds freely around the yard. It creates many seedlings the following season that may or may not be welcome.

Shearing: the pruning technique whereby plant stems and branches are cut uniformly with long-bladed pruning shears (hedge shears) or powered hedge trimmers. It is used in creating and maintaining hedges and topiary.

Slow-acting fertilizer: fertilizer that is water insoluble and therefore releases its nutrients gradually as a function of soil temperature, moisture, and related microbial activity. Typically granular, it may be either organic or synthetic.

Sucker: a new growing shoot. Underground plant roots produce suckers to form new stems and spread by means of these suckering roots to form large plantings, or colonies. Some plants produce root suckers or branch suckers as a result of pruning or wounding.

Tuber: a type of underground storage structure in a plant stem, analogous to a bulb. It generates roots below and stems above ground (example: dahlia).

Variegated: having various colors or color patterns. The term usually refers to plant foliage that is streaked, edged, blotched, or mottled with a contrasting color, often green with yellow, cream, or white.

White grubs: fat, off-white, wormlike larvae of Japanese beetles. They reside in the soil and feed on plant (especially grass) roots until summer when they emerge as beetles to feed on plant foliage.

Wings: (*a*) the corky tissue that forms edges along the twigs of some woody plants such as winged euonymus; (*b*) the flat, dried extension of tissue on some seeds, such as maple, that catch the wind and help them disseminate.

Bibliography

American Horticultural Society. *A–Z Encyclopedia of Garden Plants*. Ed. Christopher Brickell. New York: Dorling Kindersley, 1997.

Bagust, Harold. *The Gardener's Dictionary of Horticultural Terms*. Strand, London: Cassell Publishers, 1992.

Barash, Cathy Wilkinson. *Edible Flowers from Garden to Palate*. Golden, Colo.: Fulcrum, 1993.

—. *Evening Gardens*. Shelburne, Vt.: Chapters Publishing, 1993.

Baron, Robert, ed. *The Garden and Farm Books of Thomas Jefferson*. Golden, Colo.: Fulcrum, 1987.

Bown, Deni. *Encyclopedia of Herbs and Their Uses*. New York: Dorling Kindersley, 1995.

Cox, Jeff. *Perennial All-Stars*. Emmaus, Pa.: Rodale Press, 1998.

Cresson, Charles O. *Charles Cresson on the American Flower Garden*. New York: Prentice Hall Gardening, 1993.

Cutler, Sandra McLean. *Dwarf and Unusual Conifers Coming of Age*. North Olmsted, Ohio: Barton-Bradley Crossroads Publishing Co., 1997.

Dennis, John V., and Mathew Tekulsky. *How to Attract Hummingbirds and Butterflies*. San Ramon, Calif.: Ortho Books, 1991.

Dirr, Michael A. *Manual of Woody Landscape Plants*. Champaign, Ill.: Stipes Publishing, 1998.

DiSabato-Aust, Tracy. *The Well-Tended Perennial Garden*. Portland, Oreg.: Timber Press, 1998.

Fell, Derek. *The Pennsylvania Gardener*. Philadelphia: Camino Books, 1995.

Greenlee, John. *The Encyclopedia of Ornamental Grasses*. New York: Michael Friedman Publishing Group, 1992.

Hart, Rhonda Massingham. *Deer Proofing Your Yard and Garden*. Pownal, Vt.: Storey Communications, 1997.

Healey, B. J. *A Gardener's Guide to Plant Names*. New York: Charles Scribner's Sons, 1972.

Heriteau, Jacqueline, and Charles B. Thomas. *Water Gardens*. New York: Houghton Mifflin, 1994.

Resources

Hightshoe, Gary L. *Native Trees, Shrubs, and Vines for Urban and Rural America*. New York: Van Nostrand Reinhold, 1988.

Klein, William M., Jr. *Gardens of Philadelphia and Delaware Valley*. Philadelphia: Temple University Press, 1995.

Krussmann, Gerd. *Manual of Cultivated Conifers*. Portland, Oreg.: Timber Press, 1985.

Loewer, Peter. *The Annual Garden*. Emmaus, Pa.: Rodale Press, 1988.

McVicar, Jekka. *Herbs for the Home*. New York: Viking Studio Books, 1994.

Ney, Betsey, ed. *Ornamental Grasses*. Kennett Square, Pa.: Longwood Gardens, 1993.

Ottesen, Carole. *The Native Plant Primer*. New York: Harmony Books, 1995.

Roth, Susan A. *The Four-Season Landscape*. Emmaus, Pa.: Rodale Press, 1994.

Seitz, Ruth Hoover. *Philadelphia and Its Countryside*. Harrisburg, Pa.: RB Books, 1994.

Still, Stephen M. *Manual of Herbaceous Ornamental Plants*. 4th ed. Urbana, Ill.: Stipes Publishing Co., 1994.

Stokes, Donald and Lillian. *The Butterfly Book*. Toronto: Little, Brown, 1991.

—. *The Hummingbird Book*. Toronto: Little, Brown, 1989.

Thomas, Charles B. *Water Gardens*. New York: Houghton Mifflin, 1997.

Tice, Patricia M. *Gardening in America 1830-1910*. Rochester, N.Y.: Strong Museum, 1953.

Todd, Pamela. *Forget-Me-Not: A Floral Treasury*. Boston: Bulfinch Press, 1993.

Tomlinson, Timothy R., and Barbara Klaczynska. *Paradise Presented*. Philadelphia: Morris Arboretum of the University of Pennsylvania, 1996.

Welch, Humphrey J. *Manual of Dwarf Conifers*. New York: Theophrastus Publishers/Garland STPM Press, 1979.

INDEX

Index

Index

Index

Index

Index

Index

Index

Index

Index

ABOUT THE AUTHOR

*L*IZ BALL is a horticultural writer, photographer, speaker, and researcher whose articles and photographs have appeared in numerous catalogs, books, and magazines. An occasional contributor to *Green Scene*, the magazine of the Pennsylvania Horticultural Society, she also writes regularly for Burpee *Home Gardener* magazine and has written a column for her hometown weekly newspaper for six years.

Over the last sixteen years she has collaborated with her business partner, Jeff Ball, on nine books on plant and landscape care, including *The 60 Minute Vegetable Garden, Easy Composting, Yardening*, and *Smart Yard Lawn Care*; she has also written a Smith & Hawken book on backyard composting. She wrote *The Philadelphia Garden Book: A Gardener's Guide for the Delaware Valley* in response to the discovery that the "horticultural heaven" in which she lives has never had its own book on its better plants.

A long-time gardener, Liz abandoned a 25-year career teaching writing, literature, and history at the secondary level to focus on horticulture. She has taught courses on gardening at local community adult and arboretum programs and on garden writing for the department of special programs at Temple University, Ambler Campus. She is currently teaching writing to Professional Gardening students at Longwood Gardens. She speaks often to garden clubs, horticultural societies, and civic groups.

Liz is on the education committee of Scott Arboretum at Swarthmore College and is a recording secretary for the local chapter of the North American Rock Garden Society. She is both a national director of the Garden Writer's Association of America and chair of their membership committee. In her spare time, Liz manages her photography business, Garden Portraits, maintaining a small slide library of images of plants and residential yards and gardens which she licenses for publication. She presides over a suburban yard that serves as an informal laboratory and demonstration garden for ongoing plant and equipment testing, research, workshop presentations, and occasional TV/video spots.

GARDENING TITLES
FROM COOL SPRINGS PRESS

The What, Where, When, How & Why
of Gardening in Your Area